THE FEDERAL COURT OF CANADA

The Federal Court of Canada

A History, 1875–1992

IAN BUSHNELL

Published for The Osgoode Society
for Canadian Legal History by
University of Toronto Press
Toronto Buffalo London

ISBN 0-8020-4207-4 (cloth)

Printed on acid-free paper

Canadian Cataloguing in Publication Data

Bushnell, Ian, 1937–
The Federal Court of Canada : a history, 1875–1992

(Osgoode Society for Canadian legal history)
Includes index.
ISBN 0-8020-4207-4

1. Canada. Federal Court – History.   2. Canada. Exchequer
Court – History.   I. Title.   II. Series.

KE8265.B88 1997   347.71'04   C97-931224-8
KF345B88 1997

University of Toronto Press acknowledges the financial assistance to its
publishing program of the Canada Council for the Arts and
the Ontario Arts Council.

For my family

Lucienne
Anne
Eric
Paul

and

my mother, Jean
(1910–1994)

Contents

Foreword

THE OSGOODE SOCIETY FOR CANADIAN LEGAL HISTORY

The purpose of The Osgoode Society for Canadian Legal History is to encourage research and writing in the history of Canadian law. The Society, which was incorporated in 1979 and is registered as a charity, was founded at the initiative of the Honourable R. Roy McMurtry, a former attorney general for Ontario, now Chief Justice of Ontario, and officials of the Law Society of Upper Canada. Its efforts to stimulate the study of legal history in Canada include a research support program, a graduate student research assistance program, and work in the fields of oral history and legal archives. The Society publishes volumes of interest to the Society's members that contribute to legal-historical scholarship in Canada, including studies of the courts, the judiciary, and the legal profession, biographies, collections of documents, studies in criminology and penology, accounts of significant trials, and work in the social and economic history of the law.

Current directors of The Osgoode Society for Canadian Legal History are Jane Banfield, Tom Bastedo, Brian Bucknall, Archie Campbell, Susan Elliott, J. Douglas Ewart, Martin Friedland, Charles Harnick, John Honsberger, Kenneth Jarvis, Allen Linden, Virginia MacLean, Wendy Matheson, Colin McKinnon, Roy McMurtry, Brendan O'Brien, Peter Oliver, Paul Reinhardt, Joel Richler, James Spence, and Richard Tinsley.

The annual report and information about membership may be obtained by writing The Osgoode Society for Canadian Legal History, Osgoode Hall, 130 Queen Street West, Toronto, Ontario, Canada M5H 2N6.

In 1991 the Federal Court of Canada asked The Osgoode Society to assist in planning and developing a history of the Federal Court and its predecessor institutions to mark, in 1996, the twenty-fifth anniversary of the Court's establishment. The Society entered into the project enthusiastically and with complete editorial independence. For its part, the Court agreed to cooperate in the research and many members of the Court agreed to share their experiences with the author. The Society was fortunate in persuading Professor Ian Bushnell, Faculty of Law, University of Windsor, to undertake the task of writing the Court's history. As the author of a widely acclaimed history of the Supreme Court of Canada, Professor Bushnell was well equipped to accept this new challenge. He has carried out this onerous commitment expeditiously and creatively. His manuscript offers a sound and engaging introduction to the history of this uniquely Canadian court.

The Society expresses its appreciation to Professor Bushnell for the skill and integrity with which he has completed his work and to Chief Justice Julius Isaac and Mr Justice Allen Linden and other members of the Court for the strong support they gave to this project. We are grateful too to the members of the project Advisory Committee who met on several occasions to give the author the benefit of their experience and advice.

The Federal Court, existing from 1875 to 1971 under the name Exchequer Court of Canada, has occupied a special place in the court structure of Canada. Established primarily to adjudicate legal disputes in which the Canadian government was involved, it has, since its change of name and restructuring in 1971, become principally an administrative appeal court dealing with federal administrative tribunals in addition to its existing jurisdictions, admiralty, intellectual property, tax, and other areas. As a federal court within the nation its very existence provokes discussion and debate as the various provincial court systems claim a position of primacy for the adjudication of legal disputes. Central to the history of the Court is an examination of the judges who have sat on its bench. Who the judges were is presented, and their work is examined, with particular focus on the judges' views of the proper approach to decision making.

R. Roy McMurtry
President

Peter N. Oliver
Editor-in-Chief

Preface

When I was asked by the Federal Court of Canada in March 1993 to write the history of the court in honour of its twenty-fifth anniversary (June 1, 1996), it took some time to realize that this was really happening. Such an opportunity had not arisen before (at least to my knowledge) and my desire to accept this precedent-setting task was considerable. When I was assured that the book was to be a work of independent scholarship, any reservations I had were removed.

From a research and writing perspective it was unfortunate, but perfectly understandable, that there was a time limit for creating the manuscript. Work began in May 1993 and the manuscript was delivered to the publisher in April 1996. In addition to the time limit the book had a length restriction; these two factors combined meant that I clearly could not include everything of interest, or even of importance. I needed to select and focus on only certain aspects of the life of the court, and had to make difficult choices throughout the three years of writing about what to include and what not.

The nature of the book was left to me, as befitted the emphasis on its being an independent work. It was agreed, however, from the beginning that the book was not to be a history of the various areas of substantive law within the court's jurisdiction, but of the court as an institution made up of judges and established for the settling of disputes. The court's work in various areas of substantive law was to provide illustrations of the functioning of the court in adjudicating disputes.

The coverage of the court's history begins with the creation of the Exchequer Court of Canada in 1875, and ends with the coming into force of the 1990 reforms in 1992. With the 1990 reforms the court may be seen as taking on a new life; although the changes were not as dramatic as some that had taken place in the past, they were still significant. The study of their effects is that of the present court, which remains for future examination.

Given the time limit, I needed help in the research and preparation of the manuscript, and those who provided that much-needed assistance are acknowledged in a special section of this book. Nevertheless, one aspect of this study deserves special mention at this point: the series of interviews that were conducted with both retired and active judges. These interviews, in which the judges talked about themselves and their work, were unprecedented, and added immeasurably to the book. However, the use of statements made by judges, other than those in their written decisions, is a very sensitive issue. As a result it was decided not to attribute any statements to individual judges, but simply to 'a judge,' or 'some judges.'

The first requirement in writing this history was to develop themes to provide a focus for the historical information (including the cases that the judges had decided). These themes (which are described below) related to the life of the court as a dispute resolution body and were developed without any preconceived notion of what would be found. It would be problematic if someone doing historical research (to discover the past) formulated tentative conclusions (based on the present), which having been created would inevitably pull the writer in one direction or another. The themes were allowed to develop themselves based on the information I uncovered. At different periods in the life of the project the different themes would contend for attention.

History provides an identity (it may not be the one that you want, but it is defining). A knowledge of history is challenging, because it raises questions about origins and about the foundations of what are maintained to be long-standing ideas. A knowledge of history also dampens the tendency to make absolute statements in the present. For some it can represent a threat to the promotion of current values, since those values may not have existed in the past and thus have to be advocated as change. Without previous historical works about the Federal Court (or courts in general), there has been a tendency to create myths and make up history. This study may frequently challenge what was created.

THE THEMES

Judges and Judging

A court is as good as the judges who sit on its bench. This history examines the judges, past and present, of the Exchequer Court and the Federal Court, and how and why they were appointed. It makes special mention of the presidents of the Exchequer Court and the chief justices of the Federal Court, whose names have been used to designate the various periods in the court's history.

The next step was to turn to the topic of 'judging,' and to examine the judges' work. The judges' views about the approach they should take with regard to decision making were of particular interest. The life of the legal system revolves around the model of decision making adopted by the members of the legal profession, whether they are judges, practising lawyers, or law teachers. I had not expected that the theme of judging as it related to the choice of model would prove as obvious and pervasive as it did; it became a central feature of this work. The topic of models of judicial decision making is a very controversial and sensitive one within the legal profession, but its importance to the life of the legal system made an exploration of it imperative. At present the models of judicial decision making carry the titles 'formalism' and 'contextualism.'

The prime source of information about judging is, of course, the cases that the judges decided and the reasons they gave for reaching their conclusions – this is the product of their work, wherein resides the law that will guide other judicial decision makers. For this history a number of important cases, selected primarily for public importance and notoriety, were studied, and the work of the judges in those cases analysed.

The Role of the Court

This history also examines the role that the court was expected to play at various times in its history – from the government's perspective as well as that of the legal profession and the public. The court's place within the overall legal system of Canada was a very important aspect of this theme. When examining the court's role I focused on the jurisdiction that had been given to it and the various changes that had taken place over the years and why they were made.

The Relationship of the Individual to Society

This theme grew out of the study of the role of the court mentioned above. From the beginning the Exchequer Court of Canada was involved in adjudicating disputes between individuals and government, which was a central feature of the court's jurisdiction. Respect for the individual as a member of the community has been an identifying feature of our constitution for many centuries. This brings a constitutional issue into play in cases where there is a dispute between an individual and the government, and that issue quickly became a central feature of this study.

A Government Court

This theme arose from the court's role in adjudicating disputes involving the government, which also engaged the question of the relationship of the individual to the state. The issue is the perception on the part of the public and the legal profession of the Federal Court as an agent of government, and the reality behind that view. Was it a government court? This question has been an ever-present fact of life for the court, and it must never be ignored. The thought that the court can be perceived as a government court will swirl around it continuously, and those who work for or support the court must always be aware that nothing should happen to make it a specific issue. The idea of the independence and impartiality of its judges is crucial for the integrity of the court.

Relationship with the Supreme Court of Canada

Since the court has always existed as a lower federal court with an appeal to the Supreme Court of Canada (which is also a federal court), its relationship with the Supreme Court is of vital importance. The rule is that all cases of interest and importance are appealed to the Supreme Court of Canada. This work examines the relationship between the two courts by looking at selected cases.

A Federal Court

This theme is more crucial today than in the past, although discussion about two systems of courts has existed since Confederation. Since the creation of the 'Federal Court of Canada' in 1971 the existence of a dual legal system – one for matters of federal law and another for provincial law – has become a significant and sensitive issue.

A National Court

As a national (as opposed to provincial) institution, the court generates special interest in a federal state such as Canada. This history examines how the court reflected a 'national' character and its success in doing so. Naturally, in a federal state, the accommodation of the various provinces and regions is a concern. Because of the nature of this country, how the province of Quebec perceived the court and how cases from Quebec were handled are of special interest. An issue of major importance is how the court, as a national institution, accommodated two official languages, French and English, and two legal traditions, the law of England and the civil law of continental Europe.

The Two Divisions of the Federal Court

This last theme concerns the post-1971 Federal Court of Canada. When it was created in 1971 the Federal Court was divided into two parts – the Federal Court of Appeal (Appeal Division) and the Trial Division. Because the Court of Appeal is – among other things – the appeal court for the Trial Division, the relationship between the two divisions is extremely important. Essentially, the history of the Federal Court after 1971 is a history of two courts.

THE PERIODS OF TIME

My study and reflection centred on the above themes as they manifested themselves over three distinct periods in the life of the court:

1875–1887

This period beings with the creation of the Exchequer Court of Canada in 1875 as a trial court connected to the Supreme Court of Canada. The judges of the Supreme Court of Canada (which was created at the same time) were expected to travel and conduct trials sitting as individual judges of the Exchequer Court.

1887–1971

In 1887 the Exchequer Court of Canada was separated from the Supreme Court of Canada and established as a distinct entity. In this lengthy period of eighty-four years, the court continued to function with hearings before a single judge, now its own. Until 1912 the court had only one judge; in that year a second judge was appointed. There were two judges until 1945. In 1923 the title 'President' was chosen for the head of the court. After 1945 additional positions were created periodically, reaching a total of eight just before the establishment of the Federal Court in 1971.

1971–1992

The name 'Exchequer Court of Canada' was abandoned in 1971 and the Federal Court of Canada with its two divisions was created. The judges of the Exchequer Court were brought into the new court and divided between its divisions. Essentially, the jurisdiction of the Exchequer Court (with some changes) was carried over into the Trial Division, which was identifiable as the old court with a new name. The Federal Court of Appeal was entirely new, and as such attracted special attention in this study.

An idea that recurred continually during the research and writing of this history was that the Exchequer Court and then the Federal Court existed in virtual anonymity – completely unknown entities. While I doubt that the court is any more anonymous in the eyes of the public than any other specific court in Canada – for the public there are courts, judges, and lawyers – what was significant about this court was that a great many members of the legal profession considered it an unknown, which gave it a certain sense of mystery.

I hope that the excursion into the unknown provided by this history of the Exchequer Court of Canada (1875–1971) and the Federal Court of Canada (1971–1992) will inform and illuminate a part of the Canadian identity.

Acknowledgments

In order to complete this project in the time allowed a great deal of help was needed. First of all I must acknowledge a grant from the Federal Court of Canada paid to the University of Windsor, which made possible the hiring of a replacement to undertake my teaching and administrative duties and freed me for two years to work on the project. For the third year of the project I used a sabbatical leave. There was another grant to hire contributors to undertake research notes and papers, and to employ the indispensable student research assistants. Professor Denis Lemieux from the University of Laval in Quebec City was hired by the Federal Court as a special contributor, to provide information and insights into the view of the Exchequer Court and Federal Court from the province of Quebec, to deal with issues of Quebec civil law as they related to the working of the court, and to lend his expertise in administrative law matters as needed for an understanding and appreciation of the vital administrative law work of the court over the years.

The Federal Court also established an Advisory Committee consisting of former Chief Justice Wilbur Jackett, present Chief Justice Julius Isaac, Justices Arthur Stone, Robert Décary, and Allen Linden (who chaired the committee), as well as Peter Oliver, editor-in-chief of the Osgoode Society, and Professors Peter Russell (Political Science, Toronto), David Mullan (Law, Queens), John Evans (Law, York), Patrick Glenn (Law, McGill), and Richard Risk (Law, Toronto). Annual meetings with the committee were arranged, and its members were available to consider queries and offer suggestions at various stages of the project.

Particular mention should be made of the work of Mr Justice Allen Linden, who chaired the Advisory Committee and was instrumental in having the project undertaken and steering it through. He also arranged for two researchers to be hired as law clerks, and their work proved invaluable for the completion of the study.

I also wish to acknowledge the contribution of the judges who agreed to be interviewed for this book. When the opportunity was presented of having a researcher hired as a law clerk, it became possible to conduct interviews with the sitting judges, which enriched the project considerably. I was inspired to arrange the interviews mainly by the existence of a series of interviews which the Federal Court had commissioned from the Osgoode Society for the court's twenty-fifth aniversary, as part of the oral history work being carried out by the society. The interviews had been conducted by Christine Kates and were available when I started work on this book. The transcripts contained a wealth of information and comments that Christine had been able to obtain from both judges and others and they showed the potential of interviewing – that judges would actually talk about themselves and their work.

Time did not allow us to interview all of the judges currently on the court, but significantly not one judge who was asked refused to be interviewed. The interviews were conducted by Lynne Watt and Marnie McCall while they each held the position of law clerk. A list of those interviewed appears in Appendix B, along with the names of the interviewers.

It is doubtful that anyone had such research talent available to them as I did with Lynne Watt and Marnie McCall. Lynne took the law clerk position to act as researcher for the project after graduating in law from the University of Ottawa and while she waited to go to England on a Fox Scholarship. Marnie had obtained an LL B from Calgary and an MA in legal studies from Carleton, and was teaching law there part time when she accepted the position of part-time law clerk.

Special thanks go to Marnie, who contributed two research papers, did research in and outside the court, surveyed archival material, reviewed the part of the manuscript dealing with the Exchequer Court, and discussed issues with me on my visits to Ottawa and by electronic mail. The completion of the project on schedule owes a great deal to her extensive involvement.

I also want to acknowledge the indispensable help provided by Bev Greene, my colleague at the Faculty of Law, University of Windsor, who reviewed the chapters dealing with the Federal Court and offered suggestions that allowed me to breathe life into the narrative and forced me to rethink various points. Also at the University of Windsor, Professor Brian Etherington offered comments on parts of the manuscript dealing with administrative law. Thanks also go to Professor John McEvoy of the University of New Brunswick, who dealt with several queries that I sent his way.

I would also like to thank the anonymous assessors who reviewed the manuscript for the Osgoode Society and who offered many helpful suggestions and thought-provoking queries.

Throughout the three years of research and writing many student research assistants worked on various topics. I must mention specifically three major assistants who participated in the project while they were students at the University of Windsor. Jennifer Bucknall ably gave the project a good start, Megan Ellis kept it moving in its second year, and Eleanor Pawelski brought it to a close in the final year. The work of all three was greatly appreciated.

On the thorny question of the jurisdiction of the Federal Court as it developed out of the language of section 101 of the constitution, I would like to thank former Law Clerk Ron Barem for a copy of his unpublished paper 'For BETTER or for Worse: A Historical Interpretation of s. 101 of the Constitution Act, 1867 and Federal Court Jurisdiction.'

I would also like to thank Mrs Pat Levac, executive assistant to the administration of the court, for her help in collecting the photographs that have been used in the book.

I was glad to know, when I undertook this major project, that the book was to be published by the Osgoode Society. Throughout the years of preparation I felt the full support of the society for the publication of an independent scholarly work. I would like to thank Professor Peter Oliver, the society's editor-in-chief, and Marilyn MacFarlane, its secretary and administrative assistant, for their support and patience in dealing with queries and comments of all sorts, and for their encouragement.

Sir William Buell Richards. Richards was chief justice of the Supreme Court from 1875 to 1879, during the period when the judges of the Supreme Court of Canada were also the judges of the Exchequer Court. (From a portrait; National Archives of Canada C80528)

Sir William Johnstone Ritchie, Chief Justice of the Supreme Court, in October 1880. Ritchie served as a puisne judge of the Supreme Court from 1875 to 1879 and as chief justice from 1879 to 1887, during the period when the judges of the Supreme Court of Canada were also the judges of the Exchequer Court. (National Archives of Canada, PA26661)

George Wheelock Burbidge, Judge of the Exchequer Court 1887–1908. Burbidge was the first judge appointed exclusively to the Exchequer Court, and took over the duties previously exercised by the judges of the Supreme Court of Canada. (Federal Court of Canada)

Walter Gibson Pringle Cassels, Judge of the Exchequer Court 1908–1920 and President of the Exchequer Court 1920–1923. Cassels was the first judge to be named President of the court. (Federal Court of Canada)

Alexander Kenneth Maclean, President of the Exchequer Court 1923–1942 (Federal Court of Canada)

Joseph Thorarinn Thorson, President of the Exchequer Court 1924–1964 (Federal Court of Canada)

Wilbur Roy Jackett, President of the Exchequer Court 1964–1971 and Chief Justice of the Federal Court 1971–1979. (From a portrait by Robert S. Hyndman; Federal Court of Canada)

Arthur Louis Thurlow, Judge of the Exchequer Court 1956–1971; Justice of the Federal Court of Appeal 1971–1975; Associate Chief Justice of the Federal Court 1975–1980; Chief Justice of the Federal Court 1980–1988. (From a portrait by Robert S. Hyndman; Federal Court of Canada)

Frank Iacobucci, Chief Justice of the Federal Court 1988–1991 (Federal Court of Canada)

Julius Alexander Isaac, Chief Justice of the Federal Court from 1991 (Federal Court of Canada)

Ceremonial sitting of the Federal Court of Canada for the presentation of the silver oar of the Admiralty, June 21, 1996. *From left to right*, The Honourable Judges (*standing*): L. Marcel Joyal, Barbara J. Reed, Alice Desjardins, Allison A.M. Walsh, Q.C., Marc Nadon, Danièle Tremblay-Lamer, Marc Noël, Marshall E. Rothstein, Sandra J. Simpson, Robert Décary, Max M. Teitelbaum, Donna C. McGillis, John D. Richard, Mark R. MacGuigan, P.C., Bud Cullen, P.C., Pierre Denault, Frederick E. Gibson, Douglas R. Campbell, Louis Marceau, Gilles Létourneau. *Sitting*: Yvon Pinard, P.C., Joseph T. Robertson, Howard I. Wetston, F. Joseph McDonald, Chief Judge Jon Newman, U.S. Court of Appeals (2nd Circuit), Chief Justice Julius A. Isaac, Associate Chief Justice James A. Jerome, Chief Justice Michael Black, Federal Court of Australia, Frank Iacobucci (Supreme Court of Canada), James K. Hugessen, Jean-Eudes Dubé, P.C., Arthur J. Stone, Barry L. Strayer, Louis Pratte. (Couvrette Photography Inc., Ottawa)

Former Supreme Court building. Originally built as a workshop, this building was occupied by the Supreme and Exchequer Courts from 1881 until 1946. It was also home to the National Art Collection from 1881 until 1960, after which it was demolished. (National Archives of Canada PA52668)

Present Supreme Court building. From 1946 until 1971 the Exchequer Court shared this building with the Supreme Court of Canada. When the Federal Court of Canada was created in 1971 it also shared the building with the Supreme Court, but as the number of judges grew, facilities for carrying on the work of the Court were placed in various other buildings in Ottawa. Today the building houses the Supreme Court of Canada and the Federal Court of Appeal. (Couvrette Photography Inc., Ottawa)

The silver oar of the Admiralty. The silver oar of the Admiralty is a replica, except for the Canadian coat of arms, of the one which serves as a mace in the Admiralty Court in London, England. It is the visible symbol of the Federal Court of Canada's right to try cases concerned with admiralty law. The silver oar has had a long association with the exercise of admiralty jurisdiction in North America, dating from early colonial times when British Vice-Admiralty Courts in both Canada and the United States used it as a mace symbolizing their right to try admiralty cases. This oar was presented to the Federal Court of Canada on June 21, 1996, by the Canadian Maritime Law Association. (Couvrette Photography Inc., Ottawa)

The Federal Court of Canada

PART 1

Introduction

1

Introduction

A LEGAL HISTORY

The history of a court can be written from different perspectives. As a social institution, the court can be examined from a social and political perspective, focusing on its institutional characteristics and its role in the governing of society. Another perspective would focus on the court as part of the legal system and that system's legal profession. From this point of view, the subjects of examination would be the judges and their work – the cases they decided and the reasons for a particular conclusion.

The individuals who constitute the court – the judges – are the heart and soul of the institution. This history of the Exchequer/Federal Court uses the second perspective, examining the judges and their work in the context of the legal system and the legal profession.

Two legal traditions exist within Canada, the law of England and the civil law of continental Europe. The law of England, frequently termed 'the common law,' developed through the work of judges. The common law consists of judge-made law, developed on a case-by-case, pragmatic basis. The law, which will govern or guide other judges, resides within the explanation given by the judge for reaching the particular solution to the dispute – the reasons for judgment.

Today, and for some time, judge-made law no longer dominates the Canadian legal system. Legislation enacted by the federal and provincial legislatures has come to replace much of the judicially developed law. The judges have now, in the main, the task of interpreting words in legislation that constitute the law, rather than that of finding appropriate words in previous reasons for judgment and then interpreting them. This said, a significant quantity of judge-made law is still operative. The tradition of judge-made law enhances the stature of the judges and influences their behaviour.

The civil law tradition of continental Europe centres on a code of law created by the political process. The code contains general rules, which judges apply to particular fact situations. The words of the code constitute the law, and the decisions of the judges are treated as particular applications that may or may not be followed.

The civil law tradition operates within the province of Quebec, while the tradition of the law of England applies in the other provinces and the territories of Canada. While the civil law tradition is acknowledged to be part of the Quebec identity, a considerable quantity of law derived from the law of England does apply in Quebec, primarily through the application of federal law, which is based on the law of England. There are also areas of Quebec law that have been deliberately based on English law, most notably regarding business and commercial matters. In addition, all constitutional law is based on the law of England.

Because of the mixing of the two systems of law within Quebec, and the dominance in the past of English-speaking Canadians in the federal political process, the approach of lawyers educated in the civil law of Quebec has not differed markedly from that used by lawyers from common law Canada. As a result the history of the federal court is primarily that of an institution with the characteristics of a common law court and with common-law judges.

The writing of a legal history such as this one which focuses on judges and their work presents considerable difficulties. Judges are special.[1] While one might agree with Sir John A. Macdonald who, over a century ago, said: 'I think a Court of Justice ... which cannot stand investigation cannot stand very high in the estimation of the country,'[2] critical examination of public institutions in general has not been characteristic of Canadians, and that of judicial institutions, exceedingly rare. According to the late Bora Laskin, chief justice of Canada, writing as a law professor in 1952, the public's attitude towards judges was to view them as 'trusted friends.'[3] Naturally, it follows that criticism would be unthinkable. While critical comments about decisions of judges frequently appear in professional journals, they focus predominantly on the Supreme Court of Canada. These journals are by and large inaccessible to the general public. Discussion of judges and judging has in the vast majority of instances been doctrinal in nature, focusing on the legal rules and not on the judges themselves or their approach to decision making. In recent years examinations of judges and judging have appeared in public newspapers and magazines, and on one occasion there was even a television special,[4] but, again, this coverage has overwhelmingly targeted the Supreme Court of Canada. The position of the Supreme Court at the top of the court hierarchy gives it a certain remoteness (for the profession as well as the public) that insulates it, and any criticisms of it do not reflect directly on the daily administration of justice in the provinces.

As an indication of change there has been an upsurge in public criticism of judges, particularly in the lower trial courts, for their conduct during a case, most notably because of inappropriate comments that reveal their social attitudes. Media coverage of such incidents gives judges a human side and suggests that traditional social barriers to the open discussion of judges and judging are breaking down. These incidents, however, are still generally viewed as isolated examples of individual shortcomings rather than something that reflects on the overall functioning of the legal system.

Even lawyers who teach the law appear reticent to engage in any significant discussion of the functioning of the judiciary. Academics would seem ideally suited to becoming critics of the legal system because they are not involved in the day-to-day practice of law, which might require them to face the same judges they have commented on, and they have the time to engage in scholarly study and writing. However, a professional and social resistance to such criticism has had a muzzling effect here too.

Willes Chitty's reaction to a statistical study of judicial behaviour in 1968 illustrates the perils of the study of judges by academics. A Canadian law professor who had studied in the United States, and who emphasized a behavioural approach to law, examined certain Supreme Court of Canada decisions for how the judges had voted in particular areas of law (e.g., whether pro-government or pro-taxpayer in taxation cases, or pro-accused or pro-prosecution in criminal cases) and discussed the resulting statistics.[5] A Bencher of the Law Society of Upper Canada, at the time, Chitty charged that such a study might have a tendency to undermine confidence in the judiciary. He may have overreacted, but his words echoed the language of the crime of sedition; his admonition that law journals should hesitate to publish such work was unequivocal.[6] The fact that the statistical study had been newsworthy and reported on by the press may have increased his vehemence.

One might think that such reactions – a sharp case comment bringing murmurs of contempt of court, or (as with Chitty) threats of writing to journal editors to prevent future publication, or critical comments about legal personages causing minor blacklisting – are things of the past, but perhaps not. At a symposium convened in 1991 to honour the twentieth anniversary of the Federal Court of Canada, political scientist and eminent court watcher Peter Russell of the University of Toronto commented on an article he had co-authored about the appointment of judges. Many people, he said, regarded it as 'a rather cheeky little article.'[7] What had distressed them was Russell's examination of the political background of those appointed as judges.

A great deal of the trepidation about open discussion of judges stems from the pervasive nature of partisanship in both politics and society in Canada. The need to portray judges as politically neutral, and therefore impartial and independent (which the notion of partisanship immediately negates), makes any suggestion that judges have or had political views a very sensitive issue. Even raising the question of political affiliation, as Russell noted, can generate a reaction. In 1988 two judges of the Trial Division of the Federal Court used the Charter of Rights and Freedoms to challenge the constitutional validity of the law that prohibited them from voting in federal elections. While they were successful on the basis of the right to vote of 'every citizen of Canada' stated in the Charter,[8] the judge hearing the case, Allison Walsh, sitting as a deputy judge, was deeply concerned about the effect of the decision on the public. He thought that allowing a judge to cast a ballot in an election, which would recognize that the judge had political views, might affect the public's perception of judges as impartial. Walsh felt a need to protect judges from any possible criticism of not being completely apolitical. What was crucial was that the judges had to be perceived to be politically neutral by the public. Walsh declared that it had never been suggested that judges allowed their previous political views to affect their judgments.[9] The case was not reported.

The integrity of the legal system depends on the independence and impartiality of the judiciary, qualities which are intimately connected with our foremost constitutional principle, the rule of law. Because these qualities are so vital, many feel that the public must believe, as a matter of faith, in an independent and impartial legal system, and that nothing should be done to shake that faith. This perceived need to project the image of the judiciary as independent and impartial adjudicators of disputes represents the greatest barrier to the study of judges as individuals and the evaluation of their approach to decision making. Members of the legal profession often express the opinion that judges must be protected from criticism.[10] Criticism by politicians (from whose influence judges must maintain their independence) is an obvious concern, but the ban is all-encompassing. It is commonplace to find exclamations that maintaining confidence in the law is one of the underpinnings of civilized society, with the result that the judiciary must be protected from anything that is calculated to bring the legal system into disrepute.[11]

Politicians are conscious of the issue, which is certainly not surprising given the high number of lawyers involved in the political process. Debates in the House of Commons and the Senate reflect the idea that care should be taken when discussing judges.[12] In 1955 one senator was forced to comment that lawyers in the legislature might not be able to take an unbiased view of a measure intended to correct some defect in the legal system: 'On each and every occasion when there is any discussion on a matter affecting judges every member of Parliament who is a lawyer seems to feel it is his bounden duty to come to the aid of the judges.' He went on to say that this attitude did not indicate a robust democracy.[13] With disarming ease, members of the legal profession can allege that some critical comment about a judge affects the independence of the judiciary. Since the integrity of the legal system is at stake, lawyers are required to uphold the stature and dignity of the courts as a matter of professional ethics.[14] For the lawyer as legal historian, this poses the problem of balancing that professional concern with the desire to examine developments which influence judges and judicial history.

However, the desire of the Federal Court of Canada to have a work of independent scholarship suggests a changing attitude towards the study of judges and judging. In that spirit I have undertaken the challenge of writing this history of the Exchequer Court and the Federal Court of Canada, always keeping in mind the need to maintain a proper balance between the competing elements.

MODELS OF JUDICIAL DECISION MAKING

The approaches that judges have taken to decision making will naturally dominate any history of a court that focuses on judges and their decisions. In spite of the extensive literature on judicial decision making, only two easily identifiable models exist. The judges of the past probably did not identify themselves as following one or the other model: participants in an event are rarely conscious of what is happening as history. The most important part of knowing and understanding the past is its tendency to soften the absolute nature of thoughts in the present.

The two models of decision making are known as 'formalism' and 'contextualism.' They will be explored in detail in the chapters that follow; the discussion at this point simply highlights their basic features. While the term 'formalism' has a solid place within the literature, the model identified as 'contextualism' has had various titles throughout the years, a fact which is itself a repercussion of the tension between the two.

Formalism as a model developed in the nineteenth century. In this model of decision making the solution of problems and resolution of disputes are achieved by applying fixed principles to facts. The principles are identifiable as 'fixed' because they are found in sources deemed authoritative (the standard query with respect to the source of a rule or principle would be: 'Is it an authority?') and the prime source is a previous decision by a judge (precedent). The authority of the earlier case was 'fixed' by the legal doctrine of *stare decisis*. Under *stare decisis*, judges are bound by the principles of law that have been articulated in past decisions of judges, and which judges are powerless to change. This requirement was not adopted as a matter of practice to achieve predictability and fairness of treatment, but as a principle of constitutional law. The development of *stare decisis* began in the middle of the nineteenth century[15] and was declared to be settled at the end of that century.[16]

The finding of an 'authority' gave a judge the appearance of simply 'finding' the law and not 'making it.' If the principle that had been 'found' was thought to be in need of change because of new social conditions, the formalist would declare that such a change was the responsibility of the political system through the enactment of legislation. A judgment written by a formalist would display a search for the right form of words (the law) and not a discussion of the problem and a proposed solution.

The formalists found support for their approach in what is known as the declaratory theory of law, originating in the writing of William Blackstone in the eighteenth century. Blackstone presented law as a complete body of rules, existing from time immemorial and unchangeable except to the limited extent that legislatures changed the rules by enacting statutes.[17] The use of this theory permitted formalism to project the appearance of value-neutral decision making.[18] Judges found existing principles in the law (precedents), and had no choice but to follow those principles.

Policy considerations (social values) did not enter the picture. Although as influential a legal scholar as John Austin, working in the 1860s, might attack the theory, calling it a 'childish fiction employed by our judges, that judiciary or common law is not made by them, but is a miraculous something made by nobody, existing, I suppose, from eternity, and merely declared from time to time by the judges,'[19] the development of the formalist model armed with the declaratory theory proceeded throughout the nineteenth century.

A crucial aspect of formalism was that the fixed principles were general propositions and not fact-specific. To engage the general rules, only certain facts (viewed as socially crucial) were significant. If a society accepted values as indisputable, then the use of general propositions worked, because deviations from what was generally accepted would not be identified as social behaviour worthy of recognition by the law.[20]

Formalism thus provided judges with the appearance of objectivity; the legal process was seen as separate from the political process, where policy could be discussed and a socially acceptable solution reached. The knowledge possessed by a lawyer or a judge within the legal system was characterized as 'technical knowledge,'[21] since the rules of law were viewed in the same way that one would see the rules of a technical trade.[22] The growth of formalism as a model was very attractive to the legal profession because one could speak of a 'legal' point of view as opposed to a moral or political point of view; there was also 'legal' reasoning, and a 'legal' question. The formalist model offered the legal profession a distinct identity. The requirement of 'legal' knowledge of a technical nature gave lawyers an expertise that was exclusive; it acted as a barrier to those who lacked the training necessary to discuss the law and lawyering (or judges and judging).

In the nineteenth century, the growth in statute law (as opposed to judge-made law), was pronounced – in part as a result of the adoption of *stare decisis*. Statutes eliminated the need for judges to search for the appropriate rule: it was presented to them in the relevant statute. In order to maintain the appearance of objectivity and impartiality in legal decision making, formalism required that judges concern themselves only with the plain meaning of words. The words were identified as so controlling that judges could announce that they were not responsible for the social consequences of their decisions – they merely applied the law. Law was formal and abstract, with a life of its own. Law had become separated from the notion of justice. If the law did not produce a just decision, then it was left to the politicians to adjust the situation by creating new law.

When the language of a rule is clear (plain), a judge has no legitimate (reasonable) choice to make in determining the meaning of the words in question. In such circumstances the proper role for the judge is to follow the language (the law), and refrain from altering the effect of the words. This elementary proposition is justified by the application of our constitutional principle of 'rule of law.'

As with other aspects of formalism, the 'plain meaning rule' was adopted as an imperative legal doctrine in the nineteenth century.[23] Adoption of the doctrine gradually replaced the approach of examining the purpose behind a rule, that is, the policy behind its creation (its spirit), and then giving the words the meaning that would best carry out the policy. The practice of giving effect to the spirit of a law went back to cases that originated in the sixteenth century,[24] and had been in operation for at least three centuries before formalism started to push it aside. Under formalism words were not to be given meaning, they were to be treated as if they were plain and unambiguous on all occasions. In the nineteenth century, society became more and more moralistic, with dreams of ideal images, and social values were to be taken as clear and absolute. In such an environment words would correspondingly have clear and absolute (plain) meanings, because of unquestioned (and hence unstated) social assumptions. The passion for certainty meant conformity to social values. This is reflected in the characteristic of the formalist model whereby there is a single correct answer to a problem in law because there is a 'correct' interpretation of the words of a rule.

In 1885, as the mainstream of the legal profession became convinced that there was a distinct body of legal knowledge and a distinct legal methodology, the confidence of the profession was aided immeasurably by the English jurist, A.V. Dicey, who articulated the fundamental constitutional principle known as 'rule of law.'[25] Law was to be supreme, and the members of the legal profession were its guardians.

There is no doubt that rule of law has been and is today the fundamental principle of our society and constitution.[26] The Supreme Court of Canada has recently asserted that it is the very basis of our constitution, and the foundation of any constitution.[27] As with all things fundamental, it is general in nature, and for those who seek absolutes, it disappoints. It does not provide answers, but provides the milieu for the process of humane decision making in an attempt to reach answers. What is it? Rule of law consists of the government of laws and not of persons. Those with political power render obedience to a law that is other than their own will, or whim. In a government of laws, there is law superior to the will, or the whim, of those with political power. As a contemporary scholar says, 'That is all there is to it.'[28]

But Dicey added something that proved irresistible to the legal profession.[29] Of three meanings he promoted for rule of law, the most significant one was, 'no man is punishable or can be lawfully made to suffer in body or goods except for a distinct breach of law established in the ordinary legal manner before the ordinary courts of the land.'[30] The word 'ordinary' is key – 'ordinary legal manner' and 'ordinary courts' signify the ordinary legal profession. Dicey's identification of rule of law (supremacy of law) as a characteristic of the English constitution could not be questioned, but the meaning he assigned to it suited a purpose he had. Dicey wanted to attack the growth of government in the economic regulation of society. As the American legal scholar Morton Horwitz noted, 'Dicey's conception of the rule of law acquired a permanent place in all subsequent discussions of the growth of the administrative state.' The administrative state and the regulation of an individual's actions were fuelled (at least in part) by socialist sentiments and Dicey wanted no part of that ideology.[31] Horwitz went on to say of Dicey,

He brought to the rise of administration all of the conservative common lawyer's antipathy to public law as coercive, political, and redistributive. His great ideological – and intellectual – achievement was in successfully asserting the existence of a conflict between the rule of law and the rise of administrative regulation.[32]

Rule of law would become the rallying-cry for those who favoured judicial control of government (administrative) action.[33]

Dicey advocated that 'wide, arbitrary, or discretionary powers' should not be given to persons in authority, and asserted that 'wherever there is discretion there is room for arbitrariness.'[34] Formalism had adopted the position that decision making within the legal system involved the selection of correct answers; judges had no choice, once they found the applicable rule. In giving meaning to words within a rule, there was no choice. If the existence of choice was acknowledged, it followed (using language provided by Dicey), that discretion (choice) was being exercised, which led to arbitrariness. As a result all decision making which did not conform to the formalist model became, by definition, the exercise of discretion and arbitrary in nature, and involved a breach of rule of law.

By the end of the nineteenth century formalism as a defining methodology had been adopted by the mainstream of the legal profession. It was 'legal' – and any other approach was not. There could not be competition – one model was correct and any other had to be wrong. The contextual model lived on as an alternative approach, although it would occupy a secondary role until late in the twentieth century.

In the contextual model restrictions (formalities) placed on the process of reaching a solution are rejected as artificial. 'Legal reasoning' becomes simply 'reasoning.' Nothing about the process of resolving a dispute within the legal system is recognized as inherently unique. The contextualist is concerned primarily with the substance of the problem that has caused the dispute requiring adjudication. Procedure is important for orderliness, but form and procedure never dominate substance. Proponents of the model could identify it with the approach of the judges before the rise of formalism.

Because contextualism rejects formalism, the formalists identified contextual decision making as involving the exercise of discretion and not the application of law. Because the approach was not proper legal methodology there was no reason to give it a name, and, in fact, every reason not to name it and thereby acknowledge its existence.

A variety of terms have been used by those who wished to keep this alternative model alive and advocate its readoption by the mainstream of the legal profession. The term used in this work (contextualism) is the one currently used by the Supreme Court of Canada in its promotion of the methodology. Contextualism also accords nicely with the view that the words of a law acquire meaning within three contexts: the context of the language of a law, that is, the ordinary meaning of the words within the society at the time in question; the context of the law, namely, guides to meaning found within recognized existing legal sources, such as other legislation, cases, and writings; or the social context, which gives the words meaning as determined by the values of the society at the time.[35] Formalists accept only the language context as legitimate.

Other labels which have been used throughout the years (many still current) to designate approaches which embrace contextual thinking are 'sociological' jurisprudence (which has enjoyed considerable popularity over the years – even among formalists, because 'sociological' can be semantically distinguished from 'legal');[36] instrumentalism;[37] pluralism;[38] and functionalism.[39]

A contextual analysis of law is sometimes referred to as the 'purposive' approach. In 1982, the very general language used in the Charter of Rights and Freedoms, such as 'freedom of expression,' and 'principles of fundamental justice,' forced a shift from a simple linguistic analysis to contextual thinking. The prime articulation of a 'purposive' analysis was made by Mr Justice Brian Dickson (as he then was) in an early case involving the application of the Charter:

[The] proper approach to the definition of the rights and freedoms guaranteed by the Charter was a purposive one. The meaning of a right or freedom guaranteed by the Charter was to be ascertained by an analysis of the purpose of such a guarantee; it was to be understood, in other words, in the light of the interests it was meant to protect.

In my view this analysis is to be undertaken, and the purpose of the right or freedom in question is to be sought by reference to the character and the larger objects of the Charter itself, to the language chosen to articulate the specific right or freedom, to the historical origins of the concepts enshrined, and where applicable, to the meaning and purpose of the other specific rights and freedoms with which it is associated within the text of the Charter. The interpretation should be ... a generous rather than a legalistic one, aimed at fulfilling the purpose of the guarantee and securing for individuals the full benefit of the Charter's protection.[40]

Each of the three contexts is mentioned: 'the language chosen' (the language context); 'the character and the larger objects of the Charter itself' (the legal context); and 'the historical origins of the concepts' (the social context). '[O]ther specific rights and freedoms' points to the legal context and perhaps the social context.

In an earlier work, I suggested the use of the term 'creative decision making,' by which I meant thinking out a problem and *creating* a solution which would serve as a guide to the solution of future problems.[41] However, some readers understood the word 'creative' as equivalent to 'activism.'

The word 'activism' is used to describe three types of judicial behaviour. There is a law-making potential within the legal system when judges are evaluating an existing judge-made rule (common-law rule), and also when evaluating existing interpretations of legislation. A willingness to undertake change in the law is not activism per se, but the extent of the change brought about may earn a judge the label 'activist.' This was the meaning that Madame Justice Beverly McLachlin had in mind in a Supreme Court of Canada judgment in 1989 in which a power to reform law was recognized as existing within the judicial process, to which she added the comment 'some judges are more activist than others.'[42] The term is also used in constitutional law with regard to the power of the judiciary to declare a law invalid because of conflict with a provision of the constitution. A judge who wields the power of judicial review of legislation may similarly attract the label 'activist,' depending on the ease with which the power is used. In both of the instances discussed above the question of whether a judge is an activist or not is a question of degree. Finally, the word is used to describe judicial behaviour on those rare occasions when a judge moves beyond the judicial role and becomes purely a political actor. Here, the judge uses the power within the legal system to reach a conclusion that he or she prefers. The judge may create law to reach a solution, but in the process ignore the language and legal contexts, and proceed directly to the social context to invoke the social values that the judge personally thinks are appropriate, rather than those that exist outside the judge's personal desires. Activism in this instance involves a negation of the principle of rule of law. There is no question of degree involved. The judge's behaviour is considered to be inappropriate.

In an very valuable article Roger Traynor, late chief justice of California, pointed out that a lawyer and a judge must have 'an actively analytical mind,' and that a judge must be an 'active analyst,' which he pointed out was different from being a judicial activist. Traynor asserted that there must be a difference between 'judicial analysis' and 'legislative innovation,' that the legal system cannot be 'the engine of social reform.'[43]

A study of those rare decisions which illustrate this third type of activism reveals that the judges who were activists were formalists. What appears to have happened in each case was that the judge experienced a strong reaction against the social values expressed in the law that the judge was being asked to apply, and which were bearing in on the judge. The reaction caused the judge to break loose from the constraints within the rule of law, and essentially to make a political decision.

In addition to the language, legal and social contexts already discussed, it becomes necessary to acknowledge a fourth. This is the 'professional' context. The social values to which members of the legal profession personally adhere will potentially affect decision making within the system, but a sincere commitment to serve the interests of clients (who may have other values) can attenuate lawyers' personal values. However, if a particular lawyer is unable to set aside his or her personal values in favour of the clients', that lawyer will inevitably decide to serve only those clients who have compatible values. The professional context also becomes a concern when the rules created by lawyers for lawyers (procedural rules) begin to determine the outcome of cases. With the creation of something distinctly 'legal,' such as 'legal' evidence and 'legal' reasoning, which, as one scholar pointed out, made lawyers indispensable actors,[44] the professional context intruded significantly. In the contextual model, the impact of the fourth context would lessen with the reduction in the amount of 'lawyer's law.'

This history of what was initially the Exchequer Court of Canada, now the Federal Court of Canada, examines more than one hundred years of activity which saw fundamental changes occur in law and lawyering and judges and judging. The text chronicles the solidifying of formalism as the 'legal' methodology late in the nineteenth century. Armed with the new method of dispute resolution, the legal profession assumed the role of the most suitable and accomplished resolvers of disputes. Now, however, many are questioning that role and establishing alternative methods for the adjudication of disputes – known within the legal profession as alternative dispute resolution (ADR).

Over the same one hundred years came the rise of the administrative state, which the legal profession tried to combat, though a small contingent of lawyers supported it. This struggle is also part of the history of the Federal Court.

The century studied has been a time of considerable change in the law, none greater than the rise and fall of formalism as the defining methodology of the profession. It took decades of the nineteenth century for formalism to obtain dominance, and its grip is only now loosening. The changes may continue well into the next century.

2

Establishment

Throughout the ninety-five-year history of the Exchequer Court of Canada, from 1876 to 1971, and the almost quarter-century of existence of the Federal Court of Canada, from 1971 to 1992, the one word, more than any other, that characterizes them is 'anonymity.'

The Exchequer Court was created in anonymity, its existence and work hidden behind the bulk of the Supreme Court of Canada. The road that had led to the establishment of the Supreme Court of Canada in 1875 had not been easily travelled, and had taken eight years following Confederation, even though the creation of a national appeal court had been considered a priority in the pre-Confederation negotiations.[1] The two more-or-less equal parts of the dual Province of Canada that had existed from 1840 until 1867 had each, for their own reasons, been concerned about vesting any power in the new central authority housed at Ottawa. Ontario (known officially as Canada West before Confederation, though many still preferred its older name, Upper Canada) showed concern about protecting its legal system from potential incursions by Ottawa. Quebec (called Canada East in the Province of Canada era and Lower Canada from 1791 to 1840) had a deeper concern with the potentially centralizing, and hence unifying, forces inherent in national institutions. In addition national legal institutions posed a potential threat to its law. The law of Quebec, housed in its Civil Code, was a symbol of nationality and a distinguishing mark.[2]

From the beginning it was accepted that Ottawa would have the power to create courts to administer federal law, in addition to the authority to establish a national court of appeal.[3] In the end the power appeared in section 101 of the constitution:

The Parliament of Canada may, notwithstanding anything in this Act, from Time to Time provide for the Constitution, Maintenance, and Organization of a General Court of Appeal for Canada, and for the Establishment of any additional Courts for the better Administration of the Laws of Canada.[4]

The existence of the Exchequer Court of Canada, and that of its successor, the Federal Court of Canada, has been based on this provision, in particular on the words 'additional Courts for the better Administration of the Laws of Canada.' These words have given the two courts their identity.[5]

With regard to courts there is also section 129 of the constitution, which provides that 'all Courts of Civil and Criminal Jurisdiction ... shall continue ... as if the Union had not been made; subject nevertheless ... to be repealed, abolished, or altered by the Parliament of Canada, or by the Legislature of the respective Province, acording to the Authority of the Parliament or that legislature under this Act.' More will be said about this provision later.

The constitution for the Dominion of Canada that came into being in 1867 contained powerful forces for the creation of a legislative union (apparently desired by Sir John A. Macdonald, the driving force behind Confederation). Such a union could have broken down those elements of federalism in the constitution where the power of the provinces lay. If the unifying forces had been let loose they would have resulted, more or less, in one unified country, or at the very least such forces would have been promoted at the expense of those that tended towards provincial rights and a federal system. The experience of the United States of America, whose Civil War – fought in great part over the issue of the rights of its component states – had ended just two years before Confederation and was vivid in the minds of Canadians. The violent struggle that had dominated the life of the United States for four years was seen as having arisen from a weak central government. British North Americans were determined to avoid a similar catastrophe.

The constitution of 1867 – with particular reference to the centralizing forces within it – has come to be known as the 'Macdonaldian constitution.'[6] A survey of the provisions of the constitution reveals that there was to be 'One Parliament for Canada,' which would include the ruling sovereign,[7] while for the provinces there were to be 'legislatures,'[8] and rather than the sovereign there would be 'an Officer, styled the Lieutenant Governor.' The lieutenant-governor would be appointed by the Canadian government at Ottawa[9] and thus in essence a federal public servant, thereby giving Ottawa a voice in the enactment of all provincial legislation. The lieutenant-governor had the power to reserve provincial bills for consideration by the federal government. In addition the federal government was given the enormous power to disallow any provincial statute that had been enacted.[10]

With respect to the legal system, Ottawa was given the authority to appoint the judges of the principal provincial courts, leaving the provincial governments to appoint the judges of local courts of the time.[11] The judges who presided over these courts were not necessarily lawyers. Through the appeal process, all provincial courts would ultimately come within the control of the one court of appeal for Canada that Ottawa had the power to create.[12] The potential for unification of law through the judicial process was very real.

However, the constitutional provision with greatest potential for creating uniformity of laws and destroying the federal system as we now know it was the section which specified that the provinces could abandon their power to enact laws and pass the authority to Ottawa, thus effectively ending the provincial legislatures and reducing the provinces to the position of municipalities in relation to the central authority at Ottawa.[13] There was however a crucial exception to this highly centralizing provision, namely, the province of Quebec. If the other provinces had made use of this provision, the result would probably have been two primary law-making institutions, the Parliament of Canada and the Legislative Assembly of Quebec, creating in effect two separate parts of the country. However, there is a major qualification to this picture: under the Macdonaldian constitution the provinces could only enact laws affecting private persons, 'property and civil rights.' The major areas for legislative action lay within the federal sphere. But for Quebec control over the day-to-day affairs of its citizens was of primary importance, and, since it had been specifically excepted from the provision providing for the unification of law, from Quebec's perspective the existence of a general court of appeal with a unifying potential then became highly suspect.

Indeed, in any consideration of the Macdonaldian constitution and its potential, or any speculation about what the country would have looked like had that potential been harnessed, the position of Quebec has to be viewed as an enigma. Or can one simply accept that there would have been two distinct political entities governing matters of property and civil rights and 'matters of a merely local or private nature,' such as hospitals and licensing of shops?[14] Matters that fell within the legislative authority of Ottawa would have been common.[15]

It was in the spirit of a unified nation, rather than a confederation, that Macdonald made the first move to exercise the federal government's constitutional power to establish a federal court. In 1869 he introduced a bill in the House of Commons that would have established a Supreme Court for Canada. The fact that nothing more was ever publicly heard about this bill indicates its extraordinary nature. In today's terms, the proposed court can be seen in the same light as the words 'Supreme Court' of a province. In other words, the court would have represented the legal system for the entire country. It was indeed to be a 'general court of appeal' that would hear appeals from provincial courts on matters involving provincial law, including from Quebec, but it was also to have an extensive original or trial jurisdiction. It was to have exclusive jurisdiction over cases in which the constitutionality of a provincial law was challenged; cases involving federal revenue laws; cases in which a party was the British government, a British colonial government, a provincial government, a foreign government, or a consul of a foreign state; and cases involving federal law that had been enacted to carry out the terms of an Imperial treaty. It would have a wide jurisdiction over cases in which Parliament had enacted a statute and had specified that it was to be applied exclusively by the court. In addition the court would have jurisdiction to issue the writ of *habeas corpus ad subjiciendum* in extradition cases, and also jurisdiction over admiralty law.

Further, there was concurrent jurisdiction with the provincial courts, such as when the parties were from different provinces, or when one party was from outside the country.

If the Conservatives under Macdonald had not already set off alarm bells in the provincial capitals with the above provisions, the ultimate wake-up call was the provision giving a judge of the proposed court jurisdiction to consider matters involving purely provincial law and the administration of justice within the province, such as the 'trial of all issues of facts in actions on the common law side of the ... Court,' the 'hearing of causes in suits on the equity side of the ... Court,' and in Quebec to exercise the jurisdiction of a single judge of the Superior Court of the province. The court would effectively replace the provincial superior courts.

Macdonald later said that this 1869 bill was only for discussion purposes, but its provisions appear unbelievable, even in terms of the state of

Confederation in 1869. Out of the provisions relating to the original jurisdiction of the Supreme Court would arise the Exchequer Court of Canada, but with a very much reduced scope of jurisdiction. The attempt at
such an extensive original jurisdiction not only failed, but may have left
as a legacy the thought that the jurisdiction of a court of first instance created by Ottawa was a threat to the existence of the provincial courts.[16]

The intent behind the drafting of the 1869 bill remains a mystery. Its
author was Henry Strong, a judge of the Chancery Court in Ontario, who
has been identified as a friend and adviser of Macdonald. The mystery
becomes more pronounced when one realizes that, after being one of the
initial six appointees to the Supreme Court in 1876, Strong was to leave
no doubt about his sympathy for provincial legislative jurisdiction. He
was to prove no friend of the Macdonaldian constitution.[17]

Although Macdonald viewed the original jurisdiction as the foundation of his new federal court, it had to be effectively abandoned.[18] In
a subsequent attempt to create a federal court, only revenue cases
remained from the vast original jurisdiction that had initially been proposed. Macdonald considered it wise to confine the jurisdiction to cases
in which the Crown was a party, 'after the same fashion as causes
between the Crown and the people are conducted in Courts of Exchequer
in England.'[19]

In a renewed attempt in 1870 to create a court, the 'principal object' had
become the establishment of an appeal court,[20] with the extensive trial
jurisdiction being abandoned. In addition, Macdonald had felt it necessary to propose a more restricted appellate jurisdiction than that of the
earlier bill. But in the end this did not prove sufficient to ensure acceptance of the court, although it was doubtful whether anything would
have worked at the time. Macdonald's party was dependent on support
from Quebec and the spectre of the new national court with non-Quebec
judges forming a majority and applying the civil law of that province was
too much for the Quebec members of Parliament. This was Macdonald's
last attempt to create a federal court and it failed primarily because of a
lack of support by his own party.

What Macdonald and the Conservatives failed to accomplish was
finally brought about by the Liberal government of Alexander Mackenzie, which came into power following the general election of 1874. The
bill to create the federal court was introduced in February 1875 by the
Liberal Minister of Justice, Télesphore Fournier, and was in essence a
copy of Macdonald's revised bill of 1870. When Fournier introduced the
bill he announced that, because of the objections that had been made to

the original jurisdiction that Macdonald had tried to give the court, he had tried to avoid the problem by creating two courts, one of appellate jurisdiction, the Supreme Court of Canada, and the other, a tribunal of original jurisdiction, to be called the Exchequer Court of Canada. While the two courts were to be composed of the same judges, Fournier wanted to assure everyone that they were really totally different courts.[21] They had different names at least.

During the course of introducing the bill, Fournier alluded to the fact that 'every one admitted that it was very important that the Federal Government should have an institution of its own in order to secure the due execution of its laws.' He went on: 'There might perhaps come a time when it would not be safe for the Federal Government to be at the mercy of the tribunals of the Provinces.'[22] One is left to wonder whether these views were expressed tongue-in-cheek, and by someone who, at the time, was confident that the federal government was in no danger. Perhaps there was a hidden threat aimed at the provinces, namely, that the new federal court could have its jurisdiction extended if that was thought necessary.

With its reduced jurisdiction, the new Exchequer Court was not the subject of any extensive comment during the debate that ensued. There were some objections on the grounds that the provincial courts could deal with the matters assigned to the new court, and that it was thus entirely unnecessary.[23] The fact that one of those speakers, Aemilius Irving, was a Bencher of the Law Society of Upper Canada, may have indicated some antagonism in Ontario to this federal equivalent of the provincial courts.

The provision for appeals from a judge of the Exchequer Court to the Supreme Court of Canada merely evoked one passing comment from a member, that it was unsatisfactory.[24] The eventuality that a judge presiding as the Exchequer Court might also sit on the Supreme Court bench to hear an appeal from his own decision was obviously not seen as any problem at all by the great majority, or was simply unforeseen.

On April 8, 1875, The Supreme and Exchequer Court Act[25] received royal assent and a federal court system was brought into existence almost eight years after Confederation. However it remained for life to be breathed into the structure by the issuing of proclamations.[26] On September 17, 1875, a proclamation brought the Act into force with respect to the organization of the court, which included the appointment of the judges, the registrar, clerks and other employees. The judges and registrar were appointed on October 8, 1875. The judicial functions took effect by proclamation on January 11, 1876.

As stated earlier, Ottawa's authority to create the Exchequer Court appeared in the words of section 101 of the constitution: 'Establishment of ... Courts for the better Administration of the Laws of Canada.' At the time the court was created, there was no dispute at all concerning the constitutional power to create it. It would be a century later before intense controversy burst upon the successor Federal Court of Canada over the meaning of the words 'Laws of Canada.'

PART 2

The First Court, 1875–1887

3

Jurisdiction

The Supreme and Exchequer Court Act gave the Exchequer Court juris-diction partly concurrent with provincial courts and partly exclusive to itself. The concurrent jurisdiction dealt with any proceedings that involved the enforcement of the revenue laws of the Dominion, and any action of a civil nature, as opposed to criminal, in which the government of Canada initiated the proceedings. The part that was exclusive con-sisted of litigation in 'cases in which demand shall be made or relief sought in respect of any matter which might in England be the subject of a suit or action in the Court of Exchequer on its revenue side against the Crown, or any officer of the Crown.'[1]

The references to revenue and the Court of Exchequer in England give an obvious clue as to why the name 'Exchequer Court of Canada' was chosen for the new federal court. The name 'Exchequer' came with exten-sive baggage attached to it and that baggage, more coincidentally than deliberately, was to characterize the new Canadian court throughout the years, and even to continue to the present under its new name, the Fed-eral Court of Canada.

Following the Norman conquest in the eleventh century, the financial department of the government of England was called the Exchequer. The name came from Normandy where it had been 'the ancient and sovereign court ..., to which appeals from all inferior courts were heard.'[2] The name itself was said to derive from a chequered cloth resembling a chessboard, which was laid on a table on which an accounting of the King's money would be carried out. The squares were to aid in calculations.[3] As the financial department, it possessed both an administrative side and a dispute resolution side, and it was from this latter part of its role that there had evolved a distinct court by the beginning of the fourteenth century. One historian has stated that the judicial side was the nearest approach to an administrative court.[4] Over time as a court it acquired both an equity jurisdiction and the jurisdiction of a common law court, and in the seventeenth century ceased to be a specialized revenue court. It was the only common law court to have an equity jurisdiction.[5] While it had the same jurisdiction as that possessed by the other two superior courts of common law, Court of Queen's (King's) Bench, and the Court of Common Pleas, it had an exclusive jurisdiction dating back to its origin over matters of revenue and matters of interest to the government.[6]

In England in 1875, the year that the Canadian court was born, the Court of Exchequer was abolished. It was merged with the other two common law courts, and with the Chancery and Admiralty courts, to become the High Court of Justice.[7]

One historian has called the history of the equity jurisdiction of the Court of Exchequer by far the most obscure of all jurisdictions in England.[8] When it came to the adoption of the jurisdiction of the English court for the new Canadian court, a lack of understanding appears to have gone further.

For the Exchequer Court of Canada, the jurisdiction over the enforcement of revenue laws and that concerning actions by the government, both of which were concurrent with the provincial courts, were not questionable at the time, but the exclusive jurisdiction did have some flaws in it. What exactly did the words in the provision establishing jurisdiction mean? '[C]ases in which demand shall be made or relief sought in respect of any matter which might in England be the subject of a suit or action in the Court of Exchequer on its revenue side against the Crown, or any officer of the Crown.'[9]

Three months after the judicial functions of the court were proclaimed in force, and before any case was heard, those words were changed. The Minister of Justice admitted that the jurisdiction had been ill-defined and that some powers that were supposed to have been given to the court had not been, since they did not exist on the 'revenue side' in England.[10] Added to the concurrent jurisdiction were 'cases in which demand shall be made or relief sought in respect of any matter which might in England be the subject of a suit or action in the Court of Exchequer on its plea side against any officer of the Crown.'[11] Jurisdiction over actions against officers of the Crown did not fall under the 'revenue side' of the English court and was thus eliminated.

The apparent problem with adopting the jurisdiction of the court of Exchequer in England for the Canadian court stemmed from the evolutionary development of the English court. Out of the original dispute resolution aspect of the work of the revenue department, there had survived a 'revenue side' of the jurisdiction of the court, namely the settlement of disputes between the government and taxpayers. Over the years a common law jurisdiction was added in a grab for work (the judges were paid by fees),[12] and there was the somewhat mysterious equity jurisdiction, not possessed by any other common law court. The 'plea side' referred to the bringing of common law actions. The officer of the Crown subject to such an action would be a private person and thus the action would have to be brought on the 'plea side,' while actions against the Crown could only come on the 'revenue side,' which contained an equity component.

When the Court of Exchequer in England was reincarnated in the Exchequer Court of Canada, the jurisdiction of the new Canadian Court potentially included both the revenue and equity sides of the old, plus the plea side regarding actions against officers of the government. Eight centuries of experience as a judicial institution waited to be used.

CROWN LIABILITY

The jurisdiction of the new court over actions against the Crown[13] raised the issue of the liability of the Crown (government) in an action by an individual. This question was becoming more and more important as government became more involved in the affairs of the country, particularly the Dominion government, with its commitment to the building of public works.

In 1846, prior to Confederation, the Province of Canada began to use public arbitrators to resolve disputes between the government and an individual with respect to public works. This system, based on the practice in the State of New York, replaced the use of private arbitrators, who had apparently made some extensive damage awards that were considered unjustified.[14] Some question did arise with regard to the independence and impartiality of the arbitrators, who would be government employees and 'a species of court,'[15] but such concerns failed to dissuade the government. However, the new legislation provided for an appeal to the courts from the decisions of the new public arbitrators.[16]

After Confederation, the new Dominion adopted the use of arbitrators, following the system of the Province of Canada.[17] Unlike the Province's legislation, however, the new federal law did not provide for an appeal to the courts. There was an appeal from a single arbitrator to the full Board of Arbitration, 'from which decision and award,' the legislation expressly stated, 'there shall be no further appeal whatever.'[18] As with the earlier law, the arbitrators were to be concerned with matters of property, but in 1870 their jurisdiction was extended to deal with claims 'arising out of any death, or any injury to person or property on any railway, canal or public work.'[19] At the time that the arbitration system was adopted for the Dominion, certain members of Parliament from New Brunswick had pointed out that in that province, actions against the government in relation to injuries sustained on government railways were tried in the law courts,[20] but any attempt to have the use of arbitrators reconsidered was of no avail.[21]

The Court of Exchequer in England had been the court concerned with matters of the Crown and because of that the history of the court that carried the name 'Exchequer' was intimately entwined with the issue of Crown liability.[22] Crown liability is a constitutional issue, since it is the power of government that is being examined. The policy and law concerning claims against the government for personal injuries developed from the idea that the individual who received some injury because of the actions of government should be able to obtain some sort of relief against it.

The rules and principles of Crown liability developed from the thirteenth century onwards, and began with a period when the King (government) could not be sued in court, and an individual had to rely on a request (petition) to the monarch for relief for any injury. In the sixteeth century, the theory developed that the King could do no wrong, which gelled into a constitutional principle and maxim of the law. The result was that the government was not considered liable for any personal injuries caused by the actions of its employees. The citizen (subject) had recourse only in cases involving property rights. When a petition was presented to the sovereign for compensation the government would investigate the matter and gather information, which could take a long time. Following completion of the investigation a decision would be made one way or another.

If a person were injured by a fellow citizen, he or she would have a claim as of right against the other person for compensation. Since the word 'Crown' in this context means not the sovereign but rather the government, injuries caused by the actions of government are always caused by the actions of its employees. In what was considered the public interest, rules gave the government immunity from any action by an injured person. The government's agents or employees could be held accountable, but their financial resources were limited compared with those of the government.

Reform of the rules governing Crown liability followed on the changes in the nature of government action, always keeping pace, however, with the social value that recognized that the injured person ought to have a remedy. In the Middle Ages, property law was dominant and the restriction of petitions to property claims created no widespread grievances. The problems that arose concerned instances where the sovereign had seized or otherwise obtained possession of land to which the subject was entitled, for example, following the death of a tenant, attainder (forfeit of a person's property following a death sentence for treason or felony) or lunacy, or abuses of the sovereign's rights relating to a subject's real property as a result of feudal concepts of land holding. In other cases compensation was claimed for damage to property resulting from the erection of works or flooding caused by the digging of trenches.

From the fourteenth century to the middle of the seventeenth century there were petitions in revenue cases and cases involving debts due from the Crown: for example, payment for work done and materials provided for repair of a castle. A petition would be presented in Parliament, answered by the King, and then paid or referred to the Exchequer to be heard and determined. It is interesting to ponder what the jurisdiction of the Exchequer Court of Canada had the potential to cover, given the reference to claims against the Crown on the revenue side of the Court of Exchequer in England.

By the seventeenth century, medieval law had begun to change. The incidents of tenure became obsolete, and the property base of what was now known as a petition of right began to give way. In the second half of the seventeenth century came a judicial recognition that an individual was entitled to equitable relief against the Crown.[23] It was at this point that the Court of Exchequer came into its own with regard to Crown liability.[24]

Although the constitutional principle 'the King can do no wrong' had developed in the sixteenth century, claims against the Crown were nevertheless recognized. In *Pawlett v. The Attorney General* in 1667,[25] Baron Atkyns was reported to have been strongly of the view that the party in the case ought to obtain relief against the King, because the King was the fountain and head of justice and equity, and it should not be presumed that he would be defective in either. Baron Atkyns concluded that it would have derogated from the King's honour to imagine that what is equity against a common person should not be equity against him.

During the eighteenth century, the Court of Chancery, as the court of equity, was prepared to grant a remedy against the Crown on a petition of right, while the Court of Exchequer could do so in an action brought against the attorney general. In the eighteenth century the petition of right fell into disuse.

In the nineteenth century, the activities of government changed and the need arose for individuals to have a remedy for breach of contract and other injuries caused by government employees. Due to changes in the fiscal machinery of the state the old remedy that had existed with the Exchequer Court had become obsolete.[26] However, other changes were under way as well. As government became more involved in the day-to-day affairs of the citizenry and subjected itself to more and more potential claims for compensation for injuries, there arose the attitude that there was a need to protect the government in the public interest. In the case of *Viscount Canterbury v. Attorney General*[27] in 1843, Lord Chancellor Lyndhurst declared that a petition of right could not be used to recover compensation for injuries sustained because of the negligence of servants of the Crown. Tort liability of the government for acts of its employees was thus expressly denied. Only in cases where the Crown had taken the land or goods of an individual might a petition of right be used to try and recover the property.

In creating an immunity for the government against claims based on other than property rights the judges said that they were controlled by the fact that they could find no 'precise and distinct authority' that attached liability to the Crown for the negligent acts of a government employee. Certainly the employees involved who were negligent were still personally liable. At this time, the Lord Chancellor did not feel justified in being the first to declare the liability of the government. However, it should be pointed out that there was also no authority denying the liability: there was a choice available.

In 1860, with the enactment of The Petitions of Right Act, the procedure for using a petition of right was simplified.[28] The courts were to hear claims and the right of the government to decide the merits of a claim against it had been eliminated. Theoretically the government had to grant permission before a hearing in the courts could be otained, but permission was never refused, and thus the petitioner had sure access to the courts. While the procedure became easier, and the judiciary became the adjudicators, it was generally agreed that the new law did not extend the scope of Crown liability beyond what it had covered before.

In 1843 Lord Lyndhurst had shown restraint when asked to recognize Crown liability, but change was working. In 1874 the judges of the Court of Queen's Bench accepted the right of an individual to sue for damages for breach of contract by the Crown.[29] The judges acknowledged that the increase in the number of contracts being created between individuals and government departments made the change in the law necessary. The very existence of the fairly recent The Petitions of Right Act of 1860 inspired the judges to reform the law, increasing the protection of an individual vis-à-vis government action. Added to property claims were those based on contract.

In Canada, the same changing conditions were reflected by the copying, in 1875, of the 1860 English statute. The need to adopt the procedure established in England fifteen years earlier had arisen because of the government's requirement for 'an extraordinary number of contracts.' It was foreseen that there would be 'constant claims against the government.'[30] The government accepted that the legislation put claimants in a better position than before its enactment, and had obviously also accepted the 1874 judicial reform of the English law.

The Petition of Right Act, Canada, 1875[31] went through the legislative process at the same time as The Supreme and Exchequer Court Act and, while jurisdiction over actions against the Crown was given to the provincial courts,[32] it was the general opinion that the Exchequer Court should have had the jurisdiction.[33] A year later the 1875 statute was repealed and The Petition of Right Act, 1876 was passed, in which the Exchequer Court was given exclusive original jurisdiction over petitions of right.[34]

As a matter of substantive law concerning Crown liability the 1876 statute referred to the law in England, and provided that an application for a petition of right would be allowed in all cases in which a petition could be brought in England. The 1876 statute also eliminated a provision in the 1875 statute by which claims arising from public works were still to be dealt with through a process of arbitration, rather than by the courts. If this arbitration provision had been left intact, the great bulk of contract cases, for which the 1875 statute had been enacted, would not have been covered by the petition of right process.[35]

As in England, the jurisdiction of the court depended on the government granting permission – a fiat. Unlike England, where it was viewed as a technicality, the government of the day in Canada regarded the requirement of permission as 'the general and wholesome rule' by which unmeritorious claims could be weeded out.[36] However, over the years the government was not accused of blocking claims, although there were complaints about unwarranted delay.

Even after the 1876 Petition of Right Act, the arbitration process was still in effect; a provision of the Act allowed for a reference to arbitration by a government department head, which resulted in a claimant being unable to use the judicial system.[37] The government thought the use of arbitrators was a simpler, cheaper, and more effectual way of dealing with claims against the government; only if a principle of law was involved should the judiciary be used.[38] The continued use of public arbitrators did raise the issue of the independence of the decision maker, an arbitrator paid by the government, which was said to affect the confidence of the public, but to the government the benefits seen outweighed this theoretical problem.[39]

There were signs, however, that the days of the use of arbitrators might be coming to an end. The opposition suggested that the official arbitrators be abolished, to which the government simply replied that it preferred to wait until the statute had been in operation for a while before considering that reform. The arbitration system remained in effect throughout the period when the Supreme Court and Exchequer Court of Canada were tied together, although in 1879 the finality of the decision of the Board of Arbitration was abandoned and an appeal provided from the Board to the Exchequer Court.[40] Only appeals involving claims of $500 or more were allowed. This move was followed in 1881 by the creation of an appeal to the Court from all cases of arbitration arising under the Government Railways Act.[41]

4

The Judges

The initial appointments of the judges to the Supreme and Exchequer Court were highly unusual, and such a dramatic mix has not been seen since. The six judges appointed to the court were evenly split regarding their approach to law and legal decision making. As might be expected, battles were fought over which methodology should be used. Undoubtedly the appointments were made with the Supreme Court of Canada in mind; the fact that the judges would have trial duties in the Exchequer Court was not likely of any moment.

Edward Blake, then minister of justice in the Liberal government of Alexander Mackenzie, took charge of the appointments.[1] He had himself declined to become chief justice when it was offered to him, because he preferred at the time to stay in politics.[2] His choice was Antoine-Aimé Dorion, the recently appointed chief justice of Quebec's Court of Queen's Bench, but Dorion preferred to remain in Quebec. The position fell to the chief justice of Ontario, William Buell Richards, instead.

Richards, of Loyalist background, from Brockville, was sixty years of age. He had been a member of the Legislative Assembly as a Reformer from 1848 until 1853; from 1851 to 1853, he had been attorney general of Canada West. He was appointed to the Court of Common Pleas in 1853, and ten years later became chief justice of the court. In 1868, he was made chief justice of the Queen's Bench, which also carried the designation chief justice of Ontario. The *Canada Law Journal*, based in Ontario, produced a glowing description of him. He was described as a man of powerful intellect, taking a wide grasp of a subject and looking at it 'all round,' discussing it not only with reference to the abstract law, but also with reference to its relation to the wants and habits of a new country. He was also said to be a liberal-minded man with a far-seeing mind and brilliant common sense.[3] It is noteworthy that the characteristics considered by the profession to be highly praiseworthy were also those that identified Richards as a judge willing and able to take a contextual approach.

The next judge in order of precedence was the chief justice of New Brunswick, William Johnstone Ritchie, who was almost sixty-two. Ritchie also had a Loyalist background and a significant political career. He had been a member of the House of Assembly of New Brunswick from 1847 to 1851, and a member of the Executive Council until appointed to the bench in 1855. He was made chief justice in 1865. He was viewed as an able lawyer, with a strong will and decided views, and one who had a considerable sense of the dignity of his position. The *Canada Law Journal* pointed out that at one time he had been strongly opposed to Confederation.[4] He has been assessed as a good, conscientious, and independent judge, though not a great innovator.[5] He has also been described as a reformer and a Liberal, but this was in relation to the ultra-conservative establishment that existed in the society in which he lived. His biographer has pointed out that he was not a progressive.[6]

The third judge was Samuel Henry Strong, a judge of the Ontario Court of Error and Appeal. Unlike the previous two judges, he had no political background. Born in England, he came to Canada with his parents at the age of eleven. His father was an Anglican clergyman at Quebec City. He practised as an equity lawyer in Toronto until appointed to the bench as senior vice-chancellor of the Ontario Court of Chancery in 1869. He became a member of the new Court of Error and Appeal in 1874. Strong was fifty when appointed to the Supreme and Exchequer Courts, and the youngest of the six judges. In contrast to Richards' qualities as a judge, Strong was characterized by the term 'scientific.' His distinction came from his knowledge of law as a science and of the principles of jurisprudence generally[7] – a description indicative of a formalist.

The legislation creating the courts specified that at least two of the six judges would come from the bench or bar of the province of Quebec.[8] The two judges selected from Quebec were fourth and fifth in precedence.

Jean-Thomas Taschereau, almost sixty-one, had been a judge in Quebec for ten years, eight on the Superior Court and two on the highest court in the province, the Court of Queen's Bench. He had practised law at Quebec City and had held no public office. The Taschereau family were Quebec aristocrats. It would be an understatement to say that he was reluctant to become part of the new institution. He never took up residence in Ottawa and left the court after only three years, having wanted to leave for some time.[9] He actually requested a leave of absence before the work of the court had begun, but it was refused because another judge was ill at the time.

The problems facing the government in finding members of the Quebec bar to come to Ottawa as judges, illustrated by the Taschereau appointment, were solved with the second Quebec judge by selecting someone who had already made a commitment to Ottawa, a member of the federal cabinet. Télesphore Fournier, fifty-two years of age, was the postmaster general and the former minister of justice who, in that capacity in the Mackenzie government, had had charge of the Supreme and Exchequer Court bill when it was introduced in 1875. Following the bill's enactment into law, he had moved to the post of postmaster general in order to allow Edward Blake to enter the cabinet. Fournier had also been minister of inland revenue, a position that would have made an appointment to the new revenue court seem natural. He had practised law at Quebec City, as had Taschereau, which left the Montreal bar out. He was a leader of the *Parti rouge*, a liberal organization that was at war with the Roman Catholic Church in Quebec because of its perceived extreme radical views, one of which was the separation of church and state.[10] In addition Fournier had a newspaper background as an editor of a liberal paper.

There was one remaining position, and that went logically to someone from the province of Nova Scotia. William Alexander Henry, a Father of Confederation,[11] was fifty-eight and had been a member of the Nova Scotia legislature for more than twenty years. He had been solicitor general and attorney general of the province. At the time of his appointment, he was the only Father of Confederation who had not received a substantial political reward.[12] His political career at the provincial level had come to an end in the provincial election of 1867 in which the people of Nova Scotia turned against Confederation and those associated with it.

At the time of his appointment the *Canada Law Journal*, based in Ontario, gave a one-line assessment of him: 'Mr. Henry, from Nova Scotia, is said to be a fair lawyer.'[13] This appraisal appears to have been swallowed whole, even by Nova Scotians.[14] As will be seen from his performance in the cases to be discussed later, if ever a reassessment was needed it would be for Henry.

In addition to the brief three-year tenure of Jean-Thomas Taschereau, the chief justice, William Richards, was forced to resign after only a little over three years on the court for health reasons: he suffered seriously from asthma. As a result, two additional judges were appointed in this first period. Henri-Elzéar Taschereau succeeded his cousin Jean-Thomas in October 1878. He had been a judge of the Superior Court in Quebec for seven years, and before that had practised law in Quebec City. He had been a Conservative member of the Legislative Assembly of United Canada from 1861 to 1867. Following his defeat in 1867, he returned to the practice of law. The aristocratic nature of his family appeared clearly in his bearing and temperament. At forty-two, he was one of the youngest judges ever to be appointed to the court.[15]

Following Richards' resignation early in 1879, the vacancy was filled as a matter of course with another judge from Ontario.[16] John Wellington Gwynne had been a judge of Common Pleas in Ontario for ten years. He was the first Conservative appointee in the history of the Supreme Court, since Macdonald had been returned to power in the election of 1878. Gwynne would be noted primarily for his undying devotion to the principles of the Macdonaldian constitution. At sixty-five, he would be one of the oldest judges appointed in the history of the court. He had been born in Ireland and came to Canada at the age of eighteen. He obtained legal training in chambers in England before setting up practice in Toronto. He had one fling at elected political life, when he was defeated as a Reform candidate early in his career.

Following Gwynne's appointment came the longest period in the history of the Supreme Court in which there were no changes on the bench, January 14, 1879, to May 3, 1888 – almost nine years and four months. The Supreme Court judges would, however, only remain judges of the Exchequer Court until October 1, 1887.

Of the original six judges, Richards, Fournier, and Henry fell into the contextual camp, and Ritchie, Strong, and Taschereau were formalists. The split between the judges with respect to their approach to law and decision making went to the heart of the legal system, creating tensions and considerable friction that spilled over into the judgments. The two most dramatic examples of different views, as will be seen in the pages that follow, were Richards and Strong, both from Ontario. It is highly interesting, and says something about the legal profession of the time, that when they were appointed the *Canada Law Journal* could assess both as praiseworthy, each for their very different characteristics. Henri-Elzéar Taschereau, who replaced his cousin, was also a formalist, as was

Gwynne, who filled the vacancy created when Richards left. Thus, from 1879 until 1887, when the Exchequer Court was separated from the Supreme Court, there were only two contextualists, compared with four formalists. The two models of decision making can readily be seen in the work of the judges, particularly in their Supreme Court decisions.

The clash of models can be seen most clearly in the very first constitutional case heard on the merits by the Supreme Court, *Severn v. The Queen*,[17] which concerned the very vital constitutional power over trade and commerce that had been given to Ottawa. In addition to dissension created by their different approaches to law and decision making, the judges revealed pronounced differences over the very nature of Confederation. The result of the case was a 4–2 split in favour of federal power over that of the provinces. What is of interest in this study, however, is the question of the approaches of the judges.

William Richards considered the solution of the constitutional question concerning trade and commerce vital and expressly dealt with it. His function as a judge, he maintained, was not to take a 'technical view' of the issue, but to consider the 'surrounding circumstances,' which would include other relevant legal rules and which would put the matter into a social context. The 'technical view' that he referred to consisted of examining the words of a law alone and engaging in what had at least the appearance of being simply a linguistic analysis – the process required by the declaratory theory of law, believed by the formalists.

In giving meaning to the words of the constitution, Richards sought their spirit, which would guide him. The social circumstances existing when the constitution was created would give the words a social context and, in turn, allow him to give them socially relevant meanings. He noted, for instance, that at Confederation the horror of the American Civil War was part of the consciousness of the time, and was seen as something that had to be prevented in the new Canadian federal system.

Richards' approach was approved by William Henry, a Father of Confederation, who asserted that the meaning of the words of the constitution should be arrived at 'not only from the words ... but from the tenor and bearing of the whole Act, the state of the law at the time, the peculiar position of the United Provinces and the object of their union, with the means for working out the Constitution provided.'[18] What the judges should not do, Henry said, was to decide the issue by a technical reading of a few words in a subsection.[19]

The contextual approach of Richards and Henry can be contrasted with that of Jean-Thomas Taschereau, who was comfortable appearing only to look at the language that existed in the constitution, and also with that of Strong and Ritchie, who both adopted without hesitation a linguistic analysis. For Ritchie, the task was to 'read the words of an Act of Parliament in their natural, ordinary and grammatical sense.'[20] For Henry Strong, the 'scientific' lawyer, the judges were not to 'interpolate constitutional restrictions'; they were to apply the law, not make it,[21] by which he meant they were to use the ordinary meaning of the words of the law.

Télesphore Fournier, at this early stage of his judicial career, seemed determined to adopted a formalist approach, although later he would abandon it. He disclaimed the use of policy and emphasized that it was the 'clear and precise terms' of the constitution that were to be used to solve the problem.[22] His basic contextualism came through when he went on to actually consider the same factors as Richards, but his apparent commitment to a linguistic analysis caused him to conclude by saying that the result was clear from the words used.

Regarding formalism, a most telling situation occurred in this case. Four judges, Ritchie, Strong, Taschereau, and Fournier, maintained that the solution to the constitutional question rested in the ordinary meaning of the words of the constitution. However, on the answer these judges split 2–2. The ordinary meaning seems to have led in two directions. Which was the best direction to take? The words had become exhausted as guides to an answer. It is little wonder that Fournier, with his experience as a political decision maker, was to abandon the formalist approach in later cases.

A further insight into the formalist thinking of William Johnstone Ritchie is available. As chief justice of New Brunswick, he had been one of the members of the judiciary invited by Sir John A. Macdonald to comment on the bill to create the Supreme Court. He was the only one who produced a substantial reply, in the form of a 24-page monograph which was discussed by the bar of New Brunswick.[23] In his paper, he made clear his view of law and the legal process. For him, the declaratory theory of law conditioned his vision: the fundamental principles of the law were unchangeable, and the judge's function was to find (declare) the law and not to make it. The judge was the interpreter of law, not its creator. Such a viewpoint needed to operate as a belief rather than as an analysis of the actual operation of law. As a belief, it created definite boundaries for the mind. Naturally, to make the declaratory theory appear to be real (as opposed to being a belief), it was necessary to adopt a linguistic analysis.

As will be seen in the discussion of the work of the court to come, there was virtually open warfare among the judges in this period.

REFEREES

The use of referees in the Exchequer Court was provided for in 1876, virtually at the beginning of the court's existence.[24] This development, which was simply termed 'most useful' by the government,[25] would relieve the judges of the Supreme Court of the time-consuming duties of a trial judge, which included hearing the evidence and coming to a conclusion on the facts, as well as assessing damages. The report of the referee would be confirmed or rejected by a judge. The time saved would naturally be channelled into carrying out the duties of a justice of the highest court of appeal in the country. There was no restriction on who could be appointed as a referee.

In this period, the full potential for the use of referees was never tested, since a significant proportion of the trial work was being carried out by the Official Arbitrators, with the judges of the Exchequer Court performing an appeal function with respect to the awards.[26]

In the few cases in which a referee was used, it was generally the registrar, Robert Cassels; the cases dealt with ascertaining the amount of damages involved in an action.[27]

5

The Work

The workload in the eleven years that the judges of the Exchequer Court were also the judges of the Supreme Court was very light. Although the court had been created to deal with revenue cases, its jurisdiction was made concurrent with the provincial courts and the federal government continued to use the local courts for revenue matters.[1]

A survey of the docket book for the period reveals eighty-five cases, an average of approximately eight per year. Actions against the government involving a contract or a property dispute accounted for sixty-seven cases (79 per cent), while there were four expropriation cases (5 per cent). There was one stated case involving a constitutional issue, namely, whether the Dominion minister of fisheries could issue a fishing licence for the Miramichi River in New Brunswick.[2] The remaining thirteen (15 per cent) consisted of actions by the government, primarily involving customs. Omitted from the total of eighty-five is a constitutional case in which the issue was whether Ottawa or the province of British Columbia owned the precious metals in the railway belt; the decision of Mr Justice Fournier in the Exchequer Court was taken by consent, without argument, in order that the case could proceed as quickly as possible to the Supreme Court.[3]

An examination of the records of the cases reveals a striking difference among the judges with respect to the number of trials conducted. The number of hearings in which each judge participated were as follows (no name was available for one case):

Fournier	25
Henry	22
H.E. Taschereau	12
Gwynne	8
Ritchie	7
Strong	5
Richards	3
J.-T. Taschereau	2

The difference between Fournier and Henry, on the one hand, and Ritchie and Strong, on the other, all of whom were on the bench for the entire period of eleven years, is particularly noticeable. The reason for the discrepancy can only be guessed at, although it seems safe to say that there was an element of choice involved. The contextual lawyers, Henry and Fournier, might have been predisposed to enjoy conducting trials where one could come face to face with the people with the problems and deal with the evidence. The so-called scientific lawyers might have felt more comfortable dealing with words on paper at the appeal level, where the level of abstraction would potentially be higher.

But the division among the judges went deeper than the level of their participation as Exchequer Court judges: their different attitudes towards law and judicial decision making made it inevitable that sharp and obvious battle lines would be drawn between them.[4] So agitated was Henry Strong that he wrote a letter in 1880 to Prime Minister Macdonald attacking Henry's ability as a judge.[5] Strong suggested that the Exchequer Court be separated from the Supreme Court and Henry be appointed as the sole Exchequer Court judge, with the Supreme Court being reduced to a complement of five judges (four judges would be a quorum). If his suggestion was not acted upon he saw the impeachment of Henry as the only alternative. In Strong's opinion only Henry's removal would save the 'unfortunate Court.' In the end only one judge was ever 'removed' to 'save' the Supreme Court. That occurred in 1902 when the legal profession openly attacked the court in the professional journals, alleging that there was complete disharmony among the judges, and effectively branding the court a discredit to the country. The blame was put squarely on the chief justice of the time, and late in 1902 he resigned.[6] The chief justice was Henry Strong.

Given Strong's attachment to formalism, Henry's contextual approach must have been galling to an extreme. As might have been expected Strong's formalism did appear clearly in his letter. He told Macdonald that it would be better for the Supreme Court if only one judgment was rendered in each case, and any dissenting judges simply recorded their dissent. The reason was 'to settle the law finally and decisively.' The belief that such a result was possible was part of the mind-set of a formalist.

In the letter Strong was also critical of the leadership of William Ritchie,[7] but, given Strong's character, this was more likely due to the fact that Ritchie was chief justice and he was not. Ritchie, being a formalist, also had problems with Henry, and was driven to condemn his approach as unconstitutional in a case to be considered shortly.

The performance of the judges can be most readily observed in the area of Crown liability, which made up almost 80 per cent of the work of the court. In these cases the relationship of the individual to the state, as illustrated through the adjudicating of disputes between them, is a fundamental issue. Disagreement over that issue again created division between the judges, indicating that formalism was much more pervasive than a simple problem-solving technique.

The times were changing. In the all-too-brief period that Chief Justice William Richards spent on the bench, he was able to demonstrate his approach and to provide an example of its potential. In 1874 the Court of Queen's Bench in England had recognized the need to adjust the law to fit the times; the court had accepted that a petition of right could lie against the government based solely on a breach of contract, whereas previously a petition could only have been used when property rights were involved.[8] A scant three years later in 1877 Richards concluded that a suppliant could recover for the actual value of work done and accepted by the government, thereby determining that a contract need not be in writing to be enforceable against the government. Crown liability was thus stretched to include implied contracts.[9] This decision was used sixteen years later, in 1893, by the then-judge of the Exchequer Court, George Burbidge, as authority for the proposition that the government was subject to implied contracts and that the principle of contract law known as *quantum meruit*, the right to reasonable compensation for goods or services provided, applied to the government in its dealings with individuals. The judge said that Richards' views had to 'commend themselves to one's sense of what is fair and just.'[10] The Supreme Court of Canada would adopt the conclusion reached by Richards and Burbidge in 1898.[11]

William Henry had given notice early of his attitude towards the government in liability cases. In a judgment rendered in the Supreme Court in 1880, he discussed the maxim that the King can do no wrong (which inevitably was mentioned whenever a party sought to attach liability to the government), and asserted that, when the sovereign allowed a petition of right to go to the court and ordered that justice be done, it meant the same justice that would be done between subjects, and by the same legal and equitable principles.[12] He went on to decide in favour of the petitioner. However, a majority of the Supreme Court, Ritchie, Henri-Elzéar Taschereau, and Gwynne, avoided direct discussion of the point, and simply decided in favour of the Crown. Fournier joined with Henry in dissent. The vote was 3–2.[13] Richards was by this time no longer on the bench.

In two cases decided in the early 1880s, the issue of Crown liability forced the judges into what must be as close to open warfare as can occur in such a setting.[14] In 1881, in *McFarlane v. The Queen*, Henry, sitting on the Exchequer Court, was faced with the following facts. The petitioner, McFarlane, was in the business of cutting timber and floating logs to the Ottawa River. In order to reach the river, McFarlane had to use a government-owned and -operated slide, for which he paid a fee. Because the operator of the slide allowed more logs over it than the main boom could hold, the boom broke and McFarlane's logs floated away, a possibility that McFarlane had warned the slide master about. There was no doubt about the slide operator's culpability for the loss of the logs. Consequently a petition of right was brought against the government for compensation. Henry found in favour of the petitioner on the basis that a contract had been created by which, in return for a fee, the government agreed that the logs would be carried in a proper manner and redelivered to the owner from the main boom. Henry dealt with the case in the same manner as if a private corporation had been involved. Dealing with the case on the basis of contract allowed it to become part of the established group of cases in which contract liability of the Crown was by then recognized.[15]

An appeal was taken to the Supreme Court, in which Henry participated. His excursion into creativity was rejected by a 4–1 vote. Henry was the dissenter. Télesphore Fournier did not sit on the appeal. The majority of the judges refused to accept that it was a contract case. Rather, they categorized it as involving a tort, namely, the negligence of the slide operator; for tort actions, the government had an immunity. The division between the judges bubbled over. William Ritchie, now the chief justice, rejected any analogy between the government and private individuals or companies. There were, for him, entirely different concerns involved. He emphasised the word 'public' as opposed to the word 'private.' What was involved was 'not private property but public property, created by the expenditure of public money for public purposes and for the public benefit.'[16] The controlling idea in Ritchie's mind, as with the other three judges who made up the majority, was that the government's actions were for the good of the public. In this way, the individual would always be forced to make an argument that went against the public interest when trying to pursue a claim against the government.

So strongly did Chief Justice Ritchie react to Henry's extension of government liability that he described the attempt as an attack on the Crown, even on the monarch personally: '[it] amounts to a direct and unwarrantable attack on Her Majesty's prerogative rights and is derogatory to the honour of her Crown and an imputation that ought not in my opinion to be permitted to appear on the records of this court.'[17] It is difficult to tell whether this personalizing of the government into the person of the sovereign and viewing the issue of Crown liability as one involving the person of the Queen herself was rhetoric or was founded on an actual belief.

Gwynne, a member of the majority, also raised the issue of the extent of judicial power. He recognized that change was being advocated and asserted that, if there was to be a reform of the law, then it should be carried out by the legislature and not the judges.[18]

This case was followed almost a year later in 1882 by *The Queen v. McLeod*,[19] one of the most fascinating decisions ever rendered by the Supreme Court of Canada. Henry was again the Exchequer Court judge and the litigation involved several claims against the government for injuries that had occurred because of a train derailment in Prince Edward Island. The Prince Edward Island Railway was owned by the federal government. McLeod had lost both his legs in the accident. The state of the track at the point where the derailment occurred had been such that, in the words of Mr Justice Henry, 'the safety of life had been recklessly jeopardized by running trains over [the track] with passengers for some time before the accident occurred.'[20] If the railway had been privately owned, there would have been no question about liability.

Henry knew of course that Crown immunity in cases of tort existed, and the *McFarlane* case would have served as a reminder if he had needed one. He had failed in *McFarlane* when he had tried to use a contract as the basis for liability; however, that could be viewed as simply an incorrect application of the law, and there was still the rule that the government could be held liable in a contract case. In *McLeod*, he proceeded to characterize the litigation as involving a contract in which the government had promised to carry the passenger safely in return for the payment of the

prescribed fare. He pointed out that there were no previous judicial decisions that would force him to add any qualifications to the word 'contract.' If there was a contract, then it would determine liability.

The appeal to the Supreme Court was heard by five judges and, not
unexpectedly, resulted in a 3–2 decision, with Ritchie, Strong, and
Gwynne in the majority, and Henry and Fournier in dissent. The minority
recognized that negligence had caused the accident, yet the action was
founded on a contract between the passenger and the railway. They were
prepared to make the government liable as if it were a private enterprise
since it was undertaking the same kind of activity, the running of a railway.

William Ritchie considered that the *McFarlane* case had already settled
the point, and that McLeod's claim was in tort and not contract law.
However, he elevated the case to the highest reaches when he accused
Henry and Fournier of acting unconstitutionally by going beyond the
permissible limits of their role as judges. Magnifying the improper behaviour of his two colleagues, as he perceived it, Ritchie characterized the
law relating to Crown liability and the rights of the Crown as constitutional law, which meant that it was not simply law that Fournier and
Henry were playing with, but the fundamental law of the society. He
stated:

This constitutional principle this court cannot ignore; it must not attempt to
make laws; it must administer the law, constitutional, local, public or private, as
it is, and leave the Dominion Parliament, on general and constitutional questions affecting the whole Dominion, and the provincial assemblies, on local
questions, each within the scope of their legislative functions, as declared by the
B.N.A. Act, to alter, or adapt the practices or principles in force, to make them, if
found expedient so to do, more suitable and applicable to the circumstances of
the country.[21]

The other two judges who made up the majority, Strong and Gwynne,
did not react as strongly as Ritchie. Strong brushed the case aside by saying that the previous decision in *McFarlane* was controlling, and Gwynne
simply rejected the idea that there was a contract.[22]

This case clearly illustrated the formalist view that there were not two
contending approaches to the nature and extent of judicial decision
making, or the nature of law itself. Rather, there was only one correct
approach. Attempting to use any other was not only wrong, it was
unconstitutional.

It is worth noting that after the train derailment the law was reformed. Ottawa enacted legislation which provided that claims arising out of any death or injury on a government-owned and -operated railway could be referred to the Official Arbitrators for investigation and report, with an appeal to the Exchequer Court being possible.[23] The government had reacted to what was thought to be a social need. Since this new law was created after McLeod's injury it did not apply to his case, but it might have conditioned a judge's approach to the issue in his case by providing evidence of the social context. However for formalists, who refused to look beyond the words of a law, it could be ignored.

Another case sandwiched between *McFarlane* and *McLeod* is worth mentioning because it is instructive about both the judges' attitude to government and the working of formalism. The litigation in *Smith v. The Queen*[24] arose when a new federal government came into office in late 1878 and attempted to cancel a contract made by the previous government for the construction of a railway. The new government had decided to change the route. The individuals concerned brought a petition of right for breach of contract. William Henry, once again the Exchequer Court judge, affirmed the view that contracts in which the government was a party were to be construed on the same principles as contracts between private parties.[25] Henry considered that what was involved in the case was a matter of common honesty and equity.[26]

On the appeal to the Supreme Court, a majority of the court had no sympathy for Henry's opinion and reversed it by a 5–1 vote.[27] Henry sat on the appeal and dissented. Fournier would have accepted part of the claim by the plaintiffs, although not the totality of it. The majority of the judges did not accept that there was a contract that was enforceable. While Ritchie and Henri-Elzéar Taschereau were not prepared to hold the government liable, they were uneasy about the result. Taschereau came right out and declared that an injustice had been done by the decision of the court.[28] Ritchie stated that he hoped that the government would not refuse a request by the plaintiffs for remuneration for work done up to the time of the cancellation of the contract. Gwynne, also, was of the view that the petitioners were entitled to the most favourable consideration of their claim out of court.

Judges who favoured the formalist approach to law and lawyering saw definite limits to the scope of both. As shown in the *Smith* case, they recognized that a line could exist between law and a concept of justice. They viewed law as something above and beyond the particular problems that produced litigation, and it was the political process that they expected to respond to particular instances of injustice, even those produced by the law. For formalists this allowed the law to remain certain and neutral in appearance, and also abstract. The contextualists believed that there should be no line between law and justice. For them, law was functional and did not possess an abstract life of its own.

6

Appeals and Attacks

There is little doubt that certain practices of the past that were considered normal in their time would today shock the sensibilities of most people. This is the way of change. However, the approach to decision making of most of the legal profession today is still very much grounded in the formalism of the nineteenth century, which also favours an attitude that things are fixed and unchanging. Therefore there is a tendency to accept the Victorian era as part of the fabric of the present-day legal system. Thus it appears incomprehensible that a value that is today considered fundamental to the legal system would be completely disregarded by our highest court in the years from 1876 to 1887. The value is impartiality. In the Supreme Court period of the Exchequer Court it was common, if not the rule, that a judge who had rendered a decision as a member of the Exchequer Court would, on an appeal of that decision to the Supreme Court, participate in the hearing of the appeal. At the time the practice appeared perfectly normal.[1]

This affront (from today's viewpoint) to the idea of impartiality did not generate any public comment in the legal journals of the time, whereas eighty years later in 1966 Mr Justice Schroeder of the Ontario Court of Appeal stated for the court: 'It is unthinkable that a member of the High Court of Justice, who is also *ex officio* a member of the Court of Appeal, should sit as a member of the latter Court hearing an appeal from the judgment pronounced by him.'[2]

The earlier practice rests on a number of factors. Primarily there is the fact that, in English law, there was no appeal unless given by statute. By contrast, in Quebec law, there was a presumption in favour of the existence of what was called the 'sacred right of appeal.'[3]

Since the existence of an appeal was not the rule in English law, it meant that there had been no need to establish a rule about judges sitting on an appeal from their own judgment.[4] A judge could and would decline to sit because of a personal bias, for instance, a financial interest in the outcome of a case, a relationship with a party, or any other reason that might incline the judge to favour one party over another. However, there was no established disqualification stemming from possible bias in favour of the previous decision. Nevertheless impartiality was still a powerful value and, as the use of appeals developed, a specific rule was needed to cover the possibility of participation by the trial judge, as arose in Ontario in 1874.

When the Court of Error and Appeal was created in Ontario in 1874, the legislation specifically provided: 'No Judge of that Court against whose judgment, decree or decision any error is assigned or appeal brought, shall sit or take part in the hearing of or adjudication upon the proceedings in Error and Appeal, in case such judge took part in the hearing in the court below.'[5] Also, in 1871, when provision was made for the appointment of four members to the Judicial Committee of the Privy Council as part of the reform of its appellate jurisdiction, the British legislation clearly specified 'that no member of the Judicial Committee of the Privy Council shall take part in the hearing of any appeal from any decision or judgment which he has given or assisted in giving.'[6]

When Christopher Patterson, a member of the Ontario Court of Appeal, was appointed to the Supreme Court of Canada in October 1888 to fill the vacancy created by the death of Mr Justice Henry, the year after the Exchequer Court had been separated from the Supreme Court, the issue of impartiality did arise. The government concluded that there was no legal provision allowing him to decline to sit. The solution was to enact a provision prohibiting a judge whose decision was being appealed from taking part in the appeal; whenever such cases arose, a quorum of four judges would be sufficient. In the Senate John Abbott, for the government, stated that it was the universal consensus of the members of the bench and bar who had been consulted that this was the proper stance to take. The legislation went through with the agreement of all parties and without comment.[7]

The federal government and its legal advisors appear to have been oblivious to this problem in 1875. This is astonishing considering they had created an appeal from the Exchequer Court to the Supreme Court, which should have raised the very real possibility of the problem arising. The Ontario legislation of the previous year should have been in their minds. Patterson's appointment made the problem very clear, although apparently it was Patterson himself who raised the question.

This blindness to the problem may have been partly due to the fact that the Exchequer Court was not viewed as a distinct court at the time. During debate on the petition of right legislation in 1876, both Sir John A. Macdonald and Edward Blake referred to the court as the 'Supreme Court.'[8]

The statistics regarding the judges of the Exchequer Court sitting on appeals from their decisions are as follows:

Judge	Appeals 1875–87	Number of times the judge sat	Percentage
Fournier	5	5	100
Henry	9	7	78
Gwynne	5	3	60
Taschereau, H.-E.	3	1	33
Taschereau, J.-T.	2	0	0

The fact that the judges were so divided on the models of decision making could very well have contributed to the frequency of an Exchequer Court judge sitting on the appeal from his own decision. With no tradition or practice to address the situation directly, together with the level of disagreement among the judges as to how they should carry out their function, Henry and Fournier, who conducted the majority of the trials, would certainly have felt the need to defend their decisions. The two appeals for which Henry did not participate were the first two of the nine that involved his decisions, and he was reversed in both.

The different tradition in Quebec, in which an appeal was a fundamental part of the legal process, did not have any apparent effect on Télesphore Fournier, and Henri-Elzéar Taschereau sat on one of the three appeals involving his decisions. Jean-Thomas Taschereau never had the chance to decide, since the two appeals from his decisions occurred after he had resigned. As part of a federal institution, the judges from Quebec would have recognized that their tradition would normally give way to that of the English law. Henri-Elzéar Taschereau was known for his strength of character and overbearing temperament,[9] which would have helped make him impervious to such pressures.

As a point of interest, the issue was dealt with openly only once by a judge of the court. In 1880 John Gwynne, in an Exchequer Court judg-ment, stated categorically that he would not sit on the case in appeal. He suggested that the government consider legislation to provide that an appeal from a single judge of the Exchequer Court be heard only by the other judges. He was concerned, not with the propriety of the practice itself, but with the integrity of the appeal process; namely, that an appeal might be rejected by a 3–2 count, with the trial judge providing the decid-ing vote.[10] He did not discuss the possibility that a 3–3 split could also occur, in which event the appeal would also be dismissed. An equally split court was common at this time. While Gwynne did not sit on this particular appeal, which was dismissed by a 5–0 vote,[11] his resolve did not hold. He sat on each subsequent appeal from his decisions in the Exchequer Court until the courts were separated.

The conflict among the judges is shown by statistics regarding the appeals to the Supreme Court. Appeals from the Exchequer Court accounted for 5 percent of the cases heard by the appellate court.

	Number of appeals 1875–87	Percentage reversed	Percentage of split decisions
Exchequer Court	25	56	68
Others	465	44	37

For individual judges the statistics are as follows:

Judge	Cases heard 1875–87	Appeals	Percentage appealed	Percentage reversed
Fournier	25	6	24	33 (2/6)
Henry	22	9	41	100 (9/9)
Taschereau, H.-E.	12	3	25	67 (2/3)
Gwynne	8	5	63	60 (3/5)
Ritchie	7	0	0	–
Strong	5	0	0	–
Richards	3	0	0	–
Taschereau, J.-T.	2	2	100	0

ATTACK ON THE COURT

Less than three years after the first hearing in the Supreme Court of Can-ada, a private member's bill was introduced before the House of Com-mons to abolish the court.[12] The ostensible reason behind the move was that the court was not worth the cost. What gave the measure significance was that, as the debate unfolded, the disaffection could be clearly identified as coming from Ontario. The bill was introduced by Joseph Keeler, a Conservative Member of Parliament from Ontario, and the voicing of the complaints was led by D'Alton McCarthy, a leading member of the Ontario bar and a prominent member of the Conservative Party, which formed the government of the day. The Liberals, who had created the court and were now in opposition, attempted to stop the debate, but the prime minister, Sir John A. Macdonald, supported its continuance. The government was sending a message. As one member noted, one thing that was certain was that the entire proceedings would have a demoralising effect on the judges.[13]

With the end of the 1879 session, the bill introduced by Keeler died, but he was not yet finished. In 1880, he once again introduced a bill to abolish the court. The irritation within Ontario that had fuelled the 1879 debate had been effectively soothed and the government was no longer prepared to support this new attack. What did emerge was the ever-present concern of Quebeckers with the court and its potential for affecting the civil law of the province, as well as a generalized suspicion of federal institutions dominated by English-speaking Canadians. After a short discussion in which grievances were voiced about the way in which the court went about its business, such as the writing of multiple judgments by the judges, this bill too evaporated.

Near the end of 1880 Keeler introduced a third bill; when he died in January of 1881, the measure was symbolically picked up by Phillipe Landry from Quebec. A bill was then introduced that proposed to remove the court's jurisdiction over issues involving provincial law, which would have answered Quebec's concerns. This bill had no chance of success since, as Macdonald asserted, either the court would be repealed or it would apply to all the provinces,[14] but it did mark the end of attempts to abolish the court. The elimination of the jurisdiction of the Supreme Court of Canada over provincial law, if it had succeeded, would have created a federal system of courts with a trial and an appeal division.

How did the Exchequer Court fit into all of this? In the attacks on the existence of the Supreme Court and its jurisdiction that part of its work carried out by the Exchequer Court also came under scrutiny. With his focus on cost, Keeler zeroed in on the first case to be heard[15] and stated that the legal costs had amounted to $51,000.[16] This would represent approximately a million dollars today. The case concerned a contract to construct a portion of a railway and the amount mentioned was only incurred in the Exchequer Court: the case had yet to go to the Supreme Court. As far as Keeler was concerned, arbitrators should have been used. He questioned the competence of the judges to deal with such matters and suggested that what was needed for cases involving railway contractors were judges with an expertise in civil engineering, rather than 'gentlemen simply learned in the law.'[17] Such an opinion from a non-lawyer (Keeler was a businessman) provoked Edward Blake – both as a Liberal who, as minister of justice, had taken personal responsibility for securing the existence of the court in the face of possible disallowance by Britain, and more so as a lawyer – to rise in defence of the judiciary. Blake asserted that expertise as an engineer was not needed when the issue was 'the legal construction of a contract,' and 'the different nice questions of an exclusively legal nature.' He went on: 'An engineer is competent to determine matters of measurement, or calculation involved in a contract; but the knowledge required to decide the meaning of a contract is another matter altogether.'[18] This shows the belief in the existence of legal knowledge (which had to be of a factual nature) that could be applied to solve a problem between people and that transcended the specifics of the problem. The idea is contained in the argument that law is a science in its own right, with its own distinct body of knowledge. Lawyers (judges) were thus to be seen as 'expert' resolvers of disputes.

When the Exchequer Court was accused of being pro-government, a charge that has hovered around the court throughout its existence, leaders of both the Liberals and the Conservatives used the point as a justification for retaining the court. Arbitrators, it was said, had tended to favour claims against the government, while only a trifling sum had been recovered against the government under the Exchequer Court. The result was that the court had saved the country much more than it had cost to maintain it.[19] The pro-government stance was attributed to the better decisions reached by judges, as opposed to arbitrators, and not to any inherent bias of the decision makers.

In the debates over the abolition of the Supreme Court, there was no doubt that the two courts were seen as tied together, as divisions of a single court. However, their rationales for existence were quite distinct. Désiré Girouard, spokesman for Quebec's attempt to abolish the jurisdiction of the Supreme Court over cases involving Quebec law, recognized the Exchequer Court as 'an essential Court for deciding questions between the Crown and the citizens of [the] country.'[20] In addition, at the time the court served the useful function of an appellate tribunal for decisions of the arbitrators.

D'Alton McCarthy suggested that the Exchequer Court should be separated from the Supreme Court completely, with a judge to be appointed specially to the Exchequer Court. The Supreme Court judges would then not be distracted by having to go on circuit and decide Exchequer Court cases and, consequently, the Supreme Court would be improved.[21]

David Mills, a Liberal member of Parliament from Ontario, took a distinctive stand in the debates. He was in favour of a dual system of courts such as existed in the United States, in which one set of courts would administer federal law and another would administer provincial law. It followed that he was opposed to the appellate jurisdiction of the Supreme Court over provincial law. He even viewed it as unconstitutional.[22] Mills, who had received his legal education in the United States at the University of Michigan, also objected to the suggestion that the work of the Exchequer Court be separated from the 'Appeal Division.' With the Supreme Court of the United States in mind, he favoured the judges of the Supreme Court of Canada going on circuit in order to come into contact with the people and learn the manner in which the business of the country was being conducted. This would enable the judges to 'read the law through the eyes of the people,' he said.[23]

The schism between the Supreme Court judges can thus also be seen in the considerable difference between Edward Blake's statement that there was a distinct legal expertise that merely needed facts on which to operate, and David Mills' opinion that something more was needed, such as relating the law to the needs of society, and therefore knowing and understanding those needs.

Although the debates concerning the Supreme Court did not pose any threat to the Exchequer Court as such, points were made that would continue to be heard throughout its existence, even when it became the Federal Court – the issue of whether it was a pro-government court, the expertise of the judges, its high cost, and the existence of a dual system of courts. The different images of law and lawyering would also continue to exist and contend with each other, although more and more the formal image would come to dominate lawyers' descriptions of how the legal system functioned.

PART 3

The Second Court, 1887–1971

7

Court of Claims

As the nineteenth century progressed, there was a growth in industrial-ization and in government involvement in the daily affairs of society. In Canada, government was involved in matters of business, building and operating public works – canals, harbours, roads, bridges, log slides, dams, locks, and buildings. Along with such activity came a growing increase in the number of contract disputes between the government and individuals. The Judicial Committee of the Privy Council noted at this time that colonial governments were acting as pioneers of improvements and had engaged in activities that might otherwise have been left to pri-vate enterprise.[1] In the Privy Council's opinion, justice required that the special rules protecting the government from liability should give way whenever possible through judicial interpretation. As will be seen, this sentiment was not shared by a significant number of Canadian legislators and judges.

The position of public arbitrator that had been created to deal with dis-putes involving public works in pre-Confederation Canada,[2] and had replaced private arbitrators, carried over into the new Dominion. But by the mid-1880s, legislators felt that a better way of dealing with claims against the government existed. It was probably natural to look to judges and the legal system at this juncture. The use of arbitrators had begun to attract criticism, primarily because they lacked legal training. The power

and prestige of the legal profession had grown in the United States, and there is no reason to believe that the situation was different in Canada.[3] The legal profession was coming more and more to regard its members as possessors of a knowledge that was distinct and technical and that separated them from other, non-legally-trained individuals. Their special training was therefore considered to make them better arbitrators of disputes. A dispute between private individuals could be taken before a superior court judge for a solution, yet disputes between private individuals and the government were being settled by adjudicators who were not legally trained.[4] Once it was accepted that a judge was better qualified to adjudicate disputes, it followed that the government should also have the benefit of that expertise.

As an example of the criticisms, the arbitrators were accused of introducing factual material too freely at the hearing of a dispute, whereas a judge with a 'technical knowledge of the rules of evidence, or of procedure'[5] would be able to apply the rules and reduce the amount of factual matter introduced. The rules of evidence were coming into their own at this time and, through the concept known as admissibility of evidence, they regulated the receipt of factual material at a hearing. It was not relevance alone that determined the introduction of evidence (facts), but rather 'admissibility' as determined by the rules. This meant that some relevant information was being excluded from the hearing of a dispute in the legal system. The rules, aptly named the 'exclusionary rules,' were, and to some extent still are, the most technical and convoluted ones devised by the profession as the grasp of formalism tightened. The legal profession believed that these rules, and others, were desirable for the adjudication of disputes.[6]

We might have expected people to have more confidence in decisions arrived at by a judge,[7] since the arbitrators were salaried employees of the government and consequently their impartiality and independence could be questioned. However, at this time, impartiality and independence were background factors; only in the future would they become a vital stock-in-trade for the judiciary and crucial to all discussions of the legal system. In 1887 the point that completely dominated discussion was that the members of the legal profession possessed expert knowledge that made them better arbitrators of disputes.[8]

Moving with the times, the government took action in the spring of 1887 to create a Court of Claims for the trial of claims involving the government, both against it and by it against individuals. An earlier attempt in 1885 had had no results. An additional court had been proposed, also called the Court of Claims, which would have consisted of a single judge and three assessors, with an appeal to the Supreme Court. When the opposition suggested using the Exchequer Court, Hector Langevin, for the government, responded that the proposed jurisdiction had no application to the Exchequer Court.[9]

It was thus a notable change in 1887 when jurisdiction over the claims was given to the Exchequer Court of Canada. But there was a new Exchequer Court. Two things happened – a court of claims was created, and the Exchequer Court was separated from the Supreme Court. While the separation would no doubt improve the sagging fortunes of the highest court in the land by freeing it to be a national appeal court only, the motivation for the change lay elsewhere. The Supreme Court judges, sitting as Exchequer Court judges, were seen by the government as having been too generous in awarding damages against it.[10] Although Macdonald had resisted the removal of the original jurisdiction from the Supreme Court,[11] which ended his dream of one Supreme Court for Canada, the new court was created with the old name. It was to consist of one judge, and have the status of a superior court.[12]

The Official or Dominion Arbitrators' work as such was ended and they became Official Referees, who would assist the single judge of the court by taking evidence and reporting on cases conducted at some distance from Ottawa.[13] They were also available for various other duties for which a referee might be needed. The provision for the use of referees, enacted in 1876, continued unchanged in the new legislation, and would prove to be very useful to the court by reducing the workload of the single judge. The term 'Official Referee,' adopted for the four existing Official Arbitrators, applied only to them and died out with them.[14]

The first court to bear the name Exchequer Court of Canada had not been a distinct court. Its title had primarily been a name for the original jurisdiction of the Supreme Court, and it was seen by the profession as a part of the Supreme Court of Canada.[15] There was now a new court, with a new role as a court of claims, and it was about to start work in a new federal state.

A NEW NATION

The separation of the Exchequer Court from the Supreme Court in 1887 had its share of symbolism. It was certainly a recognition that the idea of a Supreme Court for Canada, exemplified by the sweeping 1869 bill, had been abandoned at some point, although Macdonald resisted the change as late as 1886. The separation was, at the same time, part of the ending of the Macdonaldian constitution. The highly centralizing forces inherent in the language of several provisions of the constitution had become dead letters or were in the process of being blunted. The federal system as we know it today was being locked in place in the constitution.

All in all, 1887 was a watershed year for the country. Section 91(2) of the constitution assigned legislative authority to Ottawa over 'the regulation of trade and commerce.' This was the head of legislative power that was expressed in the widest terms. In 1878 the Supreme Court of Canada, in *Severn v. The Queen*,[16] had equated that power with the power to regulate business within the country. Times changed, and in 1887 the Judicial Committee of the Privy Council announced that the literal meaning of 'trade and commerce' had to be restricted to allow scope for provincial powers.[17] The provincial power in question resided within section 92(13), which gave the provinces authority over 'property and civil rights.' It is impossible to deal with trade and commerce, that is, business, without also engaging property and civil rights. Chief Justice Ritchie had declared in 1879 that the powers of the provinces were specially limited and defined, and that the words 'property and civil rights' in section 92(13) were to be read in a restricted and limited sense. Henry, a Father of Confederation, and Fournier, from Quebec, were able to share those views.[18] However, as early as 1881, the Judicial Committee had declared that section 92(13) was to be understood in its largest sense.[19] That sense was what had ended the wide scope for federal power in the words 'trade and commerce.' In their largest sense, the words 'property and civil rights' were to be understood as 'civil law,' as opposed to 'criminal law.'[20]

Thus the provinces effectively acquired authority over all civil law; the grants of legislative power given to Ottawa under the constitution were to be viewed as exceptions. The intended scheme, under which the words 'peace, order and good government' were meant to give Ottawa the totality of legislative power while the provinces were given jurisdiction by exception, had been reversed. The new Exchequer Court had indeed been created for a new nation and, although cases after 1887 could be identified as marking the end of the centralizing Macdonaldian constitution,[21] it was a mopping-up action.

Politically, the year 1887 was marked by the first interprovincial conference, at which the power of Ottawa, as epitomized by the centralist policies of Sir John A. Macdonald, was challenged. The conference, held at Quebec City, was called by Honoré Mercier, premier of Quebec, who led his *Parti nationale* to victory in 1886 as a champion of provincial rights and, in particular, Quebec nationalism. In 1886 a resolution for separation had passed in the Nova Scotia legislature and W.S. Fielding, the premier, attended the conference after achieving an overwhelming victory in a provincial election. He had run on a promise to take Nova Scotia out of Confederation. Ontario, New Brunswick, and Manitoba also attended. All the provinces at Quebec City, except Manitoba, had Liberal governments, prompting Macdonald to try and shrug it off as a partisan show; but there was Manitoba, with a Conservative government, in dispute with Ottawa over railways. Prince Edward Island and British Columbia, both with Conservative governments, did not attend. However, partisan politics are not to be discounted. The Liberal premier of Ontario from 1872 to 1896, Oliver Mowat, engaged in continual warfare with the Conservative government of Macdonald that was solidly entrenched in Ottawa. Partisanship, so entrenched in Canadian society, no doubt contributed to polarization on the question of the nature of the country. The nature of the country would in turn affect the role and work of the new federal court that had come into being at this crucial time.

8

The Burbidge Years, 1887–1908 (I)

THE JUDGE

George Burbidge was the judge of the Exchequer Court from October 1, 1887, until his death on February 18, 1908 – for twenty-one years and four months.[1] The new life of the Exchequer Court as an institution independent of the Supreme Court got off to a solid start with this lengthy period of continuity. At forty, Burbidge was one of the youngest judges ever appointed to a federal court. Before his appointment, he had been Canada's deputy minister of justice, a position he had held for over five years. He was a Maritimer, born in Nova Scotia, who lived and practised law in Saint John, New Brunswick. He had been in practice for ten years when he was made deputy minister. A Conservative, he became deputy minister while the Conservatives were in power and was appointed to the Exchequer Court by them. His close relationship with the minister of justice, John Thompson of Nova Scotia, continued; as a judge, he advised Thompson on matters pertaining to the Department of Justice. Thompson approached Burbidge in 1889 about drafting a code of criminal law, which he agreed to do with the deputy minister at the time, Robert Sedgewick, also a Nova Scotian.[2] The Criminal Code of Canada was completed in 1892.

As a former deputy minister, Burbidge may have been expected to resist claims against the government better than the judges of the Supreme Court had done.[3] The appointment of only one judge to do the work that had been within the original jurisdiction of the Supreme Court, as well as the work of the arbitrators involving claims against the government, might well have raised the question of workload. Only in the Senate, however, was some concern expressed, and it was pointed out that workload did not seem to be a problem, since the Supreme Court had never complained.[4] Of course, the use of the four arbitrators as referees for conducting cases would effectively increase the complement to five judges, although the government was careful to point out that they would be assigned specific cases and not engage generally in hearing disputes.[5] In addition, there was the provision that allowed the use of what were termed 'special' referees, as distinct from those who were titled 'Official Referees.'[6] The registrar was specifically mentioned as being available for work as a referee, thus adding yet another person who could arbitrate disputes.

The first registrar of the new court was Louis Arthur Audette, a francophone from Quebec who had been a member of that province's bar for seven years when he was appointed to the Exchequer Court at the age of thirty-one.[7]

The Use of Referees

While the use of referees for 'taking accounts and making enquiries' was authorized in 1876, little use was made of them during the Supreme Court period. With the creation of an autonomous Exchequer Court having only one judge, and with the additional work that had once been that of the Official Arbitrators, the situation changed. An amendment to the law in 1889 clarified the function of the referee as 'for the purpose of taking accounts or making enquiries, or for the determination of any question or issue of fact,' and the referee would make an inquiry and report.[8] With fact-finding specifically added, the referees were prepared to take their place as part of the judicial apparatus of the court.

Although the wording of the provisions authorized referees to act in their traditional role of conducting fact-finding investigations, in practice the referees were essentially conducting trials. The 'report' would constitute a decision on the merits of the case.[9] The parties would then bring motions before the judge of the court either to confirm the report or by way of appeal from it.[10] It is interesting that, when the practice was challenged in 1904 in a debate in the House of Commons as creating an appeal process within the court, the minister of justice maintained that referees were being used exclusively for gathering factual evidence. He added that it was usually the registrar who carried out the inquiries.[11]

The image referees projected was different from the role they some-times played. There were indeed instances when a referee was directed to take evidence only.[12] The effect, whichever function a referee carried out, was that Burbidge was relieved of the time-consuming work of determin-ing the facts in a case. The use of referees also allowed for the evidence in a case to be taken at or near the location of the incident that had given rise to the litigation, while the argument on the evidence would then be heard at Ottawa, before the judge. It was common to use referees in expropria-tion cases, which would have made it possible to bring local knowledge to bear on the question of compensation.

The frequent use of referees lessened following the turn of the century, and effectively came to an end shortly after Burbidge's death in 1908. The registrar, Louis Arthur Audette, played an important role as a referee when, as a francophone and a civil law lawyer, he heard cases originating in the province of Quebec and those requiring the use of French.[13]

Judges Pro Hac Vice

Since there was to be only one judge of the Exchequer Court, the legisla-tion provided that, if the judge was ill or absent from Canada, another qualified person, a judge of a provincial superior or county court or a lawyer with at least ten years' membership at the bar, could be appointed to fill in temporarily.[14] Such a temporary judge could also be appointed if the judge had an interest in any case.[15] The replacement was *pro hac vice*, meaning simply 'for this one particular occasion.'

A survey of the first three docket books of the court, which cover the years from 1876 to around 1900, reveals that temporary judges were used five times, twice in 1892 and once each in 1893, 1896, and 1897. Near the end of his life when Burbidge became too ill to work, Sir Thomas Taylor was also appointed as judge *pro tempore*. This incident will be considered more fully later.

JURISDICTION

The jurisdiction of the new court had a distinctly old appearance. It had the jurisdiction established in the original 1875 statute and its amend-ments, and in addition it had the jurisdiction previously possessed by the Official Arbitrators, for whom the Exchequer Court had also functioned as an appeal court.

Its jurisdiction displayed the character of the court as a tribunal before which the government brought actions against citizens and defended actions by citizens against it. It was the government's court. At this time the English legal scholar A.V. Dicey was engaged in a crusade in which he severely criticized the existence in France of *droit administratif* or administrative law, a body of law particular to government and its agencies, and the existence of special courts to administer that law with regard to acts of government and its officials. For Dicey, such law and courts rested on 'ideas foreign to the fundamental assumptions of our English common law, and especially to what we have termed the rule of law.'[16] It is an understatement to say, from today's vantage point, that Dicey's writings on administrative law and rule of law have had considerable influence,[17] yet in Canada at the time he was writing there was apparently no thought that the Exchequer Court flew directly in the face of Dicey's criticisms. Canada had a special court that applied the special law of Crown liability in disputes between individuals and the government. It would no doubt have shocked Canadians at the time to hear that what they were doing was contrary to the most basic of constitutional principles – rule of law. It may have been so according to Dicey, but not according to Canadians' understanding of the principle.

Like the first court, the second had two parts to its jurisdiction, an exclusive and a concurrent part.[18] The court had exclusive jurisdiction over those cases in which an action could be brought against the Crown in England: that is, cases in which a petition of right could be brought. The reference to actions brought in England meant that Canadian lawyers always had to keep abreast of legal developments in England, which blunted any tendency to create a distinctively Canadian solution.[19] At the time, the disputes in England that would allow a petition of right against the government were those involving issues of property and contract. The Canadian legislation went on to make specific reference to such actions, which was superfluous unless it was intended to make sure that tort actions were excluded, albeit indirectly. Only a few years before the issue had arisen in the Supreme Court, and two of the judges had been prepared to recognize actions based on tort if tied to a contractual relationship of some sort. In the end the Supreme Court had supported an immunity for the government against tort actions, but only by the barest of margins, three judges to two.[20]

In Canada, however, tort liability did attach to the Crown based on the previous jurisdiction of the Official Arbitrators. The specific wording of the statutory provision was to prove highly significant:

Every claim against the Crown arising out of any death or injury to the person or to property on any public work, resulting from the negligence of any officer or servant of the Crown, while acting within the scope of his duties or employment.[21]

This wording would be debated and commented upon for the next half-century, as some judges were prepared to expand liability and others to contract it.

In addition the court had exclusive jurisdiction over claims arising from the expropriation of property by the government and claims for damage to property injuriously affected by the construction of any public work.

The court's concurrent jurisdiction dealt with proceedings brought by the government in revenue cases or in cases in which it sought to impeach a patent of invention or to set aside a land grant or lease of property, or, as a catch-all, civil proceedings of any kind in which the government brought the action. In these situations, the government had a choice of court. The private individual only had a choice of court in actions against officials of the government for any injuries they might have been responsible for in the performance of a duty. The choice in each case was between the Exchequer Court or the courts of a province.

REFERENCES

The Exchequer Court also had jurisdiction whenever there was a reference to the court from a head of department.[22] Previously a head of department had been able to refer a matter to an arbitrator for investigation and report; he could now make a reference to the court for adjudication of a claim.[23]

This reference mechanism had its opponents, and the provision was called into question as being outside the normal practice of the courts for adjudicating disputes between parties. During the argument of an appeal from one such case, the Supreme Court of Canada raised the question of whether an appeal from a reference existed.[24] The judge had dealt with the case based on the documentation submitted by the department, which in this case was Customs. Pleadings had been dispensed with. The Exchequer Court Act of 1887 specified that a case could be appealed by 'any party to a suit,'[25] and the opponents of the reference system took the word 'suit' to signify an adversarial proceeding. To remove any doubts, new legislation was quickly enacted in which the words were changed to 'any party to any action, suit, cause, matter or other judicial proceeding.'[26]

The concern that the Supreme Court judges had reacted to was no doubt fuelled by the controversy over references to the Supreme Court itself. The 1875 legislation that had created the court had included a provision allowing the executive to put questions on 'any matters whatsoever' to the Supreme Court.[27] The primary use contemplated was the quick settling of constitutional questions. In 1875 it was generally accepted, for what seemed valid constitutional reasons, that a decision of the court on a reference could not constitute a judgment, and would only be considered an advisory opinion.[28] As of 1890 none of the judges had in fact rendered reasons for their answers to the questions that had been referred to them. The last reference to them had been in 1885. The Supreme Court of the United States had refused to hear such a case because it had decided that it was not part of the judicial function to do so.[29] To overcome the opposition of the judges of the Supreme Court of Canada to the use of references, the government amended the legislation in 1891; the amendment expressly directed the judges to hear and consider any matter referred to them by the Governor in Council, and to give reasons for their opinions.[30]

The cases that were called 'references' in the Exchequer Court were quite different from those being sent to the Supreme Court. In the Exchequer cases, there was a dispute between parties and the reference was the mechanism by which it was being presented to the judiciary. However, because they bore the same name, they were caught up in the controversy afflicting the Supreme Court.

THE MYSTERIOUS JURISDICTION

When in 1891 the Exchequer Court of Canada acquired admiralty jurisdiction, an aura of mystery came with it. The Admiralty Court has always been regarded by the legal profession in general as an unknown, and the domain of a highly specialized group of lawyers. For the minister of justice in 1908 it was 'a thing separate and apart,' in which those versed in 'special mysteries' practised,[31] and, over the years since the Canadian court acquired the jurisdiction, it has remained foreign to most lawyers.[32] Not to be discounted is the sense of mystery that has always surrounded the sea and those who sail it.

Acquiring jurisdiction over disputes involving admiralty law was a highly significant event in the history of the Exchequer Court. The picture of the court as an 'administrative court' was cracked; now disputes between citizens involving ships and shipping would take their place beside proceedings involving the government. One way of looking at the change, however, was to see it as the creation of a Court of Admiralty under the umbrella name 'Exchequer Court of Canada,' the same judge constituted the two courts, but otherwise they were distinct.

History of the Admiralty Courts

A feature of admiralty law that adds to the curiosity, as well as to the mystery that it can evoke, is the history of England's Court of Admiralty from its beginning in medieval times. In order to understand the developments in Canada, as well as for general historical interest, we should examine that history briefly.[33]

The title 'Admiral' had originally designated the head of the department of government that controlled naval matters. That department came to have authority to deal with disputes that arose in the fleet. Out of this power of adjudication arose the Court of Admiralty, similar in origin to the Court of Exchequer. Throughout its history, its jurisdiction has aroused controversy. Within a few years of the establishment of what can be called a court of admiralty by Edward III in 1360, legislation was enacted to restrict its jurisdiction to matters done on the high seas (matters of a maritime nature). What was excluded were contractual matters, even when ships and shipping were involved, as well as matters of wreck.[34] A crucial consequence of this early restriction of its jurisdiction by statute was that the court acquired the status of a statutory court with limited jurisdiction, meaning that its jurisdiction always had to be expressly given by legislation. Since it had developed from the dispute resolution capability of a government department, the Court of Admiralty attracted the enmity of the courts that had developed from the *curia regis*, the King's Council of the eleventh and twelfth centuries, which could also sit as the supreme court of judicature.[35] The courts that traced their origins back to the King's Council took upon themselves the role of defenders of law that was to be common for the entire realm. A special court for ships and shipping was not acceptable. These courts, the 'common law courts,' were further antagonized by the fact that the procedural rules followed in the Admiralty Court were based on civil law and juries were not used. Trial by jury was a defining characteristic of the common law of England. The universality of matters associated with the sea had naturally led the Admiralty Court to follow rules that had been developed in foreign lands if they had proved their use-fulness.[36]

The result was a continuous antagonism between the Admiralty Court and the common law courts, with the common law courts possessing the upper hand. The Admiralty Court had a jurisdiction defined by statute; the common law courts had the authority to interpret statutes and hence had the power to define the jurisdiction. A writ of prohibition could be obtained from the common law courts to prevent the Court of Admiralty from exercising jurisdiction in a particular case if the common law courts determined that the matter in dispute was beyond the court's juris-diction.

The most ferocious attacks on the jurisdiction of the Admiralty Court were those led by Sir Edward Coke, who was made chief justice of the common law court, the Court of Common Pleas, in 1606. Coke asserted the supremacy of law and lashed out at the Admiralty Court, ecclesiasti-cal courts, and the King himself, whom Coke declared to be under God and the law. Coke, who was very hostile to the jurisdiction of the Admi-ralty Court, was able, by using the writ of prohibition, to virtually bring it to its knees. The court was held not to be a court of record, thus reducing it to the status of an inferior tribunal, whose proceedings would not be recorded and which could not fine or imprison for contempt.[37]

Without detailing to any extent the restrictions placed on the Court of Admiralty's jurisdiction over the years, it went from being a court with jurisdiction over ships and shipping in the late fourteenth century to a court of little or no significance in the administration of justice in England by the end of the eigthteenth century. While its jurisdiction did encom-pass torts committed at sea (especially those involving a collision), bot-tomry bonds,[38] the wages of mariners, salvage claims, and contracts made at sea to be performed there, what was noticeably missing was jurisdiction over disputes relating to the commercial aspect of shipping.

Change began with the maritime wars in the early nineteenth century, and a revival of interest centred on the court's jurisdiction over prizes. The prize law was concerned with ships and goods captured during times of war. Under international law the nations at war would each establish a court, the Prize Court, that would determine whether a cap-ture was legal under international law.[39] In the nineteenth century indus-trialization brought about an increase in the transportation of raw materials and of the subsequently manufactured goods, thereby enhanc-ing the importance of ships and shipping and producing a need to settle the disputes that inevitably arose. The advent of steam-propelled ships added to this. These various developments resulted in 1833 in the appointment of a select committee of the House of Commons to examine the jurisdiction of the Court of Admiralty. The committee recommended that the court's jurisdiction be extended.

Beginning with legislation in 1840, the court's previously attenuated jurisdiction began to recover.[40] By 1861, the court had jurisdiction over questions of ownership of ships, salvage, damages caused by a ship, wages, bottomry, and claims for necessaries supplied to a ship, as well as claims for the building, equipping, or repairing of any ship, and claims for damage to cargo. The increased jurisdiction was to be exercised concurrently with the common law courts.[41] In addition the 1861 legislation restored the Court of Admiralty as a court of record.[42]

The conflict over jurisdiction that had plagued this British court over the years finally came to an end in 1875 when it was combined with the other superior courts into one court, the High Court of Justice.[43] No new admiralty jurisdiction resulted, but now the judge applying admiralty law could also apply the common law as a judge of the High Court.

Throughout the years of conflict, what had been securely within the admiralty jurisdiction were those matters that could readily be identified as relating to maritime concerns. The common law courts had held tightly to jurisdiction over matters that were not intimately tied to the sea, such as commercial questions relating to the carriage of cargo.

Vice-Admiralty Courts

Following the Restoration of the monarchy in 1660 James, Duke of York (later James II) became Lord High Admiral not only of England, Wales, and Ireland, but also of the lands of the Crown beyond the seas. In the exercise of his authority over the colonies, commissions were issued to judges in the colonies making them vice-admirals with jurisdiction over admiralty matters.[44] The governors of the colonies were ex-officio vice-admirals.[45] The source of the jurisdiction of the Vice-Admiralty Courts was commissions from the Admiralty in Britain.

In keeping with the mid–nineteenth century enlargment of the jurisdiction of the Admiralty Court, legislation was passed in the 1860s changing the jurisdiction of the Vice-Admiralty Courts.[46] The jurisdiction of the courts in North America was made the same as that of the courts in Britain, except for authority to deal with charter-parties or bills of lading; questions of ownership or title to vessels; disputes between co-owners and adjustment of outstanding accounts; sale of a vessel; and distribution of proceeds. These omissions were said to have seriously lessened the value of the Vice-Admiralty Courts.[47]

On Confederation in 1867, there was no change to the Vice-Admiralty Courts in the various colonies. It was thought that the new Dominion had no power to deal with admiralty matters.[48] In the 1869 bill to establish the Supreme Court of Canada (drafted by Henry Strong) admiralty jurisdiction had been given to the proposed court, but it was omitted from the bill of 1870. Sir John A. Macdonald had objected. Strong, who thought that the court should have the same jurisdiction as the Supreme Court of the United States, recognized that Imperial legislation would be needed to give effect to the proposal.[49] However, there seems to have been no controversy within Canada about the omission of jurisdiction over admiralty law from the powers of the new Dominion. Following Confederation, the Vice-Admiralty Courts continued to function as they had before, as British courts.

Admiralty jurisdiction applied to activities on the high seas;[50] however, it was not long before a problem surfaced with respect to the Great Lakes, which were classed as inland waters. Commercial and other interests involved with shipping on the Great Lakes wanted to have access to the remedies available in admiralty law, such as enforcement of claims for seamen's wages, necessaries supplied, and repairs. Of particular interest were the availability of a maritime lien and proceedings *in rem*.[51] As previously mentioned, the need for a court with admiralty jurisdiction had been recognized in the 1869 bill to create the Supreme Court of Canada. The bill would have given the Supreme Court jurisdiction in admiralty 'in respect of the navigation of, and commerce upon the inland navigable waters of the Dominion, above tide water, and beyond the jurisdiction of any now existing Court of Vice-Admiralty.'[52] This provision, along with the general admiralty jurisdiction that the court was to have, did not appear in subsequent attempts to create the court, or the final legislation that established it in 1875. The Americans had recognized the need and introduced admiralty law to the Great Lakes in 1845.[53]

Canada's need for a special court to administer admiralty law on the Great lakes finally resulted in the enactment of The Maritime Jurisdiction Act, 1877.[54] This legislation created the Maritime Court of Ontario with authority over issues 'arising out of or connected with navigation, shipping, trade or commerce on any river, lake, canal or inland water, of which the whole or part is in the province of Ontario.' However, the power and jurisdiction of the new court were immediately tied to that of the existing British Vice-Admiralty Courts,[55] introducing the established rules of admiralty.

Agitation finally did develop within Canada for taking control of the Admiralty Courts. The first overt action originated in British Columbia in 1879 when the province's legislature passed a resolution urging Ottawa to obtain control over admiralty matters, and then give the jurisdiction to the provincial courts – in effect abolishing the distinctive Admiralty Courts. The motivation was concern for local requirements.[56] In 1882, the Conservative government introduced a resolution in the House of Commons addressed to the Queen, requesting authority to create a Maritime Court for Canada to replace the Maritime Court of Ontario and the British Vice-Admiralty Courts.[57] The leaders of the Liberal party, Edward Blake and David Mills, believing such authority existed already under the constitution, favoured direct action, namely, enacting legislation to establish an Admiralty Court for Canada.[58] For Blake, the British courts were anomalies and a blot on Canada's administration of justice. The Liberals maintained that a resolution would not likely get any reaction from the British government. They were right.[59]

Although there was no response to the resolution, there was activity in London regarding the Vice-Admiralty Courts and their reform, and it appeared that the passage of control to Canada was only a matter of time.[60] One proposal, to which the government of Canada reacted negatively, was that Britain would authorize the Supreme Court of a colony to assume the jurisdiction of the Vice-Admiralty Court. The Dominion government considered the possibility of jurisdiction going to the Supreme Court of Canada unacceptable, since, by this time, the court was viewed as a purely appellate tribunal. Using the provincial supreme courts was also unacceptable, because this would detract from the national nature of the jurisdiction. The government suggested the Exchequer Court. Ottawa wanted to take over complete control of the courts that administered admiralty law.[61]

Using the Exchequer Court would satisfy the Dominion government's goal of having a national court that would produce uniform decisions across the country. However, at the time the judges of the Exchequer Court were also Supreme Court judges and there were murmurs that the Exchequer Court side of their work was taking a somewhat distant second place. The sharply unequal number of sittings by the judges indicated a problem.[62] Any additional workload could only make matters worse. One solution proposed was to appoint judges in the old Vice-

Admiralty jurisdictions to conduct trials, but nothing further developed at the time.

When Britain finally brought in the legislation ending the Vice-Admiralty Courts and passing control to the colonies in 1890, the Exchequer Court had changed and now consisted of only one judge. George Burbidge, the judge of the Exchequer Court, could not have been surprised by what followed since, throughout the crucial part of the discussions between Canada and Britain, he had been deputy minister of justice. The Imperial legislation of 1890, the Colonial Courts of Admiralty Act, 1890,[63] empowered Canada to declare a court with 'unlimited civil jurisdiction' – meaning there was no limit on the value of the subject-matter at issue or the amount that could be claimed or recovered – to be a Court of Admiralty and, failing such a declaration, any court of original unlimited civil jurisdiction would acquire the jurisdiction, which in Canada meant the provincial superior courts. Thus Britain had allowed for the selection of the Exchequer Court, which had 'unlimited civil jurisdiction,' although not 'original unlimited jurisdiction.'[64] The 'Colonial Court of Admiralty' would acquire the same jurisdiction as the High Court in England, whether exercised under the authority of statute or any other authority. The Act was to come into force for Canada on July 1, 1891.[65]

On May 11, 1891, Sir John Thompson, minister of justice in the Macdonald government, introduced the bill that would designate the Exchequer Court as the court with admiralty jurisdiction.[66] The new legislation that named the Exchequer Court as the Court of Admiralty represented a major alteration in the jurisdiction of the Exchequer Court. The separation of the court from the Supreme Court and the creation of a jurisdiction over claims against the government had been accepted without controversy. This new jurisdiction was different, and tested section 101 of the constitution, under which the federal government could provide for an 'additional court for the better administration of the laws of Canada.'[67] The Liberal opposition, which would fight and win a pivotal general election five years later on the issue of the rights of the provinces in the federation, challenged the bill on the basis that admiralty jurisdiction should be vested in the provincial superior courts.[68] The arguments from the opposition benches emphasized that the provincial courts were 'at the door of the litigant,'[69] as well as invoking basic principles of federalism, which were said to require that power be given to the provinces.[70]

Thompson justified giving the jurisdiction to the Exchequer Court on several grounds. First, the nature of admiralty law required that there be a specialized court. Second, since the Imperial Parliament had vested the power to create an Admiralty Court in Ottawa, Thompson said '[I]t seems more consistent with the dignity and authority of this Parliament that the court should be one of our own creation.'[71] He also stated, 'If we take advantage of this opportunity presented by the Imperial legislation to keep the matter within our control, we shall have the judicial system established.'[72] Later in the debate, he referred to the idea of creating a system of federal courts, an idea which would be politically incendiary a century later: 'It may be very useful to have the organization we are making by this Bill available for other purposes than mere admiralty jurisdiction.'[73]

The organization that Sir John Thompson referred to consisted of Admiralty Districts within the country and a judge appointed for each district. There would be an appeal from the judges of the various districts to the Exchequer Court judge. Thus the government had established a federal court system, on a small scale and with a specialized jurisdiction, but done deliberately. For the first time, the existence of a dual system of courts, one for provincial matters and another for federal matters, was a reality. In the Senate, Nova Scotian Lawrence Power, a Liberal and a Harvard-educated lawyer, challenged the existence of the Exchequer Court itself, and expressed fear of what the future might bring. 'It appears that there is something in the mind of the Government,' he said, 'which indicates that at some future day they may extend the Exchequer Court.'[74] However, the threat of a federal court system challenging the jurisdiction of the provincial courts was not felt by enough people to make it a serious controversy. This may have been partly because the occasion was the creation of an Admiralty Court, a court that until recently had been distinct from the common law courts. The provincial courts were not having their jurisdiction reduced in any way. The Liberal opposition's commitment to provincial rights, which at this time had to give way to the Conservative government's promotion of a dual system of courts, would finally win the day in the general election of 1896.

The proposed Admiralty Districts were ready-made, since the old areas covered by the Vice-Admiralty Courts would suffice. These were the districts of Quebec, Nova Scotia, New Brunswick, Prince Edward Island, and British Columbia. The Maritime Court of Ontario was abolished and the Toronto Admiralty District created. 'Toronto' was chosen instead of 'Ontario' because, at the time, the intention was to create other districts within Ontario. The judges of the districts, each styled 'Local Judge in Admiralty of the Exchequer Court,' were already in place as the Vice-

Admiralty judges and, in Ontario, as the judge of the Maritime Court. Thompson noted that the Canadian government was required to pay the pensions of the Vice-Admiralty judges, and consequently it would be cheaper to simply continue their employment.

Since the judges chosen to be local judges could very well be provincial superior court judges there was the potential for irritating those with provincial sensitivities because of the provision for an appeal to a single judge of the Excequer Court. An opposition spokesman suggested that there should be an alternative appeal directly to the Supreme Court, thus bypassing the Exchequer Court judge, at the choice of the litigant.[75] Local sensibilities triumphed: later in the debate, Thompson announced that the bill would be changed and an appeal would be optional, either to the Exchequer Court or to the Supreme Court.[76]

It is difficult to assess the effect on the Exchequer Court of Canada of acquiring the new admiralty jurisdiction. It had acquired a jurisdiction that went beyond that of actions involving the government, and it now dealt with actions between private citizens, but the reality of the situation belies such a simple statement. The Vice-Admiralty Courts had been brought under Canadian control, and an appeal had been provided to the Supreme Court of Canada, when previously it had been to the Judicial Committee of the Privy Council. The Maritime Court of Ontario had been added to the Vice-Admiralty Courts to create the system of courts named the Admiralty Districts of the Exchequer Court. There was an optional appeal to either the Supreme Court or the Exchequer Court, two such different courts that its strangeness cried out. It was the best that Ottawa could do in the face of an assertion of provincial rights. The Admiralty Courts had the name 'Exchequer Court' as part of their official title, but the Exchequer Court as such could be cut out of the picture easily if it were bypassed in favour of an appeal to the Supreme Court.

While the Court of Admiralty in Britain had been combined with the common law courts, in Canada the court was kept distinct as a specialized court. Its separateness contributed to the maintenance of its mystery and its existence was a source of irritation to those favouring provincial control of the administration of justice in Canada.

INTELLECTUAL PROPERTY

In keeping with the Conservative government's tendency to expand the federal presence in the legal world and edge towards its own system of courts, the authority of the Exchequer Court was further enlarged in the autumn of 1891 when it was assigned jurisdiction over actions between private individuals concerning patents, copyrights, trade marks, and industrial designs.[77] Industrialization had brought these matters, collectively known as intellectual property, into great prominence.

A patent relates to an invention, and, when issued to the inventor by the government, gives that person the exclusive right to manufacture and use the substance of what has been invented. A copyright works in a similar fashion, except that it grants exclusive rights over artistic expression, such as writings, plays, musical works, and paintings. A trade mark, on the other hand, concerns symbols used in business, and protects the exclusive use of a symbol as a means of identifying goods. The concern with protecting trade marks is to prevent the public being misled by the use of a symbol that might be identified with another business, and to prevent unfair competition in which one business attempts to profit based on the reputation of another. An industrial design is a distinctive design of goods that involves not only appearance, but also structure and operation. The design of production equipment is included. The designs of what might be considered artistic works come within copyright protection and, for certain designs, it may be difficult to know whether copyright is involved or not. Designs were coupled with trade marks and handled in the same manner.

The constitution of 1867 gave Ottawa legislative authority over patents;[78] legislation enacted in 1869 and 1872 set out conditions for obtaining a patent.[79] A Patent Office was created[80] and attached to the Department of Agriculture, with the minister of agriculture designated as the commissioner of patents. If a dispute arose over the validity of a patent based on an alleged breach of a condition, it was to be settled by the minister of agriculture or the deputy minister, and their decisions were appealable only to the Governor in Council until 1913.

In 1887 the Exchequer Court had acquired jurisdiction in cases in which the government sought to have a patent set aside.[81] Three years later the Patent Act of 1890 gave the court jurisdiction concurrent with that of provincial courts in all cases involving the impeachment of patents,[82] and exclusive jurisdiction over the forfeiture of patents for breach of conditions.[83] The jurisdiction also covered questions about the existence of a patent. Until the 1891 amendment to the jurisdiction of the Exchequer Court, an action for infringement of a valid patent could only have been brought in the provincial courts.

For trade marks,[84] if someone attempted to use a symbol or mark that was identical to or closely resembled that used by someone else, the person whose mark was being improperly used could bring a passing-off action at common law and obtain an injunction, as well as damages and an accounting of profits earned using the mark. However, the plaintiff in such an action had to establish use and reputation of the symbol sufficient to give the plaintiff a property right in it. Exclusive use was the criterion. The proof required could involve an expensive and time-consuming process. To facilitate such proof, the Dominion established a registry of trade marks in 1868.[85] The federal authority over trade mark law was recognized as coming under section 91(2) of the constitution, 'The Regulation of Trade and Commerce.' The register was kept by the minister of agriculture. Evidence of a registration would be taken as *prima facie* proof of the required exclusive use.

The change in the manner of dealing with disputes between government and an individual is vividly illustrated by the history of registering a trade mark. Following Confederation the minister of agriculture had complete discretion with regard to registration, with an appeal only to the cabinet. This changed in 1879, when a new Act provided for a hearing before the minister or deputy minister.[86] As before, however, any appeal would be to the cabinet. In 1890 the minister was given the power to defer a decision until the matter had been heard by the Exchequer Court, which was given the jurisdiction to hear disputed cases. The matter could be brought before the court on information from the attorney general or by any interested party. The order of the court was not final, however, and was to guide the minister only.[87]

Change had gathered considerable momentum by this time and in 1891 the judiciary was given complete control. The pressures that had been present when the judiciary took over the jurisdiction of the adjudicators in 1887 were present. The minister could still refer questions of registration to the Exchequer Court, but now the order of the court was determinative. The court was given the jurisdiction to settle questions of registration brought by any person affected, or by the attorney general.[88] Also at this time, the court acquired jurisdiction over an infringement action concerning a trade mark.

Under section 91(23) of the constitution, Ottawa had legislative authority over copyright law. Whereas patents, trade marks, and industrial designs protected business interests and were commercial matters, copyright went beyond those concerns and engaged matters of culture as exemplified by artistic expression. Legislation had been enacted in 1842 in Britain which purported to regulate copyrights both in the United Kingdom and in its overseas possessions.[89] In the opinion of the British government, granting the federal Parliament authority over copyright in the 1867 constitution did not repeal the 1842 statute. Canada acquiesced and, when the first copyright law was enacted in Canada in 1875, the Dominion government accepted that British legislation was needed to give it effect. The British legislation was enacted in 1876 after the Canadian statute was reserved.[90] British authors continued to be protected by the earlier statute. Canadian legislation dealing with copyright passed in 1889 was reserved for consideration by the British government and was never assented to. It would be 1921 before the 1842 Imperial statute would be repealed as it affected Canada. The Exchequer Court was given jurisdiction to deal with conflicting claims to copyright in 1890.[91] As with patents and trade marks, the Exchequer Court acquired jurisdiction over infringement actions in 1891.

In addition to its role as an administrative court, the Exchequer Court had become a Court of Admiralty, and finally a court dealing with intellectual property issues. Part of the new jurisdiction fitted into its role as an administrative court. The other part, infringement actions between private individuals or companies, gave it the role of a specialized court operating under the rubric of the Exchequer Court of Canada.

9

The Burbidge Years, 1887–1908 (II)

Burbidge's judgments were marked by an earthiness and lack of pretension. He displayed a keen grasp of the reality of everyday life in the society in which he lived. There was little doubt that he leaned towards the approach of the contextualists in his decision making.

In the area of statutory interpretation, where the different approaches show so clearly, he began the task by asking the prime question: What was the problem that the legislation in question was attempting to solve or prevent from occurring? In other words, what was the policy behind the law? The policy would imbue the words of the law with their spirit, which was to be given effect by the judge. His attitude as a contextualist shows clearly in the following statement in a case from 1894:

In construing a statute relating to the revenue, one must, I think, have regard to the general fiscal policy of the country at the time when the statute was enacted. That may be a matter of common knowledge, or of history; and if of history, he who seeks to know the truth must go to the sources of history, and they, so far as the fiscal policy of a country is concerned, are to be found not only in Acts of Parliament but in the proceedings of Parliament and in the debates and discussions that take place there and elsewhere.[1]

Chapter 5 mentions that Burbidge had adopted a decision by William

Richards in which Richards held that the government could be bound by an implied contract, and refused to accept a rule that only a formal contract in writing signed by a representative of the government was required.[2] Richards's views were said by Burbidge to 'commend themselves to one's sense of what is fair and just.'[3] While Burbidge's point followed directly from Richards' reasons in the earlier case, his adoption of those reasons was a deliberate decision: the point was not that clear-cut within the legal community and involved an exercise of judgment by Burbidge. Five years later the Supreme Court would examine the issue and by only a bare majority of 3–2 affirm Burbidge's judgment and accept the application of implied contracts to the government.[4] In a dissenting judgment in the Supreme Court, John Gwynne took the position that implied contracts should have no application to the government since the government represented the public interest and the decision would impose a burden on public funds.

Formalism in legal decision making is part of more fundamental principles, and is aligned with other attitudes, such as the status of the government in relation to those being governed. Richards and Burbidge saw no need to create a contract rule for the government when it was involved in business dealings that differed in any way from the rules applicable to private individuals involved in the same kind of dealings. For a formalist, such as John Gwynne in the Supreme Court, identifying the government as representative of the public interest made special rules follow as a matter of course, since the public interest needed protection.

Burbidge's tendency to contextual decision making can be readily seen in the area of Crown liability, which occupied the bulk of the Exchequer Court's work and in which the relationship of the individual to the state is so central. Although imbued with the characteristics of a contextual lawyer, Burbidge was also a product of his times, and at that point in history the legal profession accepted without question that the government was not liable for the tortious acts of its employees, and that this had always been the law. Even Henry and Fournier had accepted this in the early years of the court and had attempted to attach liability only when a contractual relationship between the government and the injured person existed.[5] One result of this position was that it became a ritual in the writing of judgments in Crown liability cases until the 1950s for a judge to expressly point out that the Crown's liability was founded on the language of legislation only. Such a statement pressed home the point that the liability was definitely to be viewed as an exception, and approached as such. Although Burbidge tended to take a less restrictive view of

Crown liability than many of his contemporaries, and the ritual statement would appear much more often in later years from other judges, it did appear in Burbidge's judgments.[6]

Viewing liability as an exception would have fitted with an attitude prevalent at the time to the interpretation of legislation, namely, the strict interpretation of words, and together the two would produce the tendency to impose liability on the Crown only in the clearest of cases. The defendant orientation that existed in English law in negligence actions would also have helped to shield the government from liability.

As mentioned earlier, the precise wording of the legislative provision creating Crown liability would become crucial:

Every claim against the Crown arising out of any death or injury to the person or to property on any public work, resulting from the negligence of any officer or servant of the Crown, while acting within the scope of his duties or employment.[7]

Since a claim against the government depended on a public work being involved, the government could be shielded from liability by taking a narrow view of what counted as a 'public work.' Although Burbidge might hesitate to adopt a narrow meaning, he saw himself as restricted by the law. He held that an army rifle range was not a public work in an action that followed from the wounding of the suppliant by a bullet fired during target practice at the range. Although the Expropriation Act provided that 'works of defence' were to be considered public works, and Burbidge himself thought that the range was a work of defence, because it was debatable, he was still not prepared to conclude that the rifle range was a public work.[8]

Another way in which the words of this provision allowed for the limiting of liability was the two-letter word 'on.' The legislation provided for a claim against the Crown arising out of any death or injury to the person or to property 'on any public work.' Thus the cause of any injury and the injury itself both had to occur on a public work. For instance, claims for damages resulting from fires started by sparks from train engines were unsuccessful since the fires had not occurred on a public work, that is, the railway itself.[9] However, this interpretation of the legislation was too much for Burbidge, and he took a stand against it. In a 1900 decision he was prepared to accept that, while the cause of an injury had to arise on a public work, the injury itself did not have to occur there. He did have to acknowledge that certain Supreme Court judges thought otherwise.[10] He was to stay with his opinion for his remaining years as judge,[11] and it was only after his death that the Supreme Court rejected it.

When the Supreme Court finally came to write paid to Burbidge's opinion, it was in a case in which the government had not raised the defence in the Exchequer Court that the injury had not occurred on a public work. Burbidge's position had been too strong.[12] The Supreme Court thought otherwise and used its authority to establish the rule that the injury had to occur *on* the public work involved. Notably, Mr Justice Louis Davies of the Supreme Court felt it necessary to make some sort of comment. He said,

With the policy of Parliament we have nothing to do. Our duty is simply to construe the language used, and if that construction does not fully carry out the intention of Parliament, and if a wider and broader jurisdiction is desired to be given the Exchequer Court, the Act can easily be amended.[13]

This was formalism in all its glory. Throughout the years, Judge Burbidge had read the same words. The difference must have been that he was trying to give effect to the policy of Parliament by extending liability to the extent that the words would allow. The formalists in the Supreme Court may have simply been promoting counter-values and trying to maintain immunity for the government in actions by individuals who would fail before the assertion of public interest. However, formalists could mask this, since it was their 'duty ... simply to construe the language used.'

In chapter 7, it was mentioned that the Judicial Committee of the Privy Council supported the breaking down of government immunity with respect to claims against it.[14] In an 1887 appeal from New South Wales, *Farnell v. Bowman*, Sir Barnes Peacock had provided inspiring words for those who favoured breaking down resistance to attaching liability to the government for tortious acts of employees.[15] He said:

It must be borne in mind that the local Governments in the Colonies, as pioneers of improvements, are frequently obliged to embark in undertakings which in other countries are left to private enterprise, such, for instance, as the construction of railways, canals, and other works for the construction of which it is necessary to employ many inferior officers and workmen. If therefore, the maxim that 'the king can do no wrong' were applied to Colonial Governments in the way now contended for by the applicants, it would work much greater hardship than it does in England.[16]

He went on,

Justice requires that the subject should have relief against the Colonial Governments for torts as well as in cases of breach of contract or the detention of property wrongfully seized into the hands of the Crown. And when it is found that the
Act uses words sufficient to embrace new remedies, it is hard to see why full
effect should be denied to them.

The message was clear: if the language of a law is 'amply sufficient to
include a claim for damages for a tort'[17] against the government, it should
be so interpreted. A search of the cases cited in the Exchequer Court
reveals that Burbidge cited and quoted this decision,[18] and it was cited by
counsel several times during the Burbidge era to suggest the proper
approach to the interpretation of the words of the law. However, after
1901 it no longer appeared for this purpose.[19] Formalism finally put an
end to any life force that resided in the opinion of the Privy Council
when, in 1943, Joseph Thorson, then head of the Exchequer Court,
declared,

these remarks of the Judicial Committee ... are of little, if any, value, since the
courts are not concerned with the policy of legislation but only with its interpretation and application.[20]

The tension between expanding and contracting the liability of the
Crown was present throughout the Burbidge era of the Exchequer Court,
as it had been in the Supreme Court era. After Chief Justice William Richards had resigned for reasons of health in 1879, a majority of the judges of
the Supreme Court appeared in favour of restricting liability. However,
the sharp differences of opinion that had marked the opening years of the
court still surfaced. In 1892, in *The Queen v. Martin*, several of the judges –
William Ritchie, Henri-Elzéar Taschereau, and John Gwynne – were very
reluctant to expand the government's liability, and even raised the question of whether the 1887 legislation, which had created the Exchequer
Court as a court of claims, had actually changed anything with respect to
tort liability, thus suggesting that the immunity from tort liability still
existed.[21] They wanted to stay with the opinion that they had fought so
hard for in the *McLeod* case in 1882. This attitude was in contrast to that of
Christopher Patterson, who had replaced William Henry, and who possessed some of the same values as Henry. He thought that government
railways should be placed on the same footing with regard to liability as

private companies, and was prepared to find sufficient support for this position in the Government Railways Act of 1881,[22] in which the government had accepted the same tort liability with respect to the running of railways as a private railway had.[23] The statute was to be given a 'fair and liberal construction,' and, in Patterson's opinion, its whole tenor indicated the liability of the Crown. He stated that he had difficulty with the opinion that a government railway should be seen as having a high political object, the public good, rather than as a commercial enterprise undertaken with a view to profit. As far as he was concerned, both kinds of railways were conducted in the same way and the individual had to deal with both in the same way.

In the *Martin* case Burbidge in the Exchequer Court had found for the suppliant and awarded damages. The suppliant's son had been trespassing on a train and the brakeman had forced him and his friends from it by throwing water on them. The boy fell and his leg was crushed by the moving train. On the appeal to the Supreme Court, the defence of prescription (meaning that the action had been brought outside the prescribed time limit) was raised by the judges on their own to deny the recovery of damages by the suppliant. The defence had not been pleaded, and in fact the Crown had intentionally refrained from raising it.[24] Within months of the Supreme Court's decision, Burbidge made it absolutely clear where his sympathies lay in the battle over Crown liability. He referred to the view of the minority in *McLeod*, Fournier and Henry, whose decision making had been branded as unconstitutional by William Ritchie, and which to this day is never mentioned by judges of the Supreme Court, although the conclusion of the bare majority in the 3–2 decision is taken as unquestioned authority.[25] Burbidge also referred approvingly to Patterson's judgment in the Supreme Court in the *Martin* case. It was, he said 'an opinion that adds much to the discussion, deals fully with the more important question raised but not decided by the appeal.'[26]

In another case in 1901, Burbidge espoused the same sentiments as had Patterson when he stated during the argument of counsel that it was reasonable that the government should be liable in the same way as a company when engaged in what amounted to a commercial undertaking.[27] In 1898 he pointed out that the opinion that liability would attach to the Crown only in cases in which the injury actually occurred on a public work was attributable to two judges of the Supreme Court in an early case, John Gwynne and George King;[28] it was clear that Burbidge did not consider the matter to be settled at all.

The solidifying of formalism in the Supreme Court can be seen in 1906 in a statement by John Idington, then recently appointed to the court. In his view the intention (policy) behind the legislation establishing Crown liability for tortious acts was to put the relation between the government and the individual on the same footing as that between individuals, and thus eliminate any special rules regarding the government. He acknowledged, however, 'the general trend of opinion, in and of this court, in this regard has been against such a wide, and as I conceive beneficial, interpretation.'[29] He also noted that the court had never actually declared against the implementing of the policy. That did come, however, three years later, and Idington would acquiesce without any protest. The policy would fall before 'a long series of decisions,' the 'general trend' noted by Idington, none of which, as he had also noted, was determinative, but which provided a formalist source of inspiration, rather than the forbidden reference to 'policy.'[30]

A particularly interesting aspect of Crown liability was the issue of what law to apply when deciding the extent of liability, assuming that the question of the words 'on a public work' had been dealt with. It was accepted that the liability of the Crown would be determined by the laws of the various provinces at the time the liability was imposed. It was, Burbidge had said, 'settled by the general concurrence of judicial opinion.'[31] This conclusion was based on the opinion that there could not be a national law founded on judge-made law because of the existence of a different law in Quebec. Burbidge went to the words of Mr Justice Henry Strong in the 1894 decision, *City of Quebec v. The Queen*:

It can make no difference that all the provinces save one derive their common law from that of England; the circumstance that the private law of one province, that of Quebec, is derived from a different source, makes it impossible to say that there is any system of law apart from statute, generally prevalent throughout the Dominion.[32]

Thus, when applying tort law in a matter of federal jurisdiction, such as the liability of the federal government, the provincial law would be applied in the absence of applicable federal legislation. Another factor was the recognition that liability had been imposed as of the date the Exchequer Court Act came into force, June 23, 1887. Consequently any reform of tort law undertaken by a province after that date (and essentially all reform was to come after 1887) would not increase the liability of the federal government. By a special rule the government could take advantage of any new rule that reduced liability. Although provincial law applied to Crown liability, it was only the basic law of negligence.

When the Exchequer Court was separated from the Supreme Court and made a court of claims against the government, it may have been thought that the former deputy minister of justice would tend to protect the government and that the court would become a government court. George Burbidge had a greater commitment to the law and the policy behind it which gave it its spirit. The minister of justice, Charles Fitzpatrick, lamented in 1904 that, in cases before the court, the Crown frequently received the short end of the stick and did not very often receive much sympathy.[33]

Cases involving claims against the Crown formed by far the largest single category of Exchequer Court cases, making up 52 per cent of the reported decisions in the Burbidge era, which was down from 83 per cent in the years before 1887. The new areas of jurisdiction were having an effect. For reported cases for the years 1888 to 1907, inclusive, the work of the court was divided as follows: Crown liability, 52 per cent; intellectual property, 14 per cent; expropriation, 14 per cent; admiralty, 9 per cent, customs, 8 per cent, railways, 2 per cent; and miscellaneous, 2 per cent.

RELATIONSHIP WITH THE SUPREME COURT

Crown liability raises the issue of the relationship between the Exchequer Court and the Supreme Court. The relationship between George Burbidge and a majority of the judges of the Supreme Court, although potentially stormy because of Burbidge's tendency to view law and lawyering differently, did not strike the kinds of sparks seen between judges before the two courts were separated. In the Burbidge era of 1887 to 1908, there were various judges on the Supreme Court who could be identified as contextualists. The profession was made up of both kinds of lawyers. The existence of judges on the highest court who might sympathize with the Exchequer Court judge as far as approach was concerned may have helped to soften any antagonism. Of the original judges of the Supreme Court who were contextual in approach, William Henry died in May of 1888 and Télesphore Fournier resigned in 1895. Christopher Patterson, another contextualist, took Henry's place. He was noted for being well-read and a learned individual, with creative instincts. He was sixty-five when appointed, and died in 1893 after only four and a half years on the court. There were three other contextual judges who were only on the bench for very brief periods of time. It is no doubt significant that each was over seventy when appointed. David Mills, almost seventy-one, was appointed in 1902 and died a little over a year later. He has been referred to earlier for his involvement as a legislator in the life of the court. He was in favour of viewing the law through the eyes of the people.[34] He declared in one case in his short tenure the credo of the contextualist: 'Were it necessary to do so, it would be our duty to make the words of the statute yield to its reason and expressed intention ... The courts ... have, on more than one occasion, preferred to follow the reason rather than the exact letter of the law.'[35] John Douglas Armour, like William Richards chief justice of Ontario, was over seventy-two years old when appointed in November 1902, and was dead eight months later. A legal journal complimented him on his robust common sense, and his clear conception of the conditions of life in the country, with a capacity to grasp the true spirit of a legal proposition.[36] These were words of the kind that had earlier described William Richards. James Maclennan, also from Ontario, joined the Supreme Court in 1905 as the oldest appointee to date, at seventy-two years and seven months. Three and a half years later he resigned. He was praised for being well read with a wide general knowledge – the praises bestowed on the good judges of the nineteenth century. All of these judges had obtained their legal education or entered the bar in the 1850s when formalism was only beginning to become the dogma of the legal profession. They were from an era before the dogma had set in and when representatives of both judicial styles could be easily found. Of the two, it was the contextualist who was inevitably praised by the bar. The last appointee to the Supreme Court for decades to come who would show sparks of contextualism was Désiré Girouard from Quebec. He was appointed to replace Fournier in 1895, and was the first lawyer from Quebec to come from the Montreal district. He was noted for his excellent literary credentials. He died unexpectedly in 1911 following an accident, and the Supreme Court slipped into a period of sterility.[37]

A FEDERAL COURT

The Exchequer Court had acquired jurisdiction covering private actions in admiralty and intellectual property as early as 1891, and the minister of justice could hint at the existence of a federal court system. In admiralty law there was a federal court system, with local courts, an appeal directly to the Supreme Court or the Exchequer Court, and then, if a party in an Exchequer Court case thought it necessary, to the Supreme Court.

In the 1903 debates, when once again the Supreme Court came under fire and an attempt was made to remove its jurisdiction over matters of provincial law, the Exchequer Court was not involved. The proposal was to make the Supreme Court purely a federal court.[38] The Exchequer Court already was one.

When the jurisdiction over admiralty matters and intellectual property was added by the Conservative government in 1891, the notion of a dual legal system, federal and provincial, reached its high point. The Conservatives were replaced in 1896 by a Liberal government committed to the support of provincial rights. This policy surfaced in a 1908 debate on a resolution concerning the jurisdiction over admiralty matters. The minister of justice, A.B. Aylesworth, proposed that the jurisdiction be conferred on the provincial courts. He commented on the Conservatives' giving the jurisdiction to the Exchequer Court in 1891 and stated that, at the time, the government thought that power should be centralized in Ottawa. Aylesworth asserted that he was diametrically opposed to that position, adding, 'it is in the interest of the body politic in this country that greater power, in every place where it can be given, should be given to the provincial authorities.' He also referred to the 'constitution and maintenance' of the courts, which he said had been vested in the provincial authorities by the constitution.[39] Nothing came of the proposed transfer of jurisdiction at the time, but the policy regarding the nature of the federation was clear. There was no doubt that the court was dependent on the strength or weakness of centralism within the country.

A NATIONAL COURT

In a court with only one judge, the nation obviously would not be reflected in the make-up of the bench, unless of course that single judge leaned towards the contextualist school of viewing law and decision making. A contextualist would try to see the problems with the eyes of the participants, and consequently there would be a better chance of the values and sensibilities of the various parts of the nation being respected than through a linguistic analysis with so many unstated social assumptions that were taken as unquestionable. Burbidge possessed that wider view of law and lawyering.

The registrar, Louis Arthur Audette, gave a Quebec profile to the court. Through his function as a referee, he took an active part in the hearing of cases from his province of origin. Having been appointed in 1887, he had grown with the institution.[40]

National institutions at this time were English institutions. For the

Exchequer Court, with its jurisdiction over matters of government involvement and administrative or Crown law, the law of England applied. The constitutional law of Canada was the law of England; the federal nature of the country was recognized in that, in matters of private law, contracts, torts, and property, the provincial law was understood to apply and its use was to be read into federal statutes providing for Crown liability. The provincial law could not, however, increase the Crown's liability. The fact that the public law of Canada was accepted as English law and the Exchequer Court was established as a public law court may have accounted for the absence of criticisms or even comments from Quebec about the court being an English court, criticisms which were aimed at the Supreme Court of Canada.

Travelling had continued to be part of the work in this national court. Burbidge, as its only judge, had to travel across the country, but the need for this was reduced by the use of referees and Official Arbitrators to conduct hearings locally. Occasionally the trial for the determination of facts would also be conducted locally and the argument on the facts would take place in Ottawa.

THE END OF THE BURBIDGE ERA

George Burbidge's lengthy tenure of twenty-one years created a stable period during which the second court to be called the Exchequer Court of Canada could establish itself. A vital part of the new court's success was also attributable to Burbidge's ability as a lawyer and judge. His dedication to his duty as a judge and his concern with the parties marked his final days on the court. In the summer of 1907 he travelled to Dawson in the Yukon Territory for the hearing of a number of cases involving hydraulic mining leases, which consisted of both Crown actions to cancel leases and petitions by private individuals for the grant of leases. There was also a petition of right involving the government's cancellation of a contract for the publication of *The Yukon Year-Book of 1903*. He heard these cases in the latter half of July. While in Dawson he became ill, but continued his work and, following the hearings, travelled to the east coast. Given the travelling conditions of the time, this feat alone deserves comment. At the end of 1907 he suffered an 'utter collapse.'[41]

Burbidge's conscientiousness about his work prevailed over advice to rest and, as a last act, he attempted to clear up the outstanding judgments. For some cases he wrote very brief judgments, while for others he relied upon an earlier decision of the court in which Mr Justice Fournier had pronounced judgment by consent of the parties without any arguments being presented in order that the case might proceed to the Supreme Court of Canada.[42] Burbidge decided that, since he was unable to give the decisions that he thought were required in the time left to him, he would simply render a judgment, having decided who should have the burden of proof in the higher court. In this way the case could proceed, rather than litigants having to repeat at least part of the process if the case were left unresolved at his death.[43] His final judgments are dated January 7, 1908.

Sir Thomas W. Taylor was appointed as a temporary measure (Judge *pro tempore*) during the final days of Burbidge's illness. He was the retired chief justice of Manitoba. His commission ended with Burbidge's death on February 18, 1908. George Burbidge was only sixty-one years of age, still young for a judge.

The Exchequer Court of Canada and George Burbidge had developed together. The court had taken on the characteristics that were seen in Burbidge, an 'able and conscientious judge.'[44] In the face of the growing domination of the Supreme Court of Canada by formalist judges, he had held his ground. As an indication of the prestige that Burbidge had acquired, an appreciation published after his death pointed out that, in admiralty cases, 'he presented the unique, not to say anomalous, spectacle of a single Judge constituting a complete federal appellate tribunal,' and, as the writer added, had a concurrent jurisdiction with the Supreme Court of Canada.[45]

10

The Cassels Years, 1908–1923

Two weeks after Burbidge passed away, the new judge was appointed. Walter Gibson Pringle Cassels was an intellectual property lawyer from Toronto, who had experience before the court. His brother, Robert, as registrar of the Supreme Court of Canada from 1875 to 1898, had been the first registrar of the Exchequer Court. Walter had been born in Quebec City, where he received his early education. He attended the University of Toronto, and obtained his legal education in Ontario. At sixty-two, he was older than Burbidge had been when he died.

The state of equanimity that had characterized the institution during the Burbidge era was soon disrupted. The disturbances came from two sources.

There had been few outward problems with the fact that Burbidge was both a unilingual anglophone and also had no civil law background. Louis Arthur Audette, the court's francophone registrar after 1887, compensated for any lack on Burbidge's part. His much lower status did not attract any direct public comment, and there was only the merest hint of something when a question was asked in the House of Commons in 1901 about the number of cases from Quebec handled by the court and how many were tried before a referee. The statistics as presented did not disclose any serious problem.[1] However, within weeks of Cassels' appointment, Philippe-Auguste Choquette, a Liberal and previously a superior

court judge in Quebec, expressed concern in the Senate about his language ability and knowledge of Quebec law. If he were found to be defi-
cient in both, Choquette wanted to know if a second judge would be
appointed in order that 'French-Canadian citizens shall be upon an equal
footing with English-Canadian citizens before all the tribunals of this
country as prescribed by the constitution.' The most that the government
spokesman could say was that he thought that the new judge would
address the bar in French when he opened the court in Montreal; he
pointed out that Cassels had been born in Quebec. Choquette understood
that Cassels had said he would try to give the speech in French. As far as
Cassels' expertise with the law of Quebec went, the spokesman did not
know whether Cassels was up on Quebec law, but assumed that with his
inherent ability he could master it.[2]

A second controversy involved Cassels' appointment to investigate
certain matters concerning the department of marine and fisheries at the
time of his appointment to the court. This move necessitated the passage
of legislation providing for the appointment of a substitute judge whenever the judge was ill or absent, or was engaged in other judicial duties. It
also covered instances when the judge was interested in the case, or
related to any party, or had acted in a professional capacity regarding the
case before being appointed to the bench.[3] The use of Cassels for the
inquiry struck a chord of discontent within the profession regarding
the use of judges for other than judicial work. Earlier, in 1905, the concern had resulted in legislation specifically stating that judges of the
Supreme and Exchequer Court (later expanded to all judges appointed
by Ottawa) could not engage in work other than 'judicial duties.'[4] The
controversy revolved around the legal profession's concern with keeping
the judiciary away from anything that might even hint at political partisanship. From their viewpoint partisan issues would flow naturally from
government-appointed investigations of problems. The government had
a political need to have someone called a 'judge' carry out an investigation, because of the status and prestige of the position and the aura of
impartiality that imbued it. The public's perception of the inquiry and the
government would obviously be more positive.[5] As far as the legislation
limiting judges to judicial duties, the government considered the investigation and reporting of an incident to be the carrying out of judicial
duties.[6] Those opposed naturally disagreed.

Cassels personally emerged from the fracas unscathed. The fact that he
had made it known that he had declined any payment over and above his
judicial salary certainly helped.[7] In the end, it would not have been in the

interest of the profession or of the government to level any personal attack and thus weaken the integrity of the judiciary.

The concern expressed, primarily by Philippe-Auguste Choquette, over adequate representation of the French language and the distinct law of Quebec in the Exchequer Court reaped some rewards when Audette was appointed an assistant judge in 1912.[8] There was never any doubt about Audette's appointment, as he was mentioned by name in the debates. However, reflecting a certain lingering sensitivity to the question, the government pointed out that Audette was not a judge for Quebec only.[9] The true nature of Audette's position apparently did not become clear until the creation of the position of *ad hoc* judge of the Supreme Court of Canada in 1918.

As early as 1876 it had been suggested that provision be made for appointing *ad hoc* judges to the highest court in order to maintain a quorum, if that became necessary. However, the government had responded by saying that the proposed measure was simply not thought advisable at that moment.[10] Discussion of the possibility continued, on and off, for the next forty-odd years. The legal profession was concerned that inserting different judges into the Supreme Court at different times would weaken the coherence among its judges. They felt that certainty in the law, a passion of the formalists, would be a casualty. Naturally, from an institutional perspective, any instability that might be created would affect confidence in the court.[11]

The moment finally came in 1918 when the Supreme Court was facing a crisis with respect to having a quorum of judges for hearings. Two judges were ill and, in addition, in late 1917 Lyman Duff had taken on the duties of central appeal judge under the Military Service Act, by which conscription had been introduced. As the central appeal judge, Duff sat as the final appeal court for decisions on exemptions from military service. By April, when the bill to create *ad hoc* judges was introduced, the government had decided to expand the categories of men who could be conscripted, which made an increase in Duff's work easily foreseeable.[12] There was a specific concern that a four-judge bench would create the potential for an even split among the judges.[13]

The legislation of 1918 provided that, in the absence of a quorum of the judges of the Supreme Court to carry on any session of the court, the chief justice or senior puisne judge might request the attendance, first, of the judge of the Exchequer Court and, if he was unable to sit, a judge of a provincial superior court to be named by the provincial court. If the two Supreme Court judges appointed from the bar of Quebec were not available to sit on an appeal from Quebec, then an *ad hoc* judge had to be appointed from one of the superior courts of that province.[14]

The specification that 'the judge of the Exchequer Court' would be the first to be called upon provoked a reaction from Quebec politicians when they realized that Louis Arthur Audette, as assistant judge, would not be included. Until this time no distinction had been made between him and Walter Cassels as far as judicial duties were concerned. Although the minister of justice, C.J. Doherty, might say that there had been no intention to reflect negatively on Audette, he put it very lamely.[15] Doherty ignored all further attempts to discuss the issue and the debate on the bill continued. When a Quebec MP and former member of the Liberal cabinet, Rodolphe Lemieux, moved an amendment to allow Audette to sit on the Supreme Court, the surface covering was pierced, and Doherty declared that it would not be acceptable to have three judges from Quebec sitting on an appeal from a common law province.[16] That there were three common law judges sitting on appeals from Quebec was apparently too obvious even to be mentioned. It was simply a matter of the reality of political power. As one of the two judges of the Exchequer Court was generally in Ottawa,[17] Audette might have been appointed fairly frequently. The provision in the Supreme Court Act dealing with *ad hoc* judges was changed in the 1927 revision of the statutes to read 'a' judge of the Exchequer Court,[18] but Audette was never appointed. The Quebec judges who were needed for quorum purposes continued to be drawn from the provincial superior courts.

Quebec members of Parliament experienced considerable agitation on realizing that the title 'assistant judge' meant less than they might have hoped. They were somewhat mollified when, on May 5, 1920, legislation was introduced that changed the titles of the judges. The judge was to be the 'President,' while the assistant judge was to be the 'Puisne Judge.' The reason for choosing the title 'President' rather than 'Chief Justice' remains obscure. When Arthur Meighen, acting minister of justice, gave notice in the Commons in 1919 of this and other changes contemplated, he said that the head of the Exchequer Court in England was called 'President.' The title 'President' had been given to the heads of the divisions of England's High Court of Justice when it was created in 1875. The head of the Exchequer Division was the 'Lord Chief Baron, President.' The title was used in Ontario for the heads of the divisions of its Supreme Court. 'Chief Justice' seemed to be the obvious title to use, and there appears to have been some support for it,[19] but something was blocking its adoption.

Meighen pointed out that Walter Cassels believed that 'President' was the appropriate title.[20]

Deputy Judges

In the same 1920 legislation that provided for the president and puisne judge, a section was added to the Exchequer Court Act giving the power to appoint a deputy judge as a temporary measure. Such a judge, who was to have the same qualifications as the two regular judges, would be appointed if either of those judges was ill or absent, or 'at the request of the President, for any other reason which he deems sufficient.'[21] A means had been provided to overcome any deficiency in the number of judges temporarily. Despite this provision there is no indication in the reported cases of a deputy judge having been used until 1942.

THE WORK

Based on the cases reported in the period that Cassels was head of the Exchequer Court, the workload was not particularly heavy. The issue of the volume of work had come up in 1919 when the minister of justice, Arthur Meighen, introduced a bill that increased the number of judges to three.[22] The court was expected to have extra work from divorce cases, because there was also a bill that would have provided for divorces to be heard by the court. However, the bill did not become law, and the number of judges was returned to two the next year.[23]

An indication that there was still some controversy surrounding the admiralty jurisdiction of the court occurred when Meighen stated in 1919 that the government intended to allow the provincial courts to exercise the jurisdiction.[24] However, nothing came of this at the time.

From 1908 to 1922 reported cases from the court break down as follows: Crown liability, 46 per cent; expropriation, 27 per cent; intellectual property, 13 per cent; admiralty, 5 per cent; railways, 3 per cent; others, 6 per cent. Included in the 'others' category were the first two cases involving questions of taxation. In the next decade, taxation cases would begin to grow in number, until they became the dominant area of work for the Exchequer Court in its concluding years of existence.

Following Audette's appointment as assistant judge in 1912, it is clear that it was his role to take the cases from Quebec. From 1912 until 1920 Audette carried virtually double the workload that Cassels did, and after 1920 became effectively the sole judge. Cassels, meanwhile, used his background in intellectual property and heard the great majority of these cases.

CROWN LIABILITY

Pressure for reform of the law relating to government liability was mounting. However, little of this pressure came from the Exchequer Court. Burbidge, while somewhat restrained because of his position as a lower court judge, did protest and would have helped to create a tension within the system. Whenever he could, Burbidge would give effect to the policy he identified behind the words of the law and would give recompense to injured individuals.

Pressure for change also came from the lawyers, who challenged the interpretation of the word 'on' whenever they could.[25] The government responded by bringing in reform legislation, such as that of 1908 that made the government liable whenever damage to property had been caused by a fire originating from a locomotive of a government railway.[26] Of wider scope was the legislation in 1910; the 1910 Act made the government liable for claims arising from injury to person or property as a result of negligence of a government employee acting within the scope of employment in relation to government railways.[27]

The legislative reforms followed decisions of the Supreme Court in which the court had taken its characteristically restrictive approach to the plight of injured citizens. There was a not-unexpected reluctance to comment adversely on the work of the judges, but the promoter of the 1910 legislation could not resist saying that 'the court carried technicality a very long way in arriving at a decision.'[28] Significantly, the main justification for the reform was that the interpretation adopted by the judiciary had never been intended. This meant that Burbidge's approach and his conclusion had been appropriate, but formalism seemed to have taken hold to such an extent that the judges who had followed the inappropriate policy were not to be criticized, since they were seen as simply giving meaning to words.

While the trend was towards widening liability, not everyone favoured such a move. The majority of the Supreme Court judges had allies. In a debate in the House of Commons, the minister of justice in the Liberal government, A.B. Aylesworth, had declared that he was more conservative on the issue than the leader of the Conservative Party, Robert Borden. He considered that it was one of the most valuable rights of the Crown to have immunity from being sued except upon the advice of the attorney general. He rejected the argument that the rights of a subject and the Crown be co-relative and co-equal. In his opinion, there was a reason for the established order of things that had prevailed for centuries. The attorney general was said not to be personally interested, and he could be safely trusted to decide when an action should proceed.[29] It was 1917 before the first major reform of the law that had been enacted in 1887 took place. The government was now Conservative and Aylesworth was no longer minister of justice. It began as a private member's bill.

On May 15, 1917, Ernest Lapointe, Liberal member from Quebec, who would in the 1930s become William Lyon Mackenzie King's Quebec lieutenant, introduced his bill with the intention of eliminating the interpretation that had been given to the words, 'on any public work,' and replacing it with liability whenever the negligent act of the government employee that had caused death or injury to someone had occurred on a public work. Lapointe was far less reticent than the average legislator when he specifically referred to a recent decision of the Supreme Court and to statements of judges that had made the law 'a stupid enactment,' with the result that justice had often been denied.[30] The case in question was *John Piggott and Sons v. The King*.[31] Blasting operations carried out by the government during the construction of a cement dock on the Detroit River had resulted in damage to an adjoining dock owned by the petitioners. Cassels in the Exchequer Court, and subsequently the Supreme Court, had decided that there was no liability: the damages had not occurred on a public work. In the Supreme Court, John Idington let loose with a verbal barrage against the result: 'The absurdity has continued for many years, and probably justice has often been thereby denied.'[32] For him, the case illustrated how 'absurd and barbarous' the law was.[33] He then made a direct appeal for law reform: 'I respectfully submit that the sooner the probably misplaced words, 'on any public work,' are stricken out of sub-section (c) the better.'[34] Louis-Phillippe Brodeur, who had replaced Désiré Girouard on the Supreme Court bench after Girouard's death, was not happy but said that, since the restrictive meaning given to the words by the judges had been allowed to remain, it must be assumed that it had been accepted by Parliament and, until legislation was passed to alter the law, the doctrine of *stare decisis* hamstrung him and other judges who desired change. Brodeur had been a member of the Liberal cabinet. Although Lapointe had made the first move with his private bill, the government introduced its own bill a month later, an action which finally resulted in an amendment to the law. The new provision read:

Every claim against the Crown arising out of any death or injury to the person or to property resulting from the negligence of any officer or servant of the Crown while acting within the scope of his duties or employment upon any public work.[35]

This legislation went through with no difficulty of any kind. The minister of justice, C.J. Doherty, pointed out once again that the judges of the Supreme Court had interpreted the existing words of the law very literally and had failed to fulfil the original intention of the legislators, but he was at pains in his speeches to reiterate that what the Supreme Court judges had done had been justified given the language of the law.[36]

In contrast to Burbidge, who had done battle with a majority of the judges of the Supreme Court, Cassels put no pressure on the highest court. He accepted the formalism and the values inherent in a limited liability. Audette was prone on occasion to criticise the law, but in the main his decisions, whenever he had a choice, went with a restricted liability.

PERFORMANCE

Overall, Cassels' decisions were unexceptional. There is nothing of any particular interest in his judgments, simply a rendition of the facts followed by a conclusion. This is the hallmark of a formalist judge. There is in effect no *ratio decidendi*, that is, no reasons for judgment, on which the law can develop and help to solve future problems. In between the facts and the conclusion, Cassel's judgments featured extensive quoting from previous decisions, which he had identified as 'authorities.' He was thus giving the impression that he was creating nothing, only following what had been created elsewhere sometime in the past. The appearance of objectivity and neutrality in the judicial process would be maintained. There were of course winners and losers and the litigants would have had their day in court.

Audette was of much the same judicial mould, but did on occasion let his guard down and reveal the values that were driving his thinking. For instance, in an action by a downtown merchant in Ottawa for damage to his stock caused by a fire which had started in part of a building rented by the government for use as a recruiting office, Audette determined that the offices could not be classed as a public work. He reached this conclusion 'in light of the statutes and the long series of decisions,' all of which could be called authorities, but he was driven to comment:

'While desirous of doing justice between the parties, I see no reason to condemn the crown because it is the crown and thereby mulct His Majesty's liege subjects with large damages.'[37] For policy reasons, he had set himself against finding liability except, one assumes, in the clearest of cases.

Audette was also known to criticise the law that he had to apply. On one occasion, the government, which was being sued for damages as a result of the death of an employee of the Intercolonial Railway, raised the defence of common employment, by which an employer could escape liability if the injury to the employee had been caused by the fault of a fellow worker. Audette was clearly not happy with the doctrine and pointed out that it existed only in English law and had been forced on Scotland by the House of Lords for the sake of uniformity. Were it not for a decision of the Supreme Court of Canada, he said, the legislation could have been interpreted so that the defence would not have applied in negligence actions against the federal government.[38] Five years later, he again asserted that the intention of the legislation creating the government liability was to exclude the defence of common employment, but admitted that he was bound to decide otherwise by a decision of the Supreme Court.[39] On other occasions, he expressed regrets that the law forced him to decide in such-and-such a way.[40] It is difficult to evaluate such statements. They certainly do not indicate a commitment to the integrity of the legal system. Such behaviour was dysfunctional within the formal model, and would have an unsettling effect. While denying that policy should influence a judge, Audette was declaring himself in favour of a policy different from the one previous judges had imposed on the words of the law.

An Ad Hoc Judge

Walter Cassels sat as an *ad hoc* judge of the Supreme Court thirty-three times from 1918 to 1922.[41] This was an era when every judge of the Supreme Court tended to write a judgment, yet Cassels was well below the average. The seven judges who were on the Supreme Court for these years wrote judgments 89 per cent of the time, while Cassels wrote in only 43 per cent of the cases he sat on. The percentage of cases where the Supreme Court upheld a lower court decision is interesting: Cassels as a trial judge might have been thought to be more sensitive on this point, yet he had one of the lower percentages among the individual judges.

Percentage of Decisions in Favour of Lower Court

Idington	80
Fitzpatrick	80
Duff	75
Brodeur	73
COURT	67
Anglin	62
Cassels	52
Davies	50
Mignault	46

A FEDERAL COURT

In the Cassels era, there was only one incident that raised the issue of a federal court and a federal legal system. In 1909 the government, with Aylesworth as minister of justice, was able to get through the House of Commons, without any serious controversy, a bill under which the Crown would have been allowed a right of appeal from the Exchequer Court to a provincial court of appeal. Aylesworth's declared sympathy for government immunity from claims by individuals had apparently overwhelmed any concern he might have had for the status of the federal court. The measure never made it through the Senate.[42] The primary objection to the bill was that only the government would have the right, not the party claiming against it. Aylesworth's advocacy of special rules for the government – let alone adding to them – was out of step with the times. Aylesworth was adamantly opposed to giving both parties a right of appeal and, in the face of objections, he did not proceed with the proposed legislation.

Concern with the very nature of a federal court was mentioned only briefly; comments focused on the possibility of diverse decisions by the various provincial courts interfering with the uniformity of federal law across the country. Quebec members of Parliament, with general support, identified the proposed legislation with support for provincial rights. In the debate in the Senate two people did express concern with the status of the Exchequer Court. Two Liberals, L.G. Power, a lawyer from Nova Scotia, and, somewhat surprisingly, George Ross, who had been premier of Ontario from 1899 to 1905 and who was not a lawyer, felt that the court was higher than a provincial court of appeal. Raoul Dandurand, a lawyer from Quebec and also a Liberal, maintained that the court was not higher that the superior court of a province, but was coequal with it.[43]

In general terms, what this incident probably reveals was a certain amount of hostility in Quebec to a federal court, and a lack of commitment by the Liberal government of the time, certainly in the person of the minister of justice, A.B. Aylesworth (a very prominent lawyer from Ontario) to a federal court system in principle.

END OF THE CASSELS ERA

Walter Cassels died on March 1, 1923, at the age of seventy-seven. As head of the Exchequer Court he had had a somewhat controversial start, but overall it had turned out to be a quiet fifteen years. He was able to follow Burbidge's example of a lengthy tenure, which provided stability. At the time of Cassels' death Louis Arthur Audette was sixty-seven and had been associated with the court for thirty-five years, twenty-four as registrar and eleven as a judge.

Following Cassels' death the *Canadian Bar Review* published two brief eulogies. One was by Pierre-Basile Mignault, a Supreme Court of Canada judge from Quebec and a noted civil law expert who had written a nine-volume encyclopedia of Quebec law; the other was by William Meredith, the chief justice of Ontario.[44] There was no question that the status of the writers added to the lustre of the late judge's career. The only mention of Cassels' contribution to the law was Mignault's statement that it was not for him to speak of the 'contribution to the science of jurisprudence' made by Cassels as a judge of the Exchequer Court.

11

The Maclean Years, 1923–1942

Eight months after the death of Walter Cassels, on November 23, 1923, Alexander Kenneth Maclean was appointed president of the court. The Liberal government of Mackenzie King appears to have given some thought to the selection. Although Louis Arthur Audette was the choice of certain francophones, it was almost certainly assumed that the leadership of the institution would fall to an anglophone.[1] Audette was almost sixty-seven at the time. Maclean was fifty-four. He had been born on Cape Breton Island, Nova Scotia, and had received both his legal and general education in the province. Following his graduation from Dalhousie University in law in 1892, he practised in Lunenburg and later Halifax.

One problem with Maclean as far as the Liberal government of Mackenzie King was concerned was that he was alienated from the leadership of the party. He did have extensive and varied political experience, having alternated between provincial and federal politics for a number of years. He was elected to the Legislative Assembly of Nova Scotia in 1901, to the federal House of Commons representing Lunenburg in 1904 and 1908, and then again to the provincial legislature in 1909, becoming attorney general of Nova Scotia. In 1911 he was elected to the House of Commons again and became the financial critic for the Liberal opposition. His problems within the party began when he joined the Union government of Robert Borden in 1917 and became acting minister of finance in 1918. He could have been minister of public works in a Borden government, but resigned from the cabinet in 1920 since he considered that it was the duty of the Union government to resign once the war was over. In addition to his defection to the Union government, he supported William Fielding in 1919 for the party leadership over the ultimately successful candidate, William Lyon Mackenzie King. Following his resignation from the Union government, he did return to the Liberals and was re-elected in 1921, but was not brought into the government. Whatever was behind his appointment to the bench by King and J.L. Gouin, the minister of justice, the loss for the political process became a gain for the judiciary. Maclean's abilities as a judge would make him one of the greatest ever to sit on a Canadian bench.

Maclean was known as a direct person, with a straightforward manner: one knew where one stood with him. He was independent of spirit and a man of principle. As with Burbidge, there was an earthiness and lack of pretension about his judgments.

Audette remained on the court until December 1931, when he became the first judge of the Exchequer Court to be mandatorily retired at seventy-five under legislation enacted in 1927.[2] As the registrar of the court, he had conducted hearings as a referee, and had later been granted jurisdiction as a Judge in Chambers.[3] He was made an assistant judge in 1912, and a puisne judge in 1920. In total he was associated with the court for forty-four years. He died in Ottawa in 1942, at the age of eighty-five.

Audette's position was taken by Eugene-Réal Angers, a francophone and a member of the Quebec bar who had been in private practice in Montreal for twenty-four years. He was appointed by the Conservative government of R.B. Bennett. Angers was the nephew of Sir Auguste-Réal Angers, a leading Conservative politician of the late nineteenth century, who had been a member of the federal cabinet in 1895 and 1896 and the leader in Quebec of the federal Conservative Party.

Performance

The performances of the three judges were quite different. Maclean was definitely a contextualist who was sensitive to the facts of a case and used a common-sense approach. He was capable of undertaking law reform, if needed, by moulding the words of the law to deal with changed circumstances. It was the spirit and purpose of the law that dominated his thinking. He analysed previous decisions not merely to produce quotations, but to understand why the particular result had been arrived at. At the heart of his decision making was his ability to think out a problem and to create a solution. Audette could generally produce a good workmanlike job. While he tended definitely to the formalist school, his judgments could have a moral tone to them, and he was once accused of moulding the law to agree with his conception of justice.[4] Angers, unfortunately, produced what can only be described as lazy judgments. He used extensive quotations from cases, and even headnotes, for his statements of the law, and then produced an extensive amount of undigested facts. He would conclude with a statement of who won and who lost.

The following cases illustrate the performance of these three judges. Throughout the more than eighty years that the second court existed, 1887–1970, it heard only one highly significant constitutional case. The case was *The King v. Eastern Terminal Elevator Co.*[5] The Canada Grain Act[6] had been created in 1912 to regulate the grain trade in Canada. The litigation involved a challenge to the constitutional validity of a provision of the Act that had been added in 1919. The section in question specified that a certain percentage of the grain in a terminal elevator was to be sold by the Board of Grain Commissioners and the proceeds retained by the board.[7] Maclean concluded that the section was invalid since it could not be justified as coming within the federal constitutional authority over trade and commerce. The purpose of the challenged law was to regulate profits, he said, which was a matter of property and civil rights and within provincial jurisdiction. Maclean showed himself sensitive to the facts of the case, including the history behind the creation of the law, which pointed clearly towards the result he reached. He also engaged in a very knowledgeable discussion of the trade and commerce power in the constitution and explained why it could not be used. Overall, Maclean's decision was highly competent, one in which the problem was thought out and analysed. The quality of what he had produced is highlighted when compared with what happened in the Supreme Court of Canada.

The Supreme Court affirmed Maclean's conclusion, but Lyman Duff delivered a very mechanical-looking judgment. There was no reference to the purpose behind the enactment of the challenged law. Duff adopted the rule that, under the trade and commerce power, Ottawa could not regulate particular occupations in a province. Since the challenged section attempted to regulate elevators, which were a particular occupation, it was invalid. The judgment contains virtually nothing else apart from these assertions.

Pierre-Basile Mignault did outline the facts, borrowing heavily from Maclean, but he too made no mention of why the law had been brought into being. Though he dealt fairly extensively with the facts, his discussion of the legislation was stark. He stated that he was forced to conclude that the entire Grain Act was invalid because of 'successive pronouncements of the Judicial Committee.' These judgments had settled the law, he said.[8]

The different models of judicial decision making are dramatically exposed by Maclean's factual analysis[9] and Mignault's non-analysis and statement of conclusion. Duff aligned himself with Mignault by adopting a test that could be applied in a mechanical fashion, allowing the judges to appear to be neutral and objective and not to be dealing with the particular problem that had created the litigation. One commentator pointed out that Duff had no regard for the facts of the situation and had chosen to deal with the matter in rigid abstraction.[10]

Duff's biographer, David Ricardo Williams, branded the judges of the Supreme Court in this period as 'mainly a collection of mediocrities,' who did not consciously render decisions to respond to social conditions, and were not innovative.[11] Even Duff, he felt, was not an original thinker. What Williams was seeing was formalism at its purest, particularly in the judgments of Pierre-Basile Mignault. Formalism was intended not to particularize decision making by a close analysis of all of the circumstances involved, but to deal with generalities – and, in theory, operated independently of the inherent abilities of the particular judge. A sense of neutrality and objectivity could be produced by the level of abstraction – a judge appeared to be following the words of a rule without concern for policy. Maclean's presence would be a constant reminder that formalism was a choice, and that there was an alternative method of decision making.

While Angers never posed a threat to the formalism of the Supreme Court, Audette was prepared on occasion to expand his horizons. However, those occasions appear to be examples of activism, when he would simply react to a particular problem and produce a result regardless of the direction suggested by the law. A notable example occurred in 1931.

In *The King v. Krakowec*,[12] the government had seized a small truck in which three bottles of home-made liquor had been found. Krakowec pleaded guilty to the possession of the illegal liquor, and the government sought to have the truck forfeited to it. The vehicle was being used under a conditional sales agreement and was legally owned by a loan company, which disputed the forfeiture. Krakowec made no claim for the truck and did not participate in the litigation.

Audette was faced with a law that stated that all vehicles which had been or were being used for the purpose of removing spirits were to be forfeited.[13] He was not happy with what appeared to him to be a punishment 'out of all proportion' to the offence.[14] He found that, in the provision imposing a penalty for possession of illegal liquor, the words 'whether the owner thereof or not' appeared, while these words were missing when the law was dealing with forfeiture. This provided him with his justification for saying that the language of the law did not compel any particular result. Once he accepted that he had a choice, then he had no difficulty in refusing to order a forfeiture. Given that choice, the law was to be read in favour of the individual against whom it was being applied: strict construction of such laws was to be the rule.

The government appealed the decision to the Supreme Court of Canada and the higher court wanted no part of Audette's excursion into some form of creativity. Thibaudeau Rinfret from Quebec challenged the Exchequer Court judge directly by declaring that a judge should not 'mould a statute as to make it agree with his own conception of justice.'[15] Once again it was shown that, for the formalist such as Rinfret, to appear to go beyond the words was by definition to inject something personal, which was, again by definition, to exercise discretion. Without a doubt criticism would be legitimate if 'own conception' meant a purely personal decision, but criticism would lose its sting and be barren intellectually if the words meant a judge's perception of social values, which must naturally be the judge's 'own.' Audette was said by the Supreme Court to have engaged in an 'equitable construction' of a statute which was not appropriate when the words of the law were clear – as, the Supreme Court said, they were in this case. The limited role assigned to the judiciary by the formalist model meant that, if the result were considered harsh, then the remedy rested with the government, which could exercise political power to remit a forfeiture. 'The Court ... is vested with no discretion, it must decide according to law,' Rinfret affirmed.[16]

Perhaps this case did illustrate a personal reaction by Audette. He did not employ a contextual style consistently in the cases that he heard, and his work, which could generally be described as satisfactory, did evidence a tendency to reaction in given cases. He was not adverse to questioning the wisdom of a law[17] and, if given the opportunity, could lapse into a discussion of a moral issue, as he did when the government was taxing income obtained from bootlegging when it was illegal under provincial law.[18] Audette found for the government and held that the boot-legger could not avoid paying taxes by arguing the illegality of the activity. The Supreme Court took a higher road and, while wanting to appear to be only interpreting the words, decided that the law had never contemplated that income from illegal operations would be taxable. The Judicial Committee of the Privy Council brought the litigation back to earth, declaring that, for taxing statutes, 'the question is never more than one of the words used.'[19] Income was income, and taxable. Occasionally words only will suffice.

Audette's lapses from the appearance of formalism can prove highly informative with respect to the social values that were controlling his thinking. In a case from the Cassels era decided in 1916, Audette was faced with the question of whether the government could order the removal of Micmac Indians from a reserve in Sydney, Nova Scotia. The natives did not want to leave the small, two-acre (0.8 ha) property, which was within the city and apparently blocking municipal development. The government had offered the natives a larger rural area. Audette con-cluded 'without hesitation' that removal from the reserve was obviously in the interest of the public. The natives, as wards of the nation, were to be treated with great consideration and kindness while being moved. The dominant social value conditioning Audette's thinking was articulated clearly: 'The racial inequalities of the Indians as compared with the white man, check to a great extent any move towards social development, a state of affairs which under the system now obtaining can only grow worse every day, as the number of Indians is increasing.'[20] Native people could not function within a white, urban, twentieth-century society, and could only sustain a rural agricultural existence, because of their inherent 'racial inequalities.' Racism dominated.

An Ad Hoc Judge

Maclean sat sixty-seven times as an *ad hoc* judge of the Supreme Court of Canada. He and Cassels together accounted for 48 per cent of all *ad hoc* sittings.[21] Like Cassels, Maclean did not write as many judgments as the regular judges of the Supreme Court. For instance, between 1925 and 1942 Maclean sat twenty-two times, but only wrote one judgment. While Cassels never sat on an appeal from the Exchequer Court, Maclean did sit on one in 1924, in which he was in the majority in a 3–2 reversal of a deci-sion by Audette.[22] Maclean had to sit on thirty-eight cases in 1924 and may not have had a choice regarding Audette's.

THE WORK

During the years that Maclean was president of the court the francophone judges, Audette and Angers, undertook the hearing of cases in Quebec as a specific function. Of the reported cases involving hearings in Quebec, Audette sat on 82 per cent in the years 1924–31, and Angers sat on 90 per cent in the years 1932–42.

Beginning in 1924, the rights of the government ceased to be the single most popular area of law for the reported cases; intellectual property and taxation cases vied for the distinction of being the prime area of work. Crown litigation now comprised approximately 15 per cent of the reported cases, compared with what had initially been over 80 per cent of the workload.

CROWN LIABILITY

After the end of the Great War in 1918 the reform of the law regarding Crown liability continued, but it was now joined by another concern of the legal profession, the increase in the regulation of the economic aspects of society by government.

Shortly after the war, the federal government created a tribunal known as the Board of Commerce of Canada, whose task it was to administer a system of price controls in order to deal with the inflation that had occurred after the end of hostilities.[23] The legal profession reacted negatively. They were suspicious of the new 'court,' which had less formal proceedings and did not use many of the procedural rules of the regular courts. Of greater social import was the board's role in the regulation of business by government. A constitutional challenge was made to the existence of the board.

Perhaps indicating the division within society on the issue of government regulation, the Supreme Court split evenly, three judges to three, on the question of the validity of the law under which the board operated.[24] Two of the judges who declared the law to be invalid left no doubt about the values and policy concerns that had shaped their thoughts. For John Idington, the power possessed by such a body was 'repugnant to the ideal of British law and justice.' To him, the threat was socialism.[25] From Lyman Duff, the law evoked a parade of horrors involving socialistic controls over the economy. To allow this measure to stand, he warned, might pave the way for such things as nationalization of industry and the compulsory allotment of labour.[26]

On appeal from the Supreme Court, the Judicial Committee of the Privy Council held the law to be invalid on the basis that it had become well accepted that the power to legislate with respect to profits of retail merchants was within the power of the provinces.[27]

Members of the legal profession were prepared to assume the mantle of defender of citizens against intrusion by government into their lives. 'The administration of justice is the first thing in every civilized country,' declared W.B. Ross, a Conservative senator from Nova Scotia, in 1920. Ross, a lawyer with considerable business interests who would go on to become leader of his party in the Senate, postulated that confidence in the legal system was 'the only thing that will save us from Bolshevism and all the wild things which are floating around to-day.'[28]

The resistance to government regulation of economic matters brought with it a change in the people's attitude to government. Whereas in the past, the government's actions had been identified as being in the public interest, some now viewed those actions with distrust, as against the 'public' interest. Regulation by government required a bureaucracy to carry out the many and various tasks involved, and it was the bureaucracy that became the focus of attention and the target. A rallying point for the opponents of government regulation was a book written in 1929 by the Lord Chief Justice of England, Lord Hewart, in which he warned of the growing power of government and its bureaucracy. The title was *The New Despotism*.[29]

The debate over the decisions that government might make regarding regulation of the economy through rules of administrative law brought out profound differences between those in favour of regulation and those opposed. In the other branch of administrative law, Crown liability, the two contending groups were able to reach a common position. Those who opposed special protection for government in the area of Crown liability (so that the individual harmed by government action might exercise a legal right to receive compensation) were in favour of government economic regulation, since they saw it as helping the individual. However, those opposed to government economic regulation desired control of government by the legal process, and were now prepared to increase Crown liability as a means of control. Government involvement using bureaucrats would become more perilous as a result of widening liability.

The Canadian Bar Association added its weight to the move to reform Crown liability law when, in 1935, the association's Committee on Comparative Provincial Legislation and Law Reform sought and received authority to investigate the subject of 'The Crown as a Litigant.' The committee presented its report at the association's annual meeting in 1936. Its position was that reform was long overdue and that there was general agreement on this within the country, among judges, lawyers, and the public. The committee went so far as to append a draft bill to the report for discussion purposes.[30] The report maintained that the government should be treated in the same way as a private person with respect to tort or contract liability, and generally for all types of relief that an individual might seek against it. It was recommended that the petition of right and the requirement of a fiat be abolished. The report was adopted by the members of the association at the annual meeting and a copy was sent to each attorney general in Canada.

The link that was being formed between support for greater legal control over administrative decisions and 'rule of law' appeared in the report's proposal that the jurisdiction over claims against the Crown be taken from the Exchequer Court and given to the courts of the provinces. Control of government by law, through rule of law, favoured the 'ordinary courts' and rejected the use of special courts, such as the Exchequer Court, which had been created as a court of claims in 1887. There was no explanation or discussion of the proposal in the report; it was apparently considered self-explanatory.[31]

The standard rationale for the increased interest in reforming of the law of Crown liability and increasing the scope of the liability was, again, the growth of government activity with regard to what had once been private enterprises free of government control and regulation.[32]

In both branches of administrative law, 'bureaucrats' were identified as the enemy. In a 1938 article Emmett Hall, later a judge of the Supreme Court of Canada, related that the registrar of the Exchequer Court had told the annual meeting of the Canadian Bar Association in 1936 how his sense of justice had been repeatedly offended by government employees appearing in court and claiming immunity in the name of the Crown for their actions.[33] Hall also referred to the opinion expressed by Sir Carleton Kemp Allen in his book *Law in the Making*, when he wrote about the readiness of government workers to avail themselves of 'all technical, and many unmeritorious expedients in order to resist substantially just claims.'[34] The minister of justice of the time, Ernest Lapointe, added his voice by commenting in the House of Commons in 1937 that, because of strong objections within the public service, it would be difficult at that time to bring in wide-ranging reform of Crown liability.[35]

By 1936 a major reform of the law was only a year away but, before examining it, the work of the Exchequer Court judges in the years leading up to it merits study. Shortly after his appointment, Maclean made his presence felt with a vengeance, both in the specific area of Crown liability and generally as a judge. The year was 1925 and the case was *Schrobounst v. The King*, in which the claimant had sustained personal injuries when hit by a truck on a street in St Catharines, Ontario. The truck was being driven by an employee of the Department of Railways and Canals and was being used to transport workers to a public work.[36] The government lawyers questioned whether the injuries had been sustained 'upon any public work' as required by the words of the law. While Maclean may have felt constrained by institutional concerns from criticizing previous judicial decisions too overtly, nevertheless he gave some indication that he believed that the restrictions placed by the judges on the words 'on a public work' before 1917 had not been appropriate. He then took a giant step in the direction of widening the liability of the government.

In 1917 the words 'on a public work,' which had qualified the location of the death or injury, had been eliminated from the law and replaced by the words 'any death or injury ... resulting from the negligence of any officer or servant ... while acting within the scope of his duties or employment upon any public work.' Maclean said that the 1917 change had created a 'quite different law,' whose spirit and purpose was to govern. After the hiatus of the Cassels era, a contextual lawyer once again led the Exchequer Court. The 'purposive' approach to the interpretation of statutes was the most distinctive characteristic of the model.

The government argued that the injuries had not been sustained 'upon a public work,' which, if successful, would have brought back the previous restrictions. Such an argument might have been successful if made to Cassels, or even Audette, but not to Maclean. For him, the spirit or the policy of the law required that the words 'upon any public work' need only mean that the government employee whose negligence had created the injuries be employed at the time of the negligent act on a public work and that the duties being undertaken relate generally to the employment on the public work. Maclean had rendered a judgment for the era of the motor vehicle. He perceived that, in many instances, the duties of a government employee could take that person off a public work, for most or even all of the time. This would certainly happen to drivers of trucks on government business. Maclean could not imagine that such a person would not be working on a public work.

The persuasive nature of a contextual judgment was demonstrated by the fact that a unanimous Supreme Court affirmed Maclean's decision with a mere one-page judgment,[37] prompting a case comment in which the precedent-setting nature of the Supreme Court's decision was noted.[38] Maclean's approach did not appear to have any effect on Audette, who was still inclined to intone that 'where there is no statutory authority ..., no [tort] action lies against the Crown.'[39] Nothing else of note involving issues of Crown liability appeared in Audette's judgments.

In spite of the affirmation in the *Schrobounst* case, the approach that Maclean had taken to Crown liability had set him on a collision course with the Supreme Court of Canada. His contextualist approach to law and decision making, which had much greater importance for the legal system than the law of Crown liability, virtually guaranteed a confrontation with the highest court. By its very existence, Maclean's approach was a repudiation of the formalism exemplified by Duff and especially Mignault in the Supreme Court. Mignault's judgment for the court in *Schrobounst*, affirming Maclean's decision, had simply declared: 'We are of the opinion that the words "upon any public work" ... qualify not necessarily the presence but the employment, of the negligent servant or officer of the crown.'[40] At some point there would be a clash, as there had been in 1882 in the *McLeod* case. The moment came in 1935.

The case that became the battlefield was *Dubois v. The King*,[41] which also involved a motor vehicle collision. The Radio Branch of the Department of Marine was involved in detecting and eliminating radio inductive interference and used specially equipped cars, which carried a radio electrician and investigator as well as a driver. In October 1931, one of the cars had been in use in the area around Ottawa. While returning to headquarters, the driver was forced to stop on the side of the road to wipe the windshield because driving conditions had become very bad, with darkness, rain, and fog. An oncoming car collided with the radio car; its driver was injured and a passenger was killed. In an action against the government for the death and injuries sustained based on the negligence of its employees, the government raised preliminary questions of law: whether the government-owned car was a 'public work,' and whether the two government employees were acting within the scope of their duties or employment on a public work at the time of the accident.

Sensing the importance of the case for the law and the legal system, Maclean briefly reviewed the history of Crown liability for torts and surveyed the trend of the decisions. He referred to the decisions rendered by Burbidge and those of the Supreme Court in which Burbidge had been reversed. His review gives the impression that the Supreme Court was erratic. Maclean concluded that the cases showed 'some judicial doubt' about the extent of the immunity that the government needed in order to defeat the claims of the complainant. He thus outlined the crucial issue in the case.

To indicate that the legal context had evolved since the Burbidge era, he referred to the 1917 amendment and his own 1925 decision in *Schrobounst*, which the Supreme Court had unanimously affirmed. That case had been followed by the Supreme Court in 1933 in another unanimous decision in which Mr Justice Crocket for the court stated: 'The [*Schrobounst*] case decides that the words "upon any public work," as they now appear in the subsection, are not to be given the restricted meaning which they bore before the amendment.'[42]

On the question of the meaning of the words 'public work' in the Exchequer Court Act, Maclean pointed out that, since there was no definition of them given in the statute, he was allowed to look at what they had been taken to mean in other statutes. He was also able to refer to a judgment of the then chief justice of Canada, Lyman Duff, in which Duff had rendered a very pro-petitioner opinion by giving a wide meaning to a 'public work.'[43] Maclean concluded that, in the Exchequer Court Act, the meaning was intended to be more comprehensive than when the words were used in the other statutes. A common-sense approach was to be used, and a 'public work' should mean 'any work carried on by the Crown to serve the public with some necessity or convenience which is required by the public as such, and which requirement is made available by a parliamentary vote of public moneys.'[44]

Of specific importance in the case was Maclean's conclusion that the public service in question was a 'public work' and that the car was also a 'public work.' He made it clear that the result was being driven by the intention; that is, the policy behind the law. He identified the policy as an attempt 'to place the Crown under the same liability as the subject in respect of claims arising from injury or death negligently caused by employees upon any public work.'[45] He saw this intention as having been prompted by a public demand. This was a law reform decision in which the basic questions were addressed and there was a solid analysis of the contexts.

The five-judge panel that represented the Supreme Court of Canada consisted of Chief Justice Duff and Justices Rinfret, Cannon, Crocket, and Hughes. Duff rendered the reasons for the judgment of a majority of the court.[46] Maclean's decision was reversed.[47] As had occurred over a half a century before in the *McLeod* case, the Supreme Court undertook a rare discussion of the proper judicial function. Maclean posed a threat to the formalist model and the court saw a need to reaffirm it. Duff declared:

The judicial function in considering and applying statutes is one of interpretation and interpretation alone. The duty of the court in every case is loyally to endeavour to ascertain the intention of the legislature; and to ascertain that intention by reading and interpreting the language which the legislature itself has selected for the purpose of expressing it.[48]

The crux of the matter, as stated by Duff, was: 'It is the duty of the courts to give effect to the language employed.'[49]

Duff had thoroughly reviewed the previous decisions, and although Maclean could detect some uncertainty, for Duff the route was clearly marked. He asserted that over the years there had been no expansion of the meaning of the words 'public work.' On the point of the proper judicial function, which was central to the case, Duff stated that, if the law should be changed, then that was a matter for the legislature and not for him as a judge. Maclean had said that the legislature had changed the law. Duff would not accept this view:

[I]t would effect a great enlargement of the field of responsibility of the crown for tort, and the courts can only accept a proposed construction of a statutory enactment accomplishing such a result, where the language is reasonably clear.[50]

With his emphasis on language, Duff could ignore other clues, no matter how strong, from the legal or social context that could give meaning to words that were not absolutely clear.

The decision of the Supreme Court caused Maclean to comment in a later case, with a touch of sarcasm, that the language of the section was practically the same as when first enacted in 1887.[51] Although he might strain at the fetters of formalism that Duff and the Supreme Court had placed on him, he was constrained by them. This appears in a later case. During the Depression the federal government had established a program under which money was granted to provinces for carrying out work projects. British Columbia proposed work on a highway through a forested area. The federal authorities selected the work crew and supervisors. To carry out the work, the crew had to burn parts of the forest. In one place, the fire went out of control and part of the petitioner's timber was lost.[52] Maclean was faced with these unusual facts but was constrained from analysing the problem, and dutifully followed the *Dubois* decision, in which, he said, Duff had reviewed the authorities 'in a very comprehensive way, and with great clarity and force.'[53] Maclean added that, according to Duff, the words 'public work' had not changed in meaning over the years from that found in 1870 legislation. However, he could not refrain from a snipe at Duff. Although apparently forced to conclude that the project was not a 'public work,' Maclean commented that 'much, I have no doubt, may be said for the contrary view.'[54]

As evidence that the two judges of the Exchequer Court functioned as individuals, Eugene-Réal Angers posed no threat whatsoever to the formalists on the Supreme Court. His style of writing judgments was typical of a formalist, although Angers tended to overdo it. He would present extensive reviews of cases that amounted to briefs, or would use a parade of cases with quotes, some so extensive that they might leave readers wondering which case they were reading. His love of quotes was pronounced.[55] He gave no analysis of the facts of a case; after the extensive review of cases, or quotations from them, would come the inevitable conclusions based on the previous law, without a statement of exactly what that law was. The overall results tended to be long, rambling judgments. On the issue of Crown liability, Angers did not experience any apparent difficulty with the restricted approach to a public work and liability. Maclean did not have an ally there.

The difference between the two judges can be seen clearly in a motor vehicle case that Angers decided at the time that Maclean was concerned with the *Dubois* decision. Angers was faced with an action against the government arising from an accident in Montreal; a member of the Royal Canadian Mounted Police had driven an automobile into a passenger who was alighting from a streetcar.[56] Angers concluded that the automobile was not a 'public work.' His judgment indicates that he had no apparent concern with establishing an institutional response based on Maclean's earlier decision in *Schrobounst*, rather than a personal one. He did refer to the 1925 *Schrobounst* decision in which the Supreme Court had affirmed Maclean's judgment, but it was Mignault's judgment, with its statements amounting to conclusions, that attracted him, and not Maclean's, which outlined Maclean's reasons for giving the words the meaning that he had given them. Angers proceeded to examine the words 'public work,' apparently unwilling to accept the point of the *Schrobounst* decision. He went through case after case, and even touched on the jurisdiction of the Official Arbitrators that had existed before 1887. He was bothered by the absence of a definition of 'public work' in the Exchequer Court Act. He did not consider it plausible or probable that the legislators had intended 'to leave to the discretion of the Judges the determination [of what was a public work] in each particular case.' He wanted broad general rules that would eliminate the necessity of deciding each case on its own particular merits through an analysis of the facts and the contexts. He said: 'I believe that the Legislature ought to define ... 'public work' in the *Exchequer Court Act*.'[57] He could not accept that a police car was a 'public work' and he declared: 'I have no other alternative but to ...,' and added, 'I regret this ...'

Angers' rejection of Maclean's contextualist approach and his acceptance of the formalist model clearly show in his characterizing the judicial process undertaken by Maclean as leaving the determination of a case to the discretion of a judge. 'Discretion' is a highly emotive word in the legal profession, and signals that there is no law. In reality the contextual approach asks the judge to come to a personal judgment based on the totality of circumstances, the facts, and the law with its language, legal, and social contexts.

There should be no doubt that, if the language of a law is clear as to what it directs, the duty of the judge is to follow the directive. Lyman Duff had said it in the *Dubois* case in 1935: 'It is the duty of the courts to give effect to the language employed.'[58] But if there is room for interpretation, meaning that there is a choice available, then what is the duty of the judge?

The spirit of reform of the law of Crown liability was stirring in the 1930s, but the judges of the Supreme Court, led by Duff, had taken the position that, given the choice, they would restrict liability.[59] Maclean, on the other hand, had made what one writer called 'gallant but apparently forlorn efforts' to change things.[60]

In the month following the *Dubois* decision, the Supreme Court, in another unanimous decision, surprisingly made the Crown in right of the province of Quebec liable for a tort for the first time.[61] While it tempts one to comment that consistency does not appear to have been high priority for the court at this point, the case did hint that reform measures might break through at any time. During a 1936 debate in the House of Commons dealing with the National Harbours Board, it was suggested that the board be made liable in tort.[62] Those who felt that it was not the appropriate time and place for such a decision won out, but in the course of the debate the minister of justice, Ernest Lapointe, acknowledged that a desire for a change in the law existed and that the only thing missing was a decision about how it should be done. One completely unexpected comment was also made during the debate which, perhaps even more surprisingly, did not generate any response. R.B. Bennett, leader of the Conservative opposition, referred to the American jurist Benjamin Cardozo, and made the point that what was needed were judges whose minds were responsive to social changes. Canada already had, in A.K. Maclean, a judge on the model of Cardozo.

Within society in general there had been no demands for reform, probably because there had been no event significant enough to act as a catalyst. That is, perhaps, until the Supreme Court denied the government's liability for injuries sustained in motor vehicle accidents in 1935. Three years after the decision in the *Dubois* case, the law was reformed. The words 'upon any public work' were removed and the new provision read:

Every claim against the Crown arising out of any death or injury to the person or to property resulting from the negligence of any officer or servant of the Crown while acting within the scope of his duties or employment.[63]

The change was made without any sign of disagreement among the political parties. The minister of justice commented: 'The words "upon any public work" have been the cause of many denials of claims which otherwise seemed to be fair.'[64] Although he referred to the *Dubois* case, he did not pick up on Bennett's comment a few years earlier about the need for judges who were capable of dealing with social change.

ADMIRALTY JURISDICTION

The first direct effect on the Exchequer Court of the changes in the Empire following the Great War was the enactment of The Admiralty Act, 1934.[65] Shipping and admiralty jurisdiction were on the agenda of the Imperial Conferences of 1926 and 1930, and had been the subject of a special conference in 1929. It was decided that the Dominions should be given power to repeal the Colonial Courts of Admiralty Act, 1890 and to establish admiralty courts under their own laws. Following the 1930 conference, a new constitutional statute was enacted, the Statute of Westminster, 1931,[66] which gave autonomy to Canada and the other Dominions within the new Empire, now called a Commonwealth. The statute also affirmed the complete power of the Canadian Parliament over Courts of Admiralty within its jurisdiction. In spite of what many Canadians may have wanted, change was under way.

When the Exchequer Court was established as the Court of Admiralty for Canada in 1891, its jurisdiction was to be the same as 'the Admiralty Jurisdiction of the High Court in England, whether existing by virtue of any statute or otherwise.'[67] A 1926 case in British Columbia brought to the fore the question of the Canadian Parliament's ability to legislate regarding jurisdiction over admiralty matters. An action *in rem* was initiated in the British Columbia Admiralty District based on a breach of a charter-party. Charter-parties had not been within the admiralty jurisdiction as it existed in 1890. However, in 1925, legislation had been enacted in Britain that put such a matter within the jurisdiction of the appropriate British court. Mr Justice Archer Martin of the British Columbia court accepted that the Exchequer Court, as the Admiralty Court of Canada, would 'march' with the same jurisdiction as the High Court in Britain, since it had replaced the British Vice-Admiralty Courts.[68] Martin was able to refer to the existing Canadian textbook on admiralty law to support his view of an 'ambulatory' jurisdiction.[69]

Louis Arthur Audette, who tended to view the jurisdiction of the court restrictively, sat on the appeal from Martin's decision and would have nothing to do with the idea that an Imperial statute could have effect in Canada without an express provision to that effect.[70] While the Canadian jurisdiction as a consequence had to be viewed as 'static and stereotyped,' he said, the constitutional considerations were clear: an Imperial statute would not apply unless the intention to do so was clearly expressed.[71] The Judicial Committee of the Privy Council affirmed Audette's decision.[72]

With the passage of the Statute of Westminster in 1931, it was up to Canada alone to take action. A bill was introduced in the House of Commons in 1934 that repealed the earlier law and enacted a new Admiralty Act. However, the Minister of Justice emphasized the need for uniformity in admiralty matters throughout what was now the Commonwealth, and the jurisdiction over admiralty that the Exchequer Court was to have was that possessed at the time by the British courts. The Canadian jurisdiction remained static: only the point of reference had been moved forward.[73] The bill went through Parliament without a murmur of opposition or even comment.[74]

As part of the new legislation, there was an interesting change in the way appeals from the district judges were to be handled. Appeals were now to be heard by more than one judge of the Exchequer Court. Since at the time there were only Maclean and Angers on the Court, it meant that both of them would have to sit. The appeal from the judges of the Admiralty Districts to a single judge of the court was such an anomalous situation that it is strange that no open discussion of it had ever occurred. Nevertheless, with only the two judges, and signs of considerable delay in rendering judgments setting in, the new scheme did not seem workable. Not surprisingly, a year later, the requirement that more than one judge hear an appeal in admiralty was repealed.[75] The minister of justice reported that the president of the court had pointed out that both judges were seldom in Ottawa at the same time.[76] The new legislation included a provision for a district judge to sit as an *ad hoc* judge, but there is no evidence that any attempt was made to implement this.

ATTITUDE TO JURISDICTION

Maclean showed no inclination to restrict the jurisdiction of the court beyond what would reasonably follow from the language bestowing the jurisdiction, but this was not true of Audette, who definitely viewed the jurisdiction of the court in a restrictive manner. In his opinion,

Statutory provisions giving jurisdiction must be strictly construed and that is especially true when the statute confers jurisdiction upon a tribunal, like the Exchequer Court, of limited authority and statutory origin, and in such a case a jurisdiction cannot be said to be *implied*.[77]

The status of the court in Audette's eyes is reflected in his language: 'a tribunal,' 'limited authority,' 'statutory origin.' There was a felt need to constantly monitor the jurisdiction.

A few years earlier, Audette had made the same point about restrictively interpreting words that bestowed jurisdiction, but at that time the Supreme Court told him that he had gone too far. The Canadian National Railway Act contained a section stating that the provisions of the Expropriation Act applied to expropriations by the railway. Under the Expropriation Act, the Exchequer Court had jurisdiction, but not under the Railway Act. The railway sought a warrant of possession under the Expropriation Act, but Audette declined jurisdiction. He said that there had to be unmistakable language granting jurisdiction, which he could not find.[78] So important was the case that, while an appeal from Audette's decision was pending, a reference case was instituted. Audette was reversed and, in a brief unanimous decision, Supreme Court of Canada recognized that the jurisdiction of the Exchequer Court under the Expropriation Act applied to expropriation proceedings under the Railway Act. The national character of the railway, created by statute for the management, operation, and control of a national railway system, made the jurisdiction of the national court appropriate, Anglin stated for the Supreme Court.[79]

Perhaps Audette, as a judge from Quebec, was favouring the jurisdiction of the provincial courts. However, Angers showed no such tendency, and in the railway case Mignault, the champion of Quebec civil law, and Rinfret, also from Quebec, recognized the jurisdiction of the Exchequer Court over matters of a national character.

A NATIONAL COURT

The years of the Depression increased pressure for a greater degree of control of society by Ottawa and the establishment of uniform services across the country.[80] As a national court, the Exchequer Court would be concerned with the establishment of any national law. How went the nation, would go the court. An example of the problems associated with establishing a uniform national law occurred in 1933, when the Conservative government tried to make the law covering money paid to the Crown under a mistake of law uniform throughout Canada.[81] Members of Parliament from Quebec took objection to the following provision:

[T]he Exchequer court shall not have jurisdiction to entertain any action heretofore or hereafter commenced for the recovery of any sum or money paid to His Majesty voluntarily in mistake of law, if the recovery of such money might not in England be the subject of a suit or action against the crown.

The measure was seen as putting the province of Quebec under the English common law. The government attempted to justify it on the basis that the Exchequer Court was founded on the law of England and, as a federal court, had jurisdiction throughout Canada, irrespective of the provinces. This naturally was a way of saying that federal law was the law of England. The opposition, through Quebec member Ernest Lapointe, pointed out that the Exchequer Court had to apply the laws of the various provinces. For him, the law relating to property and civil rights was always that of the provinces, even when federal concerns were involved. In matters pertaining to citizens of the province, the law of the province would apply. So strong was the feeling within the legal profession in Quebec that the bar of Montreal adopted a resolution protesting the bill. In addition the deputy attorney general of Quebec had written Lapointe giving his opinion that the law would be unconstitutional.

Although the Prime Minister, R.B. Bennett, maintained that the idea of a federal court required that there had to be uniformity of treatment, he conceded the strength of the opposition to the law, and it was abandoned.

As a point of interest, the law of Quebec differed from English law in that it allowed the recovery of money paid under mistake while, under English law, money paid in settlement of a claim or of a litigated matter, and money paid under a mistake of law, could not be recovered. Money paid under a law subsequently declared to be ultra vires, that is, unconstitutional, also could not be recovered.

In the end, the strength of the constitutional power of the provinces over 'property and civil rights' was Quebec's protection for its law, and the greatest block to the establishment of uniform national laws.

DELAY

The Exchequer Court, which had been somewhat noted for the speed of its decision making in the mid-1920s,[82] began in the 1930s to show considerable delay between hearing a case and rendering a judgment. The reported cases from this period provide evidence of a considerable problem. The reported cases for 1924, 1929, 1934, and 1939 produce the following statistics:

Year	Number of cases	Average number of days before judgment was rendered			
		COURT	Maclean	Audette	Angers
1924	23	41	64	27	–
1929	23	56	69	44	–
1934	19	130	65	–	218
1939	10	270	176	–	310

For 1924 and 1929 the judges were Maclean and Audette, and for 1934 and 1939 they were Maclean and Angers. As the table shows, Angers had the most pronounced difficulty. Maclean was seventy in 1939, but Angers was only fifty-six. This was only the beginning of a major delay problem for the court.

12

The Thorson Years, 1942–1964

A.K. Maclean died on July 31, 1942, at the age of seventy-two, after several years of battling cancer. Noted for his independence of spirit and the breadth of his culture (acquired through his voluminous reading), Maclean had illustrated the contextual approach to law and lawyering. Although he had apparently been on very friendly terms with Sir Lyman Duff, the chief justice of Canada, and had seen Duff through his notorious drinking bouts, the two men were virtually polar opposites when it came to the nature of their decision making.

The new president was appointed on October 6, 1942, two months after Maclean's death. He was Joseph Thorarinn Thorson, then fifty-three years old. At the time of his appointment he was minister of national war services in the Liberal government of Mackenzie King. His appointment continued the pattern of selecting the head of the Exchequer Court from outside the court, rather than promoting from within, which was the tradition at the Supreme Court of Canada. The new appointment also continued the practice of having an anglophone as president and a francophone as the puisne judge.

Thorson had been born in Manitoba of Icelandic heritage. He attended the University of Manitoba and became a Rhodes Scholar for Manitoba in 1910. He studied law at Oxford University and became a member of the English bar before returning to Canada in 1913, when he was admitted to the bar of Manitoba. He practised law in Winnipeg and was closely associated with the University of Manitoba, serving as Dean of the Law School from 1921 to 1926. During World War I he saw service in France, and was seconded to the British Army. He served as the officer commanding a prisoner-of-war camp until January 1919.

Thorson was elected as a Liberal for the riding of Winnipeg South Centre in the federal general election of 1926, but was defeated in the Conservative victory of 1930. He was re-elected in 1935 and 1940 for the riding of Selkirk. He became the minister of national war services on June 11, 1941 and held that position until his appointment as the president of the Exchequer Court. As a judge Thorson was to adopt the approach of Lyman Duff as his model. He was to have the longest tenure of any president of the court to date, twenty-two years.

For a twenty-year period beginning in 1944, additional positions would regularly be created for the court. A third judge was authorized in 1944,[1] ostensibly because of workload, but it was over a year before someone was appointed. Delay, which will be discussed later, was also alluded to in the debates at the time. Charles Gerald O'Connor, aged fifty-four, was appointed on April 19, 1945. Although born in Ontario, where he had received his legal education, O'Connor joined the Alberta bar and practised law in Edmonton. He died, at the age of fifty-eight, on November 16, 1949, after only four and a half years on the court. His brief tenure was a dramatic break in the pattern of previous judges, who had had an average tenure of almost twenty years.

Another position was created in 1946, increasing the number of judges to four.[2] Again one of the reasons given was increased work, but a more profound one was also offered. The extra judge would be available for use on government business, such as royal commissions, special boards, or other agencies. The use of provincial court judges would be reduced and, although the minister of justice acknowledged that concern had been expressed about the use of judges for such work, he felt that it had to be done and that the interests of the state were best served by using persons whom the public would identify as capable of carrying out the work in 'an impartial, competent and objective way.'[3] The spectre of the institution known as the Exchequer Court becoming a pool of people called 'judges' for use by the government did not cheer the legal profession.

Charles Cameron was appointed on September 4, 1946. Excluding the original six judges (who had also been members of the Supreme Court), Cameron was the eighth judge appointed, but only the second from Ontario. There had been two from the Maritimes, two from the west, and two from Quebec. Walter Cassels had been the only previous judge who had practised law in Ontario. Cameron was fifty-four at the time of his appointment, and had been a County Court judge for six years. During the war years he had handled several assignments at Ottawa for the Justice and Labour Departments.[4] Before his appointment as a County Court judge he practised law in Belleville and ran successfully as a Liberal candidate for the House of Commons in the general election of 1935. His appointment to the bench occurred just before the election of 1940. He has the distinction of being the only judge to have served on the Exchequer Court who had acted as a deputy judge prior to his appointment.[5]

The government's policy of using Exchequer Court judges for duties outside the court, articulated in 1946, was put into effect in 1948 when the position of chief commissioner of the Board of Transport Commissioners was designated as a judge of the Exchequer Court.[6] In addition to being an implementation of the 1946 policy, the provision was also identified in the debates as being a piece of *ad hoc* legislation that was needed to entice Maynard Archibald, a justice of the Supreme Court of Nova Scotia, to accept the position of chief commissioner. The difficult political question of equalizing the freight rate structure throughout the country had been referred to the board, hence the need for a judge as chairman.

The introduction of the legislation specifying that the chief commissioner be a judge of the Exchequer Court created a rare discussion in the federal legislature about the judiciary that included not only the question of using judges for other than their normal courtroom work, but also the perception of judges and the appropriate approach to decision making.[7] The president of the Canadian Bar Association, John T. Hackett, was an opposition Conservative member of Parliament for the Quebec riding of Stanstead at the time. He expressed concern about the effect on the reputation of the bench of using judges for other than their traditional function. The danger, as Hackett saw it, was that judges would become exposed to comments and criticisms that would lead to public disrespect for the judiciary.

Even though the government might argue that the actual position being considered, chief commissioner of the Board of Transport Commissioners, did involve a judicial function, and that what was needed at that moment was the quality of independence from government control which a judge would possess, the position was now seen as non-traditional work for a judge. The growing appearance of administrative tribunals and the negative reaction of the legal profession to 'administrative justice' had created a cleavage between a body such as the Board of

Transport Commissioners and an 'ordinary' court. Opposition member John Diefenbaker raised the point that the use of judges for government business served to undermine the public's confidence in independence; he brought up the example of the use of the chief justice of Canada, Lyman Duff, in 1942 for the inquiry into the sending of Canadian troops to Hong Kong in 1941, and the ferocious political squabbling that had swirled arout both the incident and the inquiry.[8]

The debate took a somewhat strange turn when a Conservative member of the House, J.M. Macdonnell, an Ontario lawyer, suggested that judges were human beings who would naturally lean in favour of the government that had the power to reward faithful service. The consequence would be a demonstration of the failure of the independence that was so essential. Angus MacInnis, a CCF member from Vancouver, leaped at the opening. He declared, as a self-proclaimed non-lawyer, that he was getting a little bit tired of the glorification of the virtues of judges and, by implication, lawyers. To assume, he said, that when appointed as judges, lawyers could 'in their virgin purity dispense abstract justice is of course just nonsense.' He added,

I think it is highly desirable that the judges should be kept in as close contact as possible with the economic, social and political conditions that prevail in this country, so that they will be in a position to understand what motivates and compels people to act in the way they do.[9]

This was reminiscent of the sentiments expressed in 1880 by David Mills in a House of Commons debate about the Supreme Court judges, when he said that the judges should 'read the law through the eyes of the people.'[10]

The Conservative member who had opened the door suddenly retreated from his earlier views in the wake of MacInnis' speech, and expressed the fear that sentiments such as MacInnis' (and his) would themselves undermine public confidence in the judiciary. He agreed wholeheartedly with Hackett's warnings about discussing judges at all. It seemed that, for some in the legal profession, the mere mention of a contextual approach was perceived as a danger to the integrity of the legal system.

Maynard Brown Archibald, aged fifty-seven, a justice of the Supreme Court of Nova Scotia, became a judge of the Exchequer Court of Canada – in name – when he was appointed chief commissioner of the Board of Transport Commissioners on July 1, 1948. His term as chief commissioner was for ten years, after which he would actually join the bench of the Exchequer Court. In 1951 the legislation concerning the chief commissioner was amended to provide that the person who occupied the position could be either a judge of a provincial superior court or a judge of the Exchequer Court. If the latter, then the position would be in addition to the number of judges of the court provided by the Exchequer Court Act and The Judges Act. The position of judge of the Exchequer Court then held by Archibald as chief commissioner was declared to be in addition to the number of puisne judges of the court specified by these two Acts.[11] The court had thus acquired a position for an additional judge.

On November 1, 1951, after only three and a half years as chief commissioner, Archibald resigned and joined the court. John Kearney, a career diplomat, became chief commissioner and, in name, a judge of the Exchequer Court.

Belying the concern with workload, the new position created in 1951 (by making Archibald's position an addition to the specified complement of judges) was not filled until two years later, with the appointment of Alphonse Fournier on June 12, 1953. Fournier was a francophone and a member of the Liberal government. He had joined the cabinet as minister of public works at the same time that Thorson had been moved to the Exchequer Court in 1942, and had remained in that position until his appointment to the court. He had been a member of Parliament since 1930. Fournier was born in the United States and came to Canada at the age of eleven. After being admitted to the Quebec bar, he practised law in Hull.

The Exchequer Court had been characterized by the long tenures of its judges, but in the mid-1950s the changes came with a vengeance. Fournier briefly made a third Quebec lawyer on the bench, but in the early fall of 1953 Angers resigned for reasons of health after twenty-one years and eight months on the court. Earlier in the year Maynard Archibald, the former chief commissioner of the Board of Transport Commissioners, had died after only a year and a half on the bench. The vacancy left by Archibald's death was filled by another Nova Scotian, thus establishing a practice of having a Maritimer as a puisne judge. The new judge was William Pitt Potter, aged sixty-three. Unfortunately he too spent only a year and a half on the bench before he passed away. Once again the replacement came from the Maritimes. Louis Ritchie from New Brunswick was appointed, but he preferred to live and work in New Brunswick and, nine months after joining the Exchequer Court, he was appointed to the Supreme Court of that province. Arthur Thurlow from Nova Scotia agreed to join the court. The constant turnover in this particular position stopped; Thurlow, who came from legal practice in Halifax and Bridgewater, Nova Scotia, and had been a Liberal member of the Legislative Assembly of Nova Scotia from 1949 to 1953, went on to sit for almost thirty-two years, retiring in 1988 after the longest tenure of any judge of the court to date.

More than two years after Angers had resigned, a third judge with a Quebec background was appointed to fill the vacancy. Jacques Dumoulin joined the court on December 1, 1955. Dumoulin was fifty-six years old, and in legal practice in Quebec City. He had been a Liberal member of the Quebec legislature from 1939 to 1948.

In January 1957 John Kearney left the Board of Transport Commissioners after five years and joined the court. Since Kearney was also a Quebec lawyer, Quebec held half of the places on the court at this time.

The number of judges had grown from two in 1944 and, although workload would be mentioned from time to time as the reason for the increase, the evidence indicates that it was not a real problem. It had taken more than two years to fill the vacancy created by Angers' resignation, and there had also been a two-year gap between the death of O'Connor and Archibald joining the court from the Board of Transport Commissioners. The only sign of some urgency was the search for a Maritime representative between Archibald's death and the appointment of Arthur Thurlow in 1956, when Potter and Ritchie were selected and in turn had to be replaced.

In 1961 yet another position was added to the court, increasing the number of judges to seven.[12] The delay in rendering decisions that had marked the court for twenty years could no longer be ignored, and now, for the first time, the backlog of cases was used as evidence of the workload being too heavy for the number of existing judges. There was, however, new and additional work for the judges because of the creation of the Court Martial Appeal Court. This court had been established in 1959 with the judges of the Exchequer Court and additional judges from provincial superior courts as its judges.[13]

Earlier, in 1950, the Court Martial Appeal Board had been created in a move to treat service personnel more fairly and humanely by providing an appeal tribunal for members of the armed forces found guilty at a court martial.[14] Charles Cameron was made the chairman of the board, but he was the only Exchequer Court judge involved at the time.[15] He continued as president of the new Court Martial Appeal Court when it was created in 1959. The creation of a 'court' that was a superior court of record continued the normalizing of the military legal system that had begun with the establishment of the appeal board. Now service personnel would have the same rights as other citizens, who could appeal to a provincial court of appeal.[16]

When the judges of the Exchequer Court changed hats and sat as judges of the Court Martial Appeal Court, they assumed a jurisdiction that was foreign to them. They were to be judges of a court with a jurisdiction in criminal law. There was, and continues to exist, a sensitivity to a federal court exercising such jurisdiction, which is seen as traditionally entrenched in the provincial court system. There was no noticeable negative reaction to the creation of the Court Martial Appeal Court, probably because the legal profession viewed the military justice system as something special, and outside the normal criminal justice system.

Nine months after the new seventh position on the court was created, Alexander Cattanach, aged fifty-two, was appointed. He had been a career public servant working with the Companies Division of the Department of the Secretary of State. He was born in Manitoba, where he spent his early years; he obtained his legal education in Saskatchewan, and joined the bar of that province. During World War II he was a member of the Royal Canadian Air Force. He served in the judge advocate general's office, and attained the rank of group captain. He also participated in war crimes trials regarding offences against Canadian air force personnel.

Two weeks before Cattanach was appointed, Camilien Noël from Quebec was named to the position left vacant five months before on October 8, 1961, by the death of Alphonse Fournier. Noël had practised law in Quebec City throughout his career. The appointments of Noël and Cattanach marked the first by a Conservative government in thirty years.

Deputy Judges

The use of additional personnel known as 'deputy judges' had been authorized in 1920,[17] but it was not until 1942 that the first was used. In the Thorson period a deputy judge sat forty times, primarily in 1945 (thirteen times) and 1952 (nineteen times). Thirty-two of the forty sittings were in western Canada.[18]

An Ad Hoc Judge

Thorson sat as the last *ad hoc* judge on the Supreme Court to date. In all, he sat four times, all in 1944, and participated in three judgments. In one case, he was present at the hearing, but the matter was adjourned to the next session of the court and he was not present at the second hearing.[19] Thorson wrote a judgment in one of the cases, indicating a willingness to make his own mark on the work of the Supreme Court.[20]

THE WORK

In the Maclean era cases involving intellectual property and taxation had displaced Crown litigation as the leading areas of work. Between 1942 and 1964, the court became primarily a tax court. The change began in 1949 when taxation cases began to account for more than 50 per cent of the reported cases.

In 1944, as part of the workload issue, Conservative member of Parliament John Diefenbaker suggested that the Exchequer Court might be the appropriate appeal court from administrative tribunals.[21] However, more than a quarter of a century would elapse before work of that kind became the staple diet of the court.

CROWN LIABILITY

The agitation for reform of the law in order to eliminate the special rules that shielded the government in actions brought against it had resulted in the legislation of 1938. Under that legislation, liability was imposed if injuries were sustained by someone as a result of negligent conduct on the part of a government employee acting within the scope of the particular task for which the person was employed. The spirit of change could no longer be blunted by questions of whether a 'public work' was involved, or whether the work being carried out by a government employee was 'upon any public work.' However, there was still a possibility that a special rule could be recognized that would immunize the government, given the will to do so.

With Canada on a war footing since 1939, someone was bound to be injured by action of the military. The moment came in the simple scenario of a pedestrian being struck by an army vehicle driven by a soldier carrying out assigned duties. In a claim based on negligence, the government argued that a member of the armed forces was not an 'officer or servant of the crown' and thus liability could not exist, given the words of the statute. The judge who heard the case was Joseph Thorson.[22]

The spirit of change was strong enough that Thorson expressed agreement with the various criticisms of the law of Crown liability. Nevertheless, he asserted that the government was not to be held liable unless clearly made so by legislation, and declared that it was not open to a judge to deny the existence of that rule. While Thorson acknowledged the approach of Burbidge and Maclean, and their results, even after the reform of 1938 he chose Lyman Duff as his model. It was no part of the judicial function to change the law, he asserted, and only the legislature could do that. But would a change of the law be involved?

Thorson had a choice, and he opted to accept that a member of the armed forces was not an officer or servant of the Crown for the purpose of the provision of 1938. For him, the government employees for whose negligent actions the government would be liable were those who worked on a public work. He had brought back the idea abandoned in the 1938 legislation; he sustained the spirit of the old law that had been developed by the Supreme Court of Canada and, at the same time, proclaimed that judges were not concerned with the policy of legislation, only with its interpretation and application.

However, the spirit of change afoot in the legal system swept Thorson's decision aside effortlessly. Two and a half months after his decision, the government brought a motion in the House of Commons to have the House consider a resolution that would eliminate the case as part of the law.[23] The resolution was considered and legislation enacted that received assent on July 24, 1943, a mere four months after Thorson's decision. The statute provided that members of the armed forces should be deemed to be servants of the Crown, retroactive to June 24, 1938.[24]

One ramification of the case was that Thorson's stand against the spirit of change in favour of the spirit of the older law brought another special rule that applied to the government to the fore. The government had its own special court, and a citizen could not bring an action in the provincial courts, as would occur if another private party was being sued. For the Exchequer Court, this was a significant matter. Thorson's decision provided fuel for an attack on the Exchequer Court, since he had made it appear to be a little too 'special.'[25]

Eugene Angers continued in the same way after Thorson became president as he had before, as might have been expected, since in judicial style the two judges were the same. Angers' fondness for quoting from judgments in previous cases was such that in one instance the editors of the Exchequer Court Reports eliminated the quotations, thus removing what purported to be the statement of the law.[26] As well, Angers shared with Thorson a tendency to delay in rendering judgments.

As additional judges joined the court beginning in 1945, no noticeable change in approach or attitude to Crown liability appeared. Thorson still emphasized the restricted nature of the liability,[27] and as authority for his stance he cited his earlier decision in which he had held that a serviceman was not a servant of the Crown.[28] General acceptance of the model of formalism shielded him from criticism when he ignored the legislation overruling his decision, even though it could be viewed as part of the general legal context. Opinions signifying restriction of Crown liability also came from other judges, especially Alphonse Fournier from Quebec.[29]

Thus the judges of the Exchequer Court in the Thorson era indicated a preference for restricting Crown liability and in contrast to the image of defender of the individual that had characterized it in earlier years, the court now appeared to be a defender of the government. Nevertheless, reform of the law continued in the legislature. In 1950 Crown corporations, although affirmed to be agents of the government, were put in the position of ordinary corporations in that legal proceedings could be brought against them in the provincial courts.[30] This was followed in 1951 with the abolition of the need for a fiat in actions against the government.[31] These reforms came in the wake of extensive changes to the law of government immunity in both the United States (in 1946) and Britain (in 1947). There it was accepted that the government should bear the same liabilities as an individual because of its expanding role and the activities that caused it to come into contact much more frequently with the daily affairs of people. The view was that the more the government competed with private enterprises, the more it should be treated as they were.[32] A complete overhaul of the law in Canada finally occurred in 1953 when the Crown Liability Act was brought into being.[33] There was no debate by this time on the principle of the bill, which was that the government was to be treated as if it were a private person with respect to tort actions brought against it. There was no political will left to prevent this constitutional change from taking effect.

In Britain one scholar attributed the reforms to the spirit of A.V. Dicey: 'The Act adopts the Anglo-Saxon principle of treating the State (or "the Crown") for the purposes of litigation as nearly as possible in the same way as a private citizen, instead of borrowing the Continental idea of a separate system of Administrative Law.'[34] A great majority of Canadian lawyers (at least those who were anglophones) would probably have subscribed to these sentiments, but there was a problem in Canada in that Canada had a separate court with jurisdiction over such matters, and hence naturally a separate system of law. Consequently, as the road of change was travelled, the exclusive jurisdiction of the Exchequer Court came under fire and demands were made that its jurisdiction over Crown liability be given to the provincial courts, as had occurred with Crown corporations in 1950. Adopting Dicey's version of rule of law, the tendency was to characterize the provincial courts as the 'ordinary' courts, which meant that the Exchequer Court had to be a special court.[35] The provincial superior courts were also called the 'Queen's courts,'[36] which left the Exchequer Court as the government's court.[37] Throughout the 1940s and early 1950s, the issue of the jurisdiction over Crown liability was kept constantly alive.

One aspect of the political process that limited debate was the presence of so many lawyers in the legislature. The late nineteenth century had given rise to the idea that members of the legal profession had specialized knowledge and expertise not possessed by the ordinary person.[38] This had apparently become accepted by a majority of both lawyers and non-lawyers. Legislators who were not lawyers would generally become self-conscious when dealing with legal matters and if they soldiered on, they risked being attacked by the lawyers in the legislature with cries of 'Are you a lawyer?'[39] Only members of the Co-operative Commonwealth Federation (CCF), forerunner of the New Democratic Party, seemed not to be intimidated by the mystique.[40]

While government liability was being expanded, one special rule survived the reforms of this time intact. It was the rule known as 'Crown privilege.' The government was able to block access to documents in its possession that might have been available from a private litigant through the process of discovery. Thus it had an immunity from having to disclose information. The government need only declare that it was not in the public interest to release information and the judges would not question the decision.[41] The ability to bring an action against the government was seriously hampered by the difficulty of obtaining facts on which to prosecute the action. While this special rule came under attack from John Diefenbaker in the House, it was not seriously in danger, and government leaders in the Senate defended it enthusiastically.[42] Not for over a decade following the 1953 reforms did it become vulnerable.

DELAY

The delay in rendering judgments that was becoming noticeable near the end of the 1930s, particularly with Angers, became chronic under Thorson's leadership. Of the reported decisions that President Thorson rendered over the twenty-two years of his tenure, 52 per cent took over one year to render, and 30 per cent took over two years. An astonishing 7 per cent actually took more than three years. Eugene Angers continued his procrastination, reaching what appears to have been his peak in 1946. He heard ten cases in that year that were reported and the average amount of time between the hearing and the judgment was 844 days – two and one-third years. After that time his reported decisions number only one, two, or three per year, until he resigned because of ill health in 1953.

Writing in 1988, some twenty years after Thorson's retirement, a commentator focused on a delay in one Supreme Court of Canada case of two years and five months: 'Delays of this magnitude are inexcusable, and strongly suggest some serious malaise in the Court's *modus operandi*.'[43] Delay has always been a matter of concern for the legal profession,[44] and the saying 'justice delayed is justice denied' has been linked to the language of Magna Carta.[45] The malaise reached further and deeper than simply the operation of the Exchequer Court since, from 1942 until 1964, while there were occasional references in the House of Commons and Senate to the delays, there was silence in the professional journals.

While the delay would naturally affect the interests of the parties to the litigation, it could also acquire more questionable aspects. In *Nakashima v. The King*,[46] Thorson presided over the hearing of the petition by Japanese Canadians challenging the sale of their property by a Custodian established by Order in Council.[47] Their property had been vested in the Custodian, who was the secretary of state and who had wide discretionary powers to deal with the property. The petitioners did not challenge their internment and evacuation from their homes, but they contended that the sale of the property was not related to the conduct of the war, and had nothing to do with the evacuation. Thorson in the end decided against the petitioners, but delay cast an added pall over the proceedings. The sale of the property was authorized in January of 1943 and the petition was lodged against the secretary of state as Custodian in July. The case was not heard until the end of May 1944, by which time the bulk of the property had been disposed of. Thorson's decision against the petitioners was rendered on August 28, 1947, three and a quarter years after the end of the hearing. To add to the discomfort that some might feel about the case, it should be noted that Thorson had been a member of the government when the initial Orders in Council were created to regulate the lives of the Japanese Canadians.

In the early years, the delays had been created by Thorson and Angers.

As additional judges were appointed, like O'Connor and Cameron, the average delay lessened; the new judges rendered their decisions within reasonable times. This changed in the late 1950s and a general slowness developed among the judges. For example, for cases heard in 1962, the average number of days between hearing and judgment for reported decisions were Dumoulin (366 days), Thurlow (323 days), Kearney (398 days), Noël (235 days), and Cattanach (338 days), as well as Thorson, who was still the slowest (713 days). It would remain for the next president, Wilbur Jackett, to bring an end to this situation.

THE END OF THE THORSON ERA

One curious set of facts regarding the reported decisions of President Thorson is worth recounting. In the last seven years of Thorson's tenure as president, none of his decisions are reported in the *Exchequer Court Reports*. One appeared in the year following his retirement.[48] In that same year, a special volume appeared that was to be cited as [1956–1960] Ex. CR, containing decisions of Thorson's that had been rendered in the years 1956 to 1960 inclusive. The reason given for the late publication of the special volume was that Thorson had wanted to write his own headnotes, which had delayed the publication of the judgments.

When, on March 15, 1964, Joseph Thorson reached the age of mandatory retirement, seventy-five, and left the court, he had served longer than any head of the court before or since – twenty-one years and five months. He was to achieve far greater notoriety than he had as a judge of the Exchequer Court when he launched a campaign following the enactment of the Official Languages Act in 1969[49] to end official bilingualism in federal matters and make English the only official language of Canada. In the legal arena, his name would forever be associated with the first clearly declared, and one of the most pronounced, law reform decisions rendered by the Supreme Court of Canada: *Thorson v. Attorney General of Canada*.[50] Thorson had been blocked in his attempt to fight in the courts the acceptance of the French language as official by a rule that required him to show that he was specially affected or exceptionally prejudiced by the law that he was challenging, namely, the Official Languages Act.[51] The Ontario Court of Appeal denied him standing to proceed with the constitutional case, but the Supreme Court, by a majority, overturned the standing rule and gave him the go-ahead by creating a new one. At the same time, the question of the validity of the Official Languages Act was being litigated in New Brunswick. This case made its way to the Supreme Court before Thorson's, but the ex-president of the Exchequer Court was allowed his day when he presented the argument against the validity of the law in the New Brunswick case. He lost when the Supreme Court decided unanimously that the law making French an official language of Canada for federal matters was valid.[52]

The remarkable stability within the Exchequer Court, as far as tenure was concerned, had continued under Thorson. There had been only four presidents of the court between 1887 and 1964, while in the same period there had been ten chief justices of the Supreme Court of Canada. For the puisne judges, longevity was more the rule than the exception, with Eugene Angers having served the longest at the time of his retirement, twenty-one years and eight months. Audette had been a judge for nineteen years and eight months, and, before being appointed assistant judge, had been the registrar of the Court for twenty-four years and five months, during which time he had acted frequently as a referee. Charles Cameron, who retired shortly before Thorson, had been on the court for seventeen years and five months.

Thirteen judges, including Thorson, had sat on the bench of the Exchequer Court between 1942 and 1964. The contextualism that had been evident in the work of A.K. Maclean was not apparent in any of these judges. Thorson himself was more than comfortable with the approach of Lyman Duff, with whom Maclean had done battle. For Thorson, if a judge undertook more than the examination of the words of a law and perhaps other sections of the statute in which the words were found, then the judge was acting improperly.[53] This highly formal as well as sterile approach to judicial decision making coming from the president, combined with a strong personality, may have set the standard when additional judges were appointed beginning in the mid-1940s. Angers, whose tenure dated from the Maclean period, had not been touched by Maclean's approach and was noted for rambling judgments containing chunks of undigested material.

If there is any validity in the saying that justice delayed is justice denied, then the chronic delay in rendering judgments that characterized the court under Thorson had made the institution vulnerable. This was especially troublesome at a time when rules which had shielded the government in the adjudication of claims against it were breaking down and the special position of the federal government with its own court was attracting attention.

13

The Jackett Years, 1964–1971

THE JUDGES

Wilbur Jackett was fifty-one years of age when he was appointed president of the Exchequer Court following Joseph Thorson's retirement. The appointment followed the established practice of selecting someone from outside the court as president. At the time the practice for the Supreme Court of Canada – selecting the chief justice by seniority – had coincidentally produced alternating anglophone and francophone chief justices since 1944. With direct appointments for the Exchequer Court, the government continued to choose only anglophones.

Jackett had been born, raised, and educated in Saskatchewan. After graduating from the University of Saskatchewan in law, he went to Oxford as a Rhodes Scholar and obtained the equivalent of a graduate degree in law, a BCL, in 1937. On his return to Canada, he joined the federal Department of Justice and entered upon a career in the public service.

He was made deputy minister of justice by Prime Minister Louis St. Laurent on April 15, 1957, the day that a general election was called. Another lawyer from Saskatchewan then achieved an unforgettable place in the history of Canada: in the general election of June 1957, John Diefenbaker led the Progressive Conservatives to victory after more than twenty years of Liberal rule, and became prime minister with a minority government. With his government in a tenuous position, Diefenbaker went back to the people to try to obtain a majority of seats in the House. In the election held in March of 1958, he obtained the greatest majority ever achieved in terms of the percentage of seats won.[1]

A difficulty facing the new Conservative government was that the public service had worked under Liberal governments for such a long time. Tensions existed.[2] Wilbur Jackett remained deputy minister of justice until June 20, 1960, when he left the public service and joined the Canadian Pacific Railway as a counsel. After almost six years of Conservative rule, the Liberals were returned to power in 1963 under Lester Pearson. On May 4, 1964, Jackett became the new president of the Exchequer Court.

Another judge was appointed on the same day as Jackett. Hugh Francis Gibson was a lawyer who had spent his life, personal and professional, in Kingston, Ontario, except for his time in the army during World War II. These two new judges were followed on July 1, 1964 by an unusual appointment, to a new position that had been created for that particular person.[3] When Allison Arthur Mariotti Walsh was appointed, he was not expected to assume duties on the court, but was to be the Commissioner of Divorces as an officer of the Senate. A Quebec lawyer, Walsh had been in private practice in Montreal. He had accepted the position of Commissioner of Divorces on the understanding that he would be made a judge of the Exchequer Court.[4] The tale of the Exchequer Court and the divorce jurisdiction is a special story, which is told in the next section.

The last judge to be appointed to the court in its days as the Exchequer Court of Canada was Roderick Kerr. Like Maynard Archibald and John Kearney before him, Kerr served as chief commissioner of the Board of Transport Commissioners prior to joining the court. Unlike them, he had not held the title of Judge of the Exchequer Court while head of the board (1959–67). The use of that title for the chief commissioner had lasted only from 1948 to 1951, after which the requirement was that the position be filled by a judge of a superior court of Canada or a lawyer with at least ten years' membership in the profession. Kerr qualified in the latter category. He was the last chief commissioner; after he joined the court on November 1, 1967, the board became part of the new Canadian Transport Commission, to be headed by a 'President,' the same title as that of the head of the Exchequer Court.[5] While the title of President may have enhanced the image of the new commission, it also carried the implication that the Exchequer Court of Canada was a government agency of the same sort.

Kerr was a Nova Scotian who, after graduation from Dalhousie University, practised law in Glace Bay on Cape Breton Island. Following service with the army during World War II, which consisted primarily of work with the judge advocate general's branch, he did legal work for the Unemployment Insurance Commission and the Board of Transport Commissioners in Ottawa. At the time of his appointment to the court he had spent twenty years in the public service in Ottawa.

DIVORCE JURISDICTION

An examination of the constitution reveals that Ottawa has jurisdiction to make laws in relation to matters such as trade and commerce, navigation and shipping, lighthouses, fisheries, postal service, defence, banking, and so on, while the provinces have authority to deal with local and private matters, which, in the words of Mr Justice Gwynne of the Supreme Court, meant family matters.[6] The provinces were also given jurisdiction over 'The Solemnization of Marriage in the Province.'[7] Yet included in the list of subjects over which the federal Parliament has jurisdiction is 'Marriage and Divorce,' an apparent anomaly.[8]

When the constitution was created in the mid-1860s, religious forces within the country were at work shaping society. Marriage was placed within federal control so that Ottawa could provide national recognition of a marriage contracted in any province (under the power over the solemnization of marriage), thereby preventing one province from refusing to recognize a marriage that had been contracted in another.[9] Legislative authority over divorce was given to Ottawa in order to make it as difficult as possible to obtain a divorce. Divorce law existed in Nova Scotia and New Brunswick at the time of Confederation, but not in Ontario and Quebec. Thus, while divorce had to be dealt with in the constitution, it was placed within federal authority. Because divorce was a highly sensitive religious issue, and Ontario and Quebec were opposed to the establishment of a divorce law, the federal government would be inhibited from establishing a national divorce law for over a century.[10]

From Confederation until 1930, when divorce was permitted within the provincial legal system, residents of Ontario required the passage of legislation through the Parliament of Canada in order to obtain a divorce. Quebec, and later Newfoundland, retained the need for legislative action until 1968.

Since the federal Parliament had authority over divorce law, it was not altogether surprising that the Exchequer Court would eventually come into contact with the subject. What was involved was the issue of providing a judicial process for obtaining a divorce in Quebec and, after 1949, also in Newfoundland. The Exchequer Court entered the picture because those who advocated a judicial process accepted that there would be problems with judges in Quebec and Newfoundland who were Roman Catholics having a jurisdiction in divorce matters, since their religion would prohibit them from exercising it. The Exchequer Court was consequently proposed as a surrogate court for those people in Quebec and Newfoundland who wanted a divorce.[11]

On those occasions when the question of the Exchequer Court handling divorce cases did arise, concerns were rarely expressed about the court itself. However, a momentary glimpse of how the court was perceived as a federal and national institution occurred in 1919, in a debate in the House of Commons over having the court act as the divorce court for Quebec residents. The debaters must have assumed that the Exchequer Court judge would not be Roman Catholic. Walter Cassels, the judge at the time, was Anglican. When a Quebec member of the House pointed out that Audette, the assistant judge, was Roman Catholic, the proposer of the legislation responded by stating that, should the senior judge die, a replacement would probably be appointed quickly.[12] The underlying assumption was that the senior judge would always be a Protestant, which held true for the next seventy-two years, until the appointment of Chief Justice Julius Isaac in late 1991. Aside from this, most Quebec legislators prior to the 1960s opposed divorce and wanted no part of any divorce process for Quebec residents, whether or not it was to be in the Exchequer Court.[13]

As social attitudes to divorce changed, it became increasingly difficult for many to accept the need for an Act of Parliament in order to obtain a divorce. For residents of Ontario (from 1867 until 1930), Quebec (from 1867 until 1968), and Newfoundland (from the union in 1949 until 1968), getting a divorce required a petition to Parliament. A hearing would take place before the Standing Committee of the Senate on Divorce, and the committee would make a recommendation. A committee of the House of Commons would also consider the matter. A bill would be introduced, and, if the legislators thought that the divorce was appropriate, the bill would become law.[14]

As the move towards judicial divorces gained momentum in the 1950s and 1960s, the Exchequer Court became a constant feature of the discussions. There was some uneasiness about having the Exchequer Court judges deal with divorce, since their normal diet consisted of claims against the government, intellectual property, admiralty law, taxation, and the like cases.[15] To overcome any concern about the ability of the judges to handle divorce cases, it was suggested that judges be added to the court for divorce petitions.[16]

A step towards eliminating the old system was taken when the law was changed in 1963. The Senate could now dissolve a marriage by means of a simple resolution, with Parliament having the power to review the resolution.[17] The process was further judicialized by having the evidence heard by an officer of the Senate designated by the Speaker. The officer would report to the Senate Standing Committee on Divorce, which would in turn refer the matter to the Senate where the resolution would be adopted. Allison Walsh was designated as the divorce commissioner on November 19, 1963.[18]

To help Walsh with the divorce petitions, Charles Cameron, who retired as a judge of the Exchequer Court on February 1, 1964, was designated as a commissioner. Cameron handled the contested cases. Even in 1964, Quebec Senators still protested that judicial divorces were being created, which was unacceptable to them.[19] However, by 1967 values had changed sufficiently that the federal government, with Pierre Trudeau as minister of justice, determined to bring the divorce laws 'more in line with the present social climate.'[20] A century after Confederation, a uniform divorce law was created for Canada.[21] With it came the creation of judicial divorces for Quebec and Newfoundland, to be granted by a special division of the Exchequer Court.[22] Divorce was still sufficiently sensitive that the government felt it necessary to use the federal Exchequer Court rather than the provincial courts of the two affected provinces, but that was seen as a temporary measure, and there was a mechanism for allowing the jurisdiction to be transferred to the provincial courts.[23] According to Pierre Trudeau, while the government had no wish to force judicial divorces upon any province, yet 'in the meantime we take out of parliament this outmoded way of proceeding.'[24]

To address the unease about the capability of regular Exchequer Court judges to handle divorce matters, the law entrusted the new Divorce Division of the court to the judge who had been the divorce commissioner, Walsh. In addition, at the request of the president, any person who held or had held office as a judge of a provincial superior or county court could sit for a specific period. The regular judges were made ex officio members of the new division. An appeal from the Divorce Division lay to the Exchequer Court.[25] Three judges were to constitute the panel for an appeal, and the trial judge in the case could not sit on the appeal.

The Quiet Revolution in Quebec and social attitudes in general across the country had their effect and, before the jurisdiction of the Exchequer Court could come into play, both Quebec and Newfoundland acted to vest jurisdiction in their provincial courts. What was left to the Exchequer Court was the jurisdiction to deal with divorce petitions if both husband and wife presented petitions on the same day in different provinces.[26]

In 1969, Allison Walsh, who had taken a leave of absence from his work as a judge in order to carry out his duties as Commissioner of Divorces, took up his judicial duties on the court.

THE INDIVIDUAL AND THE STATE

Cases involving claims against the government for damages now consisted mainly of an analysis of the facts and a determination of whether liability should be recognized or not. The legislation reforming the law of Crown liability had had the desired effect and there were no significant differences observable between negligence actions against the Crown and those against any private person.

Now cases began to appear in which the traditional grounds for an action – negligence, breach of contract, or injury to property – were no longer the basis for the claim for damages. The owner of a mail-order business claimed damages for interference with property rights because of a suspension of his postal service by the Post Office Department.[27] An assistant deputy minister claimed damages for being dismissed from the public service without being given the opportunity to present his side of the case.[28] In an appeal under the Canada Shipping Act, within the admiralty jurisdiction of the court, the issue was whether, following a collision in the St Lawrence River, an investigating commissioner should have ordered a pilot's licence suspended.[29] These were cases in which damages were no longer sufficient recompense, and what was wanted was resumption of postal service, retaining a position in the public service, or restoration of a pilot's licence. Decisions made by officials of the state were being called into question. The aspect of administrative law concerned with Crown liability was being replaced in importance by the aspect involving a review of the decisions made within the administration of government.

Having quickly established a firm control over the administration of the court, in particular the problem of delay, the new president just as quickly let it be known that something was different on another front. In 1965 Wilbur Jackett took an opportunity to openly discuss the issuing of writs of assistance. A writ of assistance was a search warrant that was general in nature and did not relate to any particular offence or any specific matter that was the subject of a search. Writs were issued to named members of the Royal Canadian Mounted Police and other government officials and remained in effect as long as the named person held the position which justified the holding of the writ. Writs of assistance were used in the enforcement of the laws relating to customs and excise, narcotic control, and food and drugs.[30] In Jackett's mind, 'certain questions' arose with regard to them.[31]

He acknowledged that writs of assistance had been issued by the Exchequer Court judges 'as a matter of course for many years,' but the 'extraordinary wide powers'[32] that they conferred seemed to him to be out of step with the times. Since the legislation that authorized these special search warrants made it mandatory for the judge to issue them once it was shown that the person to whom the writ was to be issued was an appropriate officer, the only thing that Jackett felt able to do to effect change was to shine some light on the situation by describing the authorizing legislation and explaining what the writs were, how they worked, and what power he had as the person who issued them. He hoped that an informed public would create a demand a change in the legislation. He added no commentary, other than the obvious description of the power to search as 'extraordinary.' It was a very mild style of judicial law reform.

Jackett pointed out that a person exercising the power granted by such a writ was exercising it as granted by statute, not executing an order of the court. The only meaningful involvement of the judiciary was to ensure that the wording of a writ was as carefully chosen as possible. Thus in the particular application that he was concerned with, Jackett required that the wording of the writ be revised to follow the language of the statute in question.

While the president of the Exchequer Court may have thought that the time was ripe for change with regard to the writs of assistance, it did not occur. For one thing, his written decision did not attract public attention, nor that of legal commentators. Times did change, however, and, given the warmth with which the legal profession in general embraced the Canadian Charter of Rights and Freedoms in 1982, it soon became apparent that the writs could not sustain a challenge based on the provisions of the Charter. In 1985 the provisions that had authorized them were repealed.[33] In 1987, in two cases involving writs that had arisen before the repeal, the Supreme Court of Canada held that writs of assistance could not survive in the face of the Charter prohibition against unreasonable searches and seizures.[34]

THE CANADIAN BILL OF RIGHTS

The Charter of Rights and Freedoms created in 1982 had a predecessor, the still-existing declaration of rights and freedoms called the Canadian Bill of Rights.[35] The coming into effect on August 10, 1960, of the Canadian Bill of Rights carried the potential for making a monumental change in our constitution as far as individual rights were concerned.

Until this time the legal process had undertaken to protect the individual within the realm of rule of law, while the political process protected the individual with respect to the substance of the law. In both areas, the driving force was a concern with the dignity and worth of the individual human being. In this division of functions between the legal and political process the legal profession adopted the role of the guardian of individual rights vis-à-vis the executive, while the rights themselves were created by the legislators, who would act as their protectors. With the Canadian Bill of Rights, the legal system acquired a direct means of monitoring the content of law based on ideas of the liberty of the individual within society.

The Bill was clearly applicable to federal law and, as a federal court administering federal law, the Exchequer Court could not avoid encountering it. However, it was in the area of criminal law that the Bill would be most frequently used and, except for the Court Martial Appeal Court work, and the inactive criminal jurisdiction under the Combines Investigation Act that the court had acquired in 1960,[36] criminal law was not an area that the judges of the Exchequer Court were concerned with.

The flirting with civil libertarian ideas that had occurred in the Supreme Court of Canada in the 1950s, which amounted to the creation of an implied bill of rights,[37] seemed to have had no impact on the judges of the Exchequer Court. It is doubtful if there had been any significant impact on the legal profession in general. Thus a definite challenge was faced by the judges who had little or no experience in dealing with such issues, which previously would have been viewed as political in nature. Potentially the judges were being asked to deal with the social context of the law, an area that the formalists had maintained was beyond the proper role of a judge.

While the Bill of Rights was enacted in 1960, during Thorson's tenure as president, no cases were brought before the Exchequer Court in the first four years of the Bill's existence. The first ones arrived in 1965 when the Court was under Jackett's leadership. By that time, the Canadian Bill of Rights had been emasculated by the judges of the provincial courts.[38] These judges had not been receptive to the new law, and within a few years it was finished. All that was left of any significance was the idea that it was an interpretation statute,[39] which still gave it some potency as a law intended to enhance individual rights vis-à-vis the state.[40]

An early stance taken by judges in the provincial courts was that a particular statute was not to be considered repealed by a subsequent general statute. The Bill of Rights articulated general principles such as a right to life, liberty, security of the person, enjoyment of property, due process of law, freedom of speech, and equality before the law, which meant that, for legislation in existence when the Bill came into being, it could have no effect.[41] This idea, a devastating one for the Bill of Rights, retreated from view because its application obviously ignored the dictate of Parliament evidenced by the very existence of the Bill. By 1973, however, the idea was revived by the Supreme Court of Canada, ending at that time whatever was left of the moribund statute.[42] Roland Ritchie in the Supreme Court was even prepared to say that that was what Parliament had actually intended. The idea that judges had never been intended to use the Bill of Rights to render law inoperative had appeared earlier.[43] Judges had in the past declared themselves to be guardians of the liberty of the people, but the powerful social values creating a collectivist mentality had made judicial action relatively unnecessary.

Because judges were reluctant to review the substance of legislation and because of the legal concept of parliamentary supremacy, the judiciary, early in the life of the Bill, maintained that the potentially very powerful civil liberties contained in the concept of 'due process of law' meant the law of the land, that is, simply the law as it existed.[44] At its most civil libertarian, the phrase was said to mean the traditional fundamental principles of justice.[45]

While Jackett's decision in the *Writs of Assistance* case was motivated by a perception of changing social values regarding individual liberty, he made no mention of the Canadian Bill of Rights. Indeed the Bill had made an appearance in the Exchequer Court, but in keeping with the approach of the judges of the provincial courts, it had made little or no impact.[46] Nevertheless its spirit appeared to be working.

In *Randolph v. The Queen*,[47] Jackett asserted that an individual's right to be heard and to be given a fair opportunity for correcting or contradicting what was alleged against him or her was a fundamental rule of British justice that was to be read into statutes in which power had been conferred on someone to make decisions that affected the individual. In Jackett's mind, there was consequently no need for the Bill of Rights.

Randolph conducted a mail-order business and the Post Office Department had suspended his postal service temporarily for the purpose of an investigation. Samples of films, books, and photographs that were for sale were sent to the department and, after they were examined, an interim prohibitory order was made. Randolph filed a petition of right for damages against the Crown alleging interference with property rights in the mail addressed to him. Jackett concluded that no law existed that allowed for the temporary suspension and he categorically rejected the government's contention that there was an implied power, that is, a power 'to interfere with the property rights and statutory privileges of presumably law-abiding citizens.'[48] As far as the prohibitory order was concerned, it was true that the process outlined in the legislation suggested that a hearing had not been intended. However, given the importance of the postal service to Canadians in general, coupled with the strength of the fundamental rule of justice that a person had a right to be heard, Jackett concluded that a person in that situation had to be afforded a hearing and that the order in question was invalid.

While Wilbur Jackett seemed willing and able to deal with the notions of civil liberty that had been given voice in the Bill of Rights by the Diefenbaker government, the Supreme Court of Canada would have nothing to do with them. At this time the core of the judges of the Supreme Court were highly conservative in their approach to decision making and social values. Since the Bill of Rights had been created by a Conservative government, there is some irony in this.

On appeal to the Supreme Court, Jackett's decision was reversed by a unanimous decision of seven judges.[49] John Cartwright rendered the judgment for the court, which occupied a mere one-and-a-half pages. For Cartwright, the conclusion seemed simple: 'on its true construction s. 7 ... authorizes the making of an interim prohibitory order without prior notice to the party affected. There is no doubt that Parliament has the power to abrogate or modify the application of the maxim *audi alteram partem*.'[50] For the Supreme Court, the fundamental rule of justice recognized by Jackett existed, its name Latinized by Cartwright as *audi alteram partem*, but it had to give way before the government's need to be able to act swiftly to protect the public. With respect to the illegal temporary order, Cartwright held that a claim for damages against the government was precluded by a provision of the Post Office Act, a special statutory provision that was an exception to the general terms of the Crown Liability Act.[51] Under the section, a claim arising from the loss, delay, or mishandling of anything deposited in a post office was prohibited. Cartwright allowed it to also cover an illegal act.

Whereas Jackett had been reticent about using the Bill of Rights, Camilien Noël used it forcefully in a case in which a pilot had been reclassified to a lower classification by the Department of Transport following a marine collision, but without any form of hearing having taken place.[52] The pilot brought an action for a declaration that he was entitled to his old classification and, alternatively, that the Orders in Council that had created the various grades of pilots were invalid because they were beyond the authority granted by the enabling statute.

Noël minced no words. The reclassification, he said, was the sole arbitrary decision of the Superintendent of Pilots for the department, and it had been made in complete disregard of the Bill of Rights. There had to be a fair hearing in accordance with the principles of fundamental justice.[53] So crucial was the application of the Bill of Rights in Noël's mind that he discussed the hearing issue only on the basis that the rules were assumed to be valid.

Again there was a unanimous Supreme Court of Canada,[54] for which Louis-Philippe Pigeon rendered the judgment. He was a most formidable opponent of the existence of the Bill of Rights and was not impressed by the stand that Noël had taken. There was no mention of the Bill of Rights in Pigeon's judgment, and he criticised the Exchequer Court judge for rendering a judgment on the basis that the Orders in Council were assumed to be valid: 'he cannot accede to contradictory claims,' Pigeon asserted. He also criticized the trial judge for a lack of clarity in his reasons. A very minimal criterion for a good judgment is that it be clear; thus Pigeon's criticism was extremely severe. Noël had held that the action against the minister of transport could not proceed, based on previous decisions that controlled him. So settled was the point in the opinion of the government litigators that no appeal was taken on this conclusion, but, during the hearing before the Supreme Court, the judges thought otherwise and gave permission to enter an appeal on the issue. It was in Pigeon's opinion the principle question and one of great importance. The question of the need for a hearing disappeared.

The treatment of the Bill of Rights by the other judges of the Exchequer Court could be quite varied. Cartwright's statement in *The Queen v. Randolph*, 'There is no doubt that Parliament has the power to abrogate or modify the application of the maxim *audi alteram partem*,' was used by Allison Walsh to nullify any effect of the Bill of Rights.[55] Despite these decisions, the Bill could still provide inspiration for civil-liberties decisions: Roderick Kerr referred to the preamble of the Bill in a citizenship appeal in which he held that someone who was a conscientious objector with regard to military service could still become a citizen.[56]

THE JUDICIAL FUNCTION

At this time, and for the first time, a judge of the court publicized his ideas about the judicial function. In a lecture to students at Queen's University, Kingston, Ontario, Wilbur Jackett articulated the declaratory theory of law as the one that controls the thinking of lawyers within the legal system, but he acknowledged that, as 'a practical fact,' the theory was not true. He did not explain to the students why they were being educated to think in a formal manner that he admitted existed for some reason other than the rational solution of problems. He simply asserted that, for the lawyer, it is the language of statutes and cases that provides the solutions to problems.[57]

It followed from Jackett's acceptance of the formalist view of judicial decision making that such decision making had to be limited to that of dispute resolution only, and have no law-making role.[58] Indeed, with the formalist mind-set, any attempt at law-making would be perceived as an act of will or exercise of an absolute discretion on the part of the judge, in that there was nothing for the judge to consider other than words and the judge's own personal inclinations. Seen as an act of will, it would be considered to be a denial of the rule of law.

One can clearly see in the decisions rendered by Jackett his commitment to this model of decision making. There is the appearance of thoroughness conveyed by an extensive analysis of cases. An analysis of precedents replaces an analysis of the problem that has created the litigation. Even when Jackett recognized that there were no binding precedents, he still engaged in a review of cases – for a formalist, there was nothing else.[59] He also showed a commitment to the doctrine of *stare decisis* at a time when there were signs that it was beginning to weaken.[60] Since he recognized that the formal model was artificial, he had to have made a conscious and definite decision not to engage in the contextual analysis illustrated by judges of the past, such as Burbidge and Maclean.

As a formalist, Jackett liked to create lists, which always presented an appearance of objectivity and certainty. However, he added a feature to his judgments that was unprecedented and has not been copied: he occasionally used appendices. They were informational pieces which were in addition to what he wrote in the reasons for judgment. Their existence kept the judgments themselves neat and clean in the formalist tradition. Since they were not traditional in the judicial system, it is not clear how they should have been approached. Were they 'quasi-judgments,' or formalized statements in the nature of obiter dicta? They bear a certain resemblance to advance rulings or policy memoranda associated with the administrative process. Their existence at this time was more intriguing than their contents.[61] Jackett also had a habit of writing lengthy memoranda to the other judges about matters of law that he had studied, and the appendices could have been the equivalent provided for the members of the bar.

The other judges of this era did not publicly pronounce on their understanding of their function as a judge, either in writings or addresses, or in their reasons for judgment. In one case where counsel attempted to deal with policy considerations behind a law, Allison Walsh overreacted and declared, 'Questions of policy are for Parliament to decide.'[62] This point was never in doubt. The issue was identifying and using the policy behind the law. The judge's statement completely excluded of any such concerns, and left the participants with the words of the law only.

CHANGE

In the last years of the 'Exchequer Court of Canada,' under its final president, Wilbur Jackett, there were many signs of change, both for the court and for the country.

No change had been more dramatic for the court than the complete turnaround in the court's performance in rendering judgments. The following numbers illustrate the change starkly:

Year	Number of reported reserved decisions	Average number of days between hearing and judgment
1962	48	341
1965	58	49

Another change concerned appeals in admiralty cases. The anomaly of appeals from the Admiralty Districts being heard by a single judge was ended and a standard appeal court panel of three judges instituted. The reported cases indicate that, from 1964 until 1971, nine appeals were heard by a three-judge panel; no appeals were heard by a single judge of the court. Two of the appeals in which a three-judge panel was used involved inquiries under the Shipping Act by a provincial superior court judge. The use of a three-judge panel was evidence of a certain sensitivity that had developed between the judges of the provincial superior courts and the judges of the Exchequer Court with respect to status. In admiralty law, the practice also arose of Exchequer Court judges handling trials in the admiralty districts.

In the late 1960s, the new federal government of Pierre Trudeau, with John Turner as the minister of justice, began contemplating changes to the court. Perhaps as a result of the general sense of change, the reticence that had existed over the years concerning the Exchequer Court and courts in general momentarily slipped away, and the court, now in its final years, came in for an unprecedented amount of comment and debate. The minister of justice, John Turner, was thrust into the role of defender of the court.

Not surprisingly, the discussions that developed had a partisan flavour and must be interpreted accordingly. However, they did bring to the surface various matters that were no doubt of concern to the legal profession as a whole.[63] Needless to say, members of the legal profession dominated any discussion of the court.

Eldon Woolliams, an Alberta lawyer and Conservative member of Parliament, began in 1967 with comments describing the Exchequer Court as 'a special federal court,' and 'a court set up for the crown,' and suggesting that some of its jurisdiction should go to the provincial courts, and that it was an expensive court.[64] His comments and criticisms gathered strength the next year. In a debate dealing with mineral resources and Indian reserves in British Columbia, Woolliams began with the suggestion that, because of complicated procedure and the high cost of litigation, the court was not accessible to the average person. Shortly after, in a debate involving the appointment of judges for Ontario and Quebec, Woolliams alluded to the opinion that the court tended to favour the government.[65]

This comment about the court being pro-government went to the heart of the integrity of the institution and naturally provoked a strong response from the minister of justice. He asserted that Woolliams could not have meant any reflection upon the independence or impartiality of the judges, and that he had the fullest confidence in the court.[66] Woolliams, no doubt realizing that he might have overstepped the proper bounds of any discussion of the judiciary, later softened his words:

'When I say that that court is pro-crown, naturally I am not passing a slight on the judges of the court, but I do say that court is set up more to serve the crown than to serve Canadian citizens.'[67] The minister of justice did, however, grudgingly accept that the centralization of the court's administration at Ottawa did create a degree of expense that could be reduced by decentralization. Turner went on to mention two other potential reforms that were being considered, namely, the handling of appeals from administrative tribunals, and the creation of two divisions, a trial and an appeal division.[68] Change was definitely in the air.

Another and more threatening issue raised by Woolliams was why, for some matters, there was a need to use 'a special court called the Exchequer Court,' rather than the provincial courts.[69] An NDP member, John Gilbert, a lawyer from Toronto, added his voice in agreement.[70]

Woolliams would continue his criticisms into the next year, and the year after,[71] focusing on the idea that the court was special and different. As far as the legal profession was concerned, this was critical; the Exchequer Court was unfamiliar to the average lawyer and carried with it the worries associated with something unknown. Its jurisdiction was seen as being of a 'fairly complicated and specialized nature.'[72] The mystery long associated with the admiralty jurisdiction now tended to pervade the court as a whole. The areas of law within its jurisdiction were those for which lawyers tended to specialize, such as taxation, intellectual property, and admiralty law, areas unfamiliar to most members of the profession. These specialized areas were the court's main reason for existence: the lawyers practising in these areas wanted a court with the necessary knowledge and expertise to deal with the problems that were litigated. The Exchequer Court fulfilled that role, although it had diverse specialties.[73]

Another justification for the court was advanced: as a federal court, it could provide uniformity in decisions across the country in areas of federal law.[74] Unfortunately, important areas of federal law such as criminal law, bankruptcy, and the liability of government railways were handled by the provincial courts, a fact that could prove embarrassing if mentioned in this context. It was also accepted that uniformity of application across the country was not a constitutional requirement for a federal law, and it could have a local application which resulted in variations from place to place.[75] A major difficulty latent in this argument was the spectre of the dual system of courts it tended to create.

One of the matters that Woolliams raised to make the point that the court was peculiar was that its rules were closer to the English rules than to those used in the provincial courts. 'In fact,' Woolliams stated, 'if one reads the whole book, dealing with the procedure in English courts, he would almost think we had English courts functioning here in Canada, in the name of the Exchequer Court.'[76] By 1969, the continuing reliance on law made in England was definitely not sitting very well in Quebec and was beginning to create an uncomfortable feeling in English Canada.[77]

While another Alberta member of Parliament calling the Court 'a faceless monster in the capital city' was obviously overreacting,[78] there was a sense of a need for change. The minister of justice said that, for one thing, the name would be changed, since nobody understood what the name 'Exchequer' meant.[79]

Great change was also under way for the country. When the 1950s began, Canada and its national institutions were still English-speaking. Quebec was a bilingual province; within it, French had a status equal to English in law, if not in practice. During the 1950s, a strong sentiment developed within Quebec that it should be 'mistress in its own house.' At the time this end was seen to be achievable through the federal system.[80] With the 1960s began what is known as the Quiet Revolution and, while it is seen as having brought change within Quebec, it also created a revolutionary change across the country. The domination of the francophone majority by the English-speaking minority in Quebec came under attack. Francophone Quebeckers wanted a full share of what the twentieth century had to offer, including a share in the political power within Quebec. The highly conservative English within Quebec were seen as a privileged class and the relationship between them and the francophone majority identified as colonial in nature.[81]

In April 1963, shortly after the political awakening within francophone society, the Liberal government of Lester Pearson came to power in Ottawa and within a few months established the Royal Commission on Bilingualism and Biculturalism (the B & B Commission). The government accepted that there was an equal partnership between English-speaking and French-speaking Canadians, and the commission was to recommend ways to recognize this partnership. Francophones, who were seeking greater control over their destiny within Quebec were being offered a share of the power across the country. The federal government wanted francophones to view Canada, rather than Quebec, as their nation. One result was the coming into force of the Official Languages Act in September 1969, when Canada became officially bilingual for federal matters.[82] The change was reflected in the following year's *Exchequer Court Reports* (published in 1971), when the judgments began to appear in both French and English.[83]

As went the country, so went the court. The powerful changes under way in the country provided the climate that would allow for the creation of a third court, and this time it would have a new name.

PART 4

The Third Court, 1971–1992

14

Creation of the Federal Court

The Federal Court Act[1] was proclaimed in force on June 1, 1971. The legislation declared that the Exchequer Court of Canada would continue under a new name as the Federal Court of Canada,[2] but there was much more to it than simply a change of name.

Change was the watchword of the governing Liberals following Pierre Elliott Trudeau's selection as party leader and prime minister in April 1968, and the general election victory in June 1968. The prime minister made no secret of his government's attitude that social institutions were subject to change. Citizens were exhorted to keep pace: '[to] live is to change,' and 'to progress is to adapt and modify to such changes.'[3] After almost a century of existence the social institution known as the Exchequer Court of Canada was not immune.

The ignition of the reform process can be found in a memorandum from the deputy minister of justice, Donald Maxwell, to the minister of justice, in which Maxwell wrote that it was 'an appropriate time' to consider the nature of a federal judicial system.[4] The memorandum was dated July 2, 1968, exactly a week following the Liberals' election victory, when they had achieved the first clear majority government in a decade. A goal of the new government that had been widely broadcast by Trudeau was the creation of a 'just society,' and now the government could set about achieving it.

A few months later, the new minister of justice, John Turner, would rise in the House of Commons to say that the Exchequer Court could be used as a tribunal having a general jurisdiction to hear appeals from federal administrative tribunals. The minister of justice also noted that the court could have a trial division and an appeal division.[5] The next month Turner stated in the House that he hoped to bring forward changes to the Exchequer Court which would relieve the workload of the Supreme Court, by creating an appellate division. He also announced that the government was contemplating reform of the process of judicial review of administrative tribunals.[6] Two significant changes were being considered, the creation of an intermediate court of appeal and the creation of an administrative law court, and they were moving forward together.

Other events unfolding in the legal world helped set the stage for changes to the Exchequer Court. Maxwell sketched the details in his memorandum.

The Royal Commission on Taxation had tabled its report in 1967,[7] and one of its recommendations urged the creation of a special tax court. The deputy minister of justice made it clear that he did not favour a federal system of courts composed of separate specialized courts. Maxwell preferred to have one federal court – with divisions, if need be. He suggested that the Exchequer Court be given the jurisdiction of the tax court. He argued against a series of specialized courts on the grounds that there would be only a few judges in each (three or four), with separate staffs, and different rules of practice and procedure. Perhaps most important, Maxwell maintained that the problems people saw with the present Exchequer Court would continue to exist and require examination.

The deputy minister also expressed concern about the workload of the Supreme Court. He suggested that an appellate court be created within the federal legal system to serve as an intermediate court between the Exchequer Court and the Supreme Court of Canada, thereby relieving the workload of the highest court.[8]

Naturally the creation of the new appeal court would make the federal legal system look more like a complete system. The existing one consisted of a trial court (the Exchequer Court) and the Supreme Court of Canada as a hybrid appeal court serving both the provincial judicial systems and the Exchequer Court, as well as certain federal administrative bodies.[9] The resulting image of a legal system resembling the provincial ones may have been why the deputy minister of justice pointed out very carefully that it was an accepted constitutional fact that the provincial court system 'provides the judicial services required in that province whether or not any particular matter calls for the application of provincial or federal laws.' He also observed that no one would suggest changing that constitutional fact. Maxwell nevertheless added that the existence of federal courts must be accepted as well, perhaps for no other reason than that they were needed.

At the time that these reforms to the federal legal system were being proposed significant developments were taking place with respect to the judicial review of federal administrative tribunals. There was no question at this time that federal administrative tribunals such as the Canada Labour Relations Board were subject to control by the judges of the provincial superior courts. The worrisome issue was *which* provincial courts. Since the federal tribunals sat at Ottawa, in Ontario, it had become the practice to use the Ontario courts for judicial review. However, problems had surfaced a decade earlier, in 1959, when litigants began to use the courts of other provinces. Litigation involving the Restrictive Trade Practices Commission and the fishing industry resulted in actions in Ontario and in British Columbia with contrary outcomes. The litigation ended only after the Supreme Court of Canada rendered a decision.[10] In 1962, the British Columbia Court of Appeal decided that the courts of that province had jurisdiction over the decision of a federal tribunal if it had effect in the province.[11] The Ontario courts did not give up their jurisdiction and in 1966 the Ontario Court of Appeal did not hesitate to review a decision of the Canada Labour Relations Board, even though the same decision had already been reviewed in the courts of Quebec.[12] The problem simmered for a while until a decision of the Quebec Court of Appeal caught the attention of the Justice Department in 1968. The Court of Appeal concluded that the Quebec courts had no jurisdiction to supervise or control federal tribunals.[13]

Maxwell's memorandum highlighted the fact that, in addition to the 'harassment' of federal administrative tribunals by litigants bounding from one province to another in search of a favourable outcome, the Quebec decision had created the very real possibility that some provinces might have no jurisdiction at all. The Department of Justice suggested the elimination of all provincial court jurisdiction over federal administrative bodies, and giving exclusive supervisory jurisdiction to the Exchequer Court.

Additional reform to the substance of administrative law was also under way. Existing remedies in the area of judicial review of administrative decisions were said to be inadequate. The deputy minister acknowledged that there was no remedy for a person adversely affected by an order founded on an erroneous view of the law when that error did not appear on the face of the record. The deputy minister proposed that the

Exchequer Court be given a more extensive jurisdiction to review administrative decisions than that accorded to provincial courts of the time.

When the reform legislation was finally introduced in March of 1970,[14] the name of the court had been changed to the Federal Court of Canada. The highly symbolic nature of names or titles no doubt prompted the minister of justice, John Turner, to begin the second reading by stating that there was no hidden meaning or significance in the abandonment of the name 'Exchequer Court' and the adoption of 'Federal Court.' Essentially his point was that the name 'Exchequer Court' had lost its significance and no longer conveyed the purpose of the court.[15]

The Deputy Minister had not overlooked the matter of a name for the court. Maxwell insisted that 'Exchequer Court' had to give way. Its French origin had lost its significance centuries before and the name had been adopted from Britain at a time when 'Canadians' were first and foremost British North Americans. Though Maxwell suggested the name 'Federal Superior Court,' the word 'Superior' fell away during the process of reform.

The Supreme Court of Canada influenced the destiny of the court once again. In 1875 the Exchequer Court had been created to maintain an original jurisdiction for the Supreme Court; in 1970, the appellate division was created to relieve the workload of the same court.[16] However, while concern for the Supreme Court may have prompted the addition of an appeal division, it was the jurisdiction to review federal administrative decisions that gave the Federal Court a mandate of its own.

The burgeoning growth of government administration and the widespread delegation of decision making to public servants was not a new concern. No less a supporter of individual rights than John Diefenbaker had suggested having the Exchequer Court review decisions of administrators or government agencies, some twenty-five years earlier.[17] Concern with the relationship of the individual to society – so much a part of the life of the court over the years – was still a central theme. The minister of justice clearly recognized the creation of the court as 'a further step toward balancing the rights between the citizen and the state, providing some sort of recourse against bigness, remoteness, alienation, distance from the decision making power. I believe it will give the average citizen the power to enforce his rights against the government and against the structures that government sets up.'[18] In a subsequent debate on the Statutory Instruments Act (1971), John Turner would refer to the Federal Court Act as part of the 'continuum of law reform directed to the protection of individual rights from the power and remoteness of modern government.'[19] The government's intention in righting the imbalance in the relationship between the individual and the state was to identify new ways of increasing methods of redress, recourse, and appeal for the average citizen. Very basic constitutional principles underscored the reform of the federal court system in 1970.

The same basic concerns that were propelling the reform of administrative law at the federal level erupted in Ontario around the same time. The Conservative government of John Robarts had become preoccupied with the existence of organized crime within the province and Attorney General Frederick M. Cass introduced a bill to amend the Police Act on March 19, 1964. The proposed amendments extended the investigative powers of the Ontario Police Commission by allowing the examination of witnesses in secret, coupled with the power to order the imprisonment of any witness who refused to testify. The existence of the Canadian Bill of Rights, proclaimed in 1960, had apparently had negligible effect on the Ontario government. The public outcry which ensued could not have been anticipated and its magnitude signalled social change. Cries of 'police state' had their effect and the bill was withdrawn within the week. Cass resigned as attorney general.[20]

To allay the public agitation generated by the 'police state' imagery, Ontario appointed a royal commission. The Royal Commission of Inquiry into Civil Rights, with Chief Justice James C. McRuer as its sole member, was instructed to study the law of the province as it affected the personal freedoms, rights, and liberties of individuals, and the extent of unjustified encroachment on civil liberties by public authorities.[21] The McRuer Report was released in 1968. Its recommendations spurred a reform of administrative law in Ontario and the enactment of new laws that came into force in 1971.[22] The new legislation was heralded by the Toronto Globe and Mail as 'A new Magna Carta.'[23] The Ontario government boasted that it was providing leadership in the field by appointing the McRuer Commission and carrying out the 'unprecedented program' of law reform.[24]

There was no question that administrative law and its reform had become very topical by the end of the 1960s. A decision of the Supreme Court of Canada provided a catalyst for the federal government.

The appeal, known as the Three Rivers Boatman case,[25] was from the Quebec Court of Appeal. The Quebec court had held that the courts in the province did not have jurisdiction to review decisions of the Canada Labour Relations Board, from which it would follow that there would be no jurisdiction over any federal agency. This was the very same issue that the deputy minister of justice had pointed out in his 1968 memorandum as a cause for concern. The Supreme Court decided unanimously that provincial courts did have the authority to review decisions of a federal board. Of course, the particular decision must affect the people of the province in question and be carried out there. However, the crucial point made by the Supreme Court in its reasons for judgment was that the law to be applied by the provincial court had to be federal. Since Ottawa had not created any law dealing with the basic principles of judicial review since Confederation, one had to go back to 1867 for the law to apply.[26] Only the Parliament of Canada was competent to change it. What arose was the unappetizing prospect of two sets of laws – one for provincial administrative agencies and one for federal. The reforms under way in Ontario would not apply to a decision of a federal administrative entity. If there was already a lack of clarity regarding administrative law, one can only speculate about what the future might have been![27]

Thus, when John Turner introduced the bill to create the Federal Court and stated as an additional justification for the new law that only the Canadian Parliament had legislative jurisdiction to amend the law relating to the supervision of administrative bodies, he was echoing the opinion of the Supreme Court in *Three Rivers Boatman*.[28]

It is important to mention that there was more in the bill than the creation of an intermediate court of appeal and a national court to direct administrative law. In addition, it included jurisdiction that would allow the Federal Court to deal with litigation involving bills of exchange and promissory notes, aeronautics, and interprovincial works and undertakings (all subjects within federal legislative authority under the Constitution).[29] Turner announced, 'a member of the public will have resort to a national court exercising a national jurisdiction when enforcing a claim involving matters which frequently involve national elements.'[30] For those sensitive to the issue this new jurisdiction contained a hint at a dual system of courts – one for provincial matters and another for national. Any negative reaction was blunted by making the jurisdiction concurrent with provincial courts and giving litigants their choice of courts.

There was still more change. Alterations in the jurisdiction over admiralty law (now called the maritime jurisdiction)[31] were intended to establish jurisdiction over 'maritime causes' and to put behind Canadians the historical battles over jurisdiction which had been inherited from England. John J. Mahoney was hired to revise the admiralty jurisdiction,[32] and he advised the government that 'Canada is free to establish a Court having general jurisdiction over maritime causes subject only to restrictions arising out of the Canadian Constitution rather than restrictions arising out of any other law.'[33] Jurisdiction over 'maritime causes' was encompassed by the federal constitutional power over 'navigation and shipping.'[34] The thinking which had created the jurisdiction over the other matters within federal legislative competence (bills of exchange and promissory notes, aeronautics, and interprovincial works and undertakings) had extended to the maritime area. Perhaps to lessen antagonism to a federal judicial system, for the first time the jurisdiction over maritime matters was made concurrent with that of the provincial courts.

In addition to the changes contemplated for the maritime jurisdiction, the old jurisdiction of the Exchequer Court was carried forward, including claims against the government (Crown liability) and intellectual property. For better or for worse, the creation of the Federal Court would elevate the status of federal courts. There was unquestionably an intention to strengthen the federal system.[35]

Second reading of the bill in the House of Commons was uneventful. John Turner, the minister of justice, spoke for the ruling Liberals; Robert McCleave rose for the Progressive Conservatives; Andrew Brewin participated for the New Democratic Party. Although there was some apprehension about aspects of the administrative law jurisdiction, the various reforms and the creation of the court itself were generally well received by all parties.

When the proposed legislation moved to the Committee on Justice and Legal Affairs in May of 1970,[36] the mood was tranquil for only a moment. George Nicholls, a Professor of Law at Dalhousie University, Halifax, and former editor of the *Canadian Bar Review* (1946–57), had written a memorandum dealing with the new administrative law jurisdiction, which he distributed to legislators and members of the Justice Department alike. He was highly critical of certain aspects of the proposed reforms, advocating further study and a complete overhaul of them.[37] But for Nicholls' initiative there would have been no hearings on the bill, other than with members of the Department of Justice. The committee was unprepared for general hearings and a subcommittee was convened to discuss the procedure to be adopted for questioning witnesses. It was ultimately decided that three witnesses would be heard, along with the Ontario Administrative Law Subsection of the Canadian Bar Association, and perhaps a judge. The first witness was George Nicholls.

Professor Nicholls would have known the boundaries of his potential persuasion: he could not transform the committee's review into a hearing on the reform of administrative law, but he could perhaps halt matters and instigate further study. Nicholls launched into a vehement attack on the court's proposed jurisdiction in administrative law. Some of the questions asked by committee members make them appear to have missed the point. Other witnesses did not help. Another academic, Professor Watson from Osgoode Hall Law School, Toronto, attacked the very existence of a federal court, although he accepted the existence of the Supreme Court of Canada. Watson was also Secretary of the Ontario Civil Justice Subsection of the Canadian Bar Association, but he was not authorized to speak on the subsection's behalf.

The Canadian Bar Association asked noted Canadian lawyers Gordon F. Henderson from Ontario and Philippe de Grandpré from Quebec to examine the bill and convey their views to the minister of justice. Henderson also made a presentation to the committee, but it was unhelpful. He had prepared nothing in writing, and was concerned only with some 'technical' questions.

The next witnesses were representatives of the Canadian Labour Congress,[38] who were critically concerned about judicial control of administrative decision making, and specifically about the sensitive area of labour relations. They were direct: the traditional courts were not appropriate for the settlement of labour disputes. This point was made for symbolic purposes since that issue was not on the table at this stage of the legislative process.

With the exception of George Nicholls, the witnesses who appeared before the committee contributed virtually nothing to the process. However, a member of the committee noted that not one of them had spoken in favour of the bill. In response the minister of justice explained that a mimeographed letter had been sent out to members of the Canadian Bar Association, some fourteen thousand of them, informing them of the importance of the legislation, and offering to send a copy if they wanted. He related that he had received almost one hundred detailed letters, virtually every one endorsing the principle of the bill. Nevertheless Nicholls' presentation had generated doubt that there had been adequate study of the proposals. The minister of justice asserted that there had been twelve months of consultations with members of the legal profession, academic and practising, along with a series of meetings. When a question was asked about a presentation by the Canadian Bar Association, the Chairman of the committee reported that the Association had been contacted, and had affirmed that Henderson had appeared on its behalf.[39]

The hearing before the House of Commons committee ended on June 9,

1970, but the bill lapsed when the session of Parliament was prorogued on October 7, 1970. While the debate on second reading had suggested that the measure would proceed as a matter of course, the outspoken objections of George Nicholls had changed that.

The non-partisan nature of the bill allowed it to be revived in the following session of Parliament by agreement of the opposition parties and it was able to continue uninterrupted. When it next surfaced it was again before the Committee on Justice and Legal Affairs on October 28, 1970. However, the political and social climate in Canada had changed dramatically in the interval: Canada was a deeply troubled country. The FLQ crisis had erupted. On October 5, 1970 members of the Front de libération du Québec (FLQ) had kidnapped the British trade commissioner in Montreal, James Cross. A few days later, Quebec's minister of labour, Pierre Laporte, was also kidnapped. Within a week of Laporte's seizure the War Measures Act was proclaimed in force – for the first time in peacetime – an event thought to be impossible before it happened. The Act was intended to effectively establish a government dictatorship in a time of emergency and it consequently suspended individual civil liberties. It took effect at 4:00 in the morning on October 16, 1970, and more than two hundred persons were arrested within the first few hours. The public was notified of the state of emergency at 5:15 on the same morning. Pierre Laporte's lifeless body was found the next day. His murder challenged the prized value of stability in Canadian society.

When the Federal Court bill had been before the House for second reading in March, the minister of justice had been able to announce that the proposed reforms would provide citizens with some recourse against bigness, remoteness, alienation, and distance from the decision making power of government. By October 28, when the committee hearings started again, the spirit of the reforms supporting the creation of the new court was being tested. There was a different atmosphere in the committee. The Conservative spokesman was now Eldon Woolliams, the lawyer and member of Parliament from Alberta who had already shown himself a severe critic of the court. Woolliams had opposed parts of the bill during the earlier hearing in May, but he challenged the government's proposals vigorously in the fall of 1970. He was joined by Andrew Brewin of the New Democratic Party in expressing concern about the existence of a national court. In a short but sharp exchange between Woolliams and the minister of justice it was suggested that the court be regionalized; judges would take up residence in various regions of the country, and concurrent jurisdiction with provincial courts would be the norm. The very concept of a national court was under seige. A second thrust attacked the vital provisions dealing with jurisdiction over administrative law, and the speakers adopted the word 'confusion' as their catchword. The committee hearings ended with a sense of unease surrounding the proposed legislation. Nevertheless, the bill returned to the House of Commons and was passed without incident. It now proceeded on to the Senate.

Senator John Connolly had carriage of the bill through the upper house and as an honour to the Exchequer Court and the judges who had served on it, he read the names of the judges into the record, as well as the names of the registrars of the court. This was in contrast to the proceedings in the House of Commons where, after ninety-five years of existence, the Exchequer Court was allowed to go quietly and without a sign of remorse.

More witnesses appeared before the Senate Committee on Legal and Constitutional Affairs.[40] It was at this stage that the Senate committee received a wide-ranging brief from the Bar of Quebec.[41] The document raised a point that was to prove the most significant yet in the life of the court – the meaning of the words 'Laws of Canada' in section 101 of the constitution. Section 101 declared that the Parliament of Canada could provide for the establishment of courts for 'the better Administration of the Laws of Canada.' In its brief the Quebec Bar asserted that, even though the 'authorities' were not clear, there were strong grounds for maintaining that the term 'Laws of Canada' meant 'federal law' – legislation, regulations, and the judicial decisions which interpreted them. The Quebec position was meant to weaken the basis on which some of the new jurisdiction rested, namely, that jurisdiction could be founded on the constitutional heads of power which granted legislative authority to Ottawa. The 'strong grounds' would naturally be policy concerns. The deputy minister of justice thought that the Quebec bar's point was 'laboured to some considerable extent.'[42]

Throughout the legislative process that created the Federal Court of Canada the court was projected as a forum to deal with highly specialized areas of law. In addition to admiralty (maritime) law, expropriation, taxation, and intellectual property, matters largely unfamiliar to most lawyers, it had now acquired a new specialty, the judicial review of federal administrative decisions. But Professor Nicholls had sounded an alarm. His admonishment that 'the draftman's approach to the problem of court review of federal administrative action will be a prolific breeder of unproductive litigation'[43] generated a sense that insufficient study had gone into the key provisions. If Professor Nicholls was right, sections 18 and 28 of the Federal Court Act would amount to a flaw in the character of the new court.

It is noticeable that the justification for the court based on federalism – a federal court for the application of federal law – had been abandoned.

Also afoot at this time was a fundamental change to law and lawyering. Its potential was enormous. In 1971 a bill was introduced dealing with changes for federally appointed judges. The speaker for the government in the Commons referred to the Federal Court: 'The new Federal Court Act, just recently proclaimed, is an example of the evolution of an older institution, a necessary evolution to keep our judicial system in step with the changes in our society and the changing role of law in that society.'[44] The judiciary now had to accept a role in law reform, and recognize a duty and a responsibility to interpret law in accord with contemporary thought. The courts were expected to link the jurisprudence of the past with the cultural norms and social context of the present and the future. The Federal Court of Canada, along with other courts, would have to abandon the artificiality and limitations of formalism for contextualism. The change struck at the very meaning of judicial decision making for many judges. The Federal Court at least had the examples of Burbidge and Maclean.

15

An Administrative Court

THE BAGGAGE

When the Federal Court acquired its extensive jurisdiction to review federal administrative action, a great deal of controversial baggage arrived with it.

'Administrative law' (the law that applies to government and its activities) can be traced back to the earliest work of the Exchequer Court in England.[1] At the beginning it related to Crown liability. It is thus possible to say that establishment of the Exchequer Court of Canada as the court of claims in 1887 created an administrative court. However, the term 'administrative law,' did not develop until much later, when what preoccupied those thinking about legal control of government was the judicial review of administrative action. As a result there is a tendency to forget that Crown liability is an aspect of administrative law. Since its importance as a distinct area of law also disappeared after the reforms of the early 1950s,[2] it does not enter into the controversy over judicial review that came with the new jurisdiction.

The legislative process has long been associated with the creation of general rules, with government and its officials assuming responsibility for the day-to-day application of the rules to specific situations. The authority to apply the rules in particular cases can fall to ministers, government officials, boards or commissioners, or to courts of law.[3] As technological change created a more complex society in the nineteenth and twentieth centuries, the need for a more effective administrative system to manage the behaviour of individual citizens became obvious. Increasingly, power to make decisions was delegated to various arms of government. Changes in social values also encouraged greater government involvement in economic matters. In Canada, government had always been at the forefront of development of the country.

While a social prejudice against giving public authorities extensive powers may have existed in England,[4] it is doubtful that this attitude extended to Canada.[5] Commenting in a 1934 article on a research project at the University of Toronto that was examining how administrative boards actually functioned, W.P.M. Kennedy reflected the degree of comfort Canadians felt with administrative agencies and the delegation of decision-making power by government to individual agencies.[6] Kennedy was not at all concerned about the use of administrative boards; he cited a growing conviction that government had an obligation to aid and supervise the development of new industries, natural resources, colonization, transportation, and communications, because of the vastness of the country and the unremunerative character of these enterprises in their early stages. In Kennedy's view, government regulation was part of Canadian thinking and of Canada's social conscience, which was quite prepared to accept a wide delegation of power. In social matters, it was far better to take preventive measures rather than to rely solely on curative action!

Despite the public's general acceptance of government regulation, the legal profession began to sound warnings in the 1920s. The concerns expressed echoed those voiced in England – which were nowhere better expressed than in Lord Hewart's book *The New Despotism*, mentioned earlier.[7] In the previous decade another English judge had taken a very clear position on the role of the legal profession vis-à-vis government regulation; in 1911, in the classic administrative law case, *Dyson*, Lord Justice Farwell had declared, 'the Courts are the only defence of the liberty of the subject against departmental aggression.'[8] 'Aggression' and 'despotism' are strong and emotional words. What was it about administrative decision making that disturbed the legal profession? A description of how a Canadian administrative tribunal functioned in 1877 may provide some answers. The date is interesting because it is just prior to the time when the legal profession began to take control of the dispute resolution process for government activities.[9] At the time the minister of agriculture or the deputy minister would conduct hearings to resolve disputes over the forfeiture of patents for the breach of conditions. It was in one such case that the deputy minister, J.C. Taché, undertook to discuss how the tribunal he constituted functioned.[10] For him the tribunal was unexceptional and simply part of the administration of the country. In his view, the role of the judge on the tribunal was to be convinced of the substantial justice of his decision, which had to be based on sufficient information.

Taché elaborated on his approach to decision making. Clearly, the words of the law were crucial, for in them dwelt the spirit of the law, but the legislators could not foresee all the circumstances which might arise, and judges were called upon to use the language in a particular situation. The intention or spirit behind the legislation was what was important, and it was necessary to examine the history of the legislation, and not simply rely on the words used. Taché noted that jurisdiction had been transferred from judicial tribunals to administrative ones to avoid an over-strict application of certain provisions. Administrative tribunals could avoid over-strictness by deciding every case 'in a liberal manner,'[11] and applying common principles of justice.

The fact that the deputy minister had felt the need to defend the use of administrative tribunals and their approach to problem solving at this time was a sign that they were threatened, which was indeed the case. 'Over-strictness' was the norm for formalism, which attempted to create and apply precise rules to every situation. Taché was essentially describing a contextual approach to problem solving! But some thirteen years later, when the jurisdiction that he exercised was passed to the Exchequer Court, it was formalism – both in thought and in the nature of the proceedings – which was identified as the best way to adjudicate disputes. The use of precise rules for this purpose was accepted by a critical number of lawyers.

Despite the legal profession's advocacy of the judiciary and the use of formalism as the better means of dispute resolution, administrative tribunals proliferated. It was primarily the continued adherence to formalism that fuelled the sustained growth of tribunals. The formalities of the legal process made it slow and cumbersome, and the adversary system used in the courts was clearly not always the most appropriate method of resolving disputes. Courtroom adjudication was also expensive.

Another factor in the continuing growth of administrative decision makers was the belief that special knowledge was often required for a satisfactory decision, which lawyers per se did not possess.[12] The profession had adopted generality as a defining characteristic of law – the application of general rules to all situations. A recognized need for special knowledge would make resolution mechanisms that developed out of the government activity concerned seem ideal. In fact, the Court of Exchequer in England had developed out of the dispute resolution part of the finance department, and the Court of Admiralty had developed out of the department concerned with ships and shipping. Nevertheless, the legal profession rejected the idea that a lack of experience should prohibit a lawyer from adjudicating. When Albert Killam (a judge of the Supreme Court of Canada) was appointed chairman of the Board of Railway Commissioners in 1905, the profession defended his lack of expertise in railway matters vigorously. The *Canada Law Journal* stated the position forcefully: '[B]ut as to this every lawyer knows that any man of good intellectual attainments, who has had a long training at the Bar, and, in addition, the experience gained on the Bench, would have no difficulty in rapidly mastering all such matters of railway requirements and management as would come before him in connection with the duties of a member of the Board of Railway Commissioners.'[13]

Throughout the 1930s, in the years of the Depression, social unrest grew and with it the appeal of socialist ideas and a demand for greater government involvement in society. The hostility of many influential lawyers to that involvement also grew.[14] Since the work of a growing number of administrative boards involved the study of individual cases and a consideration of the totality of the facts involved, an open split occurred within the profession. Some voiced the belief that reliance on precise rules must give way to the use of broader rules based on the general policy involved.[15] Others even suggested that the formalism of the legal profession made its members ill-suited to the work required of a board.[16] A lawyer too committed to formalism would be unable to deal with the social factors that allowed an understanding of the problems involved.[17] However, the majority of lawyers and judges were convinced that the situation required greater control over government decision making.[18]

In 1934 the issue of the judiciary's power to control the decision making of the administrative tribunals hit the front pages of the newspapers. The Canadian Bar Association had arranged a dinner, held on January 19, 1934, to mark the ninetieth birthday of Sir William Mulock, chief justice of Ontario. Mulock had been postmaster general of Canada (1896–1905), and the first minister of labour (1900–1905) in Laurier's Liberal government. He retired from political life in 1905 and became a judge of the Ontario High Court. In 1923 he was made chief justice of Ontario. He had been called to the bar in 1868 and thus had been a lawyer during the years that saw the profession adopt formalism as its defining characteristic, and promote itself as pre-eminent in dispute resolution.

In an address Mulock warned that the preference for administrative tribunals to settle disputes (to the exclusion of the legal system) threatened the rule of law. Although the public had displayed no alarm, there was still a threat to society. Mulock characterized administrative decision makers as 'autocratic bodies' who exercised arbitrary power. The use of such powers placed the determination of a citizen's legal rights 'at the mercy of any non-judicial body, often ignorant of the law, bound by no law, free to disregard the evidence and the law, and practically at its own will, to dispose finally of his rights.' Such bodies did not have 'judicial temper, experience, procedure or authority.' Mulock became so agitated that he cried out, '[t]he spirit of John Hampden still lives'. The reference was a veiled cry for an uprising against the government![19]

The following day, the Toronto *Globe and Mail* offered the headline 'Rights of People Being Invaded, Says Mulock.' There was full coverage of the speech of 'Canada's Grand Old Man,' with photographs.[20] For the legal profession, the text of the address was also published in the *Canadian Bar Review*.[21]

In the United States formalism was under attack with the growth of legal realism. It was pejoratively called 'mechanical jurisprudence'[22] or 'slot machine' adjudication.[23] Some gave contextualism the name 'sociological jurisprudence' and it was described thoroughly and eloquently by Benjamin Cardozo in the lectures he gave in 1921, published as *The Nature of the Judicial Process*.[24] In Canada, however, contextualism within the legal system was hardly thriving. Mulock's address to the profession was imbued with the values of the late nineteenth century. The reception given his speech suggests that there were many who wanted no part of the changing social climate of the years between the wars.

Despite the profession's opposition, social acceptance of government regulation allowed it to grow. The judiciary's reaction to the policies of government created a sense of distrust of the courts within government. Attempts were made to shield the tribunals from judicial control by inserting provisions into legislation making decisions of a tribunal 'final,' or specifying that no action could be brought in the courts to question a decision, or saying that the tribunal had exclusive jurisdiction.[25] The judges termed these provisions 'privative clauses,' since they were intended to deprive the judges of their traditional supervisory jurisdiction.[26] While their intent was clear, they did not produce the desired result. Bora Laskin (later chief justice of Canada) was to write, 'no form of words designed to oust judicial review will succeed in doing so against the contrary wishes of a superior court judge.'[27]

In the challenge undertaken by the legal system – to do battle with the administrative state and its tribunals – the judiciary adopted as their talisman that most basic of constitutional principles, rule of law. The judges turned to the work of A.V. Dicey.[28] Dicey had argued that the growth of government regulation was a threat to what he defined as the rule of law, and he linked the growth of regulation with the decline of individualism and the rise of collectivism and socialism.[29]

It was difficult to criticize rule of law, that being our basic constitutional principle, but opponents of judicial intervention in administrative tribunals were able to criticize Dicey's specific definition. Contextualism as an alternative to formalism was not completely dead in Canada. It appeared in the work of W.P.M. Kennedy at the University of Toronto.[30] In his early (1934) article dealing with administrative law, Kennedy lamented that Dicey's views had taken hold of the profession, noting that a lack of reflection within the profession had blinded it to developments in government.[31] The most obvious contextualist at this time was John Willis, an English academic who came to Dalhousie University in 1933, and who later moved to Toronto and taught at both the city's law schools. Willis also took aim at Dicey. It was his view that Dicey had responded to a social prejudice against the vesting of power in public authorities, but that present social conditions were rapidly exposing the need for government agencies to exercise power. Willis charged that Dicey had 'canonized [the prejudice] with a name: the "rule of law."'[32] F.R. Scott of McGill University was another scholar who commented on the uncritical acceptance of 'Dicey's magnificently written misinformation on the subject.'[33]

Because the exercise of 'discretion' in making a decision affecting individual rights and freedoms is unquestionably anathema to the principle of rule of law, the judges chose to characterize administrative decision making as 'discretionary' or 'arbitrary.' Convinced that someone who does not purport to follow the plain meaning of words is exercising a personal discretion, the formalists were able to characterize administrative tribunals as purely subjective. An administrative decision maker attempts to follow a general rule articulating policy, but to do so in the context of the totality of facts (social, economic and political). Formalists would accuse such people of being guided by their own wishes. In the absence of a fixed standard, the formalists charged that administrative decision makers relied only on policy and expediency – both of their own making. In contrast, the judiciary were said to apply fixed and settled standards, enacted elsewhere.[34] This subjective/objective disparity came to characterize administrative and judicial functions, even for some who were not in favour of judicial review.[35] Evidence that this depiction took hold appears in a book written by a political scientist dealing with regulatory agencies: the author repeatedly uses the words 'administrative discretion' to portray 'administrative decision making.'[36]

Judges intent on controlling administrative tribunals had the same weapons available as had been used against the Court of Admiralty by the common law courts in the sixteenth century, in order to strip it of jurisdiction. These were the prerogative writs of *certiorari* and prohibition.[37] Issuance of the writ of *certiorari* would bring the decision of an inferior court before the superior court for review.[38] The writ of prohibition commanded an inferior court to stop proceedings.

Since the power of judicial review originated in the prerogative writ of *certiorari*, the legitimacy of judicial review of administrative action depended on the government official exercising a function that resembled that of a court (a 'judicial' function). This is probably the explanation for the continuing use of the word 'tribunal' to identify the administrative body being reviewed.[39] The requirement that a decision result from a judicial function was not that inhibiting. Willis commented that its scope was easily extended with the phrase, 'body exercising judicial function.' While the term originally embraced a court of justice, it was extended to apply to 'a body which decides questions similar to those decided by courts of justice,' and then to 'a body which has some right or duty to decide.'[40]

Categorization by the judiciary of the function of an administrative decision maker became the norm (rather than analyzing what exactly was being undertaken) and the result was that it could be classified as 'ministerial,' 'administrative,' 'executive,' 'legislative,' 'judicial,' and 'quasi-judicial.' The distinctions have been called pragmatic and result-oriented, and overall there was a great deal of confusion.[41]

Judicial power to review administrative action was also limited to matters of jurisdiction, or errors of law on the face of the record, and did not extend to the substance of the decision reached. 'Jurisdiction' meant only the authority to deal with the inquiry that was under way, and there was in theory no right to examine the decision itself. This obviously did not allow effective control of the administrative decision maker. To overcome this difficulty the judiciary defined the term 'jurisdiction' to include allegations of bad faith on the part of the tribunal; or that the tribunal had no power to make the actual decision; that it had breached the rules of natural justice, had considered the wrong question, had failed to deal with the right question, or had taken into account matters it had no right to consider. In 1971 Robert Reid's introduction to his textbook on administrative law began with the admonition that 'administrative law in Canada today is in a sorry state.'[42] Contradictions were apparent in judgments on virtually every issue and it was plain that there was general disorder in the law.

This dishevelled state of administrative law was not unique to Canada; it existed in all jurisdictions with the same legal traditions. Around the time that the Federal Court was created there was a flurry of activity in various countries involving reform of administrative law.[43] The most notable development in Canada was the publication in Ontario of the McRuer Commission Report. Critics pointed out that the Report of Chief Justice James McRuer had a pronounced orientation towards rule of law and judicial review.[44] The report was also said to be dominated by 'an abstract and legalistic' mind-set, consisting of an examination of the words of the law.[45] The McRuer Commission appeared to achieve a victory for formalism within the legal profession; the Report could have gone on the library shelf next to *The New Despotism*.

A complete victory for the supporters of judicial control of administrative action at the federal level occurred with the new jurisdiction of the Federal Court of Canada.

THE NEW JURISDICTION

In 1932, a British committee convened to examine the power of ministers had rejected the use of a special court to control administrative tribunals. The committee's position was entirely consistent with Dicey's version of rule of law, which required that a judge of an ordinary court render judicial decisions.[46] The idea had apparently settled into Canadian thinking, too. Commenting in 1934 on the creation of a special court, W.P.M. Kennedy suggested: 'if there is a real danger of bureaucracy, a system of administrative courts composed of persons imbued with the ideals of the civil service would strengthen the dangers.'[47] No such thoughts were articulated with respect to the Federal Court. Either times had changed, or there was something about the new court that did not stir these concerns. There was no reference to the Federal Court being an administrative court during the legislative process.

When the new Federal Court acquired a general authority to engage in judicial review of administrative action, the power was given to both the appellate division and the trial division. Because this jurisdiction was crucial to the court's future, the provisions are set out in full:[48]

18. The Trial Division has exclusive original jurisdiction

(a) to issue an injunction, writ of *certiorari*, writ of prohibition, writ of *mandamus* or writ of *quo warranto*, or grant declaratory relief, against any federal board, commission or other tribunal; and

(b) to hear and determine any application or other proceeding for relief in the nature of relief contemplated by paragraph (a), including any proceeding brought against the Attorney General of Canada, to obtain relief against a federal board, commission or other tribunal.

...

28. (1) Notwithstanding section 18 or the provisions of any other Act, the Court of Appeal has jurisdiction to hear and determine an application to review and set aside a decision or order, other than a decision or order of an administrative nature not required by law to be made on a judicial or quasi-judicial basis, made by or in the course of proceedings before a federal board, commission or other tribunal, upon the ground that the board, commission or tribunal

(a) failed to observe a principle of natural justice or otherwise acted beyond or refused to exercise its jurisdiction;

(b) erred in law in making its decision or order, whether or not the error appears on the face of the record; or

(c) based its decision or order on an erroneous finding of fact that it made in a perverse or capricious manner or without regard for the material before it.

...

(3) Where the Court of Appeal has jurisdiction under this section to hear and determine an application to review and set aside a decision or order, the Trial Division has no jurisdiction to entertain any proceeding in respect of that decision or order.

(4) A federal board, commission or other tribunal to which subsection (1) applies may at any stage of its proceedings refer any question or issue of law, of jurisdiction or of practice and procedure to the Court of Appeal for hearing and determination.

...

(6) Notwithstanding subsection (1), no proceeding shall be taken thereunder in respect of a decision or order of the Governor in Council, the Treasury Board, a superior court or the Pension Appeals Board or in respect of a proceeding for a service offence under the National Defence Act.

The jurisdiction of the Trial Division was expressed in the familiar language of the old prerogative writs, which the minister of justice had described as 'archaic legalisms.'[49] No change in the law was indicated. But in the appeal division, there was a widening of the judiciary's power over federal administrative decisions, and an abandonment of the old writs. Section 28(1)(b) allowed for review when there had been an error of law that did not appear on the face of the record. Prior to the creation of the Federal Court, the 'record' meant the formal recording of the proceedings of a tribunal; although it was not clear what else might be covered, it was commonly accepted that the reasons for judgment and the transcript of evidence were excluded.[50] The Federal Court of Appeal was free of these limitations and the court could look for any evidence of an error of law. Jurisdiction was also extended through section 28(1)(c), which allowed the Court to question the factual basis of a tribunal's decision.

The widened basis for judicial review of administrative decisions made the process essentially an appeal on questions of jurisdiction (including principles of natural justice) and on questions of law, and somewhat on questions of fact.[51] However, since it was technically not an 'appeal,' but an exercise of judicial review, the court could not substitute its own decision for that of the administrative body but was obliged to return the matter to the administrative decision maker if an error were found. Because the jurisdiction did resemble that of an appeal from administrative decision making bodies, the government thought that it was logical to give the jurisdiction to the new appeal division.[52]

The extended jurisdiction in section 28 surrounding judicial review was noticed early in the legislative process; the Conservative spokesman described it as 'generous,' and Andrew Brewin for the New Democratic Party called it 'a very sweeping jurisdiction.'[53] The forces favouring judicial control of administrative action had won the day.

The battles that had raged over the efficacy of the wording of privative clauses to exclude judicial intervention in the workings of an administrative tribunal were ended. The enactment of section 28 of the Federal Court Act extinguished the effect of privative clauses in federal law ('Notwithstanding ... the provisions of any other Act, the Court of Appeal has jurisdiction to hear and determine an application to review and set aside a decision or order'). The debate would now centre on the issue of how restrained or active a judge should be when reviewing a decision or order of an administrative decision maker.

There was no question that the thinking which had inspired privative clauses had given way. Preoccupation with the horror of 'politics,' 'politicians,' and 'people with government jobs,' identifiable as American ideas,[54] may have fuelled the scenarios that were presented at the committee hearings as justifications for judicial control, such as the threat of 'an absolutely ridiculous decision from the [board], something that was capricious, perverse and just off the top of somebody's desk,'[55] or a decision that was 'perniciously or wrongly made.'[56] The deputy minister of justice himself alluded to a board making a completely unjustified finding of fact.[57]

In 1952 Bora Laskin had postulated that if a board were to act completely irrationally, surely government or legislative control would be sufficient.[58] Writing in 1948, F.R. Scott accepted the view of the American jurist Felix Frankfurter that legislatures were the ultimate guardians of the liberties and welfare of the people, to as great a degree as the courts.[59] The change in Canadian thinking was acknowledged when, in 1971, the minister of justice commented that there had been a gradual erosion of the power of Parliament in its role as guardian of the people of Canada.[60] The legislators and government had passed to the legal profession the power to monitor the workings of the administration. The traditional protection of civil liberties through the political process was being rejected in favour of the legal process. This was in keeping with the prime minister's determination to introduce a charter of rights and freedoms, in tune with the American model of legally protected rights.

The Court of Appeal's extended jurisdiction over judicial review applied 'notwithstanding section 18,' and the Trial Division's jurisdiction to review was superseded expressly by subsection 28(3). Why then did section 18 exist?

The criticism that was to descend on these key sections began quietly when New Democrat Andrew Brewin identified what he saw as a confusing aspect of the provisions. Something about the two of them together created a jarring effect.[61] In response to Brewin's repeated observation that there was confusion, Deputy Minister Donald Maxwell offered the following rationale for the existence of section 18: 'Clause 18 is based on the philosophy that we want to remove the jurisdiction and prerogative matters from the Superior Courts of the provinces and place them in our own federal Superior Court.'[62] He then explained that the process of reform involved two steps: first, the jurisdiction over judicial review of federal administrative action had to be removed from the provincial courts and given to the new court; second, because the law regarding judicial review was in need of reform, a new reformed jurisdiction (specified in section 28) was directed to the appeal court. He justified the use of an appeal court with three-judge panels for judicial review in the following way: review by a single judge was problematic when most administrative boards were composed of three or more people; and giving the jurisdiction to the Trial Division would create a cumbersome three-step process (Trial Division to Court of Appeal to Supreme Court of Canada). Thus, in the end, only a 'residue' of cases would proceed to the Trial Division under section 18.[63]

Brewin was driven to say, 'I hate to say this in the presence of expert draftsmen but I wonder whether this is stated with the clarity that the public and the profession are entitled to.'[64] The minister of justice defended the bill and asserted that clause 28 was as clear as anything found in judicial decisions dealing with the prerogative writs. For John Turner the clarity lay in the distinction between 'judicial or quasi-judicial' (which meant that a hearing was required), and 'administrative' (which involved the determination of policy by the board). Brewin did not relent; he pointed out that there had long been problems distinguishing between administrative and judicial or quasi-judicial classifications.[65] It became apparent that there would be no reform involving labelling of the functions.

George Nicholls appeared before the committee as a witness and demanded a complete overhaul of the sections. Unable to fathom the division of jurisdiction between the Trial Division and the Court of Appeal, he warned of serious problems because of the two sections and unproductive litigation over which division had jurisdiction. He also regarded the retention of the labels 'judicial' and 'administrative' in section 28 as a breeder of litigation.[66] Nicholls wanted a fundamental examination of administrative law and an empirical inquiry into what the various tribunals actually did. He perceived a lack of expertise and study behind the provisions, and summarized his criticisms as follows: 'What I fear very much the Bill is doing in this particular area ... is making complicated, and I am almost tempted to say ivory-tower, provisions on the review of the decisions of administrative tribunals before the draftsmen know enough about what the tribunals do on the way to their decisions.'[67]

Even Gordon Henderson, the spokesman for the Canadian Bar Association, who was generally defensive about the court, and very uncritical of the bill,[68] acknowledged that he found it terribly difficult to tell whether one should be in the Court of Appeal or in the Trial Division.[69]

On the final day of committee hearings Andrew Brewin moved an amendment to strike out clause 18 in order to remove the confusion between clauses 18 and 28. The appeal division was to have the reviewing power, and questions of whether an order was administrative or not were to be eliminated. However, his attempt came to nothing.

The government was convinced that section 18 was necessary because it contained a verbal formula which would take the jurisdiction over judicial review of decisions made by federal administrative bodies away from provincial superior courts. The government held firm and when amendments to the law were proposed in 1983, the minister of justice at the time, Mark MacGuigan, asserted: 'If no reference is made to the "ancient" remedies in the Federal Court Act, the courts may find that judicial review of federal tribunals is split between the Federal Court and the superior courts of the provinces, a result which the 1971 amendments to the Federal Court Act sought to avoid.'[70] The entrenchment of formalism and its emphasis on words made it imperative to find a verbal formula that would limit the inclination of provincial superior court judges to retain jurisdiction. Clauses 18 and 28 emerged from the legislative process intact.

When the Federal Court Act came into force Robert Reid's textbook was available to the legal profession. His position was clear: he could not understand why both provisions had been included.[71] He saw them as overlapping. He could not agree that section 18 contained the words needed to end the jurisdiction of the provincial superior courts, and in section 28 he saw only the shadow of section 18, bereft of the difficulties associated with the old remedies.

Reid also considered it 'unfortunate' that the legislation contained the words 'administrative,' 'judicial,' and 'quasi-judicial' to indicate differing functions of an administrative decision-making body. Reid disparaged any distinction between 'administrative' and 'judicial' as 'almost meaningless.' He found retention of such language both unnecessary and distressing.

Reid was also sceptical about the crucial words which limited the jurisdiction of the appeal division: 'an administrative nature not required by law to be made on a judicial or quasi-judicial basis.' It would remain for the judges to give appropriate meaning to these words. The old prerogative writs had carried with them the limitation, based on their origin, of applying to inferior courts, that is, bodies exercising a judicial function, and Reid could only ponder why such a relationship was intentionally continued. If the commentators were right, the life of the new court was going to be difficult.

Peter Russell speculated that creation of the Federal Court was an 'inside job' brought about by officials in the department of justice, the minister of justice, John Turner, and possibly members of the court itself.[72] Authorship of the troublesome sections 18 and 28 became a sensitive issue. Jackett, once employed in the legislative drafting section of the Department of Justice, is generally considered the draftsman, with intellectual input being offered by the deputy minister of justice. The very establishment of the Federal Court is often attributed to Jackett, who became its first chief justice.

THE JACKETT YEARS, 1971–1979

16

The New Court

When the Federal Court of Canada came into being on June 1, 1971, it was an amalgam, with some characteristics indicating it was one court, and others pointing to the existence of two distinct courts – the Court of Appeal and the Trial Division.

The Trial Division was essentially the Exchequer Court with a broader jurisdiction, particularly with respect to maritime matters.[1] In contrast, the Federal Court of Appeal was entirely new, both as an intermediate appeal court between the Trial Division and the Supreme Court of Canada, but especially as an administrative court. That newness makes the Court of Appeal of special interest, and consideration of it dominates the remaining chapters of this study.

The judges of the Trial Division of the new Federal Court, the renamed Exchequer Court, would continue the task of travelling across the country to conduct trials. What was unusual was that the Court of Appeal was also made mobile.[2] As a travelling appeal court it was special within Canada, but this aspect of the new Federal Court of Appeal did not attract any attention during the legislative process leading up to the Court's creation.

THE JUDGES

Before its transformation the Exchequer Court had a complement of eight judges; the new Federal Court had twelve. Of the twelve, eight positions were allocated to the Trial Division, while the Court of Appeal received four.

It was never questioned that the judges of the new court would be chosen from the eight judges of the Exchequer Court, who, with the exception of President Jackett, differed from each other only in seniority. Giving the judges of the two divisions equal stature ensured a measure of peaceful co-existence. In this way the institution resembled a single court, but the fact that one of the 'courts' was the appeal court for the other demanded that the single-court notion be considerably restrained.

President Jackett wrote to each member of the Exchequer Court on February 3, 1971 (before confirmation of assignments to their respective positions in the new court), cautioning them about potential problems should there be uninhibited contact amongst them:[3]

It will be essential to the proper functioning of an appeal system that there be no tendency to involve appeal judges in the formulation of a trial judgment (because they must have open minds when an appeal is argued) and that there be no tendency for the appeal judges to take into account their personal regard for the capabilities of the trial judge (because that is not relevant to the determination of an appeal).[4]

This segregation clearly had the potential to create two distinct groups of judges, with consequent discontent. Jackett addressed that by saying that he did not want to limit communication between the judges to a purely social nature, but that he urged them to recognize 'that it is essential that there be no collaboration or personal involvement that is incompatible with a proper appeal system.' This meant that there was to be no discussion of a case until it was finally decided ('passed into "jurisprudence"'), nor 'during the period immediately after.' Jackett was clear that 'a *post mortem* cannot fail to have an improper effect on the adjudication process and may have a tendency to impair the personal relationships involved.' The President wanted a cooling-off period and, to simplify matters, he proposed that a convention be adopted that there be no discussion about a particular case until at least one year after it was finally decided.[5]

While discussion of a specific case was to be avoided, Jackett endorsed full discussion of other matters of concern to the judges. He mentioned that trial judges might help appeal judges with problems originating in boards and commissions. As judges of the administrative court, the Court of Appeal judges were to be provided (if need be) with factual information about the working of the administrative system. An internal source of facts was a characteristic of the administrative decision-making process.

The legislation did provide that the judges of each division were ex-officio members of the other division,[6] but, because of the sensitivity surrounding the appeal process, a judge of one division has rarely participated in proceedings in the other.

Four of the twelve places on the court were to be filled by Quebec-trained lawyers,[7] though as a concession to the notion of there being one court the legislation did not stipulate how they were to be allocated between the divisions. It was contemplated that if the position of chief justice were filled by a francophone, that of associate chief justice would go to an anglophone.[8]

The most significant indication that the court was one court was that the seniority of all judges would run from the moment of their appointment to the court, and not to a particular division. Thus, a judge who had been in the Trial Division for twenty years and was then appointed to the appeal division would become an appellate judge with twenty years' seniority.

The selection of a chief justice was not difficult; President Jackett of the Exchequer Court was appointed as the first chief justice of the Federal Court of Canada. The bilingualism and biculturalism of the institution was established with the appointment of Camilien Noël (a francophone from Quebec) as associate chief justice – the title given to the head of the Trial Division. Jacques Dumoulin (also a francophone from Quebec) was the senior puisne judge on the Exchequer Court, but he was seventy-three and in poor health; Noël was the fourth judge in precedence on the court. The result was that Dumoulin and Thurlow, both senior to Noël, were appointed to the Court of Appeal along with Jackett; the four judges junior to Noël joined the Trial Division. It was a fortuitous division of judicial talent.

Thus on the day that the Federal Court of Canada came into existence its members were as follows:

Court of Appeal
Wilbur Jackett, Chief Justice
Jacques Dumoulin
Arthur Thurlow

Trial Division
Camilien Noël, Associate Chief Justice

Alexander Cattanach
Hugh Gibson
Allison Walsh
Roderick Kerr

The date of appointment for each of the judges was June 1, 1971. The Trial Division was brought to its full complement of eight judges with the appointment of Louis Pratte on June 10, Darrel Heald on June 30, and Frank Collier on September 16.

Louis Pratte was a francophone from Quebec, and the fourth Quebec lawyer. Pratte was only forty-four. Both his father and grandfather had been judges on the Quebec Court of Appeal, and his brother, Yves Pratte, would later be a judge on the Supreme Court of Canada for a short time (1977–9). After practising law for a decade in Quebec City, Louis Pratte moved to the academic world and taught law at the University of Laval from 1963 until his appointment to the court. He was the first lawyer to join the court from a position as a full-time teacher of law.

Darrel Heald was from Saskatchewan. He had practised law in Regina, and had served as provincial attorney general after his election as a Liberal to the Legislative Assembly in 1964. He continued in the position until he tired of politics, and was appointed to the Federal Court at fifty-two.

Frank Collier was the first judge of the court to come from British Columbia. He had practised law in Vancouver for twenty years before being appointed to the Federal Court at forty-nine. Collier was the 'rota judge' for British Columbia – a concession to western fears that the Federal Court was an eastern institution whose members would visit the province only on occasion. The rota system ensured that a judge would be assigned to Vancouver on a continuing basis; Collier became the resident judge for the province. Without the promise of being able to stay on the coast, it is unlikely that Collier would have accepted the appointment.[9]

These first three appointments to the new court offered a wide range of backgrounds. Significantly, there was no preference for any particular background in selecting the first judges of the Federal Court's Trial Division.

Although the major innovation for the court was the judicial review jurisdiction of the Court of Appeal, no one expected that this workload would be great. Indeed the deputy minister of justice had predicted that the work was unlikely to consist of more than six cases per year.[10] This view would explain why the staffing of the Court of Appeal reflected its role as an appeal court rather than a court possessing original jurisdiction over the judicial review of administrative action. The prediction of little work as an administrative court proved correct in the early years, but the appellate workload was equally light. No significant problems arose when, because of Jacques Dumoulin's health problems, there were effectively only two judges sitting until January 1973, when Louis Pratte was moved from the Trial Division to the appeal court. Dumoulin had resigned for reasons of ill health on December 1, 1972, a few months short of what would have been his normal retirement date.

The Court of Appeal was brought up to its full complement of judges in April 1973, with the appointment of John Urie. Urie had practised law in Ottawa for twenty-five years and was appointed at the age of fifty-three. The workload of the appeal court was sufficiently manageable that Urie was allowed to undertake work in the Trial Division – an appointment he would have preferred. He considered himself to be a good practical lawyer and he identified the Court of Appeal as a place for those with an academic turn of mind. Since Chief Justice Jackett considered trial experience necessary for an appeal judge, he easily permitted Urie to become in effect the eighth judge on the Trial Division, leaving the Court of Appeal with three judges.

Finding lawyers who would come to Ottawa to serve as judges was not an easy task. Urie had grown up in Ottawa and was content to spend his legal career there. He had turned down offers of judicial positions at Toronto and other places. Francophone lawyers were particularly reluctant to leave Quebec for what was identified as an English city in both language and culture. Urie was appointed in spite of the fact that the statutory requirement that four appointments come from the province of Quebec had not been satisfied. The fourth Quebec judge was ultimately selected on September 13, 1973, when Raymond Decary was appointed to the Trial Division. Decary was fifty-one years old, and a francophone taxation lawyer from Montreal. He had been a member of the Quebec bar for twenty-eight years.

Patrick Mahoney was appointed to the Trial Division on the same day as Decary. Mahoney hailed from Alberta, and had practised corporate and taxation law in Calgary. At the time of his appointment he was a member of the Liberal government in Ottawa, as minister of state. Mahoney was given seniority over Decary.

George Addy was appointed on September 17, 1973. Addy had grown up in Ottawa and had practised law there from 1945 until 1967, when he was appointed to the Ontario High Court. He had had extensive military experience as a member of the Régiment de Hull, an armoured unit, from 1934 to 1940, and then on active service until the end of World War II. Following the war he became commander of the Canadian Officers Training Corps at the University of Ottawa (1945–56); after that he served as commanding officer of the Régiment de Hull, retiring in 1958 with the rank of lieutenant colonel. His military background gave him the credentials to be appointed to the Court Martial Appeal Board when it was created in 1953. His mother was a francophone, and he was bilingual.

Forces within Ontario had always maintained that the province should have equal or better representation than Quebec on the Supreme Court of Canada; there was also a keen and deliberate alignment of provincial and national interests.[11] In the years of a separate Exchequer Court (1887–1971), there had never been more than one judge from Ontario on the court at any given time.[12] The Ontario bar had not readily identified with the Exchequer and then the Federal Court. When Urie and Addy were appointed in 1973, the number of judges from Ontario rose to three, and would remain at that level throughout the 1970s. Their appointments may have been a response to concerns within Ontario, but given that the legal profession in Ontario centred on Toronto and that the two new judges had Ottawa origins (although Addy had been a High Court judge), there may still have been a distance between the Federal Court and Ontario's legal culture.

Four new positions were created on June 28, 1973, divided equally between the Trial Division and the Court of Appeal.[13] The change from a 2:1 ratio of trial judges to appeal judges to a 5:3 ratio (ten trial judges to six appeal judges)[14] signalled growth in the work relating to judicial review of administrative action, but it was apparent that the workload of the Court of Appeal was still not pressing. None of the positions was filled quickly. On April 11, 1974, William Ryan was appointed to the Court of Appeal; the second position in that court was filled on September 1, 1975 when Gerald Le Dain was appointed, over two years after the position had been created. A similar delay occurred in the Trial Division: Jean-Eudes Dubé was appointed on April 9, 1975, followed by Louis Marceau on December 23, 1975. These were the last appointments made while Wilbur Jackett presided as chief justice.

The last four appointments have more than usual interest. The chief justice was comfortable with a formalistic approach to law and lawyering, and was not favourably disposed towards the intellectual. He was thus not favourably disposed towards lawyers who had chosen an academic career. Jackett was also acutely aware of the need to distance the court from government, since it dealt with litigation involving government. He was instrumental in setting up the office of Commissioner of Federal Judicial Affairs, to act as a formal buffer between the government and the administrative concerns of the court. He went so far as to prohibit judges from eating at the parliamentary restaurant, because they would be seen as mixing with politicians. It is decidedly curious that the four appointments which closed his term hailed from academic and political circles! To the extent that Jackett was consulted, he apparently had no influence.

William Ryan, fifty-four at the time of this appointment, had been born and raised in New Brunswick. He started teaching law in 1950 at the University of New Brunswick, assuming responsibility as dean of the Faculty of Law throughout the years 1956–71. He was a member of the Law Reform Commission of Canada from 1971 until his appointment to the Federal Court of Appeal. The work of the reform commission was academic in nature.

Gerald Le Dain, an anglophone from Quebec, had earned his law degree from McGill University. He was fifty at the time of his appointment. While he did have some experience working in private practice in Quebec and as a corporate counsel, he was better known for his academic career. A law professor at McGill from 1953 to 1959 and in 1966/7, he became Dean of Toronto's Osgoode Hall Law School in 1967, even though he had a Quebec civil law background. He served in this capacity until 1972, and remained as a member of the law faculty until his appointment to the Federal Court in 1975. His tenure as dean was occupied to a great extent by his chairing of the Commission of Inquiry into the Non-medical Use of Drugs, 1969–73.

The third academic was Louis Marceau from Quebec. Marceau had practised law for a few years before joining the Faculty of Law at Laval University in 1958. He became dean of the faculty in 1965. In 1969 he left academic life to set up the office of ombudsman for Quebec, a position he held until his appointment.

Jean-Eudes Dubé was a francophone from New Brunswick, educated in the law of England. A career politician, he was first elected as a member of the Campbellton City Council, and after several unsuccessful attempts, became a Liberal Member of Parliament in 1962. Re-elected five times, Dubé served as minister of veteran's affairs (1968–72) and minister of public works (1972–5). He had enjoyed his time in the capital and wanted to stay; specifically, he wanted an appointment to the court.[15]

Dubé's appointment is of added interest in that it was in conflict with the requirement in the Federal Court Act that there be six judges in the Court of Appeal and ten in the Trial Division. When appointed to the Trial Division on April 9, 1975, he was the eleventh judge; however, there were only five Court of Appeal judges, so the overall complement did not exceed the mandated sixteen. When Camilien Noël resigned on July 4, 1975, the number of judges in the Trial Division was reduced to the required ten. Dubé's appointment as an 'extra' trial judge did not attract any public attention, which tends to substantiate the view that the Federal Court was operating in obscurity.

The appointments of Patrick Mahoney and Jean-Eudes Dubé prompted Joe Clark, less than a year away from becoming leader of the Progressive Conservative party and Leader of the Opposition, to rise in the House and ask whether it was the intention of the government 'to turn the Federal Court of Canada into a sort of second Senate and resting place for the relics of the treasury benches.'[16] The phrase 'second Senate' was catchy enough to have an unpleasant staying power, much to the detriment of the court.

With Marceau's appointment the number of judges from Quebec exceeded for the first time the required minimum of four. The five judges from Quebec made Quebec representation a third, rather than a quarter, which was a traditional proportion in the Supreme Court of Canada.

Other changes altered the composition of the divisions during the 1970s. Roderick Kerr resigned on September 1, 1975, at the age of seventy-three; on December 4, 1975, Darrel Heald was moved to the Court of Appeal from the Trial Division. Arthur Thurlow moved from the Court of Appeal to the Trial Division on the same date as associate chief justice, filling the vacancy left by the resignation of Camilien Noël earlier in the year. Thurlow's appointment as associate chief justice negated the intention to juxtapose a francophone and an anglophone in the leadership positions of the Court. Chief Justice Jackett and Associate Chief Justice Thurlow were both anglophones and common law lawyers.

With these changes in place, the judicial personnel of the court would remain stable for the next four years. The Court of Appeal consisted of: Wilbur Jackett (Chief Justice), Louis Pratte, John Urie, William Ryan, Gerald Le Dain, and Darrel Heald. The Trial Division judges were Arthur Thurlow (Associate Chief Justice), Alexander Cattanach, Hugh Gibson, Allison Walsh, Frank Collier, Patrick Mahoney, Raymond Decary, George Addy, Jean-Eudes Dubé, and Louis Marceau.

THE CHIEF JUSTICE

Not since the days when a single judge constituted the Exchequer Court of Canada did a judge dominate the court as much as Wilbur Jackett did during the 1970s. One judge described the situation as Jackett being half the court (the other half consisting of the rest of the judges!).

Jackett was stiff, organized, and methodical. His personal manner was domineering, which made it a challenge to work with him. Seldom would the other Court of Appeal judges on a panel disagree with him. He was committed to getting judgments out fast. One judge commented, 'He produced decisions as if they were products of some kind.' He usually delivered his judgment orally following a hearing, and it was likely to be the judgment of the Court. He would prepare the judgment during the hearing and it would be finished when the hearing was over. While the Chief Justice would not overtly insist on concurrence, the temptation for the others to concur was often overwhelming because of their own pressure of work and Jackett's personality.

Jackett had assumed responsibility for the Exchequer Court at a time when delay had reached an unprecedented level, and he changed things completely. He brought to the Federal Court of Appeal the same passion for speedy decision making.

DEPUTY JUDGES

The use of deputy judges had been authorized in 1920, and had first occurred in 1942, but it was not until the creation of the Federal Court of Appeal and their use by Chief Justice Jackett that they became noteworthy.

While it was true that the workload of the Court of Appeal was not heavy, there was the requirement that a panel of judges consist of no less that three.[17] In the early years, with Dumoulin ill, only the Chief Justice and Thurlow were available. Jackett relied on deputy judges, believing that these individuals had a positive impact because they added a local presence in the places where they were used. Jackett or Thurlow would often preside with two deputy judges.

In 1971, legislation authorized a new category of judge for provincial superior courts. Supernumerary judges were judges who elected to take a reduced workload on reaching the age of seventy with ten years' judicial experience.[18] Judges who chose to become supernumerary were no longer counted as part of the normal complement of the court and thus someone else could be appointed to occupy the vacant position. The existence of these judges meant that a group of experienced judges was available for part-time work. The legislation creating this new category of judge did not apply to the Federal Court. Chief Justice Jackett was not favourably disposed to the creation or use of supernumerary judges and preferred to rely on deputy judges. The Chief Justice was originally authorized to request a maximum of ten deputy judges;[19] in 1973 he requested and was granted authority to increase the maximum number of deputy judges who might act at the same time to twenty.[20] This remains the operative Order in Council.

The use of deputy judges caused some tension within the court. Several judges opposed the practice on the grounds that the use of retired judges gave the impression that the Federal Court was using judges past their prime. Some saw the use of county court judges as demeaning to the Federal Court. Some perceived the deputy judges as 'just bodies' who were present to constitute a quorum. Others could not credit the deputy judges with sufficient interest or commitment, since the Federal Court was not 'their' court. There was a feeling that the chief justice exerted undue influence over the deputy judges; the occasions when he sat with two of them were seen as examples of Jackett acting as the court. However, Jackett could point to two occasions when he sat with two deputy judges and dissented, at least in part.[21] Given that it was rare for Jackett to dissent at any time, these instances were quite remarkable.

17

The Life of the Court

At a conference dealing with administrative law held at the University of British Columbia in October 1979, David Mullan, a leading administrative law scholar, opened his presentation with the statement: 'Bashing the Federal Court is an easy act to get into and I am not going to hesitate.' He concluded with the comment that the procedural and remedial aspects of judicial review of federal administrative action had been complicated 'beyond anyone's wildest dreams.'[1] These two statements highlight the life of the court as an administrative court in the 1970s.

The Exchequer Court had existed in virtual anonymity, but such was not to be the fate of the Federal Court. Not only did the administrative law jurisdiction attract comment and criticism, but almost from the moment of the court's creation its very existence became a matter of debate. The role of the Federal Court was on the agenda of no less a forum than the federal-provincial conference of attorneys general and ministers of justice, held in Ottawa on March 12 and 13, 1975.[2] The province of British Columbia took the lead: Attorney General Alex Mac-Donald wasted no words and called for the Court's abolition. Quebec, at whose request the item had been put at the top of the agenda, expressed sympathy for British Columbia's position, but accepted the existence of a federal court, albeit with reduced jurisdiction.

The federal government appreciated that the provinces feared the establishment of a dual system of courts: having created the Federal

Court, the federal government might well extend the court's jurisdiction. Otto Lang (federal minister of justice) was quick to assure those concerned that the federal government had no such intention, and that he did not foresee any creation of a dual system of courts along the lines of the American system. As it turned out, there was more to the opposition than this.

The Federal Court was again on the agenda at the next federal-provincial conference of attorneys general and ministers of justice, held in Halifax on October 23 and 24, 1975. Otto Lang made a definite promise of changes to the jurisdiction of the court. He committed to creating more concurrent jurisdiction in matters such as Crown liability, and abandoning jurisdiction in matters relating to extradition and parole. Alberta concurred with British Columbia's demand for jurisdiction over judicial review of federal administrative agencies, but the federal government was adamant that the uniformity of law regarding such bodies must be preserved. The provinces of Ontario and Manitoba agreed with Ottawa on this point.

The legal profession entered the debate in 1976. Prompted by comments received from across Canada, the Canadian Bar Association established a special committee to examine and report on problems with the Federal Court. Lorne Campbell, a Winnipeg lawyer with almost thirty years of practice experience and a former president of the association (1970–71), was chosen as the sole member. The following year, the association appointed Michael (D.M.M.) Goldie and Brian A. Crane as additional members. Goldie had been a member of the British Columbia bar since 1950, practising law in Vancouver. Delivering a paper at the 1976 annual meeting of the Canadian Bar Association, he had argued that the Federal Court was 'largely unnecessary.' Goldie gave no specific reason for his challenge to the Court beyond opposition *per se* to the existence of a federal court.[3] In his view, some of the Court's jurisdiction was 'constitutionally questionable.' Brian Crane had practised law in Ottawa for fifteen years. Born and raised in British Columbia, Crane had moved to Ontario following his graduation from the University of British Columbia's Faculty of Law.

Opposition to the Federal Court from the west coast was quite pronounced, and would prove persistent. The root cause was an attitude – that British Columbia had achieved sufficient stature as a political and social entity, geographically separated from the rest of Canada, to resent being 'ruled' by people in the east. Complaints about eastern domination also pervaded other parts of western Canada, most notably Alberta.

The special committee's report was completed in 1977, and approved by the Canadian Bar Association at its annual meeting in 1978.[4] A copy was forwarded to the minister of justice. As a basic proposition the report acknowledged the existence of a federal court; it clearly rejected any suggestion of a dual system of courts similar to that existing in the United States. The Canadian Bar Association summarized the report in its newspaper *The National*, and asserted that a dual system 'would be regarded with horror by most lawyers.'[5]

The committee also reviewed the areas of law within the court's jurisdiction. Expropriation was seen as a local matter, even when it was the federal government that was taking the land. This said, the authors of the report revealed the sentiments which may have been operating to challenge the functioning of the court. The authors stated that the use of the local courts would better serve the ends of justice, since the person whose land was being taken might perceive the Federal Court, 'if only by reason of its name' as 'an arm of the executive branch.'[6] With regard to claims against the government (the issue of Crown liability, which had attracted attention at the federal-provincial conferences in 1975), the report identified a definite need for change in claims involving tort and contract disputes. The fact that there were no longer special rules of any significance applicable to actions against the government was reason enough to suggest that the exclusive jurisdiction of the Federal Court had become an anomaly.

The committee had no apparent difficulty accepting the court's jurisdiction in the traditional areas of law which were perceived as highly specialized. Admiralty, industrial property, and taxation were areas of practice which the legal profession agreed were suitable for a specialized tribunal, albeit one with a package of different specialties. The facts that admiralty had been made a concurrent area in 1971, meaning that an action could be brought either in the Federal Court or in the appropriate provincial court at the choice of the litigant, and that industrial property was concurrent for infringement actions, made the court's having jurisdiction over these areas more palatable.

Despite the criticisms that swirled about the court over its jurisdiction in administrative law, its life as an administrative court was reasonably secure. The report quietly endorsed the retention of a national court by acknowledging the need for consistency and for the expeditious processing of cases involving the review of federal administrative decisions across the country. Nonetheless, it did advocate some encroachment on the court's jurisdiction. The report recommended that unemployment insurance cases be handled by provincial court judges or by an administrative board in order to alleviate the workload of the court. Concern with workload also lay behind a recommendation that the ever-increasing numbers of immigration cases be removed from the court. The sizeable workload associated with immigration matters had the potential to overload the provincial courts as well, and an administrative board was proposed to address the need. There was no discussion about what difference there would be between using a federal administrative board and adding more judges to the Federal Court, nor was there any indication in the report that the writers were conscious of a need to do so.

Whatever the degree of disgruntlement, the government made it clear that the Federal Court's jurisdiction over judicial review of administrative action was not negotiable. By way of example, in the 1977 debates surrounding creation of the Human Rights Commission, it was proposed that an appeal to the Federal Court be provided. The minister of justice, Ronald Basford, acknowledged that the whole of the Federal Court Act was under review as a result of discussions and consultations with provincial attorneys general, but he declared that, whatever the outcome, judicial supervision over federal administrative agencies would remain with the court. Basford maintained that this was the purpose of the Federal Court.[7]

While the jurisdiction over control of administrative decisions may have been secure, the means by which it was exercised was not safe from attack. The provisions in the Federal Court Act detailing the jurisdiction (sections 18 and 28) were loudly condemned. In spite of the explanation offered in 1970 for the existence of section 18, the report's authors asserted that no good reason had ever been advanced for the division in jurisdiction between the Trial Division and the Court of Appeal. Complaints that the provisions created general confusion for lawyers caused them to be colourfully portrayed in the National's summary as 'a legal rat's nest!'

The final area of jurisdiction considered in the report was criminal law; given the legal profession's attitude to this matter over the years, the committee's negative reaction was no surprise. 'The Federal Court should not be a court of criminal jurisdiction at all,' it said.[8] The paramount factor was a considerable degree of jealousy regarding jurisdiction over criminal matters. Provincial authorities laid full claim to the administration of criminal justice.

It was the concluding sentence of both the Report and the Summary Report that synthesized the position of the Canadian Bar Association: 'It is important to reaffirm the principle that the citizen should have access to a local court unless there are compelling reasons to the contrary.'

The Canadian Bar Association was not alone in urging reform of the Federal Court. The Law Reform Commission of Canada was also scrutinizing the court's role. The commission had been established in 1970, the same year as the Federal Court. The centrepiece of what the minister of justice called a 'continuum of law reform directed to the protection of individual rights from the power and remoteness of modern government,'[9] the commission's task was to examine areas of law and to recommend changes which would ensure that the law was in tune with changing social values.

The commission undertook a study of administrative law and the Federal Court. The growing debate among members of the legal profession about the court's jurisdiction caused the commission to publish in 1977 both a working paper, which set forth the tentative views of the commission, and a thorough background paper written by David Mullan.[10]

Mullan was on record as highly critical of the jurisdiction provisions for the Federal Court in 1970. In an article published in 1973, he acknowledged G.V.V. Nicholls and his critical submissions to the legislative committee. Mullan also echoed Robert Reid, who had said in his 1971 textbook on administrative law that there existed at that time a 'confused tangle of jurisprudence' on the relevant issues, creating in effect an intellectual maze for the profession.[11] Mullan viewed the legislation as 'seriously inadequate,' and the title of his article summed up his opinion: 'The Federal Court Act: A Misguided Attempt at Administrative Law Reform?'[12]

Another writer referred to 'the byzantine structure of the Federal Court Act,'[13] while a judge who was interviewed for this book called the sections a 'dog's breakfast.'

The division of the judicial review jurisdiction between the Federal Court's Trial Division and the Court of Appeal was particularly worrisome to David Mullan and provoked him to conclude that it demonstrated 'a lack of awareness on the part of the draftsmen of modern trends in judicial review.'[14] By 1977, a major increase in the number of cases reaching the Federal Court had exacerbated the problems Mullan alluded to. The court's administrative law docket was said to be staggering, and in his background paper Mullan speculated that the court was beginning to have considerable difficulty handling the caseload. While he did not think that there was any reason to question the ability of the judges (indeed, he pointed out that some had considerable background in administrative law) he observed bluntly that they had not been able to find their way out of the 'maze.' Concluding that the judges had taken a very traditional approach to the principles of judicial review, Mullan charged that they had made no significant contribution to the law in the six years of the court's existence. The split jurisdiction and the wording of sections 18 and 28 had produced a procedural morass and had 'generated an incredible amount of litigation involving interpretative difficulties.'[15] Now more than ever, he concluded, a fundamental reordering of the judicial review jurisdiction of the court was needed.[16]

In his background paper, Professor Mullan exposed the root cause of the tangle of cases that existed in the area. When assessing the court's application of the law of judicial review, as well as the rules which made up the 'maze,' one had to be conscious of the social values that were conditioning the notions of the proper role of the courts in relation to the administrative process: '[For] some, an interventionist court may be a good thing as it ensures that the courts are being vigilant in protecting individual rights, liberties and interests against a burgeoning bureaucracy. For others, an interventionist court means simply too much interference in the affairs of allegedly expert statutory decision makers by an inexpert court.' Mullan then added a spin that showed his own perception of the role of a court. He considered an assessment of the court 'extremely difficult because of the enormous task involved in understanding all the various decision making processes that are potentially the subject of review under the Act ... Absent an in-depth understanding of all federal enabling statutes, any assessment becomes very impressionistic.'[17] In Mullan's view the judges had to become immersed in the administrative process and could not deal with the problems in abstraction. Mullan wanted the judges to abandon their formalistic approach for a contextual one.

The Working Paper of the Law Reform Commission[18] was emphatic that judicial review of federal administrative action should be undertaken by a federal court. The commission nonetheless sided with those who favoured very limited judicial intervention, which should occur 'in only a small fraction of cases.' There was concern that too much judicial interference would frustrate the operation of administrative authorities and also overload the courts. The importance of judicial review of administrative action lay in its 'symbolic value.'[19]

That the commission was aware of problems within the Federal Court itself is evident from the fact that the Working Paper went beyond administrative law to deal with certain points directed at the court and its chief justice. The paper juxtaposed the statement that the Court of Appeal might be noted for 'the efficiency and expeditiousness with which it has performed its work' with the recommendation that the court might better fulfil its appellate function if the judges were given time for reflection and for writing judgments 'that the Trial Division and the tribunals can look to for guidance that goes well beyond the particular facts of the case.'[20] The use of deputy judges (so favoured by the chief justice) attracted negative comment: they were said to create inconsistency in approach.

The Law Reform Commission recommended that the problem of the Federal Court's jurisdiction over judicial review could be resolved if the review were undertaken by the Trial Division, with an appeal to the Court of Appeal. The commission also advocated the abandonment of the prerogative writs and the creation of a single form of proceeding.

It should be noted that this had been attempted in 1971 through section 28, but the naming of the old prerogative writs in section 18 had acted as a magnet for the attention of lawyers. The legal profession perceived that the writs had been retained, which had burdened the new power of judicial review found in section 28.[21]

The commission's Working Paper gave clear notice that it was digging deep into the legal process. It acknowledged that legislated reform of the area of judicial review was difficult because of judicial attitudes. As well, the real reasons behind judicial decisions were said to be unknowable because they were so often not articulated in the judgments. The Working Paper identified judicial law making as the best method of reform, but found little evidence that Canadian courts were likely to take the initiative.[22] The paper concluded with a bold and pointed criticism of the judicial process dominant at the time: 'Too often under existing law, reasons are replaced by a judicial search for quasi-judicial elements or tags, often motivated by a preferred solution.'[23] The depth and edge of this criticism of the basic methodology of the judiciary would not have been familiar to most lawyers and judges.

In October 1979 Chief Justice Jackett resigned in the midst of what the Law Reform Commission called a 'heated debate' over the jurisdiction of the Federal Court.[24] The problems surrounding sections 18 and 28 had actually caused the government to consider eliminating the administrative law jurisdiction of the court – something that had been unthinkable only a few years before.[25]

British Columbia and Alberta opposed the court because they identified it with 'eastern interests.' Quebec favoured a restricted jurisdiction that allowed its courts to assume jurisdiction over as many cases as possible. The problems created by the administrative law jurisdiction threatened to engulf it. And there was more. The Ontario judiciary had never been favourably disposed to a federal court, and had at best tolerated it. Also, until the creation of the Federal Court, the Ontario superior court had had a claim to be the appropriate court for judicial review of federal administrative bodies. Given the open debate about the future of the federal court taking place in the late 1970s, it was not surprising that a view of the Federal Court from the perspective of the Ontario legal profession would appear publicly. This happened in a lecture given by P.S.A. Lamek, a Toronto lawyer, in the Special Lectures series of the Law Society of Upper Canada in 1978.[26]

The picture that appears in the lecture is that of a battle between the Federal Court and the provincial superior courts. The federal government is identified as the aggressor because the Federal Court Act contained 'encroachments upon the traditional jurisdiction of the provincial courts.'[27] After conversations with 'many, many lawyers,' Lamek had been persuaded that there was a 'widespread uneasiness and even suspicion about the Federal Court among members of our Bar.'[28] Behind the feeling of unease was unfamiliarity with the court. Very few lawyers had had much to do with the Federal Court, the general impression being that the court was primarily concerned with arcane and highly technical areas of the law such as income tax and patents. Lamek noted that members of the Ontario bar did not know or had not practised with most of the judges, meaning that they had been chosen from other provincial bars. He also observed that there was a vague fear that the judges were more markedly 'Crown-oriented' than the judges of the provincial courts.[29]

Ontario had squared off to reject the Federal Court because it was foreign and unfamiliar and a threat to the existing provincial system. If Ottawa should ever decide to move toward a dual system, Lamek warned that the judges of the provincial courts would use the constitution to defend themselves from any threat posed by the Federal Court. 'Jurisdictional imperialism' had always been kept within constitutional bounds, he asserted, and judges would continue to be vigilant.[30]

It would not be long before the provincial superior courts would indeed immerse themselves in the constitution, and, with the immeasurable help of the Supreme Court of Canada, assume an unprecedented amount of judicial power. There would be a declaration that a dual system of courts could not constitutionally exist in Canada.

18

The Work of the Court

As always, it is the work of the court – the cases considered – which provides information about the performance of the judges, as well as clues to the sources of future difficulties (and how they might have been avoided), and other matters concerning the court's existence.

THE *NATIONAL INDIAN BROTHERHOOD* CASE

It was not long before the Federal Court was asked to exercise its new administrative law jurisdiction. The Federal Court Act had been proclaimed in force on June 1, 1971. Just two weeks later, the National Indian Brotherhood, Indian-Eskimo Association, Union of Ontario Indians, and Canadian-Indian Centre of Toronto applied to the Trial Division under section 18 of the Act for a number of orders to be directed to the Executive Committee of the Canadian Radio-Television Commission (CRTC). One order sought would force the CRTC to decide whether it would be in the public interest to hold a public hearing about a complaint lodged by the applicants, and to give reasons for the decision. Alternatively, a second order would force the commission to forward to the court all correspondence and records concerning the complaint. A final order would direct the commission to hold a public inquiry.[1]

The complaint made by the various native groups was about a proposed broadcast of a television program. The National Indian Brotherhood, an organization that represented the Indians of Canada, the Union of Ontario Indians, an organization that represented the Indians of Ontario, and the Indian-Eskimo Association and Canadian-Indian Centre of Toronto, two organizations interested in the social, cultural, and economic advancement of the Indians and other native ethnic groups of Canada, wanted to stop the broadcast of the show *The Taming of the Canadian West*. The program was scheduled to be shown by the CTV television network on Sunday evening, July 18, 1971. The production was a documentary which dealt with the European settlement of the west; it included depictions of the native populations of the time. Originally broadcast on March 21, 1970, the program had been well received by reviewers. Its use of still photographs predated by twenty years Ken Burns' famous production *The Civil War* on the American Public Broadcasting Service in 1990.

The Taming of the Canadian West was a prestige production, and the sponsor, Canadian Pacific, did not air commercials during the show's ninety minutes. The *Calgary Herald* was impressed enough to suggest that it be rerun because the program had run opposite the Saturday night hockey game on CBC in western Canada, a point it was suggested Toronto had not taken into account.

Groups representing native people, like the National Indian Brotherhood, dated from the late 1960s and their voicing of grievances was gathering momentum. The new prime minister, Pierre Elliott Trudeau, had labelled Canadian society as 'Just' in April 1968; at the end of 1969 native activist Harold Cardinal published the book entitled *The Unjust Society*.[2] When the summer rerun of *The Taming of the Canadian West* was announced for July 1971, objections were raised by native people who alleged that the film was 'blatantly racist, historically inaccurate, and slanderous to the Indian race and culture.'[3] A similar situation would occur over twenty years later in 1993 when some members of the black community protested a production of the musical *Showboat* in Toronto.

On June 14, 1971, Mr Justice Allison Walsh of the Trial Division considered the application for the orders.[4] The law involved in the case was found in a provision of the Broadcasting Act that read: 'A public hearing shall be held by the [Canadian Radio-Television] Commission, if the Executive Committee is satisfied that it would be in the public interest to hold such a hearing, in connection with ... a complaint by a person with respect to any matter within the powers of the commission.'[5] The Executive Committee had decided on May 26, 1971, not to interfere with the broadcast and not to hold a public hearing. It was the commission's position that the broadcaster was responsible for the programs shown. This policy was said to be well established and essential to the maintenance of the right to freedom of expression in broadcasting.

Counsel for the CRTC challenged the right of the applicants to bring the application on the basis of a lack of standing, that is, a lack of a specific interest in the substance of the complaint, but Walsh rejected the argument. However, he independently raised the point that the application should be decided by the Federal Court of Appeal. The confusion between sections 18 and 28 – so strongly argued in the debate leading up to the enactment of the new law – was now making its courtroom debut. Walsh saw it as crucial that an application had been brought before the Court of Appeal under section 28 at the same time. Under section 28 the applicants sought to set aside the CRTC's decision not to hold a public hearing. Lack of clarity about which division the applicants should use had precipitated the commencement of proceedings in both.

The Court of Appeal was scheduled to hear the matter the following week: if the Court of Appeal decided it had jurisdiction, the Trial Division would have none.[6] Walsh considered it appropriate to wait. If the appeal court had jurisdiction, it would carry on; if not, then Walsh would simply proceed to render his judgment, since he had heard the matter. There would be no great delay, since the hearing before the Court of Appeal was only a week away.

Because of the uncertainty surrounding the question of the jurisdiction of the appeal division, the lawyer for the native people requested directions regarding the making of a section 28 application, and thus appeared before Chief Justice Jackett sitting alone.[7] Only that lawyer appeared. The question of jurisdiction proved to be a non-issue since the language of the law in this instance was clear: an application under section 28 'applies, ... in respect of a ... decision or order given or made after this Act comes into force.'[8] The CRTC had made its decision on May 28, 1971; the Federal Court Act had come into force on June 1, 1971. The Court of Appeal had no jurisdiction. This conclusion is so obvious that it causes one to wonder why Walsh had not reached it initially. Perhaps this is why Jackett suggested that a judge of the Trial Division should not feel reluctant to decide a question of the jurisdiction of the Court of Appeal when the jurisdiction of the Trial Division was in issue.

Chief Justice Jackett therefore concluded that the proceedings could be quashed, but this required another application in which the jurisdiction issue would be raised directly, which had not been the case in the request for directions. A three-judge panel would be needed to consider the jurisdiction question. Jackett then voluntarily formulated a number of issues 'so that counsel will be prepared to assist the Court on them when they arise in a particular matter.'[9] Jackett set up the issues which the lawyers would have to address, and seized the opportunity to educate the bar. He went even further: in the first case in which section 28 had come before the Court of Appeal, he chose to assert his opinion and not let the law develop on a case-by-case basis (as is the tradition of the common law). Most significantly, Jackett took it upon himself to define the words 'decision or order' found in section 28 of the Federal Court Act; he concluded that they meant the 'ultimate decision or order taken or made by the tribunal under its statute.'[10] In the result he narrowed the jurisdiction of the Court of Appeal as an administrative court. Interlocutory decisions were left out (to be picked up by the Trial Division) – a development the legislators never appear to have intended, and one which they consequently never discussed during the legislative process leading to the creation of the Federal Court. David Mullan commented on the peculiarity of the conclusion in his 1977 study of the court's administrative law jurisdiction: 'there is something strange about a regime where one court has original jurisdiction before a decision or order is made and another court has jurisdiction afterwards.'[11] Theoretically Jackett's opinion, since it was volunteered and not needed for the resolution of the matter before him,[12] would not compel a judge in a subsequent case to follow it, yet, because of his imposing presence in the court, and his association with the creation of the legislation, his restrictive interpretation was followed without question.

On July 16, 1971, two days before the scheduled airing of the documentary, the native organizations sought an injunction to prevent the television network from showing the film until after the court had rendered its decision. It was argued that damage would be done to native people by allowing the racist and inaccurate material to be seen, and that showing the material would render the hearing of the application for an order to force a public hearing futile. For its part, the network relied on its right to freedom of expression, which had been declared to be broadcasting policy in the Broadcasting Act. Mr Justice Roderick Kerr was the Trial Division judge.[13] He concluded that Canada's broadcasting policy was so clearly articulated in the legislation that no one could contend that the Federal Court had the power to prevent the showing of a particular program such as 'The Taming of the Canadian West' on television, unless, he added, the broadcast was legally actionable, for example, defamatory (which it was not). Kerr would not issue an injunction: the matter fell within the realm of the CRTC mandate and did not justify judicial interference. This clear exercise of judicial restraint from interference with administrative action was attenuated by Kerr's concluding comment that he would not have granted the injunction in any event: the film had aired some eighteen months earlier, and was a historical film, not one dealing with a current situation. This latter point sidestepped the fact that it was the showing itself (and not the scenes depicted) that the applicants considered socially important. Kerr's conclusion was that no legal right was being infringed; by definition the problem was political. Changes brought about by the existence of the new court with its wide power of review over government decision making had not overwhelmed the truism that the legal system is the legal system, and the political system is the political system.

The litigation concluded on December 3, 1971, when Mr Justice Walsh delivered his judgment on the merits of the application brought before the Trial Division on June 14, 1971.[14] For the first time the facts surrounding the dispute were examined in a coherent manner; only bits and pieces had appeared previously. Walsh considered the provisions of the Broadcasting Act with a closeness and precision of study that indicated the seriousness with which he took the matter. He gave every appearance of being forced to be very careful politically, and his discussion of the facts displayed a sympathy for the applicants. His review of the legislation led him to conclude that there was no intention to give the CRTC a censorship role directly; the commission's control was related to licensing. General programming, not specific programming, was its concern. Walsh concluded that the Executive Committee's decision regarding a public hearing was a matter which was not intended to be reviewed by the judiciary. He labelled it an 'administrative' decision.[15]

The traditional label of 'administrative' used by Walsh to deny judicial review was perhaps to be expected as part of the baggage that came with the continued reference to the prerogative writs, although section 28 directed attention to whether a decision should be made on a judicial or quasi-judicial basis, whether 'administrative' or not.

The proceedings received very little media coverage. Publicity for the Federal Court was certainly not helped when the *Toronto Star* identified Mr Justice Ker [*sic*] as a member of the Supreme Court of Ontario.[16] All the hearings had been held in Toronto. As a means of publicizing the political struggle waged by the native peoples of Canada the appearances before the Federal Court had not proved to be a substitute for public hearings before the CRTC.

THE *LAVELL* CASE

The court was actively involved with the *National Indian Brotherhood* litigation when another case involving native people appeared on the docket. *Re Lavell and the Attorney General of Canada*[17] was an appeal by Jeannette Lavell from the decision of the Registrar of the Department of Citizenship and Immigration to delete her name from the Indian Register. Mrs Lavell was an Indian, but she had married a non-Indian and thereby lost her Indian status by virtue of a provision in the Indian Act. This did not occur when an Indian man married a non-Indian woman. The legislation permitted Mrs Lavell to lodge a protest, which she did, and the matter was referred to a county court judge within the appropriate provincial court system. The basis of her protest was that she had been denied equality before the law as guaranteed under the Canadian Bill of Rights. The judge, from the York Judicial District in Ontario, concluded that Mrs Lavell had not been deprived of equality before the law by reason of sex because she had the same rights as other Canadian women.

A motion to review the judge's decision was made before the Federal Court of Appeal, the bench consisting of Chief Justice Jackett, Arthur Thurlow, and Louis Pratte. The three judges appeared to have no difficulty with the case. In a brief and pithy judgment rendered the day after the hearing, Thurlow (writing for the court) concluded that the section of the Indian Act that denied Lavell the right to be registered, coupled with the loss of other rights that flowed from being a registered Indian, constituted discrimination by reason of sex. The provision in question created a difference between the rights of an Indian woman who married a non-Indian and those of an Indian man who married a non-Indian. Compared with a male Indian, Mrs Lavell was at a disadvantage and thus was denied equality before the law.

No deputy judges presided in this case. Pratte was a member of the Trial Division, sitting ex officio in the appeal division.

The case involved issues that were important socially and which were highly controversial; resolving them posed considerable difficulty. There was the issue of aboriginal rights – allowing native people to govern their own affairs – versus women's rights to equality, whether they were aboriginal women or not. Working out the complex social and political issues, which once would have been left to the political process, was now before the courts.

The *Lavell* case reached the Federal Court of Appeal less than two years after the Supreme Court's surprising decision in the *Drybones* case.[18]

There, the Bill of Rights was given effect and a provision in the Indian Act held inoperative on the basis of racial discrimination. The Supreme Court's decision in *Drybones* was unexpected because by the late 1960s the Bill of Rights had ceased to be an effective source of argument within the legal system. But, a year after *Drybones*, a judge in Ontario could remark on the 'fatefully [transient] character of the majority decision' in the case.[19] While the effect of *Drybones* may have been short-lived as far as concrete results of the Bill were concerned, its existence did encourage counsel to raise the Bill in argument, as occurred in *Lavell*.

The controversial nature of the litigation may have been what motivated the Court of Appeal itself to grant leave to appeal to the highest court. It was inevitable that the case would make its way to the Supreme Court of Canada: this was true of all major constitutional litigation. Given the difficulties of the case, the apparent simplicity of the appeal court's decision suggested that that decision was but a necessary formality en route to the Supreme Court of Canada. The perceived insignificance of the Federal Court in the litigation was amply shown by the fact that no intervenors appeared to present arguments before the court. In contrast, many Indian organizations and other intervenors appeared before the Supreme Court of Canada.[20] The sense of simplicity conveyed by the short unanimous judgment of the Federal Court of Appeal was dramatically belied by a 5–4 split in the Supreme Court of Canada and the reversal of the Court of Appeal's decision.[21] Jeannette Lavell had lost. The bare majority of the Supreme Court of Canada, led by Mr Justice Roland Ritchie,[22] had in effect left the problem to be worked out within the political system and within the native community. The dissenting judges, led by Bora Laskin,[23] recognized that there had to be a classification of those who were to be considered Indians for the purpose of the constitution and those who were not. While the classification could be left with the political process and the native community as a general rule, nevertheless Laskin recognized that this classification process was subject to certain basic social values of the larger Canadian community by which reasonableness could be judged. Discrimination by reason of sex was for Laskin unreasonable, and thus it could not be supported as a value of Indian culture.

While effectively the majority had left the matter for resolution within the political arena, a disturbing feature of the case was that these judges seemed more determined to end any effectiveness that the Canadian Bill of Rights might have had for Canadian society in general than to apply it in this particular case. Ritchie, for the majority, crippled any effect that the *Drybones* case might have had in resuscitating the Bill of Rights, and the meaning of the words 'equality before the law' in the Bill was trivialized. While strong feelings were evident from the judgments rendered in the Supreme Court of Canada in this very difficult case, the Federal Court of Appeal simply upheld the decision of the County Court judge and sent the case to the Supreme Court. The judges of the Court of Appeal provided no input into the attempt to resolve the problem.

The staying power of the issue was more than amply illustrated by the fact that the provision of the Indian Act challenged in the *Lavell* case was eliminated twelve years after the decision,[24] but more than a decade later (1997) the issue was still being litigated in a constitutional challenge to the validity of the amendment to the Indian Act.[25]

A 'DYNAMITE' ISSUE

The question of the Federal Court's jurisdiction to review the decision of the County Court judge in the *Lavell* case pales somewhat beside the social importance of the rights of native people and women, but for the Federal Court of Appeal it was what one judge described as a 'dynamite' issue. The explosive point was the Federal Court's review of a decision of a judge of a provincial court sitting as *persona designata*.

When the application for review under section 28 was brought before the Federal Court of Appeal in *Lavell*, the jurisdiction question was whether the county court judge sitting in appeal under the Indian Act from a decision of the Registrar was a 'federal board, commission or other tribunal.'[26] The definition in the legislation specifically excluded 'any such body constituted or established by or under a law of a province or any such person or persons appointed under or in accordance with a law of a province or under section 96 of *The British North America Act, 1867*.' Under section 96 of the constitution the judges of superior, district, and county courts in each province are appointed by the federal government. Without question, the decisions of provincial courts and other provincial tribunals were not to be subject to review by the Federal Court. What of a judge of a provincial court appointed by the federal government under section 96, who was hearing an appeal under the Indian Act?

Chief Justice Jackett and Justices Thurlow and Pratte said that they had no difficulty in deciding that the judge in this instance was acting under a federal statute as a specifically designated person and not as a judge of a provincial court. The Federal Court had jurisdiction because the judge was a *persona designata*. The Supreme Court of Canada judgments made no mention of the issue.

The decision of the Court of Appeal was of sufficient interest to members of the bar that a comment appeared in its leading professional journal, in which the author stated that it would probably come as a shock to most lawyers that an ordinary provincial court or its judges might be subject to review by the Federal Court of Appeal. The author disagreed with the court's assumption of jurisdiction. The profession had yet another reason to worry about the existence of the Federal Court![27]

While the designation of judges of provincial courts as *persona designata* and the review of their decisions by the Federal Court troubled some individuals, the question was of little concern to the judges of the Supreme Court of Canada. In 1973 the Supreme Court gave its blessing to the concept of *persona designata*, thus favouring the jurisdiction of the Federal Court of Appeal, while at the same time offering a pointed criticism of the decision-making ability of the appeal court.

The case in question was *Commonwealth of Puerto Rico v. Hernandez*,[28] in which a decision of a county court judge acting under the Extradition Act was challenged. The judge had refused to issue a committal warrant in extradition proceedings, and the foreign government sought review in the Federal Court of Appeal. The panel was made up of Chief Justice Jackett, Thurlow, and Cameron, a retired judge of the Exchequer Court who sat as a deputy judge. In a characteristically brief and oral judgment, Jackett for the court rejected jurisdiction, but his decision was not based on the *persona designata* issue. Instead, he invoked the doctrine of *stare decisis* (he accepted that there was a previous decision which answered the question before him, and was obliged to follow it). Jackett found a case from the Supreme Court of Canada[29] in which it had been decided unanimously that a decision by an extradition judge was not a 'judgment' as defined by the Supreme Court Act. This definition also covered 'decision' and 'order,' and Jackett said that there was no basis for adopting a meaning of decision or order that differed from the one which applied to the Supreme Court Act.

The Supreme Court of Canada took a very different view of the matter. Writing for the majority, Mr Justice Louis-Philippe Pigeon turned on the Court of Appeal.[30] He said tersely: 'With respect, I fail to see on what basis a decision on the construction of the *Supreme Court Act* could be determinative of the construction of the *Federal Court Act*.'[31] In his view the Court of Appeal should have focused on section 28 of the Federal Court Act: the provision provided direction for the exercise of the new supervisory jurisdiction, and Pigeon pointed out that the jurisdiction was much broader in scope than had previously existed for judicial review. Pigeon was lecturing the Federal Court of Appeal on how to deal with the law that gave it jurisdiction! Pigeon concluded that a judge sitting as an extradition commissioner was exercising power under a federal statute and was acting as *persona designata*. The Court of Appeal had jurisdiction.[32]

Pigeon's conclusion was reached by the narrowest of margins (5–4). The dissenting judges were Abbott, Judson, and Spence, and Laskin; Laskin rendered their judgment. The basis for their disagreement was that it had been settled that there was no appeal from (nor any other form of review of) the discharge of a person in extradition proceedings. The dissenting judges did not think that the general words of section 28 should be taken to abruptly reverse the previous policy. However, like the judges in the majority, Laskin pointed out that the case followed by Jackett had not determined the application of the Federal Court Act.

The question of the review of provincial court judges sitting as *persona designata* under federal statutes had powerful symbolism for the legal profession in each province. The status of the provincial superior courts was at stake. Thus a unanimous Supreme Court of Canada restricted the application of the concept of *persona designata* quite severely just a few years later, in *Herman v. Attorney General of Canada*.[33]

Herman involved an application to the Federal Court of Appeal to review the decision of a superior court judge of a province who had been authorized under the federal Income Tax Act to adjudicate a dispute over whether documents seized from a lawyer were covered by solicitor-client privilege. The legislation provided that a client or lawyer could apply to a superior court judge of a province for an adjudication of the matter.

The Court of Appeal panel which heard the application to review the decision of the superior court judge consisted of Chief Justice Jackett and two deputy judges, MacKay and Kelly. At the conclusion of the hearing, Jackett, for the panel, rendered an oral judgment and once again found refuge in a previous decision of the Supreme Court. The decision of the higher court that he considered as controlling had concluded that the process of adjudication resulted in the whole matter being determined before the judge; no order on appeal could have any practical effect.[34] It would thus 'be entirely academic for the Court to set aside the decision or order that is under attack,' Jackett stated.[35] Regarding the jurisdiction of the Federal Court of Appeal, Jackett expressed doubt that it existed, but did not elaborate.

In the Supreme Court of Canada the majority judgment was rendered by Mr Justice Dickson.[36] He stated that the very language of the law allowed for the ready conclusion that Parliament had not intended a decision of a federally appointed judge of a provincial court to be subject to review by the Federal Court. The law in question that specified what federal bodies would be subject to review read as follows: '"federal board, commission or other tribunal" means ... any person ... exercising ... jurisdiction or powers conferred by or under an Act of the Parliament of Canada, *other than* ... any such person ... appointed under section 96 of *The British North America Act, 1867.*'

Dickson proceeded to discuss the concept of *persona designata*, pointing out that it had been used more widely in Canada than in England or the United States. He also said that he had found in the previous cases a looseness of language and thought which had created uncertainty. His examination of Canadian cases revealed a distinct need for greater certainty in the application of *persona designata*. Dickson and the other justices of the Supreme Court of Canada were about to reform the law. The court's conclusion required that the concept of *persona designata* would be reserved for exceptional circumstances. The basic approach assumed that whenever power was granted to a judge by statute, it was intended that the person would act in the capacity as a judge of his or her particular court. If the power dealt with something peculiar and distinct from that which would have been the normal jurisdiction of the person's court, *persona designata* applied. Specific to *Herman*, the Supreme Court of Canada concluded that the task presented to the judge was a very typical and commonplace judicial function. Thus when the Supreme Court applied the law which it had created, there was nothing special or peculiar about the power exercised, and hence the person was not acting *persona designata*.

The issue of law reform seems not to have been raised at the Federal Court of Appeal, but given Jackett's penchant for authorities it is unlikely that there would have been an excursion into uncharted territory without the security of a previous case.

The subject of law reform naturally raises the question of what happened to the *Hernandez* case. Mr Justice Dickson and the majority escorted it out of the way. Dickson referred to it as a recent case, quoted Pigeon, and then summarized it to make it as innocuous as possible. In Dickson's view the case involved only the application (and not the establishment) of the law, which is to say that it was accepted that judicial review existed when a judge was acting as *persona designata* under a federal statute. The lingering question of whether a judge in a given instance was acting in that capacity remained.

Chief Justice Laskin wrote a concurring judgment and was blunter. He said that the *Hernandez* decision supported his call to abandon the concept of *persona designata*; he expressed disagreement with the majority's decision in the case, albeit 'with great respect.' Laskin had dissented in *Hernandez* and he acknowledged that he had done so. He went on to articulate reasons why he thought the decision was wrong. Pigeon (whose decision in *Hernandez* was being eliminated) sat on the panel in *Herman* and recorded a simple concurrence with the decision of the majority.

When *Herman* was decided in 1978 the Supreme Court was, with the exception of Laskin, relatively restrained when it came to engaging in law reform. By the early 1980s, the court was more confident. The *Hernandez* decision was repudiated completely in 1982, in *Minister of Indian Affairs and Northern Development v. Ranville*.[37] In the Federal Court of Appeal a panel consisting of Heald, Urie, and deputy judge Kelly was prepared to reject jurisdiction to review of a judge acting under the Indian Act, but in doing so they added nothing to the jurisprudence and purported merely to be following the most recent precedent, which was *Herman*.[38]

These decisions eliminated the irritation within provincial bars that had been created by the Federal Court reviewing decisions of judges of provincial courts who were acting in special capacities under federal law. The status of judges of provincial superior courts was about to grow and grow until it became entrenched in the constitution; that story will be examined later.

The Supreme Court's reasons for judgment in *Hernandez* seem to contain a certain terseness directed at the Federal Court of Appeal. The relationship between the two courts in the mid-1970s was definitely strained, a tension explored in the next chapter.

STARE DECISIS

Adherence to precedent in treating like cases alike is naturally an ingredient of fairness in the administration of law. The legal principle of *stare decisis* obliges a judge (as a matter of law) to follow a previous judicial decision in which a legal rule was articulated, quite apart from whether the judge considers the statement of law inappropriate or even wrong when applied in the current case. This imperative originated with formalism, and the degree to which formalism had a hold over the mind of a judge could be determined by the way in which the judge handled *stare decisis*. However, a note of caution: this discussion of the doctrine of *stare decisis* concerns following decisions of judges of the same court or possibly of lower courts, not the requirement that the Federal Court follow the decisions of the Supreme Court of Canada, a higher court in the judicial hierarchy.

The doctrine has been attributed to the 'repeated assertions of one judge, Lord Campbell' in the middle of the nineteenth century.[39] *Stare decisis* had unquestionably taken hold of the legal system by the end of the nineteenth century, as articulated in the House of Lords in the famous 1898 *Tramways* case.[40] By that time, formalism had settled in quite comfortably for a significant portion of the legal profession.

Connected with *stare decisis* is the attitude that solving problems that come before judges involves a search for a previous decision (an 'authority'), and not the painstaking effort of thinking out a solution. The cases examined above provide evidence that the Federal Court of Appeal (and, in particular, its chief justice), was committed to the search for authorities and *stare decisis*. Chief Justice Jackett illustrated this approach in a foreword to a leading textbook on trade marks and unfair competition, in which he espoused the view that a textbook should 'provide references to all relevant authorities in a convenient manner,' to enable a lawyer 'to find the judicial decisions that bear on his problems and appraise the true effect of each such decision.'[41]

A major part of the changes appearing within the legal community at the end of the sixties was the abandonment in 1966 of the doctrine of *stare decisis* by the House of Lords.[42] Two years later, in 1968, the House of Lords overruled a previous decision.[43] The Supreme Court of Canada gradually reached the conclusion that it would cast aside *stare decisis* and in 1977 overruled one of its previous decisions.[44] These events no doubt forced Chief Justice Jackett in 1978 to expressly state that he was not following the principle of *stare decisis*, which he said did not apply to the court; however, he simultaneously asserted the need to follow previous decisions, even if questionable, for the purpose of 'sound judicial administration.'[45] The substance of *stare decisis* and the thinking behind it had a secure hold of the Federal Court whatever it was called. This attitude differed markedly from that of Chief Justice Laskin of the Supreme Court of Canada, who in 1978 suggested that judges would need to re-examine courses of decision when new or altered social conditions created new understanding.[46]

A SORRY STORY

In the early 1970s, land claims by Canada's native peoples had acquired a high profile. Based on a claim of aboriginal title, the chiefs of a number of Indian tribes in the Northwest Territories attempted to register a *caveat* under the Land Titles Act against approximately one million square kilometres of land. The registrar of land titles referred the question of whether the *caveat* could be registered to the Supreme Court of the Northwest Territories. The hearing of the reference began on April 3, 1973, before Mr Justice William Morrow.

The federal government then applied to the Trial Division of the Federal Court for a writ of prohibition to stop Morrow from proceeding with the case. This was astonishing! If the hearing being challenged had taken place in a provincial superior court, such action would have been impossible,[47] but the federal Department of Justice obviously viewed the superior court of the Territories as capable of being covered by the words 'federal board, commission or other tribunal.' Morrow disagreed. He rendered an unusual interim judgment on June 14, 1973 (just prior to the Federal Court's hearing) and lashed out at the proceedings, which he considered to be 'an unwarranted attack by the executive of the Canadian Government upon the integrity and independence of the Supreme Court of the Northwest Territories as the constitutional superior court of this Territory.'[48] He declared, 'To me this represents a policy decision by the Government [of Canada] which can only be interpreted as an affront to my Court and to me as the Judge of that Court.'[49]

He went on to say that such a proceeding was 'the first time in the history of Canadian jurisprudence, the first time since Confederation, when one superior court judge has been placed under attack by another superior court judge of equal status.' Since it was, in Morrow's opinion, such a breach of 'constitutional etiquette,' he had written the judgment so that the people of the Northwest Territories could hear 'their judge's side of the sorry story.'[50]

Mr Justice Morrow exposed a most sensitive aspect of the Federal Court's existence: he warned that the convening of the Federal Court for a special sitting in Yellowknife would damage the court's image and make it appear to be the government's court. The Canadian Bar Association published those portions of Morrow's judgment that were critical of the government's action in the *Canadian Bar Bulletin* of July 1973 with a heavy black border around them.[51] Regina lawyer Morris Shumiatcher wrote a comment that appeared in various newspapers, beginning with the words, 'At this moment, the pages of 350 years of history are being turned back.'[52]

The hearing before the Federal Court proceeded and was conducted by Mr Justice Frank Collier; he dismissed the application for a writ of prohibition.[53] He answered the question of jurisdiction – that is, whether Morrow sitting on a reference under the Land Titles Act was 'a federal board, commission, or other tribunal' – in the negative, and thus concluded that the Federal Court had no jurisdiction to issue the writ.[54]

Collier made no comment about the proceedings in which he was taking part. He may have thought that the best way to diffuse any criticism of the Federal Court was to play it completely by the book, but the approach adopted gave a certain picture of legitimacy to the government's action, which Morrow had described as raising a constitutional problem.[55] Eventually, Morrow heard the reference and decided that a *caveat* could be filed for certain lands, but this decision was reversed by the Northwest Territories Court of Appeal. On appeal to the Supreme Court of Canada, the position of the territorial Court of Appeal was upheld.[56]

THE *HOWARTH* CASE

The different approaches to the judicial function were illustrated in a number of cases but one of the best was *Howarth v. The National Parole Board*.[57]

Howarth's parole had been revoked by the National Parole Board and he had applied to the Federal Court of Appeal under section 28 for judicial review of the order. The government in turn applied to quash the application to review on the ground that the court lacked jurisdiction: it was the government's position that the Parole Board's decision to revoke parole was a 'decision or order of an administrative nature not required by law to be made on a judicial or quasi-judicial basis.' In other words, it was a decision of government that should not be reviewed by the judiciary.

The appeal division's panel was made up of Jackett, Thurlow, and Pratte. Chief Justice Jackett (with Mr Justice Pratte concurring), rendered an oral judgment, which because of its length and complexity tended to substantiate the view that it had been prepared before the end of the hearing. Jackett's approach to solving the problem before the court was to focus on a previous decision which was considered to be determinative of the question. Jackett's words 'it is settled' were all there was: the order revoking parole was of an administrative nature and the court consequently had no jurisdiction. While Pratte was comfortable with this approach, Thurlow preferred to render his own judgment. He stated that fairness required that the person whose parole was revoked should be allowed to state his position before any order was made, if the basis for the revocation was alleged misconduct. However, he accepted that the case that had been found by Jackett and Pratte had settled the matter, and prevented him from deciding as he wanted. He was thus prepared to live with the fact that the court was rendering an unfair decision because an 'authority' was operating.

As with all major cases, *Howarth* made its way to the Supreme Court of Canada;[58] Howarth's appeal was dismissed by a 5–3 vote. The majority was made up of Pigeon, Martland, Judson, de Grandpré, and Beetz, while the dissent consisted of Laskin, Spence, and Dickson. Pigeon rendered the judgment for the majority and the approach taken was the same as that of the majority in the Federal Court of Appeal. The statements 'the point was settled by ...' and 'conclusively determined' told the story. Pigeon made it clear that the approach to take when determining whether an administrative decision maker should act 'judicially' or not was *not* to examine the facts of the particular case, but rather to look at the nature of the decision required as set out in the law. The judges who formed the majority were obviously more comfortable dealing with words than with the facts of a particular problem.

While formalism appeared to carry the day, the dissenting judges in the Supreme Court – the 'LSD connection' – relied on contextualism. Dickson asserted the importance of the question being considered: while people accused of crimes had their civil rights protected, little attention was paid to the rights of people on parole.

Although the case involved a question of jurisdiction, and Pigeon had noted that no facts had been put in evidence, nevertheless, Dickson articulated the facts. Lenard John Howarth had been sentenced to a term of seven years' imprisonment for armed robbery. He was granted parole in May 1971 and enrolled as a full-time student at Queen's University, Kingston. Howarth was employed during the time that he was attending university. This situation continued for over two years until he was charged with indecent assault in August 1973. Howarth was taken into custody and his parole suspended. He pleaded not guilty to the charge and four days before the preliminary inquiry was to have been held the charge was withdrawn. On the day the preliminary inquiry would have started he was informed that his parole had been revoked following a meeting of the National Parole Board. He was returned to the penitentiary. Howarth had requested the reasons for the revocation of the parole but his request had been refused. The board took the position that it did not have to disclose the reasons.

Writing for the dissenting judges, Dickson took a typically contextual starting point: he articulated the purpose of the legislation involved. He stated that the purpose of section 28 was to assure judicial review of the decisions or orders of all federal boards, commissions, and other tribunals. The only decisions immune from the authority to review were administrative decisions not required to be made on a judicial or quasi-judicial basis. The question's essence was whether there was anything that required the National Parole Board to act on a judicial or quasi-judicial basis. The duty to so act might be statutory or found in the common law. Dickson maintained that the duty to act judicially, that is, to give effect to the principles of natural justice, depended on the circumstances of the particular case, as well as on the construction of the relevant statute. The duty could be implied from the nature of the power given to the decision maker.

Since the 'authority' that had controlled the thinking of the Federal Court of Appeal and the majority of the Supreme Court had been decided before the enactment of section 28, which concerned what Dickson termed 'novel type[s] of decisions,' it had been swept aside by change. This conclusion allowed the dissenting judges to analyse the function of the Parole Board. They found that in Howarth's case the Board had a duty to act judicially and, as a result, the Federal Court of Appeal had jurisdiction to review the decision.

Howarth was the first case involving section 28 to come before the Supreme Court of Canada. It generated a considerable amount of commentary, the great majority of which was highly critical of the result. Criticism focused not only on the actual decision, but also on the formalistic approach taken by so many judges in both courts.[59] Such criticisms were themselves a clear sign of change within the legal community.

19

Relationship with the Supreme Court

The relationship between an intermediate court of appeal and the highest court in the judicial hierarchy invites investigation. Though the cases presented in the previous chapter illustrate some of the points of interest, the cases surveyed in this chapter expose the tensions between the two courts acutely.

CASES OF BIAS (OR NOT)

In *P.P.G. Industries Canada Ltd. v. Attorney General of Canada* there was an unprecedented proceeding: the federal government moved for an order of *certiorari* in the Federal Court's Trial Division to quash a decision of the Anti-Dumping Tribunal because of alleged bias on the part of the chairman.[1] The tribunal had considered a complaint by a number of Canadian companies that transparent sheet glass had been dumped into Canada. The chairman had been a consultant to the companies concerned prior to his appointment; when he was appointed, he terminated his engagement as consultant.

When the complaint was brought before the tribunal the chairman informed the other two sitting members of his previous association with the companies; he did not participate in the hearings. The two remaining members of the tribunal ordered that anti-dumping duty be assessed against the imported sheet glass. The chairman read the final draft of the decision, made three grammatical changes, and signed the decision in the belief that the signatures of all three members were needed.

In addition, there was evidence that while chairman he had made inquiries about where the complaint stood. Memoranda and notes made it clear that he had also been in contact with the Canadian companies. The trial judge found that the chairman had made statements which implied connivance, and that he had apparently said that he would speak to the officers of the department conducting the inquiry to inform them about the glass industry.

What made the Federal Court proceedings unusual was that the government had not participated in the hearing before the tribunal, and none of the parties who might have been affected adversely by the tribunal's decision had challenged the result. The government's intervention was initiated some two years after the tribunal had made a decision. The attorney general of Canada claimed a general competence to have the courts inquire into any allegation of legal frailty of any decision of a federal administrative board. In doing so, he relied on the Department of Justice Act, which imposed a duty on the attorney general to 'see that the administration of public affairs is in accordance with law' (section 4).

The trial judge, Alexander Cattanach, wrote an extremely long judgment dismissing the application. He concluded that by signing the decision of the tribunal the chairman had adopted it as his own and must therefore be taken to have participated, but since the copy of the decision retained by the tribunal in its records was unsigned (the signed copy had been sent to the deputy minister of customs and excise), the answer had to be that he had not participated in making the decision.[2]

The Court of Appeal, which consisted of Mr Justice Thurlow and two deputy judges, Cameron and Bastin, unanimously reversed Cattanach and concluded that the chairman had participated in the tribunal's decision, by signing it and thus adopting it as his own. The fact that the copy retained in the records of the tribunal had no signatures did not matter, and, if anything, it suggested that those members of the tribunal named had rendered the decision, and this included the chairman.[3]

The appeal to the Supreme Court of Canada resulted in what one scholar called an embarrassing reversal of the appeal court's decision by a unanimous Supreme Court.[4] Chief Justice Laskin for the court stated that the chairman could not be said to have participated in the decision by signing it in the circumstances.[5] It was a testy judgment by Laskin.

The unusual act of the government in bringing the application was neither challenged in the Federal Court nor commented on by any of the judges. The issue of jurisdiction did arise in oral argument in the Court of Appeal, but a majority of the judges upheld the court's jurisdiction. It was different for Chief Justice Laskin. He was bothered by the government's action, and felt the need to 'underline the extraordinary nature of the proceedings,'[6] but since there was no objection he said that he was prepared to assume that the attorney general could apply under section 18 of the Federal Court Act to quash the decision of the tribunal.

Yet another embarrassing reversal[7] occurred in *Committee for Justice and Liberty v. National Energy Board*,[8] which was known as *In re Canadian Arctic Gas Pipeline Ltd.*[9] in the Federal Court. Laskin's judgment for the Supreme Court had a sharp edge to it. The issue was once again the bias of a chairman of a federal administrative board – this time, the National Energy Board.

The case had reached the Federal Court of Appeal by way of a reference from the Energy Board, and Chief Justice Jackett took the unusual step of assigning five judges to the panel to hear the case, rather than the normal three.[10] The panel was made up of Justices Thurlow, Pratte, Urie, and Ryan, with retired Federal Court judge Roderick Kerr sitting as a deputy judge.

The National Energy Board had considered competing applications for permission to construct and operate a pipeline to move natural gas from the Mackenzie River Delta and Beaufort Basin to southern Canada (the Mackenzie Valley Pipeline). A second application involved the movement of natural gas from Alaska to the United States. The competing companies were Canadian Arctic Gas Pipeline Limited and Foothills Pipe Lines Ltd. Many groups and individuals had been given standing to present their objections to granting permission to construct the pipelines (in all, eighty-eight parties participated). At the beginning of the hearings one of the applicants raised a question about bias. This applicant was actually the one in whose favour the bias might have existed. Marshall Crowe was the chairman of the National Energy Board and of the three-person panel assigned to hear the applications. He had earlier been a director, and later president, of the Canada Development Corporation; as a representative of the corporation, Crowe had participated in the deliberations and decisions of a consortium of some fifteen to twenty-seven companies considering the physical and economic feasibility of a northern pipeline to bring natural gas to southern markets. As a result of this study Canadian Arctic Gas Pipeline Limited, one of the applicants, had been incorporated. Of the eighty-eight parties, only five objected to Mr Crowe's participation on the panel.

Thurlow rendered the judgment for a unanimous Court of Appeal.[11] He identified the problem as a 'predetermination' case, given that there had been some expression of views by Crowe indicating a prejudgment. The question was whether there was reason to believe that the person whose duty it was to decide (Crowe) would not listen to the evidence or decide fairly. There was no allegation of actual bias or financial interest, nor was there evidence of any promise to anyone that any of the applications would have a particular result. Thurlow did state that 'the circumstances ... might give rise in a very sensitive or scrupulous conscience to the uneasy suspicion that he [Crowe] might be unconsciously biased.'[12] Nevertheless, he added, this was not the test in law, which he said was, 'would an informed person, viewing the matter realistically and practically – and having thought the matter through – conclude ... that Mr. Crowe, whether consciously or unconsciously, would not decide fairly.' Since Crowe did not stand to gain or lose anything personally, and the interest involved in the hearing was that of the Canadian public, Thurlow concluded that the chairman was able to approach the issues impartially and with equanimity.

Three of the interveners appealed to the Supreme Court of Canada.[13] Eight judges heard the appeal, and the result was a reversal of the Court of Appeal by a 5–3 margin.

Laskin wrote the majority judgment,[14] and saw the question as whether the principle of reasonable apprehension or reasonable likelihood of bias applied to the board. If the principle applied, then the appeal had to succeed; the board was obliged to make its decision in accordance with the rules of natural justice, which required impartiality. The position of the majority was clear: Crowe's participation in the discussions and decisions leading to the application of Canadian Arctic Gas Pipeline Limited did give rise to a reasonable apprehension of bias. Laskin noted that lawyers who had been appointed to the bench would not sit on cases involving former clients, especially if they had played a part at any stage of the case. Declaring that there must be a firm concern to ensure public confidence in the impartiality of adjudicative agencies, Laskin treated the result reached by the majority as the only outcome that was obvious. That gave his judgment its sharpness regarding the contrary result reached by the Federal Court of Appeal, which he reviewed at some length.[15]

In both cases the integrity of the administrative decision-making process was being questioned through allegations of bias – an issue on which it would seem reasonable to expect a consensus among the judges and, hence, the courts. In each case the Supreme Court of Canada reversed a unanimous Federal Court of Appeal, including one use of a rare five-judge panel. There was a definite lack of a meeting of minds between the courts.

THE CHIEF JUSTICE'S MEMO

No study of the relationship between the two courts would be complete without reference to *Antares Shipping Co. v. The Ship 'Capricorn,'*[16] a maritime law case which considered whether there should be service of documents outside Canada.[17] The substantive dispute concerned ownership of a ship. The plaintiff alleged that the ship had been sold in the United Kingdom, but before delivery a bill of sale to another company had been registered in New York. When the ship arrived in the port of Quebec City it was arrested by order of the Federal Court. A bail bond was posted by the owner associated with the New York sale as security for the ship.

The decisions of the Federal Court were not reported. In the Trial Division Pratte dismissed the application for an order for service *ex juris*, and the Court of Appeal affirmed the decision in an oral judgment delivered by Jackett. The Supreme Court reversed the appeal division, 4–1.

Writing for the majority, which also included Pigeon, Beetz, and de Grandpré, Mr Justice Ritchie stated that the issue was to be decided by applying the doctrine of *forum conveniens* – a doctrine which had not been considered by the Federal Court. His conclusion, after examining the question, was that nothing indicated a forum more convenient than the Federal Court. He acknowledged that 'special considerations apply in the administration of admiralty law and the regulation of shipping.'[18]

Ritchie's comments on the judgments of the Federal Court are noteworthy. He described them as 'so terse as to permit their being reproduced in full,'[19] which he then proceeded to do. He criticized the Federal Court judges for giving no indication of the reasons for their decisions.

Chief Justice Laskin dissented. He emphasised the element of discretion involved in the granting of service *ex juris* and the rarity with which the Supreme Court should interfere with a judge's decision. He was also of the opinion that there was an insufficient connection with Canada to advance the case. However, the most interesting part of Laskin's judgment was his statement that the proceedings in the Federal Court had taken 'an extraordinary turn.'[20]

The turn was attributable to Chief Justice Jackett, who had issued a memorandum to the court's registry requesting it to communicate with the lawyers for the parties in order to have the application for service *ex*

juris expedited. After the Court of Appeal had decided to reject service
ex juris and before the Supreme Court had granted leave to appeal, Jackett sent another memorandum entitled 'Memorandum for Counsel.' This
followed the filing of a notice of appeal of an order by Mr Justice Pratte in
a related proceeding, dismissing the statement of claim in the action. A
motion to quash the appeal from Pratte's decision was lodged.

Laskin called the memorandum 'an unusual document to come from a
Judge in respect of a motion returnable some three weeks later.'[21] Jackett
had stated in the memorandum that he could not imagine 'any fairly
arguable basis for not quashing the appeal' and thus he did not want to
set up a court of three judges at Quebec City to hear the motion. He asked
counsel either to assure him that there was 'some fairly arguable question
to be decided' or otherwise to dispose of the matter. Laskin noted that the
memorandum seemed to have had its effect, since a notice of discontinu-
ance of the appeal was soon issued.

Laskin concluded that Jackett's statements in the 'extra-curial memorandum' concerning 'an anticipated decision' of the court ' were not a
matter upon which the Federal Court of Appeal should posit any calculations on what its own course of conduct should be.'[22] Laskin had taken
the unusual step of asking for all of the files relating to the case, including
Federal Court correspondence files.

Ritchie and Laskin had delivered one-two blows which must have been
excruciating for the Court of Appeal and for the chief justice personally.
Jackett apparently thought of resigning, and, in a decision rendered the
same day as that in the *'Capricorn'* case, de Grandpré referred to him as
the former chief justice.[23]

THE *MANITOBA FISHERIES* CASE

The Freshwater Fish Marketing Act was enacted following an inquiry
into the freshwater fish business, and at the request of Alberta,
Saskatchewan, Manitoba, Ontario, and the Northwest Territories. The
legislation established a Crown corporation which engaged in the marketing and trading of fish, fish products, and fish by-products in and out
of Canada. The corporation was also given an exclusive right to market
and trade these goods in the interprovincial and export field. A section in
the legislation provided for the creation of agreements between the provinces and territory and Ottawa that would compensate private operations
rendered redundant by the legislation. Manitoba Fisheries Ltd., a private,
freshwater fish enterprise, sought a declaration that it was entitled to

compensation for property taken. The plaintiff's property claim related to loss of the business and goodwill.

Mr Justice Collier presided in the Trial Division. He determined that the legislation did not purport to take, or authorize the taking of, the property of anyone, nor did it deprive anyone of the enjoyment of property. While he said that this was 'a reasonable and fair interpretation,' nevertheless Collier had no difficulty in concluding that the plaintiff company and others had been put out of business, and 'economically erased.' He went on to comment that the businesses affected had been treated unfairly. Acknowledging that any compensation would be entirely gratuitous, Collier then stated that based on everything he had heard in the courtroom, the plaintiff was entitled to better treatment. He explained his limitations: 'This Court cannot change the law. Its function is to interpret (where necessary), and apply it.'[24] While Collier read the law as compelling him to reject the claim for compensation, he did not believe that justice had been done – the same viewpoint seen a century before![25] One thing that had not been available in the previous century was an argument based on the Bill of Rights. The company argued that it had been deprived of property without due process of law.[26] However, Collier tossed the Bill argument aside with the comment that he did not need to resort to the principles set out in the Bill to interpret the legislation.

The panel in the Federal Court of Appeal consisted of Urie, Heald, and deputy judge Mackay. Urie, for the court, agreed with Collier that there had been no taking of property, and that the legislation was involved with the orderly marketing of fish and fish products. While he accepted the rule that a statute was not to be construed as taking away the property of an individual without compensation unless there were clear and unmistakable words to the contrary, he took a restrictive view of the nature of the taking of property. He asserted that it must involve the actual, physical assumption of possession or use of the property by the government. In addition Urie agreed with Collier's handling of the Bill of Rights argument, and was not prepared to recognize the right to carry on business as a form of 'property' protected by the Bill of Rights. Last, Urie was able to say that there was considerable support for his conclusion in a recent judgment of the Privy Council. Nevertheless, along with Collier and judges of the past, he had pangs of conscience: 'I fully recognize that the result may appear harsh but, as was pointed out by the learned Trial Judge, our responsibility is to interpret the law as we see it and we must leave to others the obligation to so frame it that unfairness does not result in the implementation thereof.'[27]

A seven-judge panel of the Supreme Court of Canada unanimously reversed the Court of Appeal. Mr Justice Ritchie for the court[28] expressed difficulty with the reasoning in Urie's judgment and held that the authorities Urie had relied on were not applicable. He emphasized that the factual differences between this case and the Privy Council case were fundamental. Here, the government had expropriated the plaintiff's property and the plaintiff was entitled to compensation.[29] The Supreme Court had rejected the approach of the Federal Court judges, and had criticized them for being unresponsive to individual rights. The court's dominant role as impartial adjudicator of disputes between individuals and the government had been brought into question. The approach and language of its judges had been that of the past century, not the late 1970s.

THE *MARTINEAU* CASES

Prison discipline was the subject of the two *Martineau* cases. A disciplinary board had sentenced two inmates incarcerated in a federal penitentiary to fifteen days' solitary confinement for breach of regulations authorized by the Penitentiary Act. The prisoners challenged the decision and order of the board with applications in both the Trial Division and the Court of Appeal. Proceedings in the Trial Division were adjourned pending the outcome in the appeal division.

The customary challenge to the jurisdiction of the Court of Appeal was the first matter addressed. Counsel argued that the decision of the board was of an administrative nature that was not required to be made on a judicial or quasi-judicial basis. In a 2–1 decision, the Court of Appeal concluded that it had no jurisdiction.

Chief Justice Jackett and deputy judge Sheppard constituted the majority. Jackett rendered the judgment and characterized the disciplinary decision as part of the management operation of the prison. While he believed that disciplinary decisions should be as fair as possible, Jackett did not find that such decisions had to be made on a judicial or quasi-judicial basis; as a consequence, the disciplinary decision before the court was not subject to review by the Court of Appeal.

Mr Justice Ryan dissented and found that the Court of Appeal had jurisdiction. In his view, since internal procedural rules had been established that created a proceeding resembling that of a criminal court, the decisions had to be made on a quasi-judicial basis.[30]

The 2–1 split among the Court of Appeal judges was uncharacteristic and indicated the controversial nature of the problem. The split on appeal to the Supreme Court of Canada (5–4) removed all doubt that the issue was highly controversial. The Supreme Court also held that the Court of Appeal did not have jurisdiction.[31]

The focus in the Supreme Court was on the internal procedural rules that Ryan had accepted as giving the disciplinary process the attributes of a criminal trial, and thus creating the need for the board to perform in a judicial manner. These rules were contained in a directive of the commissioner of penitentiaries. Mr Justice Pigeon, with Ritchie, Beetz, and de Grandpré concurring, asked whether the directive was to be considered as 'law' within the wording of section 28, which referred to 'a decision ... of an administrative nature ... required by law to be made on a judicial or quasi-judicial basis.' These four judges ruled that directives prepared by the administrative head of the prison system were not 'law' for the purpose of section 28. They were administrative in nature. Noting that the commissioner of penitentiaries did not need legislative authority to issue directives, Pigeon offered additional reasons why the board should not be identified as judicial in nature: 'The members of a disciplinary board are not high public officers but ordinarily civil servants. The Commissioner's directives are no more than directions as to the manner of carrying out their duties in the administration of the institution where they are employed.' Neither Pigeon nor his three colleagues were prepared to accept the proposition that there is a duty to act judicially simply because a decision affects the right of a prisoner. The fifth judge of the majority, Judson, preferred to agree with the reasons delivered by Chief Justice Jackett in the Court of Appeal. In the Supreme Court of Canada this was a very unusual occurrence.

The four dissenting judges were Laskin, Martland, Spence, and Dickson; Laskin rendered their judgment. While he acknowledged that the issue might be viewed as narrow in a formal sense, Laskin also asserted that it went to the very heart of the jurisdiction conferred upon the Federal Court of Appeal to review decisions or orders of administrative tribunals. While the dissenting judges concluded that the directives had established a judicial or quasi-judicial process, and were actually made under the authority of statute (the formal approach), they considered the better approach to be to determine whether fairness in proceedings was required by examining the nature of the tribunal and the disputes it dealt with. In this sense, they concluded, the disciplinary board was required to act in a judicial fashion.

Thus ended *Martineau (No. 1)*. The Court of Appeal had no jurisdiction because what was involved was an administrative decision without a requirement that it be made in a judicial or quasi-judicial manner. *Martineau (No. 2)* began before the Trial Division; the proceedings which had been adjourned were revived and an order was sought in the nature of a writ of *certiorari* under section 18. The jurisdiction of the Trial Division was now challenged.

The Trial Division judge was Mr Justice Patrick Mahoney. He declared that the jurisdiction depended on some right of the applicant being abridged or denied, which was somewhat curious, in that four of the Supreme Court justices had just rejected this approach in *Martineau (No. 1)*. He concluded, 'I take it that in Canada, in 1975, a public body such as the respondent, authorized by law to impose a punishment, that was more than a mere denial of privileges, had a duty to act fairly in arriving at its decision to impose the punishment. Any other conclusion would be repugnant.'[32] It followed that of course the Trial Division had jurisdiction. Not all of the litigants were in agreement and the appeal process began again.

Wilbur Jackett sat on the Court of Appeal panel along with Darrel Heald and Arthur Kelly as a deputy judge. Jackett delivered a brief judgment for the court following the hearing. *Certiorari*, he said, applied only where the decision attacked either is judicial in character or is required by law to be made on a judicial or quasi-judicial basis. This was the criterion needed for review by the Court of Appeal! Because Jackett had already determined in *Martineau (No. 1)* that the board's decision lacked this characteristic, it followed that Mahoney's decision was overturned. The Court of Appeal held that the Trial Division did not have jurisdiction.[33]

Jackett produced an appendix to his decision in which he offered an explanation of his judgment. He opened with a measure of obvious cynicism: 'In a probably futile attempt to avoid misunderstanding as to the effect of our decision ...'[34] The text then explained that the duty to act fairly and justly did not in itself incur judicial review. Ministers and officials who have purely administrative powers are obliged to exercise those powers on a fair and just basis, but they remain accountable to their superiors or to the legislature, and not the courts. This indicated clearly that Jackett wanted no part of the development of a duty of fairness to be applied to decision makers in general (and enforceable through judicial review), a subject of considerable discussion within the legal profession at the time. This may have been the entire point of the appendix.

Between the time that Jackett rendered his judgment and the hearing of the appeal by the Supreme Court of Canada, the higher court had decided the landmark case of *Nicholson v. Haldimand-Norfolk Regional Board of Commissioners of Police.*[35] In *Nicholson*, the Supreme Court did recognize a duty on the part of all administrative decision makers to act fairly; and the duty existed quite apart from whether the actor exercised an administrative or judicial or quasi-judicial function. This duty to act fairly could be enforced by judicial review. In *Martineau (No. 2)* the Supreme Court of Canada simply applied the law which had been created in *Nicholson* to reverse the Court of Appeal.[36]

Mr Justice Pigeon, who rendered the judgment for the majority in *Martineau (No. 2),* volunteered the opinion that review under section 28 was 'a remedy which ... is in the nature of an appeal,'[37] signifying the existence of an extensive review function. Mr Justice Dickson, in a concurring opinion for himself, Chief Justice Laskin, and Mr Justice McIntyre, undertook to discuss the administrative law jurisdiction of the Federal Court. He was concerned about the lack of ability of the Court of Appeal to develop the law. His focus became the language of section 18 and 28, but he put that in the context of what he saw as the intention to create for the Federal Court an extended scope of review. Consequently he felt that the tendency should be not to diminish that scope, but to exercise it widely where the rights and interests of citizens were at issue. Dickson was prepared to accept that section 28 contained factors which could be seen as limiting the scope of judicial review, but they did not exist in the language of section 18. Development of the law, including recognition of the doctrine of fairness, could be accomplished through section 18, and he warned that a narrow reading of its language would 'virtually deny Canadians recourse against federal tribunals.'[38]

The Federal Court, and in particular the Court of Appeal, had effectively been told to abandon an approach that had restricted judicial review and rejected the development of the fairness doctrine.

A look back to the beginning of the Federal Court shows that judges had initially recognized the scope of review under section 28 of the Federal Court Act to be potentially very wide. In 1972 Mr Justice Thurlow had said that it conferred 'a heretofore unknown and non-existent right of review, broader than was formerly available by crown writ procedures.'[39] But by the time of the *Martineau* decision, Thurlow's opinion was no longer accepted by the judges of the appeal division. Dickson's comments in the Supreme Court of Canada emphasised the purpose of judicial review and implied that the appeal division had lost touch with that purpose. This was censure. When the highly critical judgments contained in the Supreme Court of Canada decision in *Martineau (No. 2)* were rendered on December 13, 1979, Jackett was no longer the chief justice of the Federal Court. He had resigned on October 1, 1979.

A pronounced aura of confusion had surrounded sections 18 and 28 from the very beginning; by 1979 it was said that the procedural and remedial aspects of the process of judicial review of federal administrative action had been complicated 'beyond anyone's wildest dreams.'[40] The problems had created a wave of nostalgia for the 'great prerogative writs'[41] and the reforms of 1970 were unravelling. Clearly something had to be done.

The episode involving the doctrine of procedural fairness signalled the need for a significant change in the Federal Court. In a thorough and well-written article published in 1975, administrative law scholar David Mullan reviewed the development of the fairness doctrine in England up to that time and discussed how it was to be applied when finally accepted in Canada. Since the rule was broadly worded (and consequently vague), judges would have to rely on a functional approach. The question for the judiciary would be, 'what kind of procedural protections are necessary for a particular decision-making process?' Mullan also thought that a very broad spectrum of decision-making functions would have to be recognized, for which varying procedural requirements would be necessary.[42] This very specific analysis was not something that formalists would be comfortable with. Contextualism had moved closer to becoming the dominant methodology.

20

The Mystery of Section 101

Whatever the difficulties associated with sections 18 and 28, or the court's new jurisdiction over federal matters such as aeronautics (section 23), or the expanded maritime jurisdiction (section 22), they did not compare with the confusion and even despair that arose from a trio of decisions of the Supreme Court of Canada that were said to have laid 'constitutional land-mines'[1] for the Federal Court. The ensuing problems raised the question of whether the very existence of the court was worthwhile. Two of these profoundly important decisions are discussed in this chapter, and the third in the next one.

THE QUEBEC NORTH SHORE PAPER CASE

The first, the *Quebec North Shore Paper* case of 1976,[2] involved a breach of contract action between two corporations. Their agreement involved the transportation of newsprint. The paper company, Quebec North Shore Paper, had undertaken to build a rail car marine terminal at Baie Comeau, Quebec; the shipping company, Canadian Pacific, had agreed to move newsprint from the terminal to the United States. The terminal was not built and Canadian Pacific brought an action in the Trial Division of the Federal Court for damages for breach of contract and for cancellation of the contract. As a preliminary step the paper company challenged the court's jurisdiction, arguing that the litigation should have been undertaken in the courts of the province of Quebec.

Such an action could not have been litigated in the Exchequer Court because the government was not a party, but was thought to be possible in the Federal Court because of the changes introduced by section 23 of the Federal Court Act. The Federal Court had been given jurisdiction in actions between subjects when 'a remedy is sought under an Act of the Parliament of Canada or otherwise in relation to any matter coming within [the] following class of subjects, namely ... works and undertakings connecting a province with any other province or extending beyond the limits of a province.'[3]

Mr Justice Addy in the Trial Division accepted that he had jurisdiction on the basis that the rail car marine terminal was part of an interprovincial system, owned and operated by Canadian Pacific railways.[4] His conclusion was affirmed by the Court of Appeal. Mr Justice Le Dain rendered the judgment of the court on the jurisdiction issue, with Thurlow and Ryan concurring.[5] The judgment gave no indication of any debate on the question.

An appeal to the Supreme Court of Canada was heard by a panel of eight judges. Writing for a unanimous Court, Chief Justice Bora Laskin rejected the result reached by the judges of the Federal Court and declared that the Federal Court did not have jurisdiction over the contractual dispute.

The solution to the jurisdiction issue in the case required an understanding of the constitution, and Laskin was a recognized constitutional law authority, both from his days as an academic and his judicial pronouncements after becoming a judge. While the unanimity of the judges of the Supreme Court suggested an uncontroversial result, what happened later was anything but. Because of the significance of this decision to the history of the Federal Court, it is worth examining Laskin's judgment in depth.

Laskin identified the constitutional authority giving the federal Parliament the power to create courts as that contained in section 101 of the Constitution Act, 1867 (then the British North America Act). Section 101 reads:

The Parliament of Canada may, notwithstanding anything in this Act, from Time to Time provide for the Constitution, Maintenance, and Organization of a General Court of Appeal for Canada, and for the Establishment of any additional Courts for the better Administration of the Laws of Canada.

The relevant language, Laskin noted, was that the federally created courts were for the 'administration of the laws of Canada.'

The jurisdiction of the Federal Court was based on the language of section 23 of the Federal Court Act:

The Trial Division has concurrent original jurisdiction as well between subject and subject as otherwise, in all cases in which a claim for relief is made or a remedy is sought under an Act of the Parliament of Canada or otherwise in relation to any matter coming within any following classes of subjects, namely ... works and undertakings connecting a province with any other province or extending beyond the limits of a province.

This meant that the meaning of the words 'under an Act of the Parliament of Canada or otherwise' found in section 23 depended on the meaning of the words 'administration of the laws of Canada' contained in section 101 of the Constitution Act, 1867.[6]

The words themselves, the language context, did not provide any apparent solution, and Laskin moved to the legal context, which in this instance consisted of previous judicial decisions of the Supreme Court of Canada and the Privy Council. Although Laskin was unquestionably a contextual thinker, it is worth noting that he rarely ventured into the third context, the social, and then only if the language and legal contexts failed completely to provide guidance. Naturally the social context exists as a web to which language and law adhere, and which, generally unobtrusively, controls thought.

In this instance Laskin preferred to focus virtually exclusively on the language used in the cases, and in a fairly short judgment was able to produce two quotations around which all discussion would take place. The cases consisted of Supreme Court decisions of 1930 and 1932, *Consolidated Distilleries Ltd. v. Consolidated Exporters Corporation Ltd.*[7] and *Consolidated Distilleries Ltd. v. The King*,[8] and the decision of the Judicial Committee of the Privy Council that reversed the Supreme Court in the second case.

The *Consolidated Distilleries* cases involved a claim by the federal government on bonds given as security for excise duty. The defendant company asked the court to have a third party notice served because of an agreement of indemnity, and in response the third party applied to set aside the notice on the ground that the Exchequer Court had no jurisdiction to deal with the third party indemnity issue. The Exchequer Court judge and a majority of the Supreme Court of Canada justices agreed that since the third party proceeding was between individuals it was not within the jurisdiction of the Exchequer Court. In his judgment in the Supreme Court, Chief Justice Frank Anglin said:

the words, 'the laws of Canada,' must signify laws enacted by the Dominion Parliament and within its competence. If they should be taken to mean laws in force anywhere in Canada, which is the alternative suggested, s. 101 would be wide enough to confer jurisdiction on Parliament to create courts empowered to deal with the whole range of matters within the exclusive jurisdiction of the provincial legislatures, including 'property and civil rights' in the provinces.[9]

Anglin's comment seems to cover the simple point that the words 'laws of Canada' means laws of federal Canada and not those of the provinces. But his use of the words 'laws enacted by the Dominion Parliament and within its competence' to give meaning to 'laws of Canada' (which was the issue in the *Quebec North Shore Paper* case) made the quote significant. Laskin was using anything that might be of help rather than abandon his reliance on the cases.

The second *Consolidated Distilleries* case involved the actual determination of the merits of the government's claim on the bonds. While the various judges each agreed that the Exchequer Court had jurisdiction, there was disagreement about which provision in the Exchequer Court Act authorized its exercise. The Privy Council was satisfied that section 30(d) of the Act applied. It read:

The Exchequer Court shall have and possess concurrent original jurisdiction in Canada in all ... actions and suits of a civil nature at common law or equity in which the Crown is plaintiff or petitioner.

Laskin reproduced a lengthy quotation from the judgment of Lord Russell of Killowen for the Privy Council. The crucial words, which served as the second quote, were

the actions and suits in sub-s. (d) must be confined to actions and suits in relation to some subject-matter, legislation in regard to which is within the legislative competence of the Dominion.

Missing were the words which had appeared in Anglin's quotation – 'laws enacted by ... Parliament.'

Laskin set out to choose which quotation was to govern. In other words, could the Federal Court have jurisdiction over an action 'in relation to some subject-matter, legislation in regard to which is within the legislative competence of the Dominion' (Privy Council), or must there be 'laws enacted by the Dominion Parliament'? (Anglin). The reliance on words only, which was not usual for Laskin, gave the reasoning a pronounced abstract flavour.

Laskin pointed out that the Privy Council had also used the words 'law enacted by' in its judgment, and when section 30(a) had been argued ('The Exchequer Court shall have and possess concurrent original jurisdiction ... in all cases relating to the revenue in which it is sought to enforce any law of Canada'), the Privy Council had said that since there was no law of Canada being enforced in the litigation, subsection 30(a) could not be the source of jurisdiction.

Laskin used the Privy Council's comment on section 30(a) to counter the argument based on the other words Lord Russell of Killowen had used, 'some subject-matter, legislation in regard to which is within the legislative competence of the Dominion.' Laskin blunted these latter words by saying that they were simply 'expressing a limitation on the range of matters in respect of which the Crown in right of Canada may, as plaintiff, bring persons into the Exchequer Court as defendants.'[10] Laskin added that some law would still be needed.

The question of judge-made law (the 'common law'), as opposed to legislation, arose quite naturally. Laskin stated that the only common law that might be called federal was the law respecting the Crown, which came into Canada as part of the public or constitutional law of Great Britain. Crown law was not part of the case that was before the court.[11]

Laskin concluded that there must be 'applicable and existing federal law' in order for the Federal Court to have jurisdiction. In the case of the contract dispute over the rail car marine terminal agreement such law did not exist and thus it was provincial law that applied.[12]

This was not a judgment that reflected Laskin's typical, contextual approach. The fact that the decision was unanimous suggests that it may have been the result of compromise, which may account for the lack of clarity in the reasons. While Laskin was never the clearest of writers, this judgment was more difficult to fathom than most. In the end, only Laskin's concluding statement that there must be 'applicable and existing federal law' seemed clear enough for the profession to use.

This judgment of the Supreme Court of Canada reversed the decision of the Federal Court of Appeal. Le Dain, with Ryan concurring, had rendered the principal judgment, and Le Dain had a certain reputation in constitutional law. Laskin appeared agitated by Le Dain's judgment, and he lapsed into what amounted to a brief constitutional law lecture on the issue of the application of provincial law to enterprises within federal jurisdiction, a gesture which would have been provoking to a constitutional law colleague. It may not have helped that Le Dain had referred to Laskin's constitutional law casebook; although the reference appeared innocuous enough, Le Dain used it as part of an argument against the position that Laskin subsequently took.

Le Dain had referred to the words 'under an Act of the Parliament of Canada or otherwise' in s. 23 of the Federal Court Act, and had stated that they applied 'to any other law that can be considered to form part of the "laws of Canada" within the meaning of s. 101.'[13] Before the Supreme Court, counsel relied on Le Dain's statement that 'laws of Canada' would cover 'any law that Parliament can validly enact, amend or repeal.' Le Dain had gone on to explain that since Parliament could enact contract law to deal with the matter, the Quebec law would come within the words 'laws of Canada.'[14] Laskin rejected Le Dain's opinion tersely and criticized the appeal judge for begging the question. Without Le Dain's judgment, the unanimous decision of the Supreme Court delivered by Laskin would have presented the appearance of there being little controversy about the question.

Curiously, on the constitutional issue Laskin's judgment made no mention of the contract aspect. It was well established in constitutional law that contractual matters were within provincial jurisdiction, and the vulnerable part of Le Dain's judgment was his view that Ottawa could enact contract law to deal with a matter of interprovincial concern. This was by no means a safe conclusion.[15] If the discussion had focused on the issue of whether the contract was part of the federal jurisdiction over interprovincial undertakings under the constitution (which Le Dain had raised), it would have been a routine constitutional decision. This did not happen.[16]

THE *MCNAMARA CONSTRUCTION* CASE

The decision in *Quebec North Shore Paper* was rendered at the end of June 1976. Early in 1977, the Supreme Court of Canada delivered judgment in *McNamara Construction*.[17] The two decisions combined to create untold difficulty. That they dealt with two quite separate legal issues simply added to the confusion.

It was true that *McNamara* involved a contract dispute, but the dispute was between the federal government and a construction company for the building of a federal prison, and not between private citizens. The litigation consisted of an action brought by the federal government for breach of the contract. While the question was again whether the Federal Court had jurisdiction, this time attention focused on a different provision in the Federal Court Act.

.   The jurisdiction of the Trial Division of the Federal Court was said to be founded on the subsection of the Act that read, 'The Trial Division has concurrent original jurisdiction in proceedings of a civil nature in which the [government] of Canada claims relief.'[18] (This was the modern equivalent of the provision in the Exchequer Court Act which the Privy Council had accepted in the *Consolidated Distilleries* case as supporting the jurisdiction of the Exchequer Court in the government's action on the bonds.)

McNamara Construction argued that Ottawa had no legislative power over contracts. This was an extension of the argument advanced in the *Quebec North Shore Paper* case. The Federal Court of Appeal reached a conclusion consistent with the position it had taken in *Quebec North Shore Paper* – not surprising since the Supreme Court had not yet rendered its decision in that case when the Federal Court became involved with *McNamara Construction*. The Court of Appeal concluded that the contractual aspect of a matter was within the scope of federal constitutional authority over the matter. In *McNamara* it was 'The Establishment, Maintenance, and Management of Penitentiaries.'[19]

The Supreme Court of Canada again reversed the Federal Court of Appeal. In another brief and unanimous judgment, Chief Justice Laskin concluded that *Quebec North Shore Paper* had established the legal rule that there must be existing federal law to be applied; since there was none, the Federal Court had no jurisdiction. Laskin asserted that the federal Parliament had no constitutional power to give jurisdiction to the Federal Court to entertain any type of civil action simply because the Crown in right of Canada was asserting a claim as plaintiff. Up to this time, it had been unquestionably accepted that the rule, 'the King has the undoubted privilege of suing in any court he pleases' allowed the federal government to bring any action in the Exchequer or Federal Court.[20] The Judicial Committee of the Privy Council had said as much in the *Consolidated Distilleries* case, mentioned earlier. The Supreme Court was therefore effecting a significant reform of the law. The principle that the government had the privilege of suing in any court it pleased (from which it followed that the federal Parliament had the power to legislate as to the court in which the Crown in right of the Dominion could bring an action) was unacceptable because it failed to consider that Canada was a federal state and not a unitary one. The Crown in Canada was divisible between the Dominion and the provinces. Federalism concerns had become potent enough to create a change in the law. Change was so imperative that for the first time Laskin for the Supreme Court expressly overruled one of its own previous decisions, *Farwell v. The Queen*. The *Farwell* case had been decided in 1894, and had stood for the proposition that the federal government could bring any action in the Exchequer and Federal Court.[21] When Laskin referred to the previous decision as a forgotten case, he was not being completely candid. Laskin had already questioned the jurisdiction of a federal court when the Crown was the plaintiff and the matter in issue was within provincial competence, in his 1966 casebook on constitutional law.[22] There he had commented that the answer given in *Farwell* did not seem satisfactory, because of Canada's federal system. He echoed these earlier conclusions in *McNamara*: '[T]he Dominion cannot require a private person to submit to the jurisdiction of the Exchequer Court merely because the federal crown is plaintiff; there must be a basis of jurisdiction in the matter in issue.'

Laskin pointed out as well that *Farwell* had not been considered in *Consolidated Distilleries*, and this was true, but the point of law had been dealt with. What had been forgotten was that in *Consolidated Distilleries* the Privy Council had declared that there were limits to the jurisdiction, in that 'the actions and suits ... must be confined to actions and suits in relation to some subject-matter, legislation in regard to which is within the legislative competence of the Dominion.'[23] That limitation had been ignored over the years and the federal government had brought negligence and contract actions with no apparent objection. The *McNamara* decision effectively reinstated the limitation. Such actions would now be brought in the provincial courts.

Neither case was earth-shattering, but the reasons for judgment soon cast a strange and mysterious spell.

REACTION IN THE FEDERAL COURT

Within two months of the release of the judgment in *McNamara* Mr Justice Addy of the Trial Division noted that the reasoning in the *Quebec North Shore Paper Co.* case 'would seem to lead to sweeping and far reaching conclusions as to the jurisdiction of this Court,' although, he added, 'the language used by the Supreme Court of Canada ... might have been broader than was actually required to dispose of the appeal as it did.' He nevertheless went on to affirm that because of the *McNamara* decision there was no doubt that the language of *Quebec North Shore Paper* should be applied in an 'all-encompassing manner.'[24] He had tied the two cases together and was prepared to allow them to roam quite widely. He referred to *McNamara* as having reversed all former jurisprudence – but that was true only of the *Farwell* point. What else was he thinking about?

The case over which Mr Justice Addy was presiding involved aeronautics, which constitutionally was within federal power and had always been given the widest scope possible.[25] The government made a claim of indemnity in an action against it for negligence. Jurisdiction was denied because there was no existing federal law. No constitutional analysis was attempted and Addy cut down the jurisdiction of the court without further thought.

Mr Justice Jean-Eudes Dubé of the Trial Division took the same simplistic approach. Based on the Supreme Court decisions, he concluded that the Federal Court had no jurisdiction in a contract case unless there was an Act of Parliament under which the relief sought in the action was claimed.[26] He went further in a subsequent case and concluded that there must be a specific Act of Parliament on which to base any action; this would require an analysis of the language to determine if the particular action was covered.[27] This was a familiar and comfortable form of analysis, but it did nothing for the jurisdiction of the court.

The need for federal legislation that specifically directed jurisdiction was often articulated in the Federal Court.[28] The overall effect of this view was that the Federal Court judges gave every appearance of being determined to limit their own jurisdiction as much as possible. Mr Justice Louis Marceau of the Trial Division expressed the opinion that the words of section 23, which bestowed jurisdiction if the action was brought 'under an Act of the Parliament of Canada or otherwise,' had to be given a 'very strict' interpretation.[29] Cases which predated *Quebec North Shore Paper* and *McNamara* and which might have suggested reining in this tendency to limit the court's jurisdiction were pushed aside.[30]

A 'WIDELY ACCEPTED VIEW'

It was commonly accepted that the Supreme Court of Canada had created a major change. Chief Justice Jackett, in *Associated Metals & Minerals Corp. v. The 'Evie W,'*[31] noted that before the 1976 and 1977 Supreme Court decisions it had been the 'widely accepted view' that section 101 allowed jurisdiction to be conferred on a federal court 'in respect of matters that are within federal legislative jurisdiction.'[32]

The foundation of the argument that section 101 did allow Ottawa to grant jurisdiction to a federal court over any matter within federal legislative jurisdiction was the language used by Lord Russell of Killowen in the *Consolidated Distilleries* case: 'the acts and suits ... must be confined to actions and suits in relation to some subject-matter, legislation in regard to which is within the legislative competence of the Dominion.'[33] Laskin had considered these words in *Quebec North Shore Paper* and had pointed out that they were 'expressing a limitation on the range of matters in respect of which the Crown in right of Canada may, as plaintiff, bring persons into the Exchequer Court as defendants.'[34] He then added the obvious, that some existing law would still have to be found.

The reference to 'existing' at first glance seems somewhat silly, for law must of course exist before it can be applied. Laskin meant that if there were an area of law which was within Ottawa's constitutional authority, but no federal law had been created, then there was no law. Provincial law, even though it might apply, was not to be used.[35]

Two questions were involved: one, What jurisdiction may the federal Parliament bestow on a federal court? and, two, When may the federal government bring an action in a federal court? Following the two cases the answer would be the same for each: when federal law, as opposed to provincial law, is involved – that is, 'applicable and existing federal law.'

The history of the so-called 'widely accepted view' and the answers to the two questions reveals that changes had occurred over time. On the jurisdiction issue, John A. Macdonald and his government had thought that the Supreme Court of Canada could be given original jurisdiction over provincial law,[36] but this idea had quickly been abandoned. In an article written in 1882 in the *Canadian Law Times*, the editor discussed the power of the federal Parliament to erect courts under section 101 and argued for a very extensive power that would allow for the creation of courts to administer provincial laws.[37] The writer, E. Douglas Armour, was motivated by a desire for a centralized state, and perceived that placing the administration of justice within the provincial courts would tend towards disunion. Armour's argument focused on the words and how they were used, and on the centralizing features contained in the constitution (the 'Macdonaldian constitution'). Armour continued to advocate extensive federal power in another article published in 1883.[38] He did note that the question was 'almost devoid of authority.'[39]

In 1882 there were certainly forces within English Canada committed to establishing a centralized system, and as a result there was considerable support for federal power. The strength of the commitment is apparent in an 1879 Supreme Court decision where the issue was whether the Dominion could impose on the Superior Court of Quebec the jurisdiction to try election issues concerning members of the federal House of Commons.[40] The federal principle was argued as requiring the establishment of a dual court system, and prohibiting Ottawa from legislating in relation to the jurisdiction of provincial tribunals. If the argument had succeeded it would have meant that Ottawa would have had to establish its own courts, or negotiate with the provinces, since the provinces could permit their courts to handle federal matters.

The Supreme Court rejected the argument, which urged the need for a dual system of courts, and recognized the power of Ottawa to confer jurisdiction on provincial courts. In the process the judges described a country in which the central authority had enormous power in relation to the provinces. Mr Justice William Henry, a father of Confederation, stated that the policy of the constitution was to limit the provinces to those civil rights in the province not specially included in Dominion power. The power of Ottawa was 'to make laws for the peace, order and good government of Canada,' which covered the totality of legislative power and was limited only by the provisions in section 92 that granted the provinces legislative power.[41]

The changing constitution has already been discussed,[42] and, by the end of the 1880s, Ottawa's power had been challenged by the provinces and largely overcome. An article published in 1891 entitled 'The Constitution of Canada' stated that the idea that Ottawa could constitute courts in place of the provincial courts, giving a wide meaning to the words 'laws of Canada,' was 'a very remarkable instance' of the existence of federal power, 'if the power existed.'[43] In his book The Law of Legislative Power in Canada, published in 1898, A.H.F. Lefroy relegated the issue to a footnote, and clearly viewed the opinion that 'laws of Canada' meant anything other than federal laws as wrong. In Consolidated Distilleries in 1933, the Judicial Committee of the Privy Council accepted that only federal law was involved, and Laskin reaffirmed this some forty years later.

The issue 'What is federal law?' still remained. Does an action for breach of contract in the construction of a penitentiary or in the building of a rail car marine terminal which would connect with an interprovincial railway come within the federal power over penitentiaries or interprovincial undertakings? From the outset, contracts were considered to be well within provincial power. The same could be said of tort actions and property disputes – provincial law applied. As a result, Ottawa could not legislate with respect to these aspects of penitentiaries or trade and commerce or interprovincial undertakings. The question of whether a contract, property, or tort dispute was within federal or provincial authority was not always answered easily, but the question was not new.

The second question – When can the government bring an action in the Federal Court? – has largely been considered.[44] It had become accepted that provincial law would apply in cases in which the government was being sued (Crown liability), and Chief Justice Laskin had acknowledged in *Quebec North Shore Paper* the existence of federal judge-made law relating to Crown liability. No distinction had been made between instances when the government was the defendant (Crown liability) and when it was the plaintiff as far as the jurisdiction of the court was concerned. Since the use of provincial law was the rule when the government was being sued, it was easy to accept that provincial law would also be used when the government was bringing an action. The limitation imposed by the Privy Council was simply passed over.

In order to make sense of the idea that Laskin had made a change in the law, one must accept that there is federal common law surrounding each matter within federal legislative jurisdiction. This proposition is historically very questionable.

At the time of Confederation the common law consisted of the basic principles of contract, tort, property, and criminal law. In the constitution the law-making power over these areas of law was divided between the provinces and Ottawa: basic principles of contract, tort, and property law went to the provinces under the 'property and civil rights,' head of power,[45] while criminal law was assigned to the central authority.[46] There is little wonder that in 1894 Mr Justice Strong of the Supreme Court of Canada could say that talk of a 'law of Canada' (other than criminal law) must refer exclusively to statute law. Quebec, with its civil-law principles of contract, tort, and property, made it impossible to have a general common law prevailing throughout the country.[47] When Strong made the above comment he was not thinking of criminal law, since the judge-made criminal law of England did apply uniformly across Canada at that time.

With respect to the phrase 'laws of Canada' found in section 101, Laskin was on record as saying, 'There is no reason in principle why it should not also include such common law or civil law principles as were in force at confederation and which afterwards could only be dealt with by federal legislation under the distribution of legislative power effected by the Constitution.'[48] But this was 'in principle,' and in fact the provincial hold over property and civil rights, particularly by Quebec, was fierce. Thus while the possibility existed that a federal head of legislative power in the constitution could be defined to include basic principles of contract, tort, and property, it never became politically feasible to do so before the 1970s.

An example of the provinces' hold over property and civil rights occurred with the development of Crown liability. This was constitutional (administrative) law and consequently the law of England applied. In the nineteenth century the proposition became established that the government had no liability in tort in the absence of legislation imposing it. Legislation was created in Canada, and elsewhere, and government immunity from tort actions slowly fell away. The Canadian federal system created a situation where the general laws of the provinces were to be taken as being read into the statutory provision that imposed the liability.[49]

All of this did not mean that there could not be a federal common law; if changing social conditions affecting a matter within federal legislative authority created the need to adapt the basic principles of contract, tort, or property, then our legal process allowed the judges to make the adjustments, and hence create 'federal common law.' Laskin himself had said that he saw no problem with a federal court fashioning the common law in a different way from that of the provincial courts.[50] But this was theory.

When the Federal Court of Appeal in *Quebec North Shore Paper* and *McNamara Construction* recognized contractual matters as within federal legislative authority, it was effecting a significant change in favour of enhancing federal legislative power. The Supreme Court of Canada, led by Chief Justice Bora Laskin, reset the constitutional balance of legislative power between the provinces and Ottawa.

THE ADMIRALTY JURISDICTION

When the Federal Court was given jurisdiction over maritime matters there was every indication that the limitations of the past had been swept away and the jurisdiction restored to a pristine condition – jurisdiction over ships and shipping. 'Canadian maritime law' was defined simply as law in relation to maritime and admiralty matters, and any federal legislation that was in relation to maritime and admiralty matters.[51] Here was an example of the common law of property, contracts, and torts being brought into the jurisdiction as long as ships and shipping (a maritime matter) were involved. Section 22(1) of the Federal Court Act gave the Trial Division jurisdiction whenever Canadian maritime law was to be applied, and also any other law relating to matters of navigation and shipping.

In the opening years of the Federal Court the response when the maritime jurisdiction was questioned was to examine the connection between the facts of the dispute and ships and shipping. For example, terminal operators were identified as closely connected with ocean carriers and an essential part of the carriage of goods by sea, so that an action involving damage to cargo in the custody of terminal operators was within the court's jurisdiction.[52] While the distinctiveness of admiralty law from other areas of jurisdiction was seemingly well established, and had been recognized by Chief Justice Laskin himself in earlier writing,[53] the advent of *Quebec North Shore Paper* and *McNamara* ensnared the judges; that distinctiveness was cast aside and admiralty cases were caught up in the confusion.

When Chief Justice Jackett confronted the problem of applying the two Supreme Court decisions to maritime jurisdiction, he created a mythical position consistent with his commitment to the declaratory theory of law. He posited that, in early times, a body of admiralty law or 'law of the sea' had governed matters of navigation and shipping and international trade in most maritime nations, including England. The statutes which had restricted the jurisdiction of the Admiralty Court did not purport to abolish this law, nor had they in fact done so. Throughout the years in which the legislation restricting the jurisdiction had operated, there had been no occasion to apply the ancient law; but when the inhibitions were removed, the old law was revived and became operative.[54] However, this thinking never caught on.[55] Something blocked the acceptance of Jackett's idea of 'unlimited' maritime jurisdiction and its distinctiveness. In the first case that came up against the effect of *Quebec North Shore Paper* and *McNamara Construction*, Mr Justice Thurlow of the Trial Division went searching for a clear legal rule that bestowed jurisdiction from the past.[56] The case involved a breach of contract action regarding the building of a ship. When his search failed to uncover a specific law that recognized the matter as within the pre-1970 admiralty jurisdiction, he held that the Federal Court had no jurisdiction. He went so far as to reject the argument that a provision of the Federal Court Act reading '[T]he Trial Division has jurisdiction with respect to any claim arising out of a contract relating to the construction, repair or equipping of a ship' could be used.[57] He concluded that the provision did not impose any new liability either specifically or inferentially and no new right was conferred. It appeared as if Thurlow did not know what to do with the two Supreme Court decisions, and consequently fell back on a simple expedient, namely, a search for a rule from the past. This response restricted the jurisdiction of the court considerably.

A pronounced self-consciousness about the jurisdiction of the court still pervaded the thoughts of the judges. When maritime law (so securely within the jurisdiction of the court since 1891) was affected, it did not bode well for other areas of the court's work.

Surprisingly, Chief Justice Laskin and the Supreme Court of Canada became caught up in the turmoil as well. In *Tropwood A.G. v. Sivaco Wire and Nail Co.* (1979),[58] the issue was whether the Federal Court had jurisdiction over an action in contract and tort for damage to cargo carried by a ship. Laskin searched through the admiralty law that had existed before the enactment of the Federal Court Act for a rule upon which the jurisdiction could be exercised. He maintained that the words in section 2 of the Act, 'any other statute,' included statutes that had actually been repealed. Thus, in the Admiralty Act of 1891 Laskin found wording sufficient for the purpose: 'all matters (including cases of contract and tort and proceedings *in rem* and *in personam*), arising out of or connected with navigation, shipping, trade or commerce, which may be had or enforced in any Colonial Court of Admiralty under *The Colonial Courts of Admiralty Act, 1890.'*[59] This provision had been repealed in 1934. He went on to acknowledge that there was a body of admiralty law which had been incorporated into the law of Canada, and the law of Canada regarding admiralty matters that the Exchequer Court had applied in 1891 was the same as that applied by the High Court in England. A search through the law of England revealed that the claim for damage to cargo had been recognized by the Admiralty Act of 1861.[60] This conclusion did not end the matter, since there remained the question of whether the law so found was within the scope of federal legislative power under the constitution (navigation and shipping). Laskin answered the question in the affirmative.

This analysis is astonishing. There was no indication in Laskin's judgment that he had paid any attention to the words in section 2 of the Federal Court Act: 'that would have been so administered if that Court had had on its Admiralty side, unlimited jurisdiction in relation to maritime and admiralty matters.' Profound concern with provincial jurisdiction is the only explanation possible.

When Thurlow's trial decision reached the Federal Court of Appeal, that court was faced with Laskin's judgment in *Tropwood*.[61] Jackett rendered the judgment for a panel which also included Pratte and deputy judge Lalande. Once again he emphasized that the Supreme Court of Canada had changed a widely held legal opinion, though this time Jackett placed quotation marks around 'widely accepted.' It is not in the formalist tradition to acknowledge that judges change the law, yet Jackett felt compelled to do so; the gesture signals an implied criticism. Taking the lead of Laskin in *Tropwood*, Jackett himself searched through the previous law, and found sufficient wording in the Admiralty Act of 1934. Jackett went on to say that if he were wrong in choosing the 1934 rule, the court still had jurisdiction by virtue of its 'unlimited jurisdiction in relation to maritime and admiralty matters.' The pristine jurisdiction had finally made an appearance. If accepted, it effectively obviated the need to sift through previous law for a specific rule.

At this time there was evidence of a different approach by at least one judge. Mr Justice Hugh Gibson of the Trial Division held that the maritime law jurisdiction covered questions relating to marine insurance.[62] He was prepared to recognize a 'large body of substantive admiralty law, much of it non-statutory in its original source' that had been incorporated into federal Canadian maritime law (by reference) through the definition section in the Federal Court Act.[63] In his opinion, this 'large body of substantive applicable federal law' fulfilled the requirement laid down in *Quebec North Shore Paper* and *McNamara*. Stated simply, the jurisdiction of the Federal Court covers actions in relation to 'navigation and shipping.' In Gibson's view the limits to the jurisdiction should be determined on a case-by-case basis, the only restriction being that the dispute relate to the navigation business or commerce of the sea or inland waters of Canada. However, the simplicity of Gibson's approach, contextual in nature, which allowed the policy behind the Federal Court Act to flow through, was an exception.

21

A Lamentable Situation

The litigation in *The Queen v. Thomas Fuller Construction Co. (1958) Ltd.*[1] began when the government halted work on the construction of a federal building in Ottawa. Blasting by the company engaged to install sewers for the new building had damaged a footing supporting part of a foundation wall. The construction company brought an action against the government based on the contract between them for damages resulting from the delay which ensued. The government issued a third party notice against the sewer company claiming indemnity. It was this third party notice that created a jurisdictional issue for the Federal Court and gave the *Thomas Fuller Construction Co.* case its significance in the court's history.

In the Trial Division, Mr Justice Raymond Decary struck out the third party notice because of a lack of jurisdiction; his decision was upheld by the Court of Appeal. The appeal taken by the government to the Supreme Court of Canada was dismissed by a 6–1 decision. Laskin did not participate in the case, and the judgment for the majority was rendered by Mr Justice Pigeon.

The judgment of the Court of Appeal was extremely brief and was rendered by Chief Justice Jackett. He asserted that there simply was no federal law and said that *McNamara* governed; he then commented that if that conclusion created a problem, the answer was to enact legislation.[2]

The Court of Appeal made no attempt to influence the thinking of the Supreme Court justices.

In the Supreme Court Pigeon began his judgment with the statement that constitutionally the Canadian judicial system possessed a 'special feature.'[3] The special feature was that the so-called provincial courts were 'provincial' only in a limited sense: they were, in fact, the courts that had a general jurisdiction, responsible for the administration of all federal and provincial laws. This arrangement had been created in order to avoid 'the difficulties of divided jurisdiction.'[4] Pigeon and a majority of the judges of the Supreme Court had decided to use the constitution to prevent the establishment of a dual judicial system.

Pigeon's next step was to note the 'extensive jurisdiction'[5] which had been given to the Federal Court, and which had created problems that could be associated with the existence of a dual system of courts. His depiction of the Federal Court as a move towards the establishment of a dual system of courts (and an erosion of the 'special feature' of the constitution) had to affect the court's future.

After setting out the basic points of his reasoning, Pigeon turned to a consideration of third party proceedings. Based on what he identified as 'conclusive authority,' Pigeon accepted that these proceedings were to be viewed as separate from the main action. There was then a need to identify applicable and existing federal law, but there was none because the claim for indemnity arose from the contract, which was within provincial jurisdiction. In Pigeon's view, any difficulties associated with his conclusion could not justify extending the general jurisdiction of the federal tribunal.

The Supreme Court's reasoning brought the constitution into the fray. By characterizing the Federal Court as an exception within the Canadian judicial structure,[6] the Supreme Court had brought the court's very existence into question.

THE *PRYTULA* AND *RHINE* CASES

The tendency of most judges of the Federal Court to restrict their jurisdiction reached its apex in two cases that were considered together by the Supreme Court.

In *The Queen v. Prytula*[7] the government applied to the Federal Court for judgment in default because the defendant had failed to enter a defence. Prytula had received a student loan from a bank pursuant to the Canada Student Loans Act, under which the government agreed to pay the interest and guarantee the loan during the period of the student's enrolment. When Prytula defaulted on the payments, the government paid the loan and then demanded reimbursement from him. The claim was for an outstanding principal of $540.00 plus interest. Prytula did not defend the action.

The application for default judgment came before Mr Justice Allison Walsh. Walsh raised the question of jurisdiction based on the *McNamara* decision, and inquired which federal law would be applied to justify the jurisdiction of the Federal Court. Following an adjournment the matter came before Mr Justice Cattanach the following month.

The government took the position that the Canada Student Loans Act and its regulations allowed the court to decide the case. Cattanach rejected the government's argument. He maintained that the proceedings must be 'founded' on existing and applicable federal law, in the sense that the word 'founded' had been used by Chief Justice Laskin in the *McNamara* case. He did not accept that the action was 'founded' on the Canada Student Loans Act. Cattanach cast the action as a breach of the agreement between the bank and the student; it was not enough that the liability arose in consequence of the statute and regulations thereunder. What was determinative was that the statute itself did not impose a liability. He asserted that the same elements existed as in the *McNamara* case.

The second case was *The Queen v. Rhine*.[8] Under the authority of the Prairie Grain Advance Payments Act, the Canadian Wheat Board made advance payments to farmers for grain that they would later deliver to the board. The defendant defaulted on his delivery of grain and became indebted to the government in the amount of $417.00. He did not defend the action and the government applied for a default judgment.

Mr Justice Cattanach was again the trial judge. Relying on *McNamara*, he demanded written representations from counsel about the court's jurisdiction. After reviewing the material submitted he concluded that the action was based on the defendant's undertaking to repay the advance, and that it was not enough that the liability arose in consequence of a statute. In his view, the statute did not impose a liability. The claim in the case was seen as completely analogous to the Crown's claim on the surety bond in *McNamara*.

The decisions of Walsh and Cattanach suggest a magnifying of the problems associated with the *McNamara* case. A fellow judge of the Federal Court was driven to comment, 'It is arguable that ... Cattanach J. has gone further ... than the Supreme Court of Canada did ..., and in so doing has accorded to the Federal Court a more restricted jurisdiction than was expressed by Laskin C.J.C.'[9]

The Court of Appeal, consisting of Heald, Urie, and deputy judge MacKay, reversed Cattanach in both cases. Heald rendered the judgments of the court.[10] In *Prytula,* the judges returned to thinking about the problem in constitutional terms; the question became whether a contract between a banker and a customer with regard to a loan was a matter coming within federal constitutional authority over 'banking.'[11] The Court of Appeal answered yes and consequently found that there was existing and applicable federal law.[12]

A curious feature of the judgment of the Federal Court of Appeal was the inclusion of an appendix, which consisted of an excerpt from the judgment of Lord Herschell in an 1898 Privy Council decision, the *Ontario Fisheries Case.*[13] The excerpt contains a very elementary proposition in constitutional law and one wonders why the judges felt it necessary to include it.

In *Rhine,* the Prairie Grain Advance Payments Act was seen as an integral part of the scheme of marketing grain; the defendant's liability arose from the legislation. The Court of Appeal said that it was not a loan based on basic contract principles alone.

Bora Laskin again rendered judgment for a unanimous Supreme Court of Canada. The two judgments, rendered together, were short and succinct.[14] Examining the legislation in each case, Laskin established the existence of a detailed statutory framework in *Rhine,* a framework which was part of an overall scheme for the marketing of grain. That framework provided a 'statutory shelter'[15] which allowed the action to be based on applicable and existing federal law. In Laskin's mind, there was a wide gulf between this and the situation in *McNamara.*

In *Prytula,* he held that the legislation governed every aspect of the relationship between the borrowing student, the lending bank, and the guarantor government; the legislation would have to support any legal claims which resulted. In both cases, the Supreme Court of Canada found that it was simply a matter of the administration of a federal statute.

Laskin, for the Supreme Court, made it clear that making a decision in the jurisdiction cases should consist not of searching for specific words in a statute upon which to found a claim (assuming that the words were constitutionally valid), but of identifying a 'statutory shelter' for the actions which had created the problems litigated. Laskin's approach would do much to release the restrictions on the jurisdiction of the Federal Court, provided its judges were willing and able to undertake the analysis required.

THE CRANBROOK AIR CRASH

The Supreme Court's decision in the *McNamara* case had cut back the jurisdiction of the Federal Court to the extent that actions by the government based on basic principles of contract, property, and tort law had been eliminated. The court's jurisdiction had been further reduced by the way in which certain Federal Court judges had reacted to the decision and had taken to viewing the Court's jurisdiction strictly. As a result, additional problems of split jurisdiction arose.

The litigation that was generally referred to as the prime example of such problems involved the Cranbrook air crash of 1978. On the afternoon of February 11, 1978, Pacific Western Airlines Flight 314 from Calgary attempted to land at the airport in Cranbrook, British Columbia; a snow-plough on the runway forced it to change course. The aircraft climbed and slewed to the left, and then crashed into the ground at the end of the runway. Forty-three of the forty-nine people on board were killed.

Pacific Western Airlines and the owner of the aircraft, Canadian Acceptance Corporation, brought a number of actions based on negligence, breach of statutory duty, and contract. They sued the federal government, the minister of transport and employees of the department of transport, the city of Cranbrook and three city employees, the Boeing Company (the builder of the aircraft) and seven of its officers, and Rohr Industries Inc., (the manufacturer of the thrust reversal system that formed part of the plane's braking system), plus four senior Rohr personnel. With the exception of Rohr Industries, all of the defendants challenged the jurisdiction of the Federal Court.

Jurisdiction over aeronautics had been given to the Federal Court in section 23 of the Federal Court Act with the intention that all litigation which arose from an aircraft accident could be tried in one court.[16] But in the Trial Division of the Federal Court, Mr Justice Collier followed what he saw as the dictates of the Supreme Court in *Quebec North Shore Paper* and *McNamara Construction*. In a judgment which offered lengthy quotations from the two cases in undigested form, he said, 'A review of all those decisions leads me to the conclusion there is no existing federal law, whether statute or regulation or common law, dealing with negligence, permitting these defendants, other than the Crown, to be impleaded in this Court.'[17]

Collier was urged to accept jurisdiction over all the defendants, since all of the claims arose out of the same occurrence, and to adopt the concept of 'pendent jurisdiction' developed in the United States. Pendant jurisdiction allows an American federal court, when it has jurisdiction over a particular case, to assume jurisdiction over all the issues that arise from the 'common nucleus of operative fact' even when issues of state law are involved.[18] To convince Collier to take jurisdiction over all the defendants the lawyers relied on a decision rendered in the previous year by Mr Justice Gibson, *Davie Shipbuilding Ltd. v. The Queen*.[19]

As the name would suggest, the *Davie Shipbuilding* case involved maritime law – an action brought by a shipbuilder against the federal government for breach of a shipbuilding contract. The government sought to counterclaim against the shipbuilder, who wanted to make a third party claim against a subcontractor. Gibson recognized jurisdiction on the basis that the main action was within the jurisdiction of the court and the counterclaim and the third party issue were ancillary to the subject matter involved in that action. This case illustrated another concept developed in the United States known as 'ancillary jurisdiction,' which allows a federal court to take jurisdiction over proceedings that are recognized as separate, such as third party notices and counterclaims, and as such outside the court's jurisdiction, but which are ancillary to the action before the court.[20]

Gibson found support for his conclusion in a statement made by Laskin in *McNamara*,[21] as well as in certain judgments from *Ship 'Sparrows Point' v. Greater Vancouver Water District*,[22] a 1951 decision of the Supreme Court of Canada. In reaching his decision to accept the idea of ancillary jurisdiction, Gibson was forced to reject an earlier decision by Collier, who had adopted a test for jurisdiction that did not accommodate the concept of 'ancillary jurisdiction.'[23] Collier had dismissed the *'Sparrows Point'* case from 1951 as no longer applicable after the decisions in *Quebec North Shore Paper* and *McNamara*.

Now in the Cranbrook air crash case it was Collier's turn. Faced with Gibson's judgment, he reasserted his contention that 'ancillary' or 'pendent' jurisdiction did not exist for the Federal Court. Unwilling to rethink his earlier decision, he then lamented the result: 'That conclusion creates an undesirable situation ... Multiplication of proceedings raises the spectre of different results in different courts.' In language that was to characterize the court and the entire issue, he went on, 'The situation is lamentable ... The jurisdictional perils must be, to all those potential litigants, mystifying and frightening.'[24]

Collier's decision was taken to the Court of Appeal. The judgment rendered by Pratte (Heald and Le Dain concurring), was very short, making it appear that there was no substance to the appeal.[25] Collier's decision was affirmed and no effort was made to decide otherwise. The Federal Court's jurisdiction over 'aeronautics' was narrowed by Pratte's assertion that the laws of negligence and of contract were clearly provincial laws; he said that aeronautics would not be treated as a distinct body of law like 'Canadian maritime law.' Pratte even said that he was not really able to understand such a proposition.

Pratte dismissed the idea of ancillary jurisdiction with the comment, '[Counsel] was unable to refer us to any law or precedent which would, for pure reason of convenience, authorize the Court to extend its jurisdiction beyond its statutory limits.'[26]

Resort to the 'no precedent' approach is the low road of judicial decision making, and the complete rejection of any creative force in the judicial process. There was no indication that the judges felt that they had any choice. Though Collier had deplored the result, the Court of Appeal accepted it without question. Gibson had thought that he had a choice, which if correct meant that the Court of Appeal had chosen to restrict the jurisdiction of the Federal Court.

Apparently no one thought that Gibson's decision in the *Davie Ship-building* case might have been distinguished on the basis that it dealt with an ancillary jurisdiction in maritime matters, probably because at the time the maritime jurisdiction had been drawn into the 'lamentable situation' so that no such distinction was available.

Le Dain had earlier participated in a 1979 case, *Bensol Customs Brokers Ltd. v. Air Canada,*[27] in which he commented on the existence of ancillary jurisdiction. He concluded that there was nothing in the language of Laskin's judgment in *McNamara* to suggest that a claim had to be based solely on federal law, and thus it could be based partly on federal law and partly on provincial law. Le Dain thought it sufficient if the rights and obligations of the parties were to some material extent determined by federal law. This language would have provided support for Gibson's opinion, and for the attempt to create an ancillary jurisdiction and relieve the 'lamentable situation.' But in the *Cranbrook Air Crash* case Le Dain remained silent, and simply concurred with Pratte.

THE LASKIN–JACKETT FEUD

At a symposium held to honour the twentieth anniversary of the Federal Court of Canada, John Turner, minister of justice at the time of the court's creation and prime minister in 1984, delivered a paper on the 'Origin and

Mission' of the court. He commented that he found it hard to understand how the Supreme Court had come to limit the jurisdiction of the Federal Court and that he found the highest court's conclusions strange. He went on to suggest that personalities might have had something to do with the cleavage between the two courts.[28]

There was no more intriguing aspect of the life of the Federal Court in its first decade than the reputed feud between the two chief justices who both presided in the Supreme Court of Canada building – Bora Laskin and Wilbur Jackett. The interviews conducted produced extensive acknowledgement of the existence of a feud, but there was a great deal of reticence when it came to details. The tendency of many to link the decisions in *Quebec North Shore Paper* and *McNamara Construction* to a personal dispute between the judges does a great disservice to the professionalism of the chief justice of Canada, and seriously questions the integrity of the other judges of the Supreme Court who joined to make the decisions unanimous. The decisions on the jurisdiction issue give strong indications that the restriction of the Federal Court's jurisdiction came primarily from within the court itself.

Bora Laskin was appointed to the Supreme Court of Canada on March 23, 1970, two days before the second reading of the bill which created the Federal Court of Canada. He was the first judge of the highest court who was Jewish. Within four years, on December 27, 1973, he became chief justice of Canada. His appointment was dramatic in that he was the most junior judge of the court at the time and was promoted over seven colleagues. Only once before had a judge been appointed over other sitting judges to become chief justice of Canada.[29] Laskin was considered a liberal thinker, and he left no doubt that as a judge he favoured a contextual approach to decision making. He had made it very clear that he rejected the approach that would allow the Supreme Court to 'be simply mechanistic about previous decisions,' and he demanded that the cases involve 'a search for an appropriate legal framework for new social facts.'[30] The history of the Exchequer Court had been marked by the contextualism of its judges colliding with the formalism of judges of the Supreme Court of Canada, but now the situation was reversed.

There is no dispute about the fact that Laskin was an avowed centralist who tended to favour Ottawa when it came to federalism issues in constitutional law, but he was openly opposed to the existence of a federal court system. No judiciary was as hostile to the Federal Court as that of Ontario, and Laskin's years as a judge of the Ontario Court of Appeal (1965–70) may have influenced his thinking.

In an address delivered at the symposium held in 1975 in honour of the centennial of the Supreme Court, Laskin commented on the existence of a dual court system. With the exceptions of the Exchequer Court (which had a limited jurisdiction) and the Admiralty Courts, he said that such a system had been resisted in Canada from the outset. With regard to the Federal Court, into which the Exchequer Court had been 'translated,' Laskin warned, 'A serious and, in my view unfortunate as well as an unnecessary upheaval in our Canadian system of judicature would result if the Government and Parliament of Canada moved now to federalize it at the level of original and intermediate appellate jurisdiction by withdrawing such jurisdiction in all federal matters from the provincial courts and reposing it in a federal court structure.'[31]

A member of the audience described Laskin's comments about a dual judicial system as being in the nature of a vicious diatribe – something which does not show up in the printed record.

The centennial of the Supreme Court of Canada was also the centennial of the Exchequer Court, but the lower court was ignored. In an exhibit in the National Library initiated by Chief Justice Laskin, nothing other than the name Exchequer in the title of the initial statute, The Supreme and Exchequer Court Act, disclosed that it had played any part in the history of the Supreme Court, even though it had been the trial division of the Supreme Court for the first twelve years of its life.

There is nothing in the judgments to indicate animosity between Chief Justice Laskin and Chief Justice Jackett. In contrast, Roland Ritchie and especially Louis-Philippe Pigeon were fully prepared to make critical comments. Was there a feud? Almost certainly. What was it about? No one would say.

THE END OF THE JACKETT ERA

The end of both the 1970s and the first period in the history of the Federal Court of Canada came with signs of change, both within the court and in administrative law. The court's first chief justice was gone and with him, his dominant control. In administrative law there was the adoption of the fairness doctrine in *Nicholson*, and in 1979 the Supreme Court delivered its decision in *Canadian Union of Public Employees, Local 963 v. New Brunswick Liquor Corporation*[32] (the *CUPE* case) in which judges were instructed to exercise restraint in reviewing administrative decisions. The *CUPE* case, an appeal from New Brunswick, would be the focus of discussion in administrative law for years to come.[33]

As for the Federal Court, the word 'confusion' dogged it. Fingers were pointed at the judges, and their decision making was criticized for being conducted in 'a rather *ad hoc* fashion ... without as much sympathy for the overall scheme and purpose of the judicial review provisions of the [Federal Court] Act as might have been expected.'[34] There was a strong call for reform and reassessment of the court.[35] The confusion and apparent difficulty of dealing with the issues presented, in particular the application of the words 'applicable and existing federal law,' caused despair; some even questioned whether having a federal court was worthwhile.[36] One writer said that the relatively short life of the rejuvenated Federal Court had been made miserable, and he suspected that the Supreme Court of Canada was trying to send a signal to the federal government: 'The message of *Quebec North Shore*, *McNamara Construction* and *Fuller Construction* is clear: curtail the jurisdiction of the Federal Court or, better yet, abolish it!'[37]

At the end of the Jackett era the future of the Federal Court was tinged with uncertainty.

THE THURLOW YEARS, 1980–1988

22

The Judges

Wilbur Jackett's resignation as chief justice of the Federal Court of Canada took effect on October 1, 1979. His successor was Arthur Thurlow, the associate chief justice. Thurlow, who had been appointed to the Exchequer Court in 1956, was the most senior judge on the court. He was sixty-six and had been associate chief justice since the end of 1975, when he had succeeded Camilien Noël. His appointment as chief justice of the Federal Court was dated January 4, 1980.

Thurlow's appointment was notable because it marked a departure from the practice of appointing the head of the court from outside. The practice for the Supreme Court of Canada was to appoint the senior judge as chief justice, although there had been exceptions.

As chief justice, Thurlow was very different from Wilbur Jackett. Jackett, the former bureaucrat, was an administrator who could take charge by force of personality and get what he wanted. He was the epitome of a 'strong' leader. Thurlow was not an administrator in that mould. Under Thurlow the day-to-day work of the court continued to be done, and for those judges who knew their role and were prepared to get on with it, such benign leadership came as a blessing. Others perceived Thurlow's management style as weakness, and thought that things tended to simply 'happen' during his tenure, without his direction or leadership.

A month after Thurlow was made chief justice, James Jerome was appointed associate chief justice. Jerome was the third judge to lead the Trial Division, and he has remained in the position to the present. The previous two appointments, Noël and Thurlow, had been from among the judges sitting on the court. It remains to be seen what the practice will be in the future, although Jerome was an obvious special case.

Jerome had been the Speaker of the House of Commons from 1974 until his appointment to the court in 1980. Although a member of the Liberal party, he remained as Speaker of the House when the Conservatives under Joseph Clark assumed power with a minority government in 1979. He was appointed to the Federal Court as associate chief justice by the Conservatives on the day of the general election that returned Trudeau and the Liberals to power, February 18, 1980. It was an accepted practice in the political arena for the Speaker to choose a reward at the end of the term, provided of course that he or she had performed reasonably well (which Jerome had clearly done). Jerome was looking for a long-term position and opted for the Federal Court. However, the vacancy on the court had been created by Jackett's resignation, and was in the Court of Appeal; Jerome's experience as a lawyer had consisted of litigation work, and he favoured an appointment to the Trial Division, preferably as its head. Thurlow was moved back to the Court of Appeal as chief justice and Jerome took his place as associate chief justice in the Trial Division. Jerome would fashion the same kind of leadership as Thurlow, so the administration of the court in the 1980s would be decidedly different from that of the previous decade.

Jerome's appointment, like Thurlow's before him, disregarded the policy of having a francophone as associate chief justice when the chief justice was an anglophone, and vice versa. The policy may have been abandoned.

JUDICIAL COMPLEMENTS

The original complements of the two divisions were structured to reflect the Court of Appeal's appellate role, since its administrative law function as a court of first instance was not expected to generate a significant volume of work. Initially the twelve judges were split between the divisions in a 1:2 ratio, four in the Appeal Division and eight in the Trial Division. This ratio was altered in 1974, following increased workload from the judicial review of administrative action. Four positions were added, two in each division, for a total of six judges in the Appeal Division and ten in the Trial Division. In the 1980s the judicial review role of the appeal court continued to increase. A further six positions were added to the court in 1983 (four in the Appeal Division and two in the Trial Division). This evened the ratio to almost 1:1, with ten judges in the Court of Appeal, and twelve in the Trial Division. Three more positions were added in 1985, one for the appeal court and two for the trial court, bringing the total to twenty-five, double the number of judges originally appointed in 1971. There were eleven judges in the Court of Appeal and fourteen in the Trial Division; this remained the complement of the court through the remainder of the 1980s.

There were also the deputy judges, who continued to be used frequently in the Court of Appeal, and occasionally in the Trial Division. Also, in 1983 the category of supernumerary judge was made applicable to the Federal Court. These judges were senior judges who elected to take a reduced workload and work part time, and were no longer counted as part of the basic complement of the court. The category had been created in 1971 for provincial superior courts as part of the changes made by the government of Pierre Elliott Trudeau in its early years, and was to further its policy of encouraging the continuing improvement of the services provided by federally appointed judges.[1] In 1971 one improvement that the government wanted to see was the recognition by the judiciary, and the legal profession in general, of the role of judges as law reformers, and hence the need to link the jurisprudence of the past with the cultural norms and social context of the present.[2]

Chief Justice Jackett had resisted the use of supernumerary judges in the Federal Court,[3] and preferred to use deputy judges. However, the use of deputy judges was quite unpopular with the puisne judges and, after Jackett's resignation, the position of supernumerary judge was finally created for the Federal Court.[4] The government said that the primary reason was to reduce reliance on deputy judges.[5] Now the Federal Court was to have 'a pool of judicial talent' that could be called on in special cases of long duration and to meet the peak workloads of the court.[6] Also, since any election to supernumerary judge created a vacancy, an additional judge could be appointed. The new judge would undoubtedly be a younger person and thus would help to rejuvenate the judiciary and further the policy of having the judiciary take a law reform role.

The first judge of the Federal Court to elect to become a supernumerary judge was George Addy, on September 1, 1983, at the age of almost sixty-eight. He was followed by Allison Walsh on June 1, 1984, a month before Walsh's seventy-third birthday. Frank Collier chose supernumerary status on November 1, 1987, at the age of sixty-five. These were the only judges who elected to become supernumerary while Thurlow was chief justice.

JUDICIAL APPOINTMENTS

Seventeen judges were appointed to the Federal Court during Thurlow's term as Chief Justice. They are listed below in order of seniority:

Name	Date of appointment	Division appointed to	Province represented	Position at time of appointment
James Jerome	18 Feb. 1980	TD	Ont.	Speaker, House of Commons
Paul Rouleau	9 Aug. 1982	TD	Ont.	County Court judge
James Hugessen	18 July 1983	CA	Que.	Assoc. C.J., Quebec Superior Court
Arthur Stone	18 July 1983	CA	Ont.	Lawyer
Frank Muldoon	18 July 1983	TD	Man.	Chair, Law Reform Commission of Canada
Barry Strayer	18 July 1983	TD	Sask.	Federal public servant
John McNair	18 July 1983	TD	N.B.	Lawyer
Barbara Reed	17 Nov. 1983	TD	Ont.	Federal public servant
Pierre Denault	29 June 1984	TD	Que.	Lawyer
Mark MacGuigan	29 June 1984	CA	Ont.	Federal cabinet minister
Yvon Pinard	29 June 1984	TD	Que.	Federal MP
Marcel Joyal	29 June 1984	TD	Ont.	Lawyer
Bud Cullen	26 July 1984	TD	Ont.	Federal cabinet minister
Bertrand Lacombe	29 Oct. 1985	CA	Que.	Lawyer
Leonard Martin	29 Oct. 1985	TD	Nfld.	Lawyer
Max Teitelbaum	29 Oct. 1985	TD	Que.	Lawyer
Alice Desjardins	29 July 1987	CA	Que.	Judge Quebec Superior Court

Barbara Reed, who joined the Trial Division on November 17, 1983, was the first woman appointed to the Federal Court. Alice Desjardins, appointed in July 1987, was the second woman appointed and the first to join the Court of Appeal.

Reed, appointed at forty-six, came from Ontario. She graduated from the University of Toronto in 1960 with a BA in philosophy and history. Later she entered Dalhousie Law School, graduating with an LL M in 1970. After teaching for a short time at the University of Ottawa, she joined the federal public service in 1973 and worked there as a lawyer until being appointed to the court.

Alice Desjardins, fifty-two at the time of her appointment, was a judge of the Quebec Superior Court. After graduating from the Université de Montréal in law, she spent a year at the London School of Economics, and also studied at Harvard University, where she obtained a graduate degree in law. She taught law at the Université de Montréal from 1961 until 1969, and has the distinction of being the first woman to teach in a faculty of law in Canada. In 1969 she joined the federal public service and worked in the Privy Council Office and the Department of Justice until 1981, when she was appointed to the Quebec court.

A good number of the appointments involved people who had made a commitment to live and work in Ottawa. James Jerome, member of Parliament and Speaker of the House of Commons, had lived in Ottawa for twelve years. Paul Rouleau had been born and raised in Cornwall but had gone to secondary school and earned his undergraduate degree in Ottawa. After graduating in law from Dalhousie University, he practised law in Cornwall, and later sought a County Court judgeship in the capital. Frank Muldoon had been chairman of the Law Reform Commission and wanted to stay in Ottawa for family reasons. Barry Strayer and Alice Desjardins had been federal public servants, as was Barbara Reed. Pierre Denault had graduated from the University of Ottawa in political science and in law. Mark MacGuigan and Bud Cullen had been in Parliament for sixteen years, and both were Liberal cabinet ministers. Yvon Pinard had had a ten-year career in elected politics in the House of Commons. Marcel Joyal had attended classical college in Ottawa, and, after graduation from McGill University, had practised in Ottawa. In all, eleven of the seventeen appointees had close connections with the city. Another judge, James Hugessen, had some connection in that his father had been a senator.

Ottawa was not particularly attractive to the legal community because of the higher concentrations of legal talent and activity in the provincial centres. Professional disdain for the city, which plagued the Supreme Court in its search for judges, may have influenced the high proportion of appointees with connections to Ottawa.

Judges from Quebec

In 1971 four of the original twelve positions were to be occupied by judges who had been members of the Quebec bar, one-third of the court's complement (the same requirement that exists for the Supreme Court of Canada). When the total number of judges increased to sixteen and then to twenty-two, the required number of judges from Quebec remained four – only 18 percent of the complement in 1983. The creation of the position of supernumerary judge in 1983 had the potential to reduce the proportion even more. It is not surprising that in 1985, when the total complement was increased to twenty-five, provision was made for at least eight judges to be selected from the Quebec bar, so that Quebec appointees would once again constitute one-third of the judges of the court.[7]

Judges from Ontario

The political power of Ontario within Confederation has made it imperative over the years to give the province a significant representation within 'national' institutions. For its part, Ontario had been essentially underrepresented during the life of the Exchequer Court. The province fared well at the outset when Walter Cassels was appointed as the court's second judge (following its separation from the Supreme Court) and became the first president, serving fifteen years in all (1908–23), but it would be twenty-three years before the next appointment from Ontario, Charles Cameron (1946–64). From 1946 until 1973, there was only one additional judge from Ontario, Hugh Gibson (1964–81). Ontario's representation began to increase in 1973 with the appointment of John Urie in April, followed by George Addy in September. With James Jerome's appointment as associate chief justice in 1980, the number rose to four (25 percent of the total complement). With the appointments in 1984 of Mark MacGuigan, Marcel Joyal, and Bud Cullen, Ontario representation finally reached one-third. By the end of the 1980s, the representation among the judges had settled into a pattern of three parts: one-third from Ontario, one-third from Quebec, and one-third from the remaining areas of Canada.

REPRESENTATION

Judges are sensitive to comments that they 'represent' anyone. The idea is thought to conflict with the fundamental notions of independence and impartiality. However, 'represent' can connote being a member of an identifiable group of people or being from a particular region of the country, as opposed to having a constituency. A federal system must recognize the former type of representation as an essential ingredient of a national institution. It is representation in that first sense that is being discussed here.

Representation may be complicated when a judge has a connection with more than one province, but such judges may be at a premium in a federal system. For Quebec, representation means specifically belonging to the Quebec bar. If we applied this criterion across the country we could call it 'substantive' representation, since a member of the bar's commitment to the legal system of that province, both in terms of time spent in the province and knowledge of the community, would be significant. We can also speak of 'ceremonial' representation when a judge has been born and brought up in a province and could still call it 'home.' The practice is to allow a judge to decide whether to be sworn in at Ottawa or in his or her home province. Swearing in outside of Ottawa serves a political function in demonstrating a judge's loyalty to a province even though the judge is assuming duties with a 'national' institution. If the home province is not where the person practised law then the swearing in serves a purely ceremonial function. Since it is the practice to recognize a judge as representing only one province, a judge's having a connection to more than one province allows the government to select the one that is the most politically expedient.

In this time of growing support for provincial power, as well as growing concern about the existence of the Federal Court of Canada as a national institution and the need for a dual court system, it is informative to notice the increase in the number of swearing-in ceremonies that take place outside of Ottawa. The judges of the Exchequer Court who became Federal Court judges were all sworn in at Ottawa. Of the eleven appointments in the 1970s, two judges (18 per cent)[8] were sworn in outside of Ottawa. In the Thurlow years of the 1980s there were sixteen appointments, with four judges (25 per cent) sworn in outside Ottawa. Examining the appointments made between Thurlow's retirement in 1988 the end of 1995 reveals a significant increase in the number of judges being sworn in at a city in their home province: of the seventeen judges appointed, eight (47 per cent) were sworn in outside Ottawa.

A number of the judges appointed during the years when Thurlow was chief justice illustrate the questions about representation that can arise. Mark MacGuigan was sworn in at Charlottetown, Prince Edward Island. He had been born and raised in Prince Edward Island, but after his graduation from St Dunstan's University there he attended the University of Toronto and later graduated from Osgoode Hall Law School in Toronto. He became a member of the Ontario bar in 1958 and taught law in the province until his election as a member of Parliament for the Ontario riding of Windsor-Walkerville in 1968. He remained a member of Parliament for that riding until his appointment to the Federal Court in 1984. Since his legal and political career of almost thirty years took place in Ontario, his substantive representation is for Ontario; his ceremonial representation is for Prince Edward Island. The government put him forward as a Prince Edward Island representative,[9] which (if the people of the island see him as such) gives them their first member on the court since it was created in 1876. Ontario has obtained a bonus member.

Arthur Stone was born, raised, and received his legal education in Nova Scotia. He became a member of the Nova Scotia bar and then moved to Ontario and was called to the bar of that province. He practised law in Toronto for twenty-five years. He is unquestionably an Ontario lawyer, and is identified as such by the federal government,[10] but he has strong family and social connections with Nova Scotia, particularly Cape Breton. He has written a book about his home county. Nova Scotia has achieved a bonus with Stone's appointment.

An interesting question of representation arises with respect to Barry Strayer. He was born and raised in Saskatchewan, and received his basic legal education at the University of Saskatchewan. After obtaining graduate law degrees at Oxford University and Harvard, he practised law as a provincial public servant and taught law at the University of Saskatchewan from 1962 to 1968. In 1968, he joined the federal Department of Justice in Ottawa and worked there until his appointment in July 1983. Strayer is recognized as representing Ontario, rather than Saskatchewan,[11] but it may be possible to think of his substantive representation as being 'Ottawa' rather than that of a province. In interviews with some of the judges, one point that emerged was that those who had a public service background in Ottawa had a distinct mentality and had lost their provincial viewpoints. Given the sensitivity about identifying the Federal Court with the federal government, though, there is no question that any idea of an 'Ottawa' representative would be resisted vehemently.

Louis-Marcel Joyal could make some claim to represent Quebec, since he has a law degree from McGill University and did join the Quebec bar, but he is a Franco-Ontarian and practised law in Ottawa from the time he graduated from law school until he was appointed to the bench. He was naturally put forward as representing Ontario.[12]

THE PATRONAGE BINGE

The court received a burst of positive publicity in May 1984 when it was announced that Gerald Le Dain of the Court of Appeal had been appointed to the Supreme Court of Canada. Le Dain was the first judge to go from the Federal Court to the highest court. His appointment was well received; unfortunately the stresses of his new position proved too great and he resigned for medical reasons in 1988.

While Le Dain's appointment had taken the Federal Court out of the shadows and had given it good publicity, a month later the court was on the front pages of the nation's newspapers with stories of the patronage binge that preceded the Liberal defeat in the 1984 general election. Of twenty-three MPs who received appointments from Prime Ministers Trudeau and Turner, three were appointed to the Federal Court. Bud Cullen and Yvon Pinard went to the Trial Division, and, most notably, Minister of Justice Mark MacGuigan went to the Court of Appeal. Matters were made worse when, in Pinard's case, the federal government did not follow the procedure that it had established with the Canadian Bar Association to obtain the association's opinion about proposed appointments. The purpose of the consultation was to obtain an assessment of the candidate's professional merit. It was the first time in the seventeen-year history of the agreement between the government and the Bar Association that this omission had occurred.

The Canadian Bar Association announced that it would undertake a study to investigate the independence of the judiciary and the appointment process for judges. The Canadian Association of Law Teachers also convened a Special Committee on Judicial Appointments. The Bar Association's report pointed out that the selection process for Federal Court judges must not display any bias in favour of the federal government, because the court adjudicated claims against that government. The report went on to say, 'At present, this court is perceived by many, rightly or wrongly, as a government-oriented court because so many former politicians and federal officials have been appointed to it.'[13] In a newspaper interview David Mullan, a leading expert on the Federal Court, pointed out, 'The appointment of federal civil servants [to the Federal Court] might tend to give the court a pro-government leaning.'[14]

In all, four of the thirteen appointments made by a Liberal government in the Thurlow years had been elected politicians (Jerome, MacGuigan, Pinard, and Cullen); two had been federal public servants (Strayer and Reed), and Muldoon had served as chair of the federal Law Reform Commission. Muldoon had also been an unsuccessful Liberal candidate in three provincial elections. Hugessen's father was a Liberal senator and McNair's father had been Liberal premier of New Brunswick. Marcel Joyal had lost a nomination bid to run for the Liberals in an Ottawa-area riding, but had remained an active member of the party. Clearly, ten of the thirteen appointees had overt connections with the appointing government.

The patronage issue emerged just as cases involving the new Canadian Charter of Rights and Freedoms were gaining public attention. The greater power that judges would theoretically possess to control political behaviour made it obvious that they should be well removed from any taint of political bias. The patronage episode resulted in the political backgrounds of the sitting judges becoming newsworthy. Of the judges then on the Federal Court, the Liberals had appointed Arthur Thurlow, the chief justice, once a Liberal member of the Nova Scotia legislature (1949–53); Darrel Heald, attorney general in a Liberal government in Saskatchewan (1964–71); Patrick Mahoney, cabinet minister and Liberal member of Parliament (1968–73); and Jean-Eudes Dubé, cabinet minister and Liberal member of Parliament (1962–75). One thing this information tends to confirm is that the 1984 patronage binge was notable only for the volume of such appointments – not their novelty.

It would be easy to conclude that the minimum requirements for appointment as a judge are ten years' membership in the bar of a province and suitable political connections. Political partisanship is such a fact of life that it would be astonishing if it did not come to mind when considering appointments. It may be the real threat to impartial and independent decision making. The blatant nature of the Trudeau-Turner appointments did a considerable disservice to the judiciary.

In the wake of the Liberal patronage binge and its significance throughout the election of 1984, the first appointments of the new Conservative government were free of signs of overt political connection. Bertrand Lacombe, a lawyer from Montreal, was appointed to the Court of Appeal in 1985. Appointed on the same day to the Trial Division were Leonard Martin, a lawyer from Newfoundland and the first judge appointed from that province to a federal court, and Max Teitelbaum, a lawyer from Montreal. In 1987 Alice Desjardins became the first woman appointed to the Court of Appeal. She had been employed as a federal public servant during a Liberal regime and had been appointed to the Quebec Superior Court by the Liberals.

23

The Work of the Court

Despite the cloud over the future of the court at the end of the Jackett years, and the patronage issue of 1984, the years of Arthur Thurlow's tenure as chief justice were not marked by the sense of turmoil which had plagued the Federal Court earlier. It was a period of relative tranquillity. 'Jurisdiction' was still a buzzword; one writer commented, 'It is almost impossible to pick up a volume of any Canadian series of law reports and not find at least one judgment in which the jurisdiction of the Federal Court is (or should be) in issue.'[1]

Criticism of section 28 continued and cries for legislative reform were heard.[2] The reform of the Federal Court Act which had occupied the Canadian Bar Association and the Law Reform Commission of Canada in the 1970s resulted in a paper prepared by the Department of Justice and released at the annual meeting of the Canadian Bar Association in August 1983.[3] It offered a noticeable reassurance that the federal government found it 'neither practical nor desirable to have two judicial systems.'[4] In his address to the Bar Association the minister of justice, Mark MacGuigan, underlined this, stating that it was a guiding principle that 'there is no desire or intention on the part of the federal government of establishing a system of dual courts in Canada.'[5] The Federal Court was described in the report as a 'specialized' court, which was deemed necessary 'in certain well-defined areas.' These areas included (1) supervision of federal administrative tribunals, in order to achieve uniformity in decisions and avoid inconsistencies; (2) specialized litigation under federal statutes, such as income tax, admiralty, and industrial property; and (3) matters which required a national forum, such as a national labour dispute, when nationwide orders would be needed.

The government had retreated from its earlier attempt to give the court jurisdiction over matters within federal legislative jurisdiction, such as aeronautics and interprovincial and international works and undertakings; in addition the jurisdiction over claims against the government, which had once been the basic justification for a separate court, was noticeably absent. Concurrent jurisdiction over actions against the government was now accepted.

The role of the Court of Appeal was delineated more clearly. The paper suggested that the judges of the Appeal Division must have time for reflection, to enable them to write judgments which the Trial Division or tribunals could look to for guidance in other cases. This could only be achieved if the original jurisdiction over judicial review of administrative action were moved from the Court of Appeal to the Trial Division. The report recommended that the combining of the two roles (an administrative court and an appeal court), in the Court of Appeal be abandoned.

In their attacks on the section 28 jurisdiction, critics had argued that the provision forced a rigid approach because it was a statutory code. In contrast, they said that the common law was flexible and allowed the judges to adapt the law to changing social conditions.[6] The Department of Justice accepted this idea and proposed that the common law remedies should be retained. The report demonstrated an acceptance and promotion of a role for the judges in changing the law, which had heretofore not been part of the formalist model. However, nothing more was heard of these proposals throughout the Thurlow years. The Liberal government that suggested them was replaced by a Conservative government one year after the proposals were made public.

In the main the decisions in this period were of a plodding nature. The Court of Appeal shied away from a law reform role and seemed content with an adjudicative one. Writing for the Court of Appeal, Mr Justice Heald stated in one case, 'The appropriate rule of interpretation, as I understand it, is that only the words enacted in the body of the statute are to be looked at unless they are of ambiguous or uncertain meaning in which event the heading may be looked at as an aid to interpretation.'[7] In another instance, Mr Justice Hugessen, with Pratte concurring, was satisfied with using an ordinary grammatical analysis for a provision in a statute; a unanimous Supreme Court of Canada reversed Hugessen's decision. Chief Justice Dickson of the Supreme Court commented that the answer to the problem could not be arrived at 'by applying strict grammatical construction to the last twelve words' of the provision in question and ignoring other contexts.[8]

Chief Justice Thurlow led the retreat from law reform in the Court of Appeal. He was prepared to say that something could be 'anomalous and capable of being unfair,' but reform was up to the Supreme Court of Canada or the legislature.[9] Judicial reform and adaptation of existing law to current need were accepted roles by this time – but not for the Federal Court of Appeal.

While the overall impression was that formalism was in control, there were instances of judges trying to break out of the narrow approach to law and lawyering. In one case in the Court of Appeal Mr Justice Arthur Stone indicated that he was not completely comfortable with the 'words could not be clearer' approach of Justices Hugessen and Urie; he dissented from their conclusion in the case.[10] There was one very interesting attempt to fashion a creative decision, which in itself counted as a change. The fact that it has come to be viewed as anomalous illustrates the hold of the formal model at this time. To add to its interest, the case occurred in the Trial Division.

THE *MARSHALL* CASE

For some years (since the days of A.K. Maclean) it had been difficult to find a decision of either the Exchequer Court or its successor that could be classed as 'creative.' While the work of the Court of Appeal might suggest otherwise, there were indications in the 1980s that the strength of the formalist model was beginning to wane. The future dean of law at the University of New Brunswick, Wade MacLauchlan, writing at the end of the Thurlow years, forcefully promoted a functional approach to the interpretation of statutes, and attacked formalism as bad interpretation.[11] Formalists had denied the legitimacy of the contextual model: now the very legitimacy of the formalist model was under attack.

But in 1985, and in particular in the Federal Court of Appeal, where most of the judges displayed no apparent concern with the need for change, reaction became pronounced when the first woman appointed to the court, Barbara Reed, fashioned a creative decision in the Trial Division. The case concerned the very sensitive issue of the court's jurisdiction, so long a preoccupation of the judges and the legal profession.

Marshall v. The Queen[12] involved litigation arising from the lay-off of an employee of the Department of National Defence. The employee brought two actions, the first against the government for various alleged wrongful acts; the second against the employee's union for alleged collusion with the employer. Since the union, the Public Service Alliance, was neither the Crown nor an agent, officer, or servant of the Crown, it challenged the jurisdiction of the court to deal with the action against it. The union maintained that the action would have to be brought in a provincial court. The plaintiff took the position that since the action against the union was intimately bound up with her claim against the government, it should be recognized as within the jurisdiction of the Federal Court.

The lamentable situation decried by Collier, but accepted as a fact of life in a federal system, had arisen once again. This time Madame Justice Reed saw a way out of the problem of multiple proceedings.

Reed acknowledged, albeit in a footnote,[13] that the concepts of ancillary and pendent jurisdiction developed in the United States had not been adopted in Canada. This meant that she could not rely directly on Mr Justice Hugh Gibson's decision in the *Davie Shipbuilding* case, because her colleague had expressly applied the ancillary concept in the maritime law area. She referred to his decision innocuously as differing from certain past decisions of the court.

In reviewing the *Quebec North Shore Paper* case and *McNamara*, Madame Justice Reed pointed out that 'laws of Canada' in section 101 had not been equated with legislation; rather, it included non-statutory law, that is, judicially created law ('common law'). Recognition of judge-made law as a legitimate part of the legal system was the opening needed to solve the problem.

Madame Justice Reed went on to note that it was accepted in constitutional law that provincial laws of general application could apply to federal entities, such as extraprovincial undertakings. Thus the view that only federal law applied in the Federal Court was not correct. She was then able to refer to a statement by Le Dain in *Bensol Customs Brokers Ltd. v. Air Canada*,[14] in which he had made the same point. Since the rights and obligations of the parties might be determined partly by federal law and partly by provincial law, it was sufficient for jurisdictional purposes that the rights and obligations of the parties were to be determined to some material extent by federal law.

Even the language of Chief Justice Laskin in *Rhine v. The Queen; Prytula v. The Queen* could be used to support her: 'It should hardly be necessary to add that "contract" or other legal institutions, such as "tort" cannot be invariably attributed to sole provincial legislative regulation or be deemed to be, as common law, solely matters of provincial law.'[15]

After her review of the existing law, she concluded that 'where there is both an element of federal statutory regulation and matters of common law in a case, the whole does not necessarily become a matter for the courts of the province.'[16]

Reed identified the plaintiff's whole cause of action as being intimately connected to the Public Service Employment Act, the regulations made under it, and the Public Service Staff Relations Act (which required the union to represent the interests of the employees properly and fairly). Thus, she concluded that the duty of fair representation was found within both provincial and federal common law, and further, that there was existing and applicable federal law. The Federal Court had jurisdiction over the action against the union.

To be legitimate, judicial creativity must be controlled by the contexts of language, legal sources, and social values. For this reason, Reed examined the language of the law. Section 17(1) of the Federal Court Act read, 'The Trial Division has original jurisdiction in all cases where relief is claimed against the Crown ...' Madame Justice Reed was satisfied that the conclusion that she had reached – which did not conflict with either the legal or social contexts – could live in the context of this language. She pointed out that the language described 'cases where relief is claimed against the Crown,' and not 'claims against the Crown.' She commented that none of the previous decisions that had reached a different conclusion had considered the wording of the law.

Reed asserted that the jurisdiction of the Federal Court depended on the intertwining of the causes of action against both parties. Faced with a choice, no judge should select a choice which would subject the plaintiff presenting a unified cause of action to multiple proceedings. The lamentable situation should be avoided whenever possible! She went on to distinguish cases in which jurisdiction had been rejected on the basis of the nature of the cases, by which she meant the degree to which the action against the Crown and the action against the other party were intertwined. She did not consider herself bound by previous decisions of the Trial Division.

As additional support, Reed was able to refer to the decision of the Supreme Court of Canada in 'Sparrows Point' (Ship) v. Greater Vancouver Water District (1951),[17] in which the Exchequer Court was held to have jurisdiction over a claim against the Harbour Commission for negligence. In Mr Justice Ivan Rand's opinion in this Supreme Court judgment, 'every consideration of convenience and justice' required a single proceeding for a single cause of action.[18] This case was part of the legal context.

Madame Justice Reed dealt with the very sensitive question of the jurisdiction of the court and extended it. Those favouring the principle of restricted jurisdiction for the Federal Court and the use of the provincial courts would react negatively.

Not surprisingly, this exercise of creativity was itself threatening to those who were more comfortable with the formal model. The use of an opinion by Ivan Rand was a clear signal of what Reed was about, for Rand was well known as having been a contextual judge. Madame Justice Reed had fashioned a rule of law that a contextualist would be comfortable using, namely, one that required a determination of the degree of intertwining, and thus would force a judge and lawyer to consider many factors and think out an answer to suit the particular situation. A formalist wants rules that appear capable of being applied in a mechanical fashion.[19]

Some members of the court were prepared to follow Reed's lead, and try to extricate litigants from the prospect of a multiplication of proceedings. Mr Justice Joyal of the Trial Division in *Roberts v. The Queen* (1986) adopted Reed's approach to the problem.[20] The Court of Appeal accepted Joyal's conclusion that jurisdiction existed in the particular instance, but one of the judges on the panel, James Hugessen, was not happy with Reed's decision in *Marshall*.[21] He began his comments with what he called a trite proposition: '[T]his court, as a creature of statute, can have no jurisdiction beyond what statute specifically confers.'[22] For Hugessen, extension of the jurisdiction of the Federal Court could only be accepted if spelled out clearly in legislation. While Hugessen had to acknowledge that the language context did not act as a barrier to the 'intertwining' approach, he pointed out that Reed's interpretation had not been adopted previously by other judges (Madame Justice Reed herself had stated that it had apparently not been considered). He was uncomfortable with the uncertainty surrounding the intertwining rule, preferring instead a rule which could be applied in a more definite manner.

In the end, a split occurred among the judges on the appeal panel. Mr Justice MacGuigan disagreed with Hugessen and was prepared to adopt Reed's analysis in *Marshall*; John Urie preferred not to comment on *Marshall*, since he saw no need to do so at the time.

The litigation made its way to the Supreme Court of Canada where it was heard by a five-judge panel made up of Dickson, Beetz, Lamer, Wilson, and Le Dain. The appeal was dismissed, and Madame Justice Wilson rendered the judgment for a unanimous Court, which consisted in this instance of only four judges, since Le Dain did not participate in the judgment.[23]

Wilson took the opportunity to discuss the *Marshall* case. In a moment of candour, she stated: 'There is clearly a substantial policy component involved in the resolution of this jurisdictional problem. Practical considerations enter in and concern over the undue extension of federal court jurisdiction where the federal Crown is not the sole defendant has to be balanced against the need for the expeditious resolution of litigation at reasonable cost.'[24]

For Madame Justice Wilson the *Marshall* decision struck an appropriate balance. If the claims were 'inextricably linked,' then the Federal Court had jurisdiction over all of them. She approved Le Dain's judgment in *Bensol Customs Brokers Ltd. v. Air Canada*,[25] in which he accepted that the Federal Court could deal with the application of provincial law as long as the rights and obligations of the parties were determined 'to some material extent by federal law.' In her opinion, the approach taken by Reed and Le Dain would avoid problems of fragmented jurisdiction.

Wilson rendered her judgment on March 9, 1989. In the two-year interval between the Court of Appeal's decision on March 2, 1987 and the Supreme Court of Canada's, activity within the Federal Court had effectively nullified Wilson's views.

On February 22, 1988, a panel of the Court of Appeal consisting of Mahoney, Hugessen, and Desjardins had rejected the *Marshall* case in *College of Physicians and Surgeons of British Columbia v. Varnam*. Hugessen rendered judgment for the court. The opinions that he had expressed in *Roberts* were now supported by the other judges on the panel. Hugessen pointed out that the concept of 'intertwining' did not arise from any language in a statute, and was 'altogether too vague and elastic a standard upon which to found exclusive jurisdiction in the Federal Court.' He did not believe that the court's jurisdiction should be 'a matter for guesswork.'[26] The judgment also said that Reed's decision went against previous decisions, which, although not binding, nevertheless represented a consistent approach and sound judicial policy.

There were two policy choices available: first, to maintain that the jurisdiction of a statutory court should not be extended beyond what had clearly been intended by the words of the statute, and that no degree of convenience or advantage which might result from extending the jurisdiction could justify going beyond the statutory limits; and second, to hold that every consideration of convenience and justice would seem to require that a single cause of action be dealt with under a single field of law, in a single proceeding.[27] The Court of Appeal chose the first policy.[28] In a candid and thorough note in the *Canadian Bar Review*, John Evans and

Brian Slattery of Osgoode Hall Law School discussed the *Roberts* case; they pointed to sensitivity about the status of the provincial superior courts (which many felt must remain the pre-eminent courts in the country) as the foremost factor hindering the Federal Court in its work. The authors also suggested that the quality of the jurisprudence produced by the Federal Court judges (which had come in for criticism over the years) contributed to the inhibiting of the Court. They saw the *Marshall* decision as an attempt to break away from the difficulties, but one that had failed because of judges who felt a greater need to restrain the Federal Court's jurisdiction.[29]

A year before, the Court of Appeal, consisting of Thurlow, Stone, and Heald, had rendered judgment in the *Oag* case, in which the issue was whether on action in tort could be taken against members of the National Parole Board.[30] The Court of Appeal allowed the action to proceed and, in doing so, they reversed the decision of Mr Justice Muldoon in the Trial Division.[31] Muldoon reacted soon after, in *Wilder v. Canada*.[32] He remarked that there was 'a *nouvelle vague* of jurisprudence' afoot,[33] and went on to find 'an enigma'[34] in the Court of Appeal's decision in *Oag*, since a previous and contrary decision of the court had not been considered.[35] Muldoon thought that 'this *nouvelle vague*' had introduced 'an element of abhorrent uncertainty into the law.'[36] The two apparently conflicting cases posed a conundrum for him and he asked what the result ought to be. By 'ought' he apparently did not mean what was rationally best or most appropriate, but rather which case should be considered the most authoritative. He opted for the more recent decision in *Oag*, and suggested that the Supreme Court of Canada should be the one to solve the conundrum.

Muldoon's decision in *Wilder* was also appealed and was heard after the *Varnam* case. He was once again reversed.[37] If he had any further comments, they did not make their way into the law reports.

In 1990, in *Bradasch v. Warren*,[38] the strict interpretation of the court's jurisdiction was finally re-established as the norm. Hugessen rendered the judgment of the court, which included Pratte and Heald. The *Roberts* case was not mentioned.

Mr Justice Joyal, who had supported Reed's decision in *Marshall*, was subsequently driven to acknowledge that unless a federal statute was the basis of an action or created a right to relief, the Federal Court had no jurisdiction. He felt strongly enough about the situation to comment that the lack of jurisdiction in certain instances was hard to accept, and prevented the effective administration of justice.[39]

Whatever scope existed for the jurisdiction of the Federal Court, it had not been accepted by certain influential members of the Federal Court of Appeal.[40]

THE ITO CASE

A highly significant case for the question of the jurisdiction of the Federal Court was *ITO – International Terminal Operators Ltd. v. Miida Electronics Inc.*,[41] a 1986 decision of the Supreme Court of Canada.

By agreement, Mitsui OSK Lines Ltd. was to carry 250 cartons of electronic calculators by ship from Japan to Montreal for delivery to Miida Electronics Inc. The goods were picked up in Montreal by ITO – International Terminal Operators (a cargo-handling company and terminal operator) and stored on behalf of Miida Electronics. While the goods were in the possession of the storage company 169 of the 250 cartons were stolen. Miida Electronics brought actions against both ITO – International Terminal Operators and Mitsui for the loss of the goods.

Both actions were dismissed in the Trial Division of the Federal Court,[42] and when an appeal was taken to the Federal Court of Appeal the issue of the court's jurisdiction was raised with respect to the action against the terminal operator. It was accepted that the maritime jurisdiction would include an action against the shipping company. The Court of Appeal split 2–1, with a majority (Le Dain and deputy judge Lalande) determining that the Federal Court had jurisdiction based on the action being governed by Canadian maritime law. Mr Justice Pratte dissented.[43]

An appeal was taken to the Supreme Court of Canada and another split decision resulted. By a narrow 4–3 result the jurisdiction of the Federal Court was upheld. Mr Justice McIntyre, for a majority consisting of himself, Dickson, Estey, and Wilson, viewed Canadian maritime law as a body of federal law relating to commerce and shipping.[44] The majority accepted an earlier decision in which stevedoring, including storage, was said to be part of shipping. The claim against ITO therefore fell within the scope of maritime law.

In addition to recognizing a wide scope for the jurisdiction of the Federal Court with respect to maritime law, and thereby taking the maritime jurisdiction in a different direction from that of the other areas, for which the restrictive approach prevailed, the Supreme Court majority accepted that Canadian maritime law encompassed the principles of the law of England concerning actions in tort, contract, and bailment. The result was that the three judges from Quebec on the seven-judge panel dissented, and went to the defence of the jurisdiction of the provincial courts.

There was an earlier decision of the Supreme Court, *National Gypsum Co. v. Northern Sales Ltd.* (1964),[45] in which Quebec law had been applied in an admiralty case. The decision there had been 3–2, with Taschereau, Fauteux, and Abbott (all from Quebec) in the majority and Cartwright and Ritchie (neither from Quebec) dissenting. In *ITO*, McIntyre agreed with the opinion of the dissenting judges of 1964. He asserted that it was imperative that the substantive law in maritime cases should be uniform across the country. The three dissenting judges in *ITO*, Chouinard, Beetz, and Lamer, agreed with Pratte's dissenting reasons in the Federal Court of Appeal. For them the proposition was straightforward: '[A] tort or delict committed in Montreal ... falls ... within the jurisdiction of the civil courts of Quebec, not that of the Federal Court.'[46]

Interestingly, the same jurisdiction issue had also arisen in 1980. A panel of the Federal Court of Appeal composed of the same judges who participated in the *ITO* case (Pratte, Le Dain, and Lalande D.J.), all of whom were educated in Quebec law, had considered the jurisdiction of the Federal Court in an action for damages by owners of goods brought against terminal operators who had stored the goods. A unanimous court said that the matter was governed exclusively by Quebec law.[47] In *ITO*, Le Dain began his judgment by stating that he had been wrong in the conclusions reached in the earlier case. Lalande said that the issue of jurisdiction needed review, while Pratte stood by his earlier opinion. For some reason, the 1980 case was not reported for two years.[48]

While the *ITO* case is important for the wide scope given the maritime jurisdiction of the Federal Court, it is better known for the fact that Mr Justice McIntyre analysed the notorious *Quebec North Shore Paper* and *McNamara* cases, and stated:

the essential requirements to support a finding of jurisdiction in the Federal Court ... are:

1. There must be a statutory grant of jurisdiction by the federal Parliament.
2. There must be an existing body of federal law which is essential to the disposition of the case and which nourishes the statutory grant of jurisdiction.
3. The law on which the case is based must be 'a law of Canada' as the phrase is used in s. 101 of the *Constitution Act, 1867*.[49]

He had provided a checklist that had the appearance of a formula. It contained nothing new in substance,[50] but since its articulation it has become commonplace to see an acknowledgement of the 'three-pronged test in

ITO,' or the 'three conditions of *ITO,*' or the 'accepted test,' followed by a conclusion going one way or the other.

Chief Justice Laskin had also articulated a 'test,' and there was more than adequate scope for the Federal Court's jurisdiction to be developed within the guideline of 'applicable and existing federal law.' In *Rhine* and *Prytula*, Laskin had also provided examples of an analysis, but he had not created what looked like a formula.

24

The Charter

When Pierre Trudeau came to Ottawa in the late 1960s, he proposed that a bill of rights be entrenched in the constitution,[1] an achievement which had eluded Prime Minister John Diefenbaker when the Canadian Bill of Rights was created because of the political and social climate in 1960. At that time the Liberals, in opposition, had felt secure about making legal protections for constitutional rights and freedoms a partisan issue. They simply argued that the proposed Bill of Rights was unnecessary. Times changed, and at a Constitutional Conference in 1971 Prime Minister Trudeau reached agreement with the provincial premiers on advancing such a project. As it turned out, the legislation failed to materialize. Trudeau's charter of rights was part of a package that included an amending formula for the constitution; when the amending formula could not be agreed on the entire package died.

Trudeau introduced the idea again in 1978, as part of a proposal for extensive constitutional reform following the November 1976 election of the Parti Québécois in Quebec. The problems which had prevented Diefenbaker from making the Canadian Bill of Rights applicable to the provinces by entrenching it in the constitution must have resurfaced, since the proposed charter was made binding on the federal government but only optional for the provinces. However, the federal government and the provinces once again failed to reach

agreement, and the charter and the accompanying constitutional reforms were stalled.

A referendum on separation was held in Quebec on May 20, 1980. The
vote went against the separatists. Trudeau had campaigned vigorously
against separation, and he promised the people of Quebec a new constitution if they voted to remain part of Canada. On the heels of the referendum result, he set about to make good his promise, but failure to reach
agreement persisted and Trudeau ultimately announced that Ottawa
would proceed on its own. His reforms included a charter of rights and
freedoms, this time binding on both the provinces and Ottawa. In the
final stages of negotiation a provision was inserted which allowed any
province, or Ottawa, to opt out with respect to a particular piece of legislation, by following a prescribed procedure.[2]

Not every province welcomed the charter, but it was difficult to argue
against, since such a stance could be perceived as opposition to the rights
and freedoms themselves. The general public was more and more sceptical about the traditional protection of civil liberties through the political
process. Finally on April 17, 1982, the Canadian Charter of Rights and
Freedoms came into being. The rights and freedoms which were suppos-
edly part of our social fabric were now enforceable by use of the legal
system.[3]

There appeared to be little hesitation in accepting that the Charter had
'greatly expanded the impact of judges on our society,' and that Canada
was 'entering a new judicial age.'[4] Speaking in 1991, Madame Justice Beverly McLachlin of the Supreme Court of Canada could look at the Charter
over its early years and see it as a breathtaking change which turned the
tables of power.[5] Parliamentary supremacy, she said, had been replaced
by the supremacy of the law, and the ultimate arbiters of the law – the
judges – had acquired a very important role. She asserted that with this
new power, the way in which judges went about their task had to change.
While formalism might still serve to resolve cases involving private law,
Madame Justice McLachlin assumed that this approach would not work
with Charter issues. Decision making under the Charter involved making
value judgments, she stated; in making such decisions the judges must
'look into themselves and base their answers on their own values and
instincts,' and also 'look outside themselves, basing their judgments on
the norms and values they see reflected in society at large.' The adoption
of contextual decision making, a change suggested at the time the Federal
Court was created, was now a necessity.

McLachlin's statement that decision making under the Charter involved making value judgments highlighted the similarity to political decision making. The general language of the Charter provisions meant that the language context provided minimal help in solving problems, and the fact that in the past the rights and freedoms had been protected through the political system rather than the legal system meant that a solid legal context was lacking. The social context was left, but the formalists in the legal system had always said that was for the political process – now it was for the legal system.

The media found it newsworthy to emphasis the political nature of the decision making that the judges would now be undertaking, and the thought followed naturally that the judges should be subject to the same public scrutiny to which politicians were subjected. Public acceptance of the impartiality of the judiciary had traditionally rested on the judge's appearance of political neutrality. Once judges are perceived as making political decisions and become subject to scrutiny and criticisms reserved in the past for politicians, there has to be a rethinking of the idea that their credibility rests on being 'value-neutrality.' The traditional sensitivity about categorizing of judges on the basis of their political leanings also has to change.

In spite of these very basic changes facing the legal profession and the likely problems, lawyers in general did not seem to view the dawn of the apparent new age with alarm; some welcomed the Charter with something akin to childlike enthusiasm. Perhaps the years of formalism had dulled their senses with regard to the nature of the decision making (political) that would be involved in reaching satisfactory solutions with the Charter.

An example of what in the past would have been a judge's nightmare occurred in October 1983, when a story about a case (complete with photograph of the presiding judge) appeared on the front page of the Toronto *Globe and Mail*.[6] The judge was Alex Cattanach of the Trial Division of the Federal Court and the article was headed 'Charter of Rights casts new role for federal judges.' The article was written as if it were dealing with a political decision maker, and included biographical information about the judge. The anonymity of the judiciary, long cherished by the legal profession, had now been pierced. Cattanach had refused to be interviewed or photographed, but he had allowed the court to release a photograph. His wife had been contacted by telephone. No article of this nature has appeared since.

There was a sense of anticipation about how the judges would take the Charter of Rights and Freedoms and wield their new 'political' power.

For those who were aware that the judiciary had reacted negatively to the Canadian Bill of Rights and had drained it of vitality, in the belief that it was not wanted, the judges' reaction to the Charter was of added interest.

THE *OPERATION DISMANTLE* CASE

The public was not disappointed when an early case also proved a very political one. It was the one which had inspired the *Globe and Mail* story on Cattanach. Known as the *Operation Dismantle* case, it involved the federal government giving permission to the United States to test cruise missiles over Canada. Public opposition to the move had taken shape as part of the disarmament movement. Polls showed that slightly more than half of Canadians were opposed to the testing. Political sensitivity about the issue was so pronounced that Prime Minister Trudeau sent an 'open letter' to newspapers across the country in which he attempted to justify granting the permission.

Following the government's announcement of final approval for the testing on July 15, 1983, various peace groups and labour unions, armed with the Charter, went to the Federal Court to try to have the testing stopped. They sought an injunction and also a declaration that the government's decision to allow the testing was unconstitutional.

The government brought a motion to have the action dismissed on the ground that there could be no basis for it. Noting that there was a major public controversy involved, Mr Justice Cattanach decided that the case could proceed. He set a very low standard for allowing the action to go ahead; there had to exist at least 'a scintilla of a cause of action,' and later he referred to 'the germ of a cause of action.'[7] The government appealed Cattanach's decision to the Federal Court of Appeal.

The seriousness with which the court viewed the matter was reflected in the selection of a rare five-judge panel to hear the appeal. The five judges were Pratte, Ryan, Le Dain, Marceau, and Hugessen. Chief Justice Thurlow did not sit.[8]

The judges of the Court of Appeal evaluated the arguments put forward by those challenging the grant of permission to test the missiles, something which made their task more difficult than Cattanach's, but much more interesting. One indication that this was not just another case was the fact that each judge wrote reasons for judgment – an uncommon practice in the Court of Appeal. Institutionally, however, the court came up short; the result was a 2–2–1 decision, or perhaps even a 2–1–1–1 decision.[9] Whether this would have happened if an appeal to the Supreme

Court had not been inevitable seems doubtful, but that must remain within the realm of speculation.

Two questions faced the judges: first, whether the cabinet's decision, which concerned national defence and international relations, was completely political in nature, or one that the judiciary had the authority to examine; and, second, whether the testing infringed the plaintiffs' rights to life, liberty, and security of the person, as guaranteed by section 7 of the Charter – and, if so, whether the infringement had been in accordance with the principles of fundamental justice.

The second question was a non-event. The lawyers for the plaintiffs were asked many times at the hearing to state the principle of fundamental justice which had been ignored, and they were unable to do so. The judges were able to dispose of this issue effortlessly, and with it the case, since they also held that there had been no breach of a Charter right. But the first question, whether there were governmental decisions not subject to the Charter and hence immune from judicial review, was a constitutional issue of some magnitude, and most of the judges could not resist dealing with it. Mr Justice James Hugessen minimized the impact of the case by ducking the first question completely. In his view, since there was no need wander into that 'difficult terrain,' he would not do so.[10] The other judges trod onward.

Two of them, Louis Pratte and William Ryan, looked at the language in section 32: 'This Charter applies to the Parliament and government of Canada in respect of all matters within the authority of Parliament.' They said that they were prepared to simply go with 'such a clear provision,'[11] and that was that. The cabinet decision could be reviewed. Neither Pratte nor Ryan had wandered very far. Le Dain and Marceau went further.

Le Dain was prepared to recognize that there were decisions made by government that were 'inherently non-justiciable,' by which he meant issues that were beyond the competence of the judiciary. The *Operation Dismantle* case posed such a question concerning the effect of the testing and the risk of a nuclear conflict, thus presenting 'factors, considerations and imponderables, many of which are inaccessible to a court or of a nature which a court is incapable of evaluating or weighing.'[12] Le Dain stepped out onto difficult terrain, and decided that it was beyond his capability to go further. In his view, the cabinet's decision was not reviewable.

Marceau rendered the longest judgment by far and one quite different from those produced by his colleagues. He justified his excursion into the first question by noting that the circumstances were exceptional. In addition, most of the argument had been directed to the question, and he did not find avoiding it satisfactory, particularly in light of the public interest in it.

Marceau examined a recent decision of the English Court of Criminal Appeal and House of Lords, as well as some classic legal writing, and concluded that a government decision relating to national defence and external relations could not be reviewed by the judiciary.[13] This proposition was an essential constitutional rule relating to executive power (the royal prerogative). For Marceau, the Charter had been enacted as part of Canada's constitution and there had been no intention that pre-existing parts of the constitution would be destroyed, particularly those viewed as essential. Marceau rejected the judiciary's right to review the decision on the testing.

The split on the court had been dramatic: Pratte and Ryan held that the government's decision could be reviewed; Le Dain and Marceau said that it could not be reviewed; and Hugessen said that he did not need to answer the question. Le Dain and Marceau split further, Le Dain stating that there could be no judicial review because of a lack of competence, and Marceau arriving at the same result because of the existence of a constitutional rule prohibiting judicial review.

Of course the bottom line was that Cattanach's decision to allow the litigation to proceed was reversed on the basis that no breach of the Charter had occurred. The judges were unanimous on this point. On the more profound issue, they had spun apart. The difference in their approaches was striking. There was the formalism of Pratte and Ryan, Marceau's contextual analysis of the 'whole' constitution, and Le Dain's analysis of the nature of the decision that had to be made, and whether the judiciary were able to deal with it, an approach which would entail considerable difficulty for judges who attempted to follow it in subsequent cases.

This early Charter decision was so eagerly awaited that the *Ontario Lawyers Weekly* made the Court of Appeal decision the subject of a centre spread, rather than waiting for the Supreme Court of Canada decision as would have been usual. The coverage was critical of the Court of Appeal. The multiple judgments were considered unnecessary and the product of 'five prima donnas.' The author's conclusion that there was 'no serious disagreement between any of the judges' reflected a belief that it would have been entirely possible for them to produce 'a single clear set of reasons.'[14] The centre spread, complete with pencil drawing of the panel, was not good press.

The opponents of the testing appealed to the Supreme Court of Canada. The Supreme Court affirmed the Court of Appeal's decision to strike out the statement of claim.[15] Six judges participated in the decision,[16] and only two judgments were rendered. The forces which allowed for an almost unanimous decision in the Supreme Court of Canada had obviously been absent from the Federal Court of Appeal. Brian Dickson, who had become chief justice of Canada by the time the judgment was rendered, produced the reasons of a majority of five judges,[17] while Madame Justice Bertha Wilson preferred to render her own reasons for judgment and concurred only in the result reached by the majority.

Dickson for the majority was content to simply accept that cabinet decisions were reviewable under the Charter, a point on which he agreed with Madame Justice Wilson, whose reasons amount to a mini-treatise on the topic. In the main, the majority was unable to accept that the threat of nuclear war could be linked factually to the government's duty not to infringe a person's right to life, liberty, and security of the person under section 7 of the Charter.

With only Madame Justice Wilson standing apart, the decision of the Supreme Court can be seen as a decision of the institution, not that of individual judges. The plaintiffs' claim of breach of the rights enshrined in the Charter was not reasonably capable of proof, and that might have ended the matter, but the important point was that a majority of the Supreme Court thought that the occasion required a firm statement that cabinet decisions were reviewable. This was of course a safe response in the circumstances, since no argument could be made that would allow an actual review to take place. The majority must have concluded that it was unnecessary to produce guidelines for when a review might or might not be appropriate,[18] which Pratte and Ryan in the Court of Appeal had also declined to do.

The most basic message sent by the Supreme Court was that the Charter had been accepted, and the experience of the Canadian Bill of Rights was behind the legal profession. The judges had recognized that the social context had changed, and they gave effect to the new social values.

IMMORAL AND INDECENT

Social values were at the core of another Charter decision that propelled the Federal Court onto the front pages. On March 16, 1985, the headline of the Toronto *Globe and Mail* read, 'Court rejects law curbing importation of pornography.'

The case was *Luscher v. Deputy Minister of National Revenue, Customs and*

Excise, a decision of the Federal Court of Appeal.[19] The Deputy Minister of National Revenue, Customs and Excise had classified a magazine as 'immoral or indecent' under the Customs Tariff Act,[20] thus prohibiting its importation into Canada. This decision was affirmed on appeal to an Ontario County Court judge, and a further appeal was taken to the Federal Court of Appeal. The three-judge panel consisted of Chief Justice Arthur Thurlow and Justices Patrick Mahoney and James Hugessen.

The judgment of the Court of Appeal was written by Mr Justice Hugessen, who went straight at the problem. He declared that the tariff classification under which the magazine had been banned was invalid because it infringed the constitutional guarantee of freedom of expression found in the Charter of Rights and Freedoms.[21] The judgment stated that the words 'immoral' and 'indecent' were too vague and uncertain to serve as legal tests, as well as being highly subjective and emotional in nature. Hugessen found social values to be in a state of flux at the time, with 'widely different opinions' being present within Canadian society. No one could disagree with the Court of Appeal that differing opinions exist in society about control over what is immoral or indecent. The question is, What should a judge do in such circumstances?

The customs prohibition against importing immoral and indecent material had been the traditional bulwark of our society against the importation of things that were thought capable of undermining its moral fabric.[22] The prohibition had existed since the beginning of Confederation. In 1948 legislation provided for an appeal to the Tariff Board from any decision of the minister of national revenue banning a book,[23] but it was not until 1958 that such an appeal was taken to the board. The 1948 legislation allowed a further appeal to the Exchequer Court,[24] but it was not exercised until the 1980s, by which time the Federal Court of Appeal had taken over. In the 1958 appeal to the Tariff Board, the publishers of the novel *Peyton Place* challenged an order banning the book; the Tariff Board, in a 2–1 decision, overturned the minister's decision. The board gave the words 'immoral and indecent' the same meaning as the word 'obscene,' defined at the time as the tendency to deprave and corrupt. The Tariff Board then criticized the test for obscenity for its lack of clarity and its subjective nature.[25] The split decision and the criticism of the law sent a clear signal that change within society was under way. In the face of changing values, the members of the board had given the words 'immoral and indecent' a meaning based on existing standards of obscenity, which they thought was more certain than a determination that something was offensive to decency.

The overturning of the minister's banning order led the government to change the law regarding appeals from such bans. The government obviously thought that the public wanted 'immoral and indecent' material kept out of the country, since it made no move to follow up on the Tariff Board's criticisms that the law was too uncertain. However, appeals were taken away from the board and given to a county or district judge, or, for Quebec, a judge of the Superior Court.[26] That judgment could still be appealed to the Exchequer Court, or, after 1971, to the Federal Court of Appeal. It was obvious that customs control over socially unacceptable material was sufficiently sensitive to require a more socially respected arbiter. Perhaps the government thought that a judge would be more in tune with the social mores that it accepted and wished to promote, than would be the members of an administrative board.

The same provision considered by the Tariff Board in 1958, which the board members had interpreted in the light of then current social values, appeared before the Federal Court of Appeal in 1985 and was eliminated from the law using the new judicial power contained within the Charter. Hugessen and the rest of the panel took the words 'freedom of expression' in the Charter and let them go to their logical extent without placing any limits on them. They did not consider it the judge's function to give socially appropriate meaning to the words 'immoral and indecent,' as the members of the Tariff Board had in 1958; the legislature should do that. The panel ignored a 1982 decision of the Federal Court of Appeal, rendered before the Charter took effect, in which a unanimous panel made up of Heald, Urie, and Kelly had decided that the words 'immoral and indecent' were to be subject to the same test as the word 'obscene,' which at that time had become a judicial measure of the community standard of tolerance for whatever material was being denied entry into the country.[27] The judicial function of using the Charter appeared to consist of destroying law and forcing the government to act.

When the Court of Appeal noted that community values were in a state of flux, they might have taken this as a signal that the entire matter should be left to political forces and that they should go with the status quo and, as the Tariff Board had done, give the law the meaning that the judges considered the most appropriate for the times. A judge's first duty must be to give meaning to law.

The Court of Appeal might find social values in a state of flux, but that did not prevent the government from identifying those values that were dominant at the time. The customs restrictions had been in place for a very long time, and were not to be easily swept aside. Customs officials initially reacted by saying that nothing would change,[28] but this, in the face of the court decision, was too strong and they later received directions not to stop any importation themselves but to call in the police if they suspected that material that should be prohibited was in the process of entering the country.[29] Two weeks after the Court of Appeal's decision the Conservative government introduced an amendment to the Customs Tariff Act. The minister of state (finance), Barbara McDougall, declared that the Federal Court of Appeal had created 'an appalling situation,' and had seriously curtailed the government's power to protect Canadian interests.[30] The customs tariff item was reworded and now bans material 'deemed to be obscene' as defined by the criminal law.[31] This is what the Tariff Board had decided was needed almost thirty years before.

There was something disquieting about the Federal Court's approach in these early Charter cases. In one case Pratte and Ryan dealt with the judiciary's power to review political decisions at the highest level, that is, cabinet decisions, on the basis of the language of the constitution, and the court was so fragmented that it could not establish a guide for future action. The other case involved a vital part of any society's existence – its values – yet the answer reached unanimously by Hugessen, Thurlow, and Mahoney was again based only on language. While these cases illustrate that the judges were willing to accept the Charter and give it effect, there was no evidence that a majority were willing to engage in the new form of analysis it required. The Canadian Charter of Rights and Freedoms contains great power to affect events within society; to simply undertake a linguistic analysis is to let that power loose without controls and is socially dangerous.

25

A Matter of Status

The Federal Court's position in Canada's judicial world depended on its status in relation to the provincial superior courts. While this had been an ongoing concern, the concern became acute in the early 1970s.

It began with the bringing of an action in the Ontario High Court for a declaration that a federal statute was invalid;[1] in an attempt to end the proceedings, lawyers for the federal government argued that the Federal Court had exclusive jurisdiction. The federal strategy suggested that the Federal Court was being used to enhance federal power, and if the argument had succeeded it would have taken jurisdiction over constitutional issues relating to federal statutes away from the provincial courts. This was an unprecedented line of reasoning and posed the clear threat of a dual system of courts for those who wanted the provincial courts to be the principal courts of an essentially unitary legal system.

Why was the argument raised? Was it simply a case of counsel making all possible arguments and leaving the judges to sift the wheat from the chaff? Was it indeed a serious attempt to obtain judicial power for the Federal Court?

In the interviews conducted for this book, one judge made the point that a good judgment is a courageous judgment – one which considers only those arguments which are truly important, and not simply every argument presented. If this is so, then the judges who came to deal with the exclusive jurisdiction argument might be said to have displayed a lack of courage. On the other hand, the fact that the issue was treated throughout with considerable respect may indicate that they took it very seriously. Certainly one result of the argument being raised was that the existence of the Federal Court had created another matter that would bedevil judges and lawyers.

A constitutional challenge to the validity of a law arises with respect to the application of the law; it follows logically that the judge who has jurisdiction over the constitutional issue will also have jurisdiction over the application of the challenged law.[2] To argue that the Federal Court had exclusive jurisdiction over constitutional issues involving federal law was to ignore this elementary principle! Success of the argument would have meant the creation of a special constitutional court for federal law – an enormous change which surely would have been at least alluded to during the legislative process that created the Federal Court. In an address at the symposium honouring the twentieth anniversary of the Federal Court in 1991, John Turner did indicate that there had been an intention to give the Federal Court exclusive jurisdiction over constitutional issues concerning federal law,[3] but this defies belief. If the federal government had indeed intended to elevate the status of the Federal Court to that of a constitutional court, the result achieved was very different – the status of the provincial courts was elevated at the expense of the Federal Court.

THE PRIMARY COURTS

The case which began the saga of the status issue was *Denison Mines Ltd. v. Attorney-General of Canada* (1973).[4] In the Ontario High Court a uranium company contended that control over atomic energy was a matter within provincial constitutional authority, and that consequently the federal Atomic Control Act was invalid. The federal legislation provided that all proceedings against the Atomic Energy Control Board were to be taken in the provincial courts. Lawyers for the federal government based their challenge to the jurisdiction of the Ontario court on language in section 17(1) of the Federal Court Act: 'The Trial Division has original jurisdiction in all cases where relief is claimed against the Crown and, except where otherwise provided, the Trial Division has exclusive original jurisdiction in all such cases.'

Mr Justice Donnelly of the Ontario High Court looked only at the language and concluded that it was sufficient to give the Trial Division of the

Federal Court exclusive jurisdiction. He rejected the counter-argument that explicit words were required to accomplish such a dramatic change.

Just how these issues bedevilled the minds of lawyers is illustrated by comparing Donnelly's conclusion with an earlier decision of the Ontario Court of Appeal, in which it had determined that the Hamilton Harbour Commissioners were a 'federal board, commission or other tribunal' and that section 18 of the Federal Court Act gave the Trial Division exclusive jurisdiction in an action for a declaration against the commissioners concerning the regulation of land.[5] This decision was completely uncontroversial, but since the resolution of the land question involved a constitutional issue, it was joined with the *Denison Mines* case as an example of how provincial courts were being excluded from deciding questions of the validity of federal law.[6]

In the early 1970s Joseph Thorson, former president of the Exchequer Court, challenged the validity of the federal Official Languages Act in the Ontario courts, and there was no mention of any exclusive jurisdiction of the Federal Court.[7] But the jurisdictional issue did arise in a constitutional challenge to the abortion law launched by Joseph Borowski in the Saskatchewan courts in 1980. Borowski sought a declaration that the provision of the Criminal Code which made abortions legal under certain circumstances was invalid. The Saskatchewan courts, both the Queen's Bench and the Court of Appeal, held that they had jurisdiction. The challenged law was a criminal law, squarely within the jurisdiction of the provincial courts. The Saskatchewan courts also found that no 'federal court, commission or tribunal' was involved.[8] This was a return to normality.

The Supreme Court of Canada heard an appeal in the *Borowski* case,[9] but did not deal with the jurisdiction issue because it had already been considered in *Jabour v. Law Society of British Columbia*.[10] The *Jabour* case was one of the most significant in the history of the Federal Court.

The *Jabour* case involved criminal law, and the issue was whether the Combines Investigation Act (now the Competition Act) applied to the Law Society of British Columbia, and, if it did, whether it was constitutionally valid, i.e., within the legislative power of the federal Parliament. The courts of British Columbia rejected the federal argument that the Federal Court had exclusive jurisdiction. Like the courts of Saskatchewan in *Borowski*, they affirmed the fundamental principle of constitutional law: since the application of the challenged law was within the jurisdiction of the provincial courts, it followed that consideration of the law's constitutional validity also rested with them. In contrast to Mr Justice Donnelly (who had relied only on words), the judges in the *Jabour* case were of the opinion that it would take very clear words to remove the jurisdiction of the provincial court over constitutional issues regarding federal legislation.[11] At this point the issue of whether the Federal Court had exclusive jurisdiction over constitutional issues involving federal law might have faded away, but the federal government appealed to the Supreme Court of Canada.

The appeal to the Supreme Court of Canada provided Mr Justice Willard ('Bud') Estey with the opportunity to make his particular mark on the question. He moved away from interpretation of the Federal Court Act and dealt with what he termed the 'more fundamental aspect.'[12] He asserted that the basic principle of the Canadian judicial system was the jurisdiction of the provincial superior courts over all law – federal or provincial. He exalted the provincial superior courts as having 'always occupied a position of prime importance in the constitutional pattern of this country,' and then gave them a pedigree as 'the descendants of the Royal Courts of Justice as courts of general jurisdiction.'[13] Estey had aligned himself with Mr Justice Pigeon and the majority decision in *Thomas Fuller Construction*.[14]

From the outset Estey appeared unable to accept the idea that Ottawa could preclude the provincial superior courts from declaring a federal statute to be invalid: 'It is difficult to see how an argument can be advanced.' He gave the matter a solid constitutional anchor when he declared that Ottawa lacked the constitutional authority to enact legislation which would prevent the provincial courts from considering the constitutional validity of federal law. He considered such judicial power to be fundamental to a federal system. Estey was concerned that taking away the jurisdiction of the provincial courts to adjudicate questions of the constitutional validity of federal law would leave provincial superior courts 'with the invidious task of execution of federal and provincial laws ... while being unable to discriminate between valid and invalid federal statutes so as to refuse to "execute" the invalid statutes.'[15] This last remark, with its emphasis on the word 'execute,' seemed to make the glorification of the provincial superior courts mere window dressing. The fundamental idea that a court with the jurisdiction to execute a law has the jurisdiction to review it on constitutional grounds was apparently left intact.

The *Jabour* decision was followed the next year by *Conseil canadien des relations du travail v. Paul L'Anglais Inc.*,[16] an ill-conceived decision of the Supreme Court of Canada. The litigation arose from a determination by the Canada Labour Relations Board that the labour relations of certain corporations in Quebec were within its jurisdiction because the companies were involved in a federal undertaking, namely broadcasting. The important issue that arose was whether the provincial superior court had jurisdiction to review a decision of the Canada Labour Relations Board when a constitutional question was involved (whether the companies were to be classed as part of federal undertakings or not). The trial judge held that the Federal Court had exclusive jurisdiction over federal agencies and declined to hear the case. The Quebec Court of Appeal unanimously reversed that decision and assumed jurisdiction on the basis that there was a constitutional issue involved.

Mr Justice Chouinard rendered the judgment of the unanimous Supreme Court of Canada and concluded that the Federal Court's exclusive jurisdiction to review the decisions of federal agencies applied to cases involving the administration of law, but not to those where the constitutional validity of the law to be applied was in question. This conclusion emerged following a lengthy parade of cases and the setting out of the arguments of counsel. Chouinard cited the *Jabour* case as a conclusive answer to the issue, which is problematic since Estey had not dealt with that particular point in *Jabour*.[17] The result was that the determination of constitutional questions regarding federal legislation was made a concurrent jurisdiction, shared between the Federal Court and the provincial superior courts. The basic and well-established principle that jurisdiction over constitutional issues follows jurisdiction over the substantive law was cast aside.

The result reached in the *Paul L'Anglais Inc.* case suggests that the Supreme Court of Canada decided to promote the provincial superior courts at the expense of the Federal Court and to bless the decision with the imprimatur of the constitution. Julien Chouinard's roots were in Quebec, as were those of Louis-Philippe Pigeon, whose judgment in *Thomas Fuller Construction* no doubt provided inspiration, and they may well have been more acutely aware of the positive ramifications of such a decision than others. However, the unanimity of the Supreme Court requires comment. At this time the court had moved into a period when unanimous decisions were a priority. It seems obvious that individual judges were giving up writing judgments, either concurring or dissenting in the belief that unanimity gave the decisions needed political and legal weight.[18]

In a legal milieu in which 'authorities' dominated thinking, the unanimous conclusion in *Paul L'Anglais* now became itself a controlling authority, until reviewed (in theory) by the Supreme Court of Canada at some future date. In a later decision in 1983, Estey simply acknowledged that the case had established a concurrent jurisdiction for constitutional questions concerning federal law.[19] He gave no hint of any thought of a power to review and possibly overrule the case.

The Federal Court of Appeal must assume some responsibility for the Supreme Court's decision in *Paul L'Anglais Inc.*, since it had declined jurisdiction on the ground that the decision of the Canada Labour Relations Board was not a 'decision' within the meaning of section 28 of the Federal Court Act.[20] This conclusion had been based solely on precedents from 1973, which adopted a restricted view of the kind of decisions reviewable by the Court of Appeal.[21] Unable to have the decision reviewed by the Federal Court, the applicant had turned to the Quebec courts.

The Supreme Court's conclusion in *Paul L'Anglais Inc.* assumes greater significance when thought of in relation to the Charter of Rights and Freedoms, which had been created in the year preceding the decision. The *raison d'être* for the existence of the Federal Court of Canada was largely the judicial review of administrative action; but the cases involving judicial review applied concepts (principles of fundamental justice and procedural fairness) which had counterparts in the Charter. In light of the *Paul L'Anglais Inc.* case, the constitutional status of the Charter would allow provincial superior courts to take jurisdiction, making the judicial review jurisdiction of the Federal Court in large part concurrent with that of the provincial superior courts.

THE CHARTER

When the opportunity arose, lawyers for the federal government were prepared to argue that the Federal Court had exclusive jurisdiction over constitutional challenges to federal legislation based on the Charter. The occasion was a constitutional challenge brought in the Supreme Court of British Columbia concerning the assessment of penalties for tax evasion under the federal Income Tax Act.

Chief Justice McEachern concluded that his provincial court had at least coordinate jurisdiction, based on the Supreme Court of Canada decisions in *Jabour* and *Paul L'Anglais Inc.* McEachern considered the case as much a Charter case as an income tax one, and said, 'I respectfully do not agree that this court should defer to the Federal Court in Charter matters.'[22] The die had been cast and the judicial review jurisdiction of the Federal Court was on the line.

The rationale put forward to justify the creation of one federal administrative court in 1971 had been that different provincial courts might decide in different ways, thereby creating a hodgepodge of results. The same problem would exist if provincial courts were acknowledged to have jurisdiction over Charter issues involving the application of federal law that would otherwise be within the jurisdiction of the Federal Court. If a non-Charter element of the matter were litigated in the Federal Court, the Federal Court could very well decide that it was not bound by the decision of the provincial court on the Charter issue. Every Charter issue would be capable of being litigated in one or more provincial courts and in the Federal Court, simultaneously or in sequence.

It would be a decade before the potential of the provincial superior courts to take jurisdiction away from the Federal Court was curbed. The issue appeared in stark form before the Ontario Court of Appeal in 1992. In *Reza v. The Queen*,[23] an applicant had sought refugee status before the Federal Court, but had been unsuccessful and was facing deportation. The applicant brought a challenge to the Immigration Act in the Ontario courts on the basis of the Charter. No Charter challenge had been launched before the Federal Court. The trial judge acknowledged his jurisdiction but declined to exercise it because he held that the Federal Court also had jurisdiction and the review of immigration matters should be left there. This result was appealed to the Ontario Court of Appeal.

The appeal panel consisted of James Carthy, Louise Arbour, and Rosalie Abella. A split decision resulted. Arbour, with Carthy concurring, was prepared to assume concurrent jurisdiction between the superior court of the province and the Federal Court for the purpose of the case. That left the question of what principles should govern a provincial superior court in deciding whether to hear an application for a remedy under the Charter or to defer to prospective litigation in the Federal Court. Madame Justice Arbour considered that the choice of courts should be left to the litigant; in a constitutional case like this one there was no reason why the Ontario court should defer. In her view, all judges were experts in matters of fundamental justice and procedural fairness. The order of the trial judge was set aside and the matter was consequently to be settled by the Ontario courts.

Madame Justice Abella dissented. She acknowledged, without hesitation, that the provinicial court had concurrent jurisdiction to decide the constitutional matter. In this case, however, she identified the Charter challenge as fundamentally linked to immigration policy and process in general, and also to the facts of the particular case. The Federal Court was an expert in immigration matters and in her view the adjudication should be left to it.

It is notable that there was no hint of deference by the judges of the Ontario court to the Federal Court's decision in the matter. While Madame Justice Arbour called it a 'juridical disadvantage,' her colleague Madame Justice Abella said simply that it was no reason to deprive the Ontario court of its jurisdiction.

As expected, the litigation wound its way to the Supreme Court of Canada, where the appeal was heard by a panel of seven judges.[24] The appeal was allowed. 'The court' rendered a short judgment, which featured a recitation of the facts followed by a review of the judgments delivered in the lower courts. The conclusion was that the judges were 'generally in agreement with the dissenting reasons delivered by Abella J.A.' This meant that the Ontario court and the Federal Court had concurrent jurisdiction to hear the application, and the trial judge had properly exercised a discretion to decline to exercise his jurisdiction because 'Parliament had created a comprehensive scheme of review of immigration matters and the Federal Court was an effective and appropriate forum.' Such an analysis would have been appropriate to the issues raised earlier by *Quebec North Shore Paper* and *McNamara*.

JUDICIAL POWER

Throughout the years, first as the Exchequer Court, and later as the Federal Court, the Federal Court of Canada has been identified as a statutory court, which must find authority for its actions in the language of legislation. In contrast, the superior courts of the provinces have been identified as 'the true successors to the original King's Justices of the Central Courts of England.'[25] The provincial courts are also frequently referred to as the 'common law courts,'[26] though technically this is only partially accurate (they are also courts of equity). The expression 'common law courts' is not used in a technical sense, but carries the mystique which surrounds the words 'common law.' The words imply something ancient, powerful, and mysterious; something to be revered.[27] A 'common law' court is understood to be able to do anything of a judicial nature that has not been expressly forbidden it by the legislature, and, armed with the Charter, the judges in such courts may be able to prohibit the legislature from interfering with their jurisdiction. So it was that in 1985, Mr Justice Estey could state that the provincial superior courts were to occupy a 'position of prime importance in the constitutional pattern of [the] country.'[28]

The question of judicial power had come up in 1975 when Mr Justice Beetz of the Supreme Court of Canada concluded that the power of the judiciary to review laws and to determine if they were valid or not according to the terms of the constitution was itself guaranteed by the constitution. He said, 'The federal and fundamental nature of the Constitution ... implies an inherent and entrenched jurisdiction in the Courts to adjudicate in constitutional matters.'[29] This was new. Up to this time the issue of a constitutional guarantee had not been a concern, since the constitutional limitations on the law-making power of the legislatures were found in the British North America Act, 1867,[30] and the Colonial Laws Validity Act, 1865 specifically authorized judicial review.[31] Perhaps as far as Mr Justice Beetz was concerned in 1975 a justification for judicial review that emanated from a view of Canada as part of a world empire, even though legally correct, did not sit that well socially, particularly in Quebec, his home province. Or he may simply have preferred to enhance the power of the judiciary by giving judges inherent powers which were constitutionally protected. This latter idea has a greater overall effect within the legal and political systems.

At the same time that Beetz was writing about an inherent power of judges to engage in judicial review of questions of constitutional validity, the issue of a constitutional guarantee of judicial review of administrative action surfaced[32] and in 1981, some five years later, the Supreme Court of Canada declared that judicial review of administrative decisions was constitutionally protected. In 1952 Bora Laskin, then a professor, could write, 'there is no constitutional principle on which courts can rest any claim to review administrative board decisions,'[33] but in 1981 Laskin, now chief justice of Canada, wrote the judgment for a unanimous Supreme Court of Canada creating constitutional protection for judicial review of administrative board decisions.[34] This surprising decision[35] enhanced the power of the judiciary; it also impacted on the making of political decisions to restrict judicial review and to create administrative tribunals.[36] Battles fought since the 1920s were now over. In the following year, Mr Justice Estey in *Jabour* would instigate the idolization of the provincial superior courts.

Canadian Union of Public Employees, Local 963 v. New Brunswick Liquor Corp., a 1979 decision of the Supreme Court of Canada known as *CUPE*,[37] was a case much heralded for deciding that there should be judicial deference for labour arbitration and labour board decisions when subject to judicial review.[38] It was perhaps natural that the enactment of the Charter in 1982 and the surge of judicial power that accompanied it would create a lack of receptiveness by judges to *CUPE*'s message. In 1984 Mr Justice Beetz, who nine years before had recognized an inherent power within the judiciary to engage in judicial review under the constitution, decided that judicial review of administrative action should be justified on the basis of the constitution. In the *L'Acadie* case,[39] he declared that the issue of judicial review in administrative law was one of judicial power with respect to governing the country, and asserted that 'The power of review of the courts of law has the same historic basis in both cases, and in both cases it relates to the same principles, the supremacy of the Constitution or of the law, of which the courts are the guardians.'[40] Beetz used rule of law as the basis for judicial review, and within the legal profession it is the version propounded by A.V. Dicey, namely, 'no man is punishable or can be lawfully made to suffer in body or goods except for a distinct breach of law established in the ordinary manner before the ordinary courts of the land,'[41] that tends to be recognized. The 'ordinary' courts, that is the legal profession, were in control in the Diceyian formulation, and the power of the judiciary was consequently enhanced by Beetz's decision.

Several commentators identified the Supreme Court's decision in *L'Acadie* as a highly significant change in the law, and although the judgment was criticised severely,[42] it nonetheless was a unanimous decision of the Supreme Court.[43] It is worth noting that, regarding the unanimity of the judges, the court was still in its phase of presenting a solid institutional profile to enhance its authority as guardian of the law.[44]

The *L'Acadie* case, which is a benchmark in the discussion of judicial power and judicial review of administrative action, provides an opportunity to catch a glimpse of the workings of the Federal Court of Appeal. The bench consisted of Louis Pratte, Gerald Le Dain, and George Miller Hyde from Quebec sitting as a deputy judge. Pratte rendered the Court of Appeal's customarily unanimous judgment, which was delivered orally following the hearing.[45] This was in dramatic contrast with the nearly two years that it took the Supreme Court to deliver its judgment, which, even making allowance for the chronic slowness of Mr Justice Beetz in writing judgments, evidences a different attitude towards the function of the two courts.

Pratte made it appear very simple – he said 'it is clear,' and then stated his conclusion. The Federal Court of Appeal demonstrated its proclivity to engage in 'the business' of rendering judgments. The guidance which a case provides for future decision makers is to be found in the reasons for judgment, but in this instance the reasons consisted of the words 'it is clear.' If the Supreme Court of Canada was, as many said, intent on creating change in a highly controversial area, then the cursory judgment of the Court of Appeal, although it actually reached the same conclusion as the Supreme Court, is very questionable.[46]

Specialist Tribunal and Generalist Court

The concern that the creation of the Federal Court of Canada was the beginning of a move towards a dual judicial system was very real.[47] The topic had arisen at a conference on the Canadian judiciary held in Toronto in February 1976 and sponsored by Osgoode Hall Law School and the Canadian Institute for the Administration of Justice.[48]

William Lederman, former dean of law at Queen's University, raised the issue in a paper on the independence of the judiciary. He asserted that Canada had, and should maintain, an essentially unitary judicial system, which meant that the jurisdiction of the Federal Court should remain limited and exceptional. This opinion was supported by commentators on the paper – the chief justice of the Supreme Court of British Columbia, N.T. Nemetz, and Brian Dickson, then a puisne judge of the Supreme Court of Canada. Both justices cautioned about a move towards a dual system – a shift which they had detected in recent activity surrounding the Federal Court. Four months later, the Supreme Court of Canada would render its decision in *Quebec North Shore Paper* (Dickson did not participate), and *McNamara* would emerge seven months later (Dickson did participate).

By the middle of the 1970s, the perception that a dual legal system had been set in motion made the very existence of the Federal Court worrisome.[49] The concern became so pronounced that the minister of justice was forced to promise at a federal-provincial conference in 1975 that there would be no dual system.[50] It was in 1979 that the Supreme Court of Canada, in the *Thomas Fuller Construction* case, decreed that there would be no dual system. In the years since these events, it has become accepted that the Canadian court system is essentially unitary,[51] and as a result the Federal Court has been relegated to a position of 'special' status.

In administrative law, a very common way to distinguish courts from administrative tribunals is to describe the court as 'generalist,' and the administrative tribunal as 'specialist.'[52]

The primary characteristic of a specialist tribunal is that its members have acquired expertise in the subject matter of the problems presented for resolution, and the specialist nature of the decision making is seen as entailing specially designed procedures.[53] The justification for judicial control of these 'experts' is the protection of general and fundamental values which are needed for fairness in decision making but may be overlooked or underestimated by an administrative agency caught up in its speciality. The generalist court is seen as ideally suited to deal with such general values.[54]

Since administrative decision making is seen as specialized and expert in nature,[55] the existence of a specialist court can be highly problematic. This may partly explain the problems of the Federal Court, which has in large part developed as a composite court of specialities (particularly admiralty [maritime], intellectual property, and judicial review of federal administrative action) within one administrative framework. Over the years demands have been made for the appointment of lawyers specialized in the areas within the court's jurisdiction, and yet if this were to occur it would unquestionably create a 'specialist' court, and, in turn, the court would tend to be identified as an 'administrative' body. The recent appointment (1994) of Mr Justice John Richards represents a departure from the practice of appointing generalists, and was made at the urging of Chief Justice Julius Isaac in response to the wishes of the members of the intellectual property bar.[56]

In 1985 the chief justice of British Columbia, McEachern, seemed prepared, in a case in which the issue of a dual system of courts arose, to accept federal courts if 'judicial specialization not available in the provincial superior courts' was required.[57] If this rationale for the Federal Court were generally accepted, the legal profession might well think of it as an 'administrative tribunal' and the future of the 'court' might be secure as such. However, such a development could leave the legal profession only a step away from thinking that the Federal Court might be subject to judicial review by provincial superior courts.

The judges of the Federal Court generally accept the specialized nature of their work. None of those asked in the interviews conducted for this book displayed any concern about being identified with a specialist court, insofar as their status within the legal system is concerned.

Federal Constitutional Power

The Federal Court Act establishes that the Federal Court is a 'superior court of record having civil and criminal jurisdiction,'[58] a change from the corresponding provision in the Exchequer Court Act, which used the words 'continues to be a court of record.'[59] If this change represented an attempt to give equal status to the Federal Court and the provincial superior courts, then it failed when developments overwhelmed it.

The enhancement of the status and power of the provincial superior courts over the years, and the solid rejection of the existence of a dual system of courts, make it politically very doubtful that a federal court could be created now with the same status as a provincial superior court. While the language of the constitution suggests that it could happen, the will to do so, combined with social conditions conducive to the move, would also be needed.

The federal constitutional authority to create courts was initially identified in section 129 of the constitution.[60] The relevant words were, 'Except as otherwise provided by this Act ... all Courts of Civil and Criminal Jurisdiction ... existing ... at the Union, shall continue in Ontario, Quebec, Nova Scotia, and New Brunswick respectively, as if the Union had not been made; subject nevertheless ... to be repealed, abolished, or altered by the Parliament of Canada, or by the Legislature of the respective Province, according to the Authority of the Parliament or of that Legislature under this Act.' The power to establish courts to administer a law was seen as part of the constitutional authority to create a particular law, which is to say that procedure went with the substantive law.[61]

Regarding section 101 of the constitution, there is little doubt that it was needed for the creation of a 'General Court of Appeal for Canada,' since that matter could not arise within section 129. That portion of section 101 which refers to 'the Establishment of any additional Courts for the better Administration of the Laws of Canada' allowed Ottawa to create courts in addition to those existing at Confederation, which were by section 129 subject to being repealed, abolished, or altered by Ottawa.

The constitutional power to establish federal courts with status and power equal to those of the provincial superior courts exists, but it is a dormant power at the moment.

THE IACOBUCCI YEARS, 1988–1991

26

The Life of the Court

Arthur Thurlow retired on May 5, 1988, at the age of seventy-five. He was the last of the judges who had served on the Exchequer Court; he had been a judge of the Exchequer/Federal Court for thirty-one years and eight months, a length of service in a federal court second only to Lyman Duff's.[1] In his years on the court Thurlow had been both a trial judge and an appeal judge, and had served as both Chief Justice and Associate Chief Justice. Whatever misgivings some may have had about his administrative ability, there was universal respect for his ability as a judge and for him as a person.

It took four months to appoint the new chief justice, the second-longest such interval in the court's history. Associate Chief Justice Jerome acted as chief justice during this period, and Louis Pratte, at Jerome's request, handled the day-to-day running of the Appeal Division.

The Conservative government of Brian Mulroney chose Frank Iacobucci, then deputy minister of justice, as the new chief justice. The perceptual problem created by the public's associating the judges and the government was obviously not significant enough to block Iacobucci's appointment. Iacobucci was actually the third of the seven heads of the court since 1887 to have served as deputy minister of justice.[2] Nevertheless, the fact that he had been deputy minister before joining the court did create problems, for there were many Federal Court files in which his name appeared as solicitor for the government. The court's administration and Iacobucci himself were scrupulous in ensuring that he did not touch or even see such cases. A list of them was prepared and kept close at hand.

Iacobucci had been born and raised in British Columbia. There had been no full-time judge from British Columbia on the Federal Court since Frank Collier had elected to become a supernumerary judge on November 1, 1987. Iacobucci chose to be sworn in at Ottawa. The new chief justice's parents were originally from Italy, and he was the first judge of Italian background within the federal judicial system. Unlike the great majority of people of Italian descent, he had been raised in the Baptist Church and later joined the United Church of Canada. He was fifty-one at the time of his appointment.

After graduating in law from the University of British Columbia, Iacobucci obtained a graduate degree from Cambridge and practised corporate law in New York. In 1967 he joined the Faculty of Law at the University of Toronto as an associate professor, and taught corporate law and taxation. He enjoyed a highly successful career within the academic community. From 1967 to 1985 he was associate dean of the Faculty of Law; vice-president for internal affairs of the university; dean of the Faculty of Law; and finally vice-president of the university. In 1985 he became deputy minister of justice in Ottawa and remained in that position until his appointment to the Federal Court as chief justice. The practice of selecting the chief justice from outside the court had been re-established.[3]

Iacobucci's appointment was well received. His prominent academic background was not controversial, because there was a general feeling within the legal profession that lawyers with an academic background were best appointed at the appeal level. Most felt that his career as a legal academic and his involvement in university administration, coupled with his appointment as deputy minister of justice, gave him impeccable credentials. In 1987 he had received the Law Society medal, awarded by the Law Society of Upper Canada for outstanding service to the profession. Superb interpersonal and political skills made him very effective in dealing with people. He was considered a very able administrator.

Iacobucci served as chief justice for just over two years. On January 7, 1991, he was appointed to the Supreme Court of Canada, the second Federal Court judge to be so honoured.[4]

Andrew MacKay of Nova Scotia was appointed to the court's Trial Division on September 2, 1988, the same day that Iacobucci was made chief justice. MacKay's appointment was an indication that the background of a prospective judge was not a controlling factor, since he had a longer academic career than Iacobucci and yet went to the Trial Division. His career as a law teacher and university administrator had been spent at Dalhousie University in Halifax. He attended that university for his undergraduate degree and his basic and graduate degrees in law. After a brief stint as a foreign service officer with the Department of External Affairs (1954–57), MacKay joined Dalhousie's Faculty of Law. He served as dean of the faculty for five years, beginning in 1964. In 1969 he moved into university administration as vice-president (academic), and remained in that position until 1980, when he became president of the university. In 1986 he left the academic world to serve as Nova Scotia's ombudsman; two years later he was appointed to the Federal Court. He was fifty-nine at the time of his appointment.

During Iacobucci's two years on the Federal Court, John Urie chose to become a supernumerary judge at the age of sixty-eight (December 31, 1988), and George Addy, who had been the first Federal Court judge to select supernumerary status, retired (September 20, 1990). Urie retired two years later at the age of seventy (December 15, 1990). Bertrand Lacombe of the Court of Appeal, and John McNair of the Trial Division, resigned for health reasons.

Robert Décary was appointed to the Court of Appeal on March 14, 1990, three months after Lacombe's resignation. Décary was forty-five. He had graduated in law from the Université de Montréal and had then obtained a graduate degree from the University of London. Décary practised law in Montreal, but later moved to Ottawa to become an agent for Quebec lawyers in cases before the Supreme Court of Canada. He also had journalistic experience, having written for newspapers including *Le Devoir* and the Canadian Bar Association's paper, *The National*.

The speediness of Décary's appointment was probably due to the need to maintain the statutory quota of eight judges from Quebec. By contrast Allen Linden, from Ontario, was appointed to the Court of Appeal a year and a half after Urie had elected to become supernumerary. Linden's appointment indicated that whatever workload pressures existed at the time, they were not sufficient to force the speedy replacement of judges who left the bench or became supernumerary.

Linden was fifty-five at the time of his appointment. Equipped with graduate degrees in law from the University of California at Berkeley (an LLM in 1961 and a JSD in 1967), he had pursued an academic career at Osgoode Hall Law School beginning in 1961. His specialty was tort law. He left teaching in 1978 to join the Supreme Court of Ontario as a trial judge, then left the bench in 1983 to become president of the Law Reform Commission of Canada, a position he held for seven years until his appointment to the Federal Court.

As head of the Law Reform Commission, Linden attracted media attention. After he made a speech to the Canadian Association of Law Teachers in 1984, a front-page headline in the Toronto *Globe and Mail* declared 'Courts impede change: Linden.'[5] He was reported as having criticised judges for not taking a broader approach and applying the policy underlying a statute, and for not recognizing that they had a duty to go beyond the simple application of the words of a statute. Contextualism was knocking at the door.

AN ASSESSMENT OF THE COURT

A candid and thorough note published in the *Canadian Bar Review* offers valuable insight into the Federal Court of Canada as it existed at the end of 1989. Authors John Evans and Brian Slattery of Toronto's Osgoode Hall Law School purported to deal with the *Roberts* case, but used the opportunity to comment generally on the Federal Court and the leading cases that had considered the court's jurisdiction.[6]

At the outset they stated that the court was 'still struggling for acceptance.'[7] The authors suggested that the reasons for this situation – after eighteen years of the court's existence – were that there were those who were disappointed in the quality of the judges' work, and others who were concerned about the dubious nature of certain appointments to the Federal Court's bench. For the authors themselves, the problem was the challenge posed by the Federal Court to the status of the provincial superior courts as the pre-eminent courts in the administration of justice in the country.

Quite understandably, the 'endless jurisdictional difficulties' dominated the authors' critique and, they wrote, could be identified as both a symptom and a cause of the problem.[8] Their conclusion was that the law of federal jurisdiction was in a shambles. They ended with a summary of the previous years:

The Federal Court Act, 1971 was an extraordinarily poorly designed piece of legislation, especially since many of its defects were anticipated by commentators and brought to the attention of the Minister of Justice of the day, Mr. John Turner. It was less easy to predict, however, that the Supreme Court of Canada would, until recently, take nearly every opportunity to reduce the Federal Court's jurisdiction through a narrow interpretation of both the Constitution and the Federal Court Act itself.[9]

ABOLITION OF THE COURT

It was during the brief tenure of Chief Justice Iacobucci that the very existence of the Federal Court became for the first time an open political issue.[10]

On June 6, 1989, the attorney general of British Columbia, Bud Smith, placed a proposal calling for the abolition of the court before a meeting of provincial ministers of justice and attorneys general in Charlottetown. Smith's plan involved each province's court system gradually taking over the work of the Federal Court. Smith was quoted by the press as saying that there was 'precious little happiness with the Federal Court system,'[11] and he focused on the continuing problem of jurisdiction. He was eager to take action before construction began on a new building for the court, saying forthrightly, 'Once that happens, you'll never be rid of it.' British Columbia's long-standing opposition to the Federal Court had now culminated in a concrete proposal. The representatives of the other provinces agreed to study the proposal and a committee was established.

In the fall of 1989 the Canadian Bar Association reconstituted the special committee that it had formed in the 1970s to study the Federal Court, this time to study British Columbia's proposal. However, on September 28, 1989, the federal government introduced a bill in the House of Commons to reform the Federal Court, and the Bar Association directed the committee to concentrate on the proposed legislation, Bill C-38.

Dissatisfaction with the jurisdictional problems that had engulfed the court was widespread. In two cases (from Ontario and Nova Scotia respectively) that reached the Supreme Court of Canada in 1990, lawyers had decided that the time was ripe to challenge the constitutionality of the court's exclusive jurisdiction over all claims against the federal government.[12] The allegations of constitutional invalidity were based on the argument that the existence of a special court for claims against the government constituted a denial of equality rights under the Charter. While the Supreme Court was ultimately satisfied that there was no denial of equality rights, Mr Justice Cory for a unanimous Court commented that the Federal Court's exclusive jurisdiction over claims against the government could 'create unnecessary hardships, delays, and additional expense for litigants.'[13] He then noted that these problems had been recognized and that Bill C-38 had been introduced with the intention of solving them.

Though the bill had been introduced in the wake of British Columbia's call for the abolition of the court, the federal minister of justice, Douglas Lewis, made no mention of that province or the broader dissatisfactions then apparent when outlining the purpose of the legislation.[14] Lewis indicated that the policy behind Bill C-38 was to provide the ordinary citizen who wished to sue the federal government with easier access to the courts. He went on to say that the Federal Court had proven to be a success, but there was a need to improve access to the system. It was decidedly telling that the minister of justice felt obliged to justify the existence of a federal court.

Lewis explained that the Federal Court was a Canada-wide court with a national jurisdiction, not impeded by territorial limitations on jurisdiction or process (essential considerations for admiralty and intellectual property cases, in the minister's view). He touched on the need for a court with specialized knowledge in certain areas, referring again to intellectual property and admiralty and adding revenue laws. In support of the administrative law jurisdiction, the minister emphasized the court's assurance of uniformity across the country – so necessary for effective, efficient, and fair operation of federal tribunals.

Regarding the jurisdiction over claims against the government, the policy of increased access to the courts had led the government to conclude that it was more convenient to launch such actions in the provincial court system. However, the intention was to make the jurisdiction concurrent, with the plaintiff having a choice of forum – the Federal Court or the appropriate provincial court. Reform of the Federal Court's jurisdiction had been promised as early as 1975, but the jurisdiction over claims against the government had been the stumbling block. The federal government had decided to remove that barrier. With this decision the reason behind the creation of the distinct Exchequer Court in 1887 had evaporated as a justification for the existence of the Federal Court. The government's willingness to transfer jurisdiction over claims against the Crown to the provincial courts was a clear victory for those who opposed dual legal systems; those who supported the primacy of the provincial courts had prevailed.

With regard to the administrative law jurisdiction, the minister spoke of the confusion about the jurisdiction of the Trial Division versus that of the Court of Appeal. Bill C-38 would remove the split between the two divisions; in addition the prerogative writs, which he said were 'loaded with arcane technical baggage,'[15] would be eliminated, and everyday language used. The new legislation would confer the review of decisions and activities of federal administrative bodies on the Trial Division and not the Court of Appeal; as a consequence, the Court of Appeal would be expected to devote more of its time to cases of broad public importance.

The Court of Appeal's jurisdiction over judicial review had been a centrepiece of the Federal Court Act in 1971 and its proposed transfer to the Trial Division signalled the creation of a new court. The prerogative writs that had been given expressly to the Trial Division in 1971 were to be abandoned for proceedings entitled 'an application for judicial review.' The grounds for review were to be essentially the same as those that had been used in the Court of Appeal since its creation. There would be an appeal as of right to the Court of Appeal from a decision of the Trial Division.

There was one exception to the Trial Division's new power over judicial review. It was proposed that the Court of Appeal would continue to review certain specified administrative tribunals. These were tribunals composed of judges or which had been constituted a court of record, and thus resembled courts. The government thought that it was appropriate that they should continue to be reviewed by the Court of Appeal.[16]

The President of the Canadian Bar Association, John Jennings, and Brian Crane, a member of the special committee (who had also been a member in the 1970s), appeared before the legislative committee for a presentation. This was a more impressive outing than had occurred twenty years before. It was possible to sense a threat when, at the beginning, Jennings announced that the association's submissions were being made on the presumption that the Federal Court would continue. Brian Crane went on to describe the court as 'a somewhat remote institution,' centred in Ottawa, and having a specialized jurisdiction. Because of its nature it would, he said, 'remain a specialized institution and somewhat remote.' A crucial point was that the association made clear that it had no desire to see the Federal Court displace the traditional role of the superior courts of the provinces.[17] The association's written submission proposed the complete elimination of the Federal Court's jurisdiction over claims against the government. The issues in such cases arose out of contract and tort disputes; since these were not seen as specialized areas of law there was no need for a specialized court. The ordinary courts – those of the provinces – would suffice. The Canadian Bar Association also pointed out that those areas of law that the legal profession recognized as being practised by specialized lawyers, such as admiralty and industrial property, allowed for 'the general acceptance of the special jurisdiction of the Federal Court.' The association felt that a technical and complex subject matter could best be handled by a single court and a specialized bar. The association followed this point with a comment about the lawyers appointed to the court: '[T]here is little to indicate that ... experience has been a factor of any importance in the appointment of judges to the Exchequer or Federal Court. In fact, the generalist lawyer is typical of the Federal Court bench.'

Two thrusts were apparent in the Bar Association's submissions and presentations. There was the pro-provincial tack, which not unexpectedly caused a reaction among members of the legislative committee. As federal members of Parliament, they expressed concern with national unity and the Federal Court's role as support for that. The second thrust emphasized the specialization of the court's work in contrast with the general nature of the work of the 'ordinary' provincial courts. In the eyes of the profession, the Federal Court was acquiring the image of an administrative tribunal. If the suggestion to appoint specialized lawyers was accepted, the picture would be complete.

Bill C-38 was assented to on March 29, 1990, and became chapter 8 of the 1990 *Statutes of Canada*. It would take effect on February 1, 1992.

The enactment of the reforms did not eliminate the unease within the Canadian Bar Association about the Federal court. In the *Ottawa Report*, a newsletter published by the association's Legal and Governmental Affairs Directorate (Legislation and Law Reform), the heading for February 1991 was 'Federal Court of Canada: Misconceived or Misunderstood.'[18] Also, the abolition proposal was still on the association's agenda. A resolution asking for the abolition of the court had come forward at the midwinter meeting in 1990 but was held over because the special committee had not yet reported. The report appeared in the summer of 1990. At the following midwinter meeting, held in Regina at the end of February 1991, the vote on the abolition resolution resulted in a tie. The chair cast the deciding vote. The resolution to abolish the Federal Court was defeated by the narrowest of margins.[19]

27

The Work of the Court

By the time that Iacobucci took over as head of the Federal Court, the Charter had settled into the legal system and newsworthy cases were common. Regular challenges to government practices and to laws which reflected conflicting social values required that the judiciary choose one over another. The traditional way of dealing with political issues within the political process – raising public awareness, discussion, debate, and lobbying in order to convince government to change its mind – not infrequently gave way to using the legal process and asking a judge to order the government to change. Even if the judge did not rule favourably, the publicity surrounding a court challenge informed and alerted the public.

The use of the judiciary and a possible successful challenge to government action promoted the image of judges as guardians of the individual citizen against the power of government, and decision makers who were neutral and above political frays. A superior moral tone pervaded what judges decided. While the stakes were higher, the crucial issue – whether it was appropriate in a given situation to involve the judiciary and remove from the government of the day the right to choose solutions for social problems – was the same as that in cases of judicial review of administrative action.

This chapter examines some of the more interesting and informative decisions of the Iacobucci period.

CONWAY V. THE QUEEN

Prisoners in a penitentiary for men challenged the use of female guards for frisk searches and patrolling cells. The prisoners asserted a right to privacy and raised a Charter argument of equal treatment, noting that male guards were not used for the same purpose in a women's prison. The much greater number of males in the prison system meant that employment opportunities for female guards would be correspondingly reduced if they were allowed to work only in prisons housing female inmates.

In weighing competing values, Mr Justice Barry Strayer of the Trial Division decided that female guards could only view male prisoners in their cells without their consent in emergency situations. Patrols by female guards were permissible if previously scheduled and announced for the general knowledge of inmates.[1] This solution was rejected by the Court of Appeal, which consisted of Heald, Marceau, and Desjardins. Madame Justice Alice Desjardins, rendered the majority judgment (Darrel Heald concurred). Louis Marceau rendered a concurring judgment.

There was no question that what was involved was a relative assessment of values. With respect to the Charter's protection against unreasonable searches and seizures, Desjardins stated: '[A]n assessment has to be made as to whether, in a particular situation, the public's interest in being left alone by government has to give way to the government's interest in intruding on the individual's privacy in order to advance its goals.'[2] The assessment was to be based on what the judge thought a reasonable person within the society would consider reasonable in the circumstances. Relying on the words of Mr Justice Antonio Lamer (as he then was) of the Supreme Court of Canada, Desjardins pointed out that the choice was conditioned by 'community values, and in particular, long term community values.'[3]

Desjardins examined information on the use of female guards in prisons and accepted the opinion that the employment of women would enhance the quality of life in prisons and the rehabilitation of inmates. She then balanced the prisoners' claim to privacy against the loss of benefits to the prison system if female guards were not used and reached the conclusion that the use of female guards in male prisons was reasonable. Desjardins' approach to the solution of the problem was the one needed for Charter adjudication, but it could hardly be welcomed by those who advocated a formalist approach.

Marceau was uncomfortable with Desjardins' approach (which he said differed markedly from his), because it involved her 'appreciation of the relative importance of the competing interests involved.'[4] While he agreed with the result, he preferred to found it on 'a straightforward reasoning revolving around only a few simple propositions.'[5] Marceau reasoned that surveillance by female guards would amount to a search, but someone who had been sentenced to imprisonment could not reasonably expect to object to being observed by certain people.

The Supreme Court of Canada unanimously dismissed the appeal, 7–0, and rendered a surprisingly brief judgment. Mr Justice Gerard La Forest, for the court,[6] considered it reasonable in the circumstances that there would be a substantially reduced level of privacy for prisoners, which would include the use of female guards. In addition, he stated, 'Given the historical, biological and sociological differences between men and women, equality does not demand that practices which are forbidden where male officers guard female inmates must also be banned where female officers guard male inmates.'[7]

The only reasoning displayed in the decision was acceptance of the conclusions. The Supreme Court had chosen not to comment on the different approaches taken by the judges of the Court of Appeal. Neither of the two women on the Supreme Court's seven-judge panel (L'Heureux-Dubé and McLachlin) chose to add any comments to the broad conclusions enunciated by La Forest, the senior judge on the panel.

The stark difference in approach between Desjardins and Marceau in the Appeal Division had the potential to make life in that court very interesting.

SECURITY CLEARANCES

The issue of security clearances for public servants brought another interesting case before the courts. A public servant failed to obtain a position because a deputy minister denied him the required security clearance. The Canadian Security Intelligence Service (CSIS) had recommended against issuing the clearance, but the Security Intelligence Review Committee had subsequently investigated the matter following a complaint by the employee and had recommended that the required security clearance be granted. The deputy minister refused to change his earlier decision.

On application by the employee to the Federal Court of Appeal, the court decided unanimously that the deputy minister had to obey the recommendation of the Review Committee. But Arthur Stone, writing the judgment for the court (Hugessen and Desjardins concurred), went on to decided that the Court of Appeal did not have jurisdiction, and that it was a matter for the Trial Division, since the decision of the deputy minister was 'administrative' in nature rather than 'judicial.'[8] It was unusual for the court to decide the substantive issue and then add that it did not have the jurisdiction to do so.

The litigation was pursued in the Trial Division and came before Mr Justice Dubé. Lawyers for the federal government asked the court not to follow the Court of Appeal's conclusion that the deputy minister was required to obey the Review Committee's decision. Whether his seven years as a cabinet minister had any influence is not known, but Dubé did not accept the conclusion of the Court of Appeal. He thought it 'extraordinary' that the Security Intelligence Review Committee could have the power to force a deputy minister to hire someone who was not trusted for security reasons.[9] Dubé classified Stone's reasons as *obiter dictum* (meaning by-the-way and not necessary to the decision) and dismissed the employee's application. In effect the way in which the Court of Appeal had dealt with the case was called into question.

In the Court of Appeal, Mr Justice Stone had emphasised the perceived intent to enhance civil liberties in the establishment of the Security Intelligence Review Committee, and took that intent (the spirit of the law) to its logical conclusion. In his conflicting decision, Dubé emphasized the existing state of the law regarding approval of security clearances and looked for an intention to change it. By implication, his concern lay with the issue of security within government.

As expected, Dubé's decision was appealed to the Court of Appeal, and the panel this time consisted of Pratte, Urie, and Mahoney. The result had the appearance of being virtually compelled. Mahoney (also a former cabinet minister) rendered an oral judgment for the court at the end of the argument and rejected the idea that Stone's reasons were *obiter dictum*. He acknowledged that a different approach could have been taken, but accepted the one which had been chosen. Mahoney declared that the trial judge (Dubé) was bound by it. Institutional integrity was a prime factor in this instance.[10]

The decision of the Court of Appeal was reversed by a 6–1 vote in the Supreme Court of Canada.[11] Mr Justice Peter Cory for the majority of the court accepted the argument that the deputy minister's decision to deny the security clearance had been made pursuant to the Royal prerogative, and consequently there had been no exercise of power 'conferred by or under an Act of the Parliament of Canada' to trigger the court's power of judicial review.[12]

'Prerogative power' meant executive power exercised by the government pursuant to a common law rule, rather than authorized by statute. The Supreme Court had given its *imprimatur* to the continuing existence of judge-made rules empowering the executive. A limitation on prerogative power would have to be set out clearly in relevant legislation, and there was nothing to restrict the power here. That the case involved government security figured prominently in the outcome.

In recent years, the existence of prerogative power as a source of executive power had receded from legal consciousness and had been replaced by a focus on statutory authority. The resurgence of prerogative power in the *Thomson* case prompted an amendment to the Federal Court Act which included judicial review of powers conferred 'by or under an order made pursuant to a prerogative of the Crown.'[13]

The Supreme Court's reversal of two panels of the Court of Appeal and consequent affirmation of the decision from the Federal Court's Trial Division did not project a comforting picture of the intermediate appeal court.

THE *SCHACHTER* CASE

The *Schachter* case achieved a very high profile with the public and the legal profession. Identified as a case which asserted judicial power, it is also noteworthy for its rare discussion of the proper approach to judicial decision making within the Federal Court.

Under the Unemployment Insurance Act, unemployment insurance benefits were available to parents of adopted children (payments could be shared between the adoptive parents) and to natural mothers following childbirth. Shalom Schachter, a labour lawyer, wanted to stay home following the birth of his child and he applied for unemployment benefits. The litigation began when Schachter's application was rejected. Schachter claimed a denial of his equality rights under the Charter, since he had been denied rights available to the father of an adopted child.

Mr Justice Barry Strayer of the Trial Division rendered a judgment in which he indicated a willingness to deal with social values openly. He granted a declaration that a natural father was entitled to unemployment insurance benefits for a period taken off work to care for his new child on the same terms as an adoptive parent of either gender. Strayer concluded that Schachter had suffered discrimination on the basis of sex that had its roots in sexual stereotyping, and stated, after examining evidence of social values, 'Canadian society is committed to equalizing the role of parents in the care of children as much as possible.'[14] Strayer had in effect amended the law.

The judges of the Court of Appeal split on the issue.[15] Heald, with Stone concurring, agreed with Strayer's conclusion. Seizing the idea that the Charter had created 'a new dimension, a new yardstick of reconciliation between the individual and the community and their respective rights,'[16] Heald relied on that dimension to read words into under-inclusive legislation and thereby create equality of treatment. The argument that the judiciary should not invade the fiscal preserve of Parliament fell on deaf ears.

This was too much for Mr Justice Mahoney. He dissented and asserted that the case raised 'in stark terms, a fundamental constitutional question': whether the judiciary had the power to extend the benefit of the law to those whom Parliament had omitted. It was Mahoney's view that: '[t]he responsibility of the courts is to define the limits of legislation permissible under the *Charter* but it remains the responsibility of Parliament to enact legislation that meets its requirements.'[17] In the circumstances, judges could only declare the under-inclusive provision in the legislation to be invalid.

A unanimous Supreme Court of Canada accepted the existence of a judicial power which allowed judges to read words into legislation based on the Charter,[18] and thus created one of the most important decisions to involve the Charter of Rights and Freedoms. However, despite this conclusion the Supreme Court reversed the Court of Appeal. What happened was that the Supreme Court put limits on the exercise of that judicial power that made it inappropriate for use in the particular case.

Lamer stated for a majority of the judges[19] that there should not be an undue intrusion into the legislative sphere. With respect to judges adding words to legislation, the added words should flow 'with sufficient precision from the requirements of the Constitution.'[20] The Supreme Court of Canada thought it more appropriate for a judge to make a declaration of invalidity and then temporarily suspend it to allow for a legislative response. The court saw this remedy as particularly useful for the problem created by under-inclusiveness. About the denied paternity benefits, Lamer said, 'Given the nature of the benefit and the size of the group to whom it is sought to be extended, to read in natural parents would in these circumstances constitute a substantial intrusion into the legislative domain.'[21] The Supreme Court of Canada was very conscious of the difference between the existence of judicial power and the appropriateness of exercising it in a given situation.

THE NANNY CASE

The 'nanny' case achieved high profile because it involved the issue of women's equality. It was a taxation case instigated by a full-time practising lawyer who was a partner in a Toronto law firm. She was also the mother of two pre-school children and employed a nanny to care for them; she deducted the money paid to the nanny as a business expense. Revenue Canada disallowed the business deduction, and substituted a child care deduction. The financial differences were significant:

	Business expense	Child care deduction
1982	$10,075	$1,000
1983	$11,200	$2,000
1984	$13,173	$2,000
1985	$13,359	$4,000

Revenue Canada considered the employment of a nanny to be a personal or living expense. Symes argued that the rejection of the deduction as a business expense violated the guarantee of equality set out in subsection 15(1) of the Charter. The trial judge was Bud Cullen, a former minister of national revenue.

Cullen took an activist stance. The absence of a definition of 'profit' in the Income Tax Act meant for him that 'judicial interpretation shall infuse the term with meaning, which will reflect the realities of the times.'[22] Over the objection of counsel for the government, he received expert evidence which highlighted the influx of women of childbearing age into entrepreneurship and the workplace, especially since the 1970s. Cullen thought that the deductibility of the salary paid to the nanny should be determined 'in view of the social and economic realities of the times.'[23] Cases decided in the 1950s and 1960s which held that nanny expenses were not legitimate business expenses were said to be founded on an 1891 English decision – a 'case from another age' when the position of women had been quite different. Cullen had no difficulty pushing the contrary authorities aside. The evidence of the expert appeared to control his thinking.

Cullen held that discrimination and denial of equality had occurred because the payments had been determined not to be business expenses when that was what they actually were, and because the denial of a deduction had been based on the taxpayer's personal characteristics of sex and family or parental status. The judgment was long, and burdened with an unfortunate parade of case synopses and extensive quotations from what Cullen identified as the most recent decision. There was no question that Cullen attempted to take a creative approach to decision making and was willing to use information about social conditions. He justified his actions as a judge on the need to interpret the law, which 'has traditionally been seen as the proper preserve of the courts.'[24] The heart of the matter as far as judicial behaviour was concerned was that Cullen rejected the legislative assessment of what should be deducted for child care expenses.

The Federal Court of Appeal reversed Cullen. Mr Justice Robert Décary rendered the judgment of the court, which also consisted of Louis Pratte and Mark MacGuigan. Though prepared to accept 'that judicial interpretation is not cast in stone and must be sufficiently flexible and sensitive to adapt to changing circumstances,' Décary considered that what was significant and indeed determinative of the dispute was the fact that the legislature had expressly dealt with the taxpayer's circumstance.[25]

For Décary, the role of the judiciary with respect to policy choices was the crucial issue in the case. He went to the words of Chief Justice Dickson of the Supreme Court of Canada to make the point that the judiciary should exercise considerable caution when confronted with difficult questions of economic policy. It was necessary to show a high degree of deference to the government's choice of strategy in combating a problem.[26]

With reference to section 15 of the Charter, Décary asserted that no obligation had been imposed on legislatures to redress all social or economic inequalities. No one could have required Parliament to adopt a child care deduction. It had exercised its discretion and made a political, social, and economic choice. Given the ample evidence of justification submitted to the court, Décary maintained that 'it is not the function of this Court to substitute its choice for the one made by Parliament, with full knowledge of the options proposed and in keeping with an overall policy of assisting the family.'[27] The judges of the appeal court considered that the law had already been adapted to contemporary reality.

The Supreme Court of Canada affirmed the decision of the Court of Appeal by a 7–2 vote.[28] The existence of a 'women's issue' was highlighted by the fact that the two female judges on the panel (L'Heureux-Dubé and McLachlin) dissented. The seven judges making up the majority were male, and their judgment was rendered by Iacobucci.[29] The use of a full panel of the court indicated the importance attached to the case.

Iacobucci's opening remarks moved away from formalism with the statement that it was not legitimate for the court simply to say that because child care expenses had traditionally been characterized as personal in nature, they must be so today. He asserted the need to examine the relationship between child care expenses and business income critically; re-examination of this specific deduction was necessary because of the social changes precipitated by women entering the workforce. Since the case involved judge-made law (the characterization of child care expenses), that law must be adapted to reflect the changing social, moral, and economic fabric of the country. Iacobucci also cautioned that previous cases should be considered in their historical context.

This said, and following a lengthy discussion of the nature of child care expenses, the controlling factor in the end was the specific provision in the legislation regarding deductions for child care expenses. As far as equality rights were concerned, Iacobucci saw nothing in the language of the law that was discriminatory.

The complete absence of any recognition of an equality issue in the judgments of the majority of the Supreme Court of Canada and the Federal Court of Appeal makes the dissenting judgment of Justices L'Heureux-Dubé and McLachlin all the more interesting. In the Court of Appeal, Mr Justice Robert Décary had expressed concern that the taxpayer's Charter argument risked trivializing the Charter. At the Supreme Court, Iacobucci raised what he called 'a very curious aspect of this case,'[30] which was the focus on self-employed women to the exclusion of female employees.

The judgment of Madame Justice Claire L'Heureux-Dubé stressed early on that the case engaged 'fundamental and complex questions about the visions of equality and inclusivity that mould our legal constructs.'[31] She later remarked that the 'case remains deeply pervaded by issues of equality' and 'reflects a far more complex struggle over fundamental issues, the meaning of equality and the extent to which these values require that women's experience be considered when the interpretation of legal concepts is at issue.'[32] Pointedly observing that the commercial needs of business had been determined primarily by men and their needs, she clearly believed that men had defined what constituted a business expense. She continued by acknowledging the judiciary's power to alter the interpretation of legislation in order to conform to a changing social framework. In her opinion the cost of child care could be covered either by the child care deduction or by a claim for business expenses and there was nothing in the language of the provisions that prevented them from co-existing. Ambiguities should always be resolved in favour of the taxpayer.

In spite of her early statements regarding equality, L'Heureux-Dubé did not want to use the Charter directly. She preferred to adopt the position that the taxpayer suffered an actual and calculable loss if child care expenses could not be deducted as a business expense.

Concern with the proper role of the judiciary was a very pronounced part of this case. Though the court unmistakably promoted a contextual approach to decision making, it also understood clearly that a contextual approach would not necessarily lead to an activist result, but more often away from one. The concern with policy choices so ably illustrated by Décary sensitizes a judge to the ramifications of a decision: Who within society should make the appropriate choice?

THE *MOSSOP* CASE

No more socially contentious issue came before the judges of the Federal Court in this period than the question of whether a gay or lesbian relationship should be recognized as a 'family.'

The question of a gay or lesbian relationship as a marital one came up around the same time that the judges of the Federal Court agreed that discrimination on the basis of sexual orientation was prohibited under the equality provision of the Charter.[33] The government had accepted that conclusion. Now the marital relationship was before the court.

Brian Mossop, a translator for the Department of the Secretary of State, did not report for work on June 3, 1985, because he was attending the funeral of his companion's father. Mossop's collective agreement provided bereavement leave for the death of a father-in-law, and the agreement recognized a 'common-law spouse.' Mossop and his companion were gay. His employer, the federal government, denied bereavement leave, but offered a day of holiday leave, which Mossop refused. After his grievance in the matter was rejected, Mossop lodged a complaint with the Canadian Human Rights Commission aimed at the Department of the Secretary of State, the Treasury Board, and his union. The prohibited ground of discrimination relied on was family status.

A single-member human rights tribunal found in Mossop's favour and held that he and his companion constituted a family, and one which had not been accorded the same treatment as other families under the collective agreement. The federal government brought an application before the Federal Court of Appeal to have the decision reviewed and set aside.

The number of intervenors appearing in support of either the government or the tribunal signalled the intense interest in the issue.[34] Intervenors did not normally appear before the Federal Court, perhaps because for high-profile cases the intermediate court was viewed as a 'pit stop' on the way to the Supreme Court of Canada. However, the federal government had given in on sexual orientation being a prohibited ground of discrimination as a result of the decision of an appeal court,[35] which may have fostered the view that it might concede the matter of family status following the judgment of the Federal Court of Appeal (assuming the judgment was in favour of Mossop).

A specialist in sociology and family policy, who had testified before the human rights tribunal, stated that there was currently no general consensus within society on the matter. What were the judges to do? The position adopted by the Human Rights Commission and the intervenors who sided with it was highly interesting and significant. They did not argue that there would be a conflict with the equality provision in the Charter if family status in the human rights legislation was not recognized as covering a gay and lesbian relationship, but rather asked the judges to engage in a creative exercise of redefining family status in general, albeit using the Charter as evidence of changed social values. Their argument thus acknowledged that the words 'family status' in the human rights legislation did not include a gay or lesbian relationship. There were definite limits to the judicial function and this argument seemed to overshoot them. In the end, it failed.

Two judgments were rendered, one by Marceau, and another by Stone, with which Heald concurred. Marceau accepted that judges should deal with human rights legislation 'as liberally and as "bravely" as possible,'[36] yet there was a limit to judicial creativity. Redefining 'family' was beyond the scope of the proper judicial function and within the realm of the legislative process. There was, he said, a core meaning of the word 'family' that was clear and generally understood.

Stone was also concerned about the limits of judicial power to change the law and he too saw the requested reform as falling within the legislative realm. The Federal Court of Appeal chose in the circumstances to leave things as they were.

The solidarity which characterized the decision of the Court of Appeal dissipated when the seven judges of the Supreme Court of Canada split 4–3.[37] The majority judges affirmed the decision of the Court of Appeal and appeared to have little difficulty in deciding against Mossop.[38] The fact that Parliament had refused to prohibit discrimination on the basis of sexual orientation at the time 'family status' was added to the human rights legislation was determinative. Chief Justice Lamer for the majority expressed dismay at having to decide the case as presented. He pointed out that the only question before the court was one of statutory interpretation, and indicated that an argument based on the Charter might have succeeded. The parties had been invited to submit new arguments, but the appellant had insisted on having the court dispose of the case solely on the basis of the meaning of 'family status.' It is true that the judges possess a degree of control over what should be considered in a case, but in this instance the adversary system, which puts the carriage of a case in the hands of the parties, had to be respected, otherwise the judges would have had to completely create the arguments.

The dissenting judges (L'Heureux-Dubé, Cory, and McLachlin) were prepared to conclude that the decision of the tribunal should be upheld, and that a new definition of 'family' could exist in today's society.[39]

MONK CORPORATION V. ISLAND FERTILIZERS LTD.

The jurisdictional question of whether a matter should be dealt with by the provincial courts or the Federal Court was still alive in the Iacobucci years. As in previous years preserving the jurisdiction of the provincial system appeared to be even more important to francophone judges from Quebec than to others.

Expansion of the federal maritime jurisdiction was the concern in the *Monk Corporation* case. The case exposed considerable diversity within the ranks of the judges of the Court of Appeal, and the split between francophone judges from Quebec and the other judges was quite apparent. The litigation involved a contract concerning a supply of fertilizer which was shipped by sea from the Soviet Union and discharged at various ports in eastern Canada. After delivery, the supplier brought an action for excess product delivered, for the cost of renting shore cranes used to unload the fertilizer, and for demurrage at one port.[40] The actions were brought in the Federal Court and its jurisdiction was challenged.

Mr Justice McNair of the Trial Division, who came from New Brunswick, recognized jurisdiction on the basis that the matters in dispute were integrally connected with maritime matters.[41] The result in the Federal Court of Appeal was not so clear-cut. The judges who made up the appeal panel were all from Quebec. While Mr Justice Hugessen agreed that the contract was of a maritime nature, his colleagues disagreed. Pratte considered that only the claim for demurrage fell within the jurisdiction of the court, and Desjardins did not accept that the Court had jurisdiction over any aspect of the dispute. Madame Justice Desjardins maintained that the contract was for the purchase and sale of a commodity and, as such, was a matter for the provincial courts.[42]

A full bench of the Supreme Court of Canada heard the appeal; Iacobucci rendered the judgment of the majority, consisting of eight judges.[43] L'Heureux-Dubé dissented. The majority stressed that the terms 'maritime' and 'admiralty' should be interpreted within the modern context of commerce and shipping and should not be static or frozen. The majority held the claims to be within the maritime jurisdiction of the Federal Court, since they related to the discharge of cargo and as such were integrally connected to maritime matters.[44] In her dissenting judgment, L'Heureux-Dubé saw the claim as falling squarely within provincial jurisdiction over property and civil rights. L'Heureux-Dubé was so apprehensive about expanding the jurisdiction of the Federal Court that she made a comment about the ideas of pendent and ancillary jurisdiction, by which the jurisdiction of the Federal Court could conceivably have been expanded to include all issues and proceedings that were connected to issues and proceedings that lay within its jurisdiction.[45] The concepts of pendent and ancillary jurisdiction had been rejected, but, perhaps fearing a revival, Madame Justice L'Heureux-Dubé took the opportunity to express her rejection of them.

Of the thirteen judges at two levels who considered the jurisdictional question, six were from Quebec. All were francophones except Hugessen. Of these, two rejected any jurisdiction for the Federal Court (L'Heureux-Dubé, Desjardins); one accepted a limited jurisdiction (Pratte), and three recognized complete jurisdiction (Lamer, Gonthier, and Hugessen). The seven judges who were not from Quebec all accepted the Federal Court's jurisdiction.

THE CONTEXTUAL MODEL

The cases featured in this chapter illustrate that as the Federal Court of Canada moved into the final decade of the twentieth century, there was some recognition of contextualism as the proper method for the analysis of legal problems.[46] Its actual use would take some time to develop.[47]

One example of a growing awareness of the need for a contextual approach has been the appearance of the phrase 'words-in-total-context' with reference to statutory interpretation. In 1985 Mr Justice MacGuigan stated in an excise tax case:

It is now settled law that there is only one principle of statutory interpretation, which might be designated as the words-in-total-context approach. As it is put by E.A. Driedger, Construction of Statutes, 2nd ed. (1983), at 87, in language approved by the Supreme Court of Canada in Stubart Investments Ltd v. The Queen ...: 'the words of an Act are to be read in their entire context and in their grammatical and ordinary sense harmoniously with the scheme of the Act, the object of the Act, and the intention of Parliament.'[48]

The contextual or purposive approach to statutes was affirmed: 'grammatical and ordinary sense' refers to the language context; 'the scheme of the Act' to the legal context; and the 'intention of Parliament' to the social context. In the same year, MacGuigan examined two Supreme Court of Canada decisions and concluded: 'It seems clear from these cases that older authorities are no longer to be absolutely relied upon. The only principle of interpretation now recognized is a words-in-total-context approach with a view to determining the object and spirit of the taxing provisions.'[49] The approach has been affirmed consistently since that time[50] and is no longer confined to taxation statutes.[51]

As contextualism takes greater hold it will generate a continuing debate about the limits of the judicial role, which is illustrated in some of the cases examined in this chapter. That topic will be crucial and ongoing.

PART 5

The Fourth Court, 1992

28

The Court Today

Chief Justice Iacobucci was appointed to the Supreme Court of Canada on January 7, 1991, filling the vacancy created by the resignation of Madame Justice Bertha Wilson. It was almost a year before Julius Isaac was appointed chief justice of the Federal Court (December 24, 1991). The Conservative government took the longest time ever taken to fill the position. In the end the person chosen was a very able administrator, known for his strong views and social-democratic leanings.

It was newsworthy that Chief Justice Isaac was black, and the first black judge to be appointed in the federal court system. Isaac had been born and raised in Grenada in the West Indies, and came to Canada to attend the University of Toronto, where he received his BA in 1955 and a law degree in 1958. Heading to Saskatchewan in the early 1960s, he worked as a legal adviser in the Government Finance Office. After the defeat of the CCF/NDP government, Isaac spent some time in private practice in Saskatchewan and Ontario before being invited back to Grenada to become senior resident magistrate. After only a year, he balked at that government's attempts to influence his decisions and returned to Canada, where he joined the federal Department of Justice in 1971 as a criminal prosecutor. He was promoted in 1987 and served as assistant deputy attorney general for criminal law for two years. In 1989, Isaac was appointed a judge of the Supreme Court of Ontario, the first black judge appointed to that court. He was sixty-three years of age when he was appointed to the Federal Court – the oldest person appointed to the court, though not the oldest to become chief justice (Thurlow had been almost sixty-seven when he was appointed to head the court in 1980).

The new year opened with the introduction of the new chief justice, and on February 1, 1992, the reforms enacted in 1990 came into force. The delay of almost two years was due to the need to constitute a rules committee to create rules for the new judicial review jurisdiction of the Trial Division.[1] The committee members were not appointed until April 30, 1991, some thirteen months after the reforms were enacted, but the new rules were completed by the end of 1991. The overhaul of the court, long discussed and advocated, was complete. Jurisdiction over claims against the government – the reason for the creation of a separate court in 1887 – was now concurrent, but the limitations associated with the jurisdiction of the Federal Court, coupled with the pronounced tendency of the bar to favour local courts, made it likely that the national court's jurisdiction as a 'Court of Claims' was all but extinguished. The attempt to sort out the notorious problems with the jurisdiction over judicial review of administrative action found in sections 18 and 28 of the Federal Court Act left the Trial Division with the jurisdiction, but certain specified boards and tribunals would still be subject to the jurisdiction of the Court of Appeal. These tribunals were described as resembling a trial court, with hearings, counsel, and a record.[2] The list of such special bodies grew ever longer and it is entirely possible that the clamour to be placed on the list resulted in a considerable part of the old jurisdiction being retained by the appeal court.

Later in 1992, extensive changes were also made to the immigration process;[3] from the court's perspective the important changes were the transfer of the review jurisdiction from the Court of Appeal to the Trial Division, with the requirement of leave from a Trial Division judge. There could only be an appeal to the Court of Appeal when the Trial Division judge certified that a serious question of general importance existed, and articulated what it was.

The removal of the original jurisdiction over judicial review from the Court of Appeal aligned its function more with that of a traditional appeal court, with less emphasis on an adjudicative role.

The number of judges in the Trial Division was increased by six to handle the increased immigration work, bringing the total number of judges in the Federal Court to twenty-nine (nineteen in the Trial Division and ten in the Appeal Division). The ratio of almost 2:1 recognized the trial and appeal functions of the divisions. The required number of judges from the Quebec bar was increased from eight to ten, maintaining the allocation of approximately one-third of the places for Quebec lawyers.

In 1992 the provincial superior courts occupied a solid and unassailable position in the administration of justice within the country. The federal power to create additional courts under section 101 of the constitution had been decidedly attenuated, and section 129 as a source of power to establish federal courts had been ignored. The Federal Court was perceived as an exception to the unitary nature of the legal system. The potential for increasing the Federal Court's jurisdiction through the analysis demonstrated in the *Rhine* and *Prytula* cases a decade earlier (the existence of a federal statutory framework would establish jurisdiction) was resisted.[4] The life of the Federal Court was seen as revolving around the adjudication of disputes in specialized areas such as intellectual property, maritime activities, immigration, and administrative law. In this respect, it resembled an administrative tribunal.

The Exchequer Court had existed in virtual seclusion from public scrutiny and had been shielded by the legal profession. Conditions had changed by the time the Federal Court was created in 1971, and while after twenty years the court was still largely anonymous to the public and to a goodly number of lawyers, it was not for lack of discussion about its real and perceived faults, which were frequently paraded before the profession.

A new development of the late 1980s and early 1990s was the attempt to publicize the court and its past. In September 1989 Chief Justice Iacobucci delivered a speech to the Lawyers' Club in Toronto entitled 'The Federal Court of Canada: Some Comments on Its Origin, Traditions and Evolution.'[5] While it tended to be glossy and completely non-controversial, the talk was informative and the coverage, although superficial, was reasonably good. It was an effort to make the Federal Court known. The chief justice spoke of 'a new and expanded identity.' This was the first historical presentation involving the court.[6]

A much more ambitious endeavour was initiated to mark the twentieth anniversary of the Federal Court; the court held a symposium in Ottawa on June 26, 1991, with the intention of having the jurisdiction of the court evaluated and receiving suggestions for improvements. Papers were presented by a variety of people, and published informally by the court under the title *The Federal Court of Canada – An Evaluation*.[7] The speakers included John Turner, who had been minister of justice at the time the court was created, Kim Campbell, who was been minister of justice at the time of the symposium, Chief Judge Dolores Sloviter of the United States Federal Court, Mr Justice Mark MacGuigan, political scientist Peter Russell, and recognized experts from various fields of legal study.

A logical extension of the desire to make the court better known was the decision to authorize and fund the writing of its history. This work is the product of that decision. This bold and innovative step, never taken before in Canada, brought with it the opportunity to interview many of the sitting judges and to question them about themselves, the court, and their work. The institution lives in the thoughts and actions of its judges. The remainder of this concluding chapter examines the opinions of the judges as expressed in the interviews. They reflect the life of the court today.

THE JUDGES

While differences of opinion on most topics were common among the judges, there was one matter on which they agreed completely – the nature of the job. The position of judge carries with it great prestige in our society, but there is a cost. The person who becomes a judge must be prepared to accept a cloistered life, and, in varying degrees of isolation, commit to work of a most demanding and intense nature.

The quality identified most often as the prime requisite of a judge was open-mindedness, with an ability to listen to different views and to understand people. Impartiality demanded such characteristics. Maturity and intelligence were also mentioned. What was not required per se was someone with a knowledge of the law as a specialized field of study.

It was somewhat remarkable that the desirable characteristics were the same as those identified a century before when the first judges were appointed to the Supreme Court of Canada – a good judge is a learned person able to look at a subject in its various aspects and take a broad view of the problem at hand. He or she should be prepared to take a common sense approach, rather than tackle a problem solely in a technical fashion.[8]

The judges acknowledged that an individual's background is always present, but it is a factor which should be controlled to allow the judge to administer the law in an impartial manner. However, life experience gained prior to appointment is valuable in allowing a judge to understand, assess, and empathize with litigants. What has to be controlled is personal values that are judgmental in nature.

BACKGROUNDS

There is a varied pool of lawyers from which the judges will be chosen. There are lawyers in general practice and those who specialize, whether in private practice or as an employee of a corporation; there are lawyers who enter the public service; there are lawyers who go into the academic world and educate those who aspire to be lawyers; and there are lawyers who enter the political world of elected office.

What is the appropriate background for a judge? Who should be appointed? Which of the above types is better qualified to be a judge? The answers to these questions are fraught with strong feelings one way and another.

Experience in the practice of law (generally taken to mean private practice) came to the fore in two contexts. Trial or litigation experience was identified as important in order for a judge to understand the reality of the legal process and be able to separate the important parts from those that were mere show. Such experience would enable a judge to understand a lawyer's problems in preparing a case, allowing for a better appreciation of the stresses and pressures of the courtroom which might affect the conduct of the case. These matters are part of the professional context, and while they were generally recognized as helpful for a judge, opinions differed as to their real importance. A few judges identified trial experience as a must, while others saw it as significant; still others saw it as unnecessary. A Trial Division judge commented that one year's service as a trial judge would provide more courtroom experience than that of any of the lawyers who could appear as counsel. There is little doubt that previous litigation experience would give a trial judge a degree of confidence at the beginning of life on the bench.

Several judges also related experience in the practice of law to the social context. The practice of law, whether one was involved in litigation or not, was said to provide life experience which would allow a judge to understand the real nature of the problems presented for adjudication. Since so much of the work before the courts is oriented to business and commerce, experience in the practice of law provided helpful exposure to the facts of life in the business world. Those in favour of practice experience as a background for judges generally thought that public servants would fall short in terms of knowledge of the workings of the business world. Similarly, lawyers who had chosen an academic career, and who were viewed as living in an ivory tower, were considered to lack both life and business experience.

A major problem associated with a public service background was the perception of the Federal Court as a government court. Those interviewed generally accepted that such a perception did exist, with the court being seen as either in the government's pocket or biased in the government's favour. This perception was fuelled whenever a former member of the public service joined the court. Those judges who were strongly in favour of a practice background expressed the view that former public servants brought a built-in bias in favour of government to their work, but others commented that former public servants tended to overcompensate for any alleged bias, deciding against the government more frequently than was appropriate. On a positive note, since much of the court's jurisdiction concerns government in a broad sense, judges with a public service background, who know how government operates, can help the court to make the most satisfactory decisions through their understanding of the reality of the problems presented.

Judges with a background as elected politicians present a different problem. The elected positions held by certain judges had inevitably been at the provincial or federal level, and generally these office holders had achieved a stature beyond that of being simply a member of the legislature. The most negative effect of appointing an elected politician is the perception that the appointment is a patronage reward, which undermines confidence in the overall competence of a court.

The expression 'Senate Two' (referring to the Federal Court) was familiar to the judges but was usually attributed to an address given by John Turner, a prime minister and former minister of justice, at the court's twentieth anniversary celebrations. The expression actually comes from a jibe Joe Clark made as a member of the Opposition in 1975.[9]

The image of the court as a place to retire from politics and a reward for partisan political service does it no good. One effect of the infamous patronage binge of 1984 has been that none of the twenty-two judges appointed to the Federal Court since then has come from elected office. In contrast, of the previous twenty-four judges appointed to the Federal Court since 1971, seven had been elected politicians (29 per cent), and of the twenty-one judges appointed to the Exchequer Court, seven had been politicians (33 per cent). If the title 'Senate Two' lives on, it may close the Federal Court of Canada to lawyers who have chosen to enter the political arena.

Since partisanship is so powerful a force in elected politics, as well as in Canadian life generally, the judicial appointment of a politician raises a strong question of partisan bias. One judge affirmed that a former politician could not have a potential bias in favour of the government, since it was the government that was being sued and not a particular political party. While there is an element of truth to this when it comes to litigation involving the day-to-day operations of government, such as labour relations in the public service, a partisanship bias would be difficult to suppress if the litigation involved the cabinet in any way.

On the plus side, a politician brings life experience to the appointment; a conscientious member of Parliament and member of the cabinet has a grasp of the realities of everyday living. A cabinet minister would also have decision making experience not dissimilar to that required of a judge.

The question of appointing academic lawyers as judges triggered some strong reactions. It is commonly thought within the profession that academics are suited to the work of appeal courts; several judges accepted that there was a place for academics in appellate decision making, while other judges were quite opposed to placing academics anywhere within the judiciary.

By the end of 1994 there had been forty-six appointments to the Federal Court. Considering initial appointments only, that is, omitting promotions to the appeal division, twelve of the forty-six had had an academic career (26 per cent), although three of these had gone from teaching into the public service. The breakdown for the divisions was:

Division	Appointments	Academics	Percentage of academics
Trial	31	5	16
Appeal	15	7	47

That five lawyers with academic backgrounds were appointed to the Trial Division is noteworthy, for it suggests a lack of concern on the part of the federal government about specific requirements for appointment to a particular division. The appointment of Mr Justice Urie is an example. When he was appointed to the Court of Appeal in 1973 he felt somewhat uncomfortable. He considered himself to be a good practical lawyer and would have preferred the Trial Division; he associated the judges of the Appeal Division with an academic turn of mind. Because the workload of the Court of Appeal was light in this early period of the court's history, Urie's request to do trial work was granted, although he officially remained a member of the Appeal Division.

There has been a sizeable number of academics in the Federal Court, which is shown dramatically by the numbers in the following table comparing it with the Ontario superior courts (the numbers are for judges on the courts as of February 1996):

Court	Total number	Academics	Percentage of academics
Ontario Court of Appeal	23	2	8.7
Ontario General Division	257	7	2.7
Federal Court of Appeal	13	9	69.2
Federal Trial Division	21	1	4.8

One effect of the large number of academics in the Federal Court is that there is less negative feeling evident within the court towards academics who join it than has occurred in provincial superior courts. Now that more lawyers with an academic background are being appointed to provincial courts, attitudes will obviously change.

The traditional image of the trial judge is of someone who presides as an umpire in adversary proceedings, and who listens to the testimony of witnesses and determines the facts of the dispute. Once the facts are found the result, that is, who was right and who was wrong, is generally thought to follow relatively automatically. In an appellate setting, the judge listens to arguments and studies written material regarding what law to apply to the facts (found at the trial level) and renders a judgment in which the law is discussed and applied. With regard to the Federal Court, several judges pointed out that the Trial Division deals most often with legal issues, not factual situations – a distinction from provincial trial courts. They said that the result was more writing of judgments in the Trial Division than in a provincial trial court, which is more demanding. This resemblance between the work of the Trial Division and that of an appeal court perhaps provides some justification for appointing academics to it.

With respect to appointments to the Court of Appeal, strong views were expressed by judges from both divisions that an appeal court judge should serve for a time as a trial judge before being appointed. It bears mentioning that those Appeal Division judges who voiced this opinion had each been trial judges, whether in the Federal Court or in a provincial court. One appeal court judge who had no trial experience stated that it was good to have a judge with trial experience on the panel of judges hearing an appeal. The acceptance of academics as appeal court judges conflicts with the opinion that appeal judges should have trial experience.

Given that the Federal Court is one of diverse specialties, and that the appointment of specialist lawyers has not been the rule, it was pointed out that the Trial Division could serve as a training ground for a judge to acquire expertise in an area before being appointed to the Court of Appeal. Requiring prior experience in the Trial Division before appointment to the Appeal Division would also involve supporting a system of promotion within the court.

Since the federal government has not evidenced any clear awareness of a difference between a position in the Trial Division and one in the Appeal Division, positions were offered as they became vacant. The result was that several trial judges who clearly had aspirations to be appeal judges accepted an appointment to the Trial Division because that was what they were offered at the time. Before 1984 prospects for advancement to the Appeal Division would have been good, but the promotion of judges from the Trial Division stopped with the election of the Conservatives that year.

Excluding the initial appointments of Exchequer Court judges to the Court of Appeal, there were eleven appointments from 1971 up to and including 1984. Of the eleven, five (45 per cent) had served as Trial Division judges. In the ten years following, nine judges were appointed, none of whom came from the Trial Division. On August 30, 1994, Mr Justice Barry Strayer of the Trial Division was appointed to the Court of Appeal. The possibility of promotions had returned.

It is not surprising that promotions from the Trial Division stopped with the coming to power of Brian Mulroney's Conservatives. All of the judges of the Federal Court since 1971 had been appointed by a Liberal government. The Liberals were returned to power in October 1993, and Strayer, a Liberal appointee in 1983, was promoted to the Court of Appeal in the year following the election. There was no question of Strayer's ability and several Trial Division judges interviewed before his appointment to the Court of Appeal mentioned him as an example of how failure to promote from within was a poor practice.

Strayer himself provided a potent example of the operation of partisanship in the appointment process. In addition, there was a rumour that his promotion had been proposed by the Department of Justice at an earlier date but had been rejected by the Conservative government at the last moment. The incident was said to have occurred at the time of the appointment of F.J. McDonald, of the General Division of the Ontario Court of Justice, to the Federal Court of Appeal in 1993. Those who sensed that something was amiss point to the French version of the news release issued by the Department of Justice, in which the announcement of McDonald's appointment begins with the words, 'est promu de la Section de première instance de la Cour fédérale du Canada à la Section d'appel.'

ONE OR TWO COURTS?

While formally there is one court, the Federal Court of Canada, with two divisions, there is no question that the two divisions operate as separate courts. Nevertheless, there are elements which point to the existence of one court in spirit. There is one chief justice, and one administrator. Seniority is measured by the date of appointment to the 'court,' rather than to a particular division. These indicia of a single court with equal status for all judges were carried over from the initial assignment of Exchequer Court judges to the two divisions. The characteristics of a single court have created expectations of equality among many of the judges of the Trial Division. However, the difference in status that arises quite naturally between a judge of an appeal court and a judge of a trial court has created a delicate situation. There must be a clear separation between the trial court and the appeal courts. Long gone is the practice of trial judges sitting on appeals from their own decisions, which existed – and was accepted – in the years when the Exchequer Court judges were also judges of the Supreme Court of Canada.

The effects of the required separation are felt more by the trial court judges, and many resent it. They tend to see the gulf between the divisions as the result more of the attitude of the members of the Appeal Division than of some inherent need for a separate existence because of the divisions' differing functions.

The relocation of the Trial Division judges to a separate building (for space reasons) in 1983 created a physical and psychological separation between the divisions. The adoption of 'J.A.' to replace the standard 'J.' following the names of the judges of the Appeal Division, a change that occurred in 1988 at the urging of Mr Justice MacGuigan, is seen as a potent symbol of the Court of Appeal's aloofness. The lack of promotions following the election of the Mulroney government in 1984 also affected attitudes, but Strayer's appointment to the Court of Appeal may alleviate some of the negative feelings.

A source of irritation for some appeal court judges is the fact that seniority is based on appointment to the court, and not to the division. Promotion from the Trial Division catapults a judge over some sitting appeal court judges. For example, when appointed Strayer was the junior judge in terms of Court of Appeal experience, but in terms of seniority he ranked third, behind the chief justice.[10]

The tensions and frictions that exist between the two divisions exceeds those that would normally exist between a trial court and an appeal court. The history of the Federal Court, with its emphasis on there being only one court, has created this problem, which is unique within Canada. The pressure in 1971 to treat the judges of the Exchequer Court as equals after their appointments to the Federal Court has led to the present situation.

GOOD JUDGING

Several judges were asked about judgments they had written that they thought were particularly good; when this failed to produce any significant responses, the question was altered to ask if there were any judgments of which they were particularly proud. Responses to this question were more forthcoming, but it was clear that there was still something missing.

Since these were the first interviews of their kind, the judges were probably somewhat reticent and uneasy. The reticence became acute for some of them when it came to naming cases. It was surprising that some judges who had been academics responded quickly and said that they did not know what a good judgment was, or that they found the question hard to answer. The most commonly articulated criteria were clarity and brevity. Many judges were either unable or unwilling to take 'good' beyond these most obvious characteristics of any competent writing.

One judge asked rhetorically, 'What makes a good novelist?' A simple and basic answer to this question would be that writing a novel requires two qualities – craft and imagination. Brevity and clarity deal only with the craft. Another judge said that there were no criteria for determining whether a judgment was good or bad. It was simply a matter of whether the problem had been considered and there was a winner and a loser. This view emphasizes the adjudicative function at its most basic level. It is reminiscent of the criticism levelled at Chief Justice Jackett, that he was concerned with turning out judgments as a product rather than committed to the reasons for judgment, which contain the law.

Several judges mentioned that a good judgment is delivered quickly. It was often suggested that one of the good things about the Federal Court was the speed with which its decisions are rendered. Unfortunately, this characteristic has a pronounced down side. One judge felt that pressure to produce a judgment quickly contributed to the writing of poor judgments, in which clarity and brevity are sacrificed and one finds a lengthy recitation of undigested facts and the use of extensive quotes from cases as statements of the law. The Court of Appeal has been criticized for the lack of reasons in its judgments, again attributed to time pressure.[11]

In contrast to those judges who could not identify good judgments and those who did not take 'good' beyond brevity and clarity, some judges identified innovation as a characteristic of a good judgment. They were also conscious of the fact that judges in higher courts could be somewhat jealous of the power to innovate or be creative.

The possibility of creating something new in finding a solution to a problem is a key aspect of contextual thinking. Those judges who identified innovation as part of the judicial function are not to be confused with 'activist' judges, who, by definition, ignore the boundaries created by the language and legal contexts, and make a political decision based on their personal values. For the activist, new law is created as 'whole cloth.' An innovative judge works within the law, and develops it to meet new situations.

In direct contrast to those judges who identified innovation as a characteristic of a good judgment, one judge unexpectedly supported the declaratory theory of law. This theory rejects creative thinking in favour of finding pre-existing solutions as illustrated by previous cases. A good judgment in this individual's opinion was one which canvassed the previously decided cases that were considered relevant. Former Chief Justice Jackett, in a speech to law students, had accepted the declaratory theory as the guiding principle for the legal profession but had recognized that it was artificial, thus making legal decision a formal exercise.[12] The artificiality of the formalist model was not noted by the judge in question.

Only one judge was prepared to discuss the judicial function in any detail. This individual stated that an argument based only on words found in the text of a law, or any argument grounded in grammatical construction, such as the placement of commas, was unacceptable. While the text of the law is a natural starting point, and establishes the boundaries of the decision making, the judge must add to this language context an argument of good, common sense. The words used by this judge were the same as those used to praise William Richards a century before.[13] The words 'common sense' are used, perhaps unconsciously, as synonymous with the social context. The legal context arises naturally as one moves from the language to the social context. 'Common sense' in the sense of the social context naturally involves a concern with policy, a word which can still agitate many within the legal profession. However, only one of the judges interviewed expressly rejected policy as a consideration, and that was a retired judge. It is possible that those judges who exhibited a formalist frame of mind would reject the idea of policy if the matter were pushed.

The pressure to produce judgments quickly, so pronounced in the first decade of the Federal Court under Chief Justice Jackett, has a much greater effect on contextual thinkers than on formalists. Formalists are generally content to produce a recitation of the facts and a series of quotations from the cases, or to state that the words of the law are clear, and then give a conclusion. Contextual thinkers want to think out a solution to the problem, and this takes time.

CONTEXTUALISTS AND FORMALISTS

It has been my experience that whenever there is a discussion of the models of judicial decision making, formalist and contextualist, and an evaluation of the performance of a judge in accordance with them, someone will question the legitimacy of applying the contextual model to earlier decisions, since that model is alleged to be the product of the late twentieth century. However, the model is not new. What has taken place in the past two decades of this century is simply that there is a greater awareness of the existence of the model and its qualities. It has been advocated and even followed by some judges and lawyers throughout this century, and it has existed as long as there have been judges.

The first Exchequer Court was dramatically made up of three contextual judges and three formalist judges, with the bulk of the court's work being undertaken by two contextual judges, William Henry and Télesphore Fournier. After the separation of the Exchequer Court from the Supreme Court of Canada there was a rotation of the models – Burbidge (contextual), Cassels (formalist), Maclean (contextual). This meant that in the Exchequer Court contextual thinking was prominent for fifty of its first sixty-five years. After this time Joseph Thorson and Wilbur Jackett accepted formalism as legal methodology, and there was little evidence that any of the other judges of the court were prepared to challenge their views. When the Federal Court was created under the leadership of Wilbur Jackett it was not surprising that its decisions displayed pronounced formalistic tendencies while he was chief justice. It was not until the 1980s that cracks began to appear in the dominance of the model in Federal Court decisions.

Lawyers can be contextual thinkers when dealing with a client's problem, and reason out the most appropriate solution by taking into account all that is considered relevant, but then adopt a formal approach when conducting litigation. If such a lawyer should be appointed a judge the same thinking processes may occur when he or she is adjudicating a dispute, that is, the judges may create a solution through contextual thinking, but translate it into a formalist guise for publication. It was not surprising to find contextual thinkers in the interviews of the judges. What was surprising was the number. The majority of the judges interviewed could be identified as falling within the contextual model. The fact that the work of the court continues to have a-formal tone may be explained by the tendancy discussed above, or by the dominance (through the power of their personalities) of certain judges who are formalists in all respects. It also has to be recognized that the emphasis on speedy decision making hinders contextual thinking.

As the formalism of the legal system in general comes under greater attack and adjudication outside the system is advocated under the name 'alternative dispute resolution' (ADR),[14] those judges who are capable of turning to contextual thinking may decide to abandon the formal style of judgment writing. In addition, there is a particular reason why the judges of the Federal Court should reassess their decision-making approach, and that is the strong consensus that the court's future lies in being primarily an administrative 'appeal' court.[15] Administrative decision making has always been recognized as contextual in nature.

At this stage in the court's history there is evidence that both the court and the legal profession are on the verge of momentous change. There will be battles, and they will be fought around the meaning given to rule of law by A.V. Dicey over a century ago, and the values underlying that meaning.[16]

No better concluding comment for this work could be found than that made by Rosalie Abella, a justice of the Ontario Court of Appeal:

We are captives, we lawyers, of an old system which we should be taming and refining rather than the other way around ... We have swallowed Dicey whole and now the beast is swallowing us. ... We should gently extricate ourselves ... We may find to our surprise that neither the Rule of Law, nor due process, nor clients, nor lifestyles will be impaired. There is even the possibility that our experiment may in fact improve justice's performance.[17]

Appendix A

The Judges

In this appendix the judges of the Exchequer Court and the Federal Court are listed in two tables. Table 1 lists judges by position and tenure on the court, and Table 2 presents them in order of seniority with date of birth, province, legal tradition, and position held at the time of appointment. While the study of the court in the text of the book ends in 1992, these tables take the information about the judges up to the court's anniversary date of 1 June 1996.

TENURE

The Supreme Court of Canada and the Exchequer Court were created at the same time by the same statute, The Supreme and Exchequer Court Act.[1] A judge of the Supreme Court sitting as a single judge constituted the Exchequer Court. This situation lasted from 1875 until 1887.

In 1887 the Exchequer Court was separated from the Supreme Court and a position was created for one judge.[2] In 1912 a second position was

---

1 SC 1875, c. 11.
2 An Act to amend 'The Supreme and Exchequer Courts Act,' and to make better provision for the Trial of Claims against the Crown, SC 1887, c. 16.

created on the court with the appointment of an assistant judge.[3] In 1920 the judge of the court was given the title of president and the assistant judge the title of puisne judge.[4] This complement of two judges lasted until 1945, when additional puisne judges began to be appointed periodically. There were seven puisne judges by the time the Federal Court of Canada was created in 1971.[5]

When the Federal Court of Canada came into being in 1971 the head of the court held the title of Chief Justice of the Federal Court of Canada. That person presided directly over the Federal Court of Appeal, while another judge headed the Trial Division as the Associate Chief Justice of the Federal Court of Canada. In each division there were puisne judges.[6] Over the years the number of judges (including the chief justice and associate chief justice) has increased from four to eleven in the Court of Appeal, and from eight to twenty in the Trial Division (as of 1 June 1996).

The total number of judges available for hearing cases, however, was increased by the creation of the position of supernumerary judge for the court in 1983. A supernumerary judge is a senior judge who elects part-time duties (eligibility is based on a combination of age and years of service). A judge who chooses to become supernumerary frees a full-time position for the appointment of a younger judge.[7]

3 An Act to amend the Exchequer Court Act, SC 1912, c. 21.
4 An Act to amend the Exchequer Court Act, SC 1920, c. 26.
5 An Act to amend the Exchequer Court Act, SC 1944–45. c. 3 (a second puisne judge was appointed); An Act to amend the Exchequer Court Act, SC 1946, c. 22 (a third puisne judge was appointed); An act to amend the Railway Act, the Exchequer Court Act and The Judges Act, 1946, SC 1947–48, c. 66 (a fourth puisne judge was appointed. However, the position created was to be taken by the chief commissioner of the Board of Transport Commissioners, who was not intended to carrry out duties as a judge of the court until his tenure as chief commissioner ended.); An Act to amend the Railway Act, SC 1951 (2nd sess.), c. 22 (one more position was acquired when the one held by the chief commissioner of the Board of Transport Commissioners was made additional to the number of judges as provided by the Exchequer Court Act and the Judges Act); An Act to amend the Judges Act and the Exchequer Court Act, 1960–61, c. 38 (a fifth puisne judge was appointed, but this judge was actually the sixth because of the 1951 legislation); An Act to amend the Judges Act and the Exchequer Court Act, 1964–65, c. 14 (a sixth puisne judge, actually the seventh, was appointed but the appointee was to be assigned the duties of divorce commissioner, as an officer of the senate).
6 Federal Court Act, SC 1970–71, c. 1.
7 An Act respecting the Tax Court of Canada and to amend the Federal Court Act, the Judges Act and the Unemployment Insurance Act, 1971, SC 1980–81–82, c. 158.

THE JUDGES OF THE EXCHEQUER COURT OF CANADA

Judges of the Supreme Court of Canada
(Exchequer Court Judges, 1875–1887)

Richards, William	8 Oct. 1875 – 9 Jan. 1879
Ritchie, William	8 Oct. 1875 – 1 Oct. 1887
Strong, Henry	8 Oct. 1875 – 1 Oct. 1887
Taschereau, Jean-Thomas	8 Oct. 1875 – 6 Oct. 1878
Fournier, Télesphore	8 Oct. 1875 – 1 Oct. 1887
Henry, William	8 Oct. 1875 – 1 Oct. 1887
Taschereau, Henri-Elzéar	7 Oct. 1878 – 1 Oct. 1887
Gwynne, John	14 Jan. 1879 – 1 Oct. 1887

Judges of the Exchequer Court

Burbidge, George	1 Oct. 1887 – 18 Feb. 1908
Cassels, Walter	2 Mar. 1908 – 16 June 1920

Assistant Judge of the Exchequer Court

Audette, Louis-Arthur	4 Apr. 1912 – 16 June 1920

Presidents of the Exchequer Court

Cassels, Walter	16 June 1920 – 1 Mar. 1923
Maclean, A.K	2 Nov. 1923 – 31 July 1942
Thorson, Joseph	6 Oct. 1942 – 15 Mar. 1964
Jackett, Wilbur	4 May 1964 – 1 June 1971

Puisne Judges of the Exchequer Court

Audette, Louis-Arthur	16 June 1920 – 14 Dec. 1931
Angers, Eugene-Réal	1 Feb. 1932 – 1 Oct. 1953
O'Connor, Charles	19 Apr. 1945 – 16 Nov. 1949
Cameron, Charles	4 Sept. 1946 – 1 Feb. 1964
Archibald, Maynard	1 July 1948[8] – 9 July 1953

8 Archibald served as chief commissioner of the Board of Transport Commissioners from 1 July 1948 until Novermber 1951, when he assumed duties on the Exchequer Court. See supra, note 5.

Kearney, John	1 Nov. 1951[9] – 29 Feb. 1968
Fournier, Alphonse	12 June 1953 – 8 Oct. 1961
Potter, William	29 Sept. 1953 – 19 Mar. 1955
Ritchie, Louis	21 Apr. 1955 – 16 Jan. 1956
Dumoulin, Jacques	1 Dec. 1955 – 1 June 1971
Thurlow, Arthur	29 Aug. 1956 – 1 June 1971
Noël, Camilien	12 Mar. 1962 – 1 June 1971
Cattanach, Alexander	27 Mar. 1962 – 1 June 1971
Gibson, Hugh	4 May 1964 – 1 June 1971
Walsh, Allison	2 July 1964[10] – 1 June 1971
Kerr, Roderick	1 Nov. 1967 – 1 June 1971

THE JUDGES OF THE FEDERAL COURT OF CANADA

Chief Justices of the Federal Court of Canada

Jackett, Wilbur	1 June 1971 – 1 Oct. 1979
Thurlow, Arthur	4 Jan. 1980 – 5 May 1988
Iacobucci, Frank	2 Sept. 1988 – 7 Jan. 1991
Isaac, Julius	24 Dec. 1991 – present

Associate Chief Justices of the Federal Court of Canada

Noël, Camilien	1 June 1971 – 4 July 1975
Thurlow, Arthur	4 Dec. 1975 – 4 Jan. 1980
Jerome, James	18 Feb. 1980 – present

Judges of the Federal Court of Appeal

Dumoulin, Jacques	1 June 1971 – 1 Dec. 1972
Thurlow, Arthur	1 June 1971 – 4 Dec. 1975
Pratte, Louis	25 Jan. 1973 – present[11]

9 Kearney served as chief commissioner of the Board of Transport Commissioners from 1 November 1951 until 15 January 1957, whe he assumed duties on the Exchequer Court. See supra note 5.
10 Walsh seved as divorce commissioner (an officer of the Senate) from 2 July 1964 until 30 January 1969, when he assumed duties on the Exchequer Court. See supra, note 5.
11 Pratte became a supernumerary judge on 29 November 1991.

Urie, John	19 Apr. 1973 – 15 Dec. 1990[12]
Ryan, William	11 Apr. 1974 – 1 Aug. 1986
Le Dain, Gerald	1 Sept. 1975 – 29 May 1984
Heald, Darrel	4 Dec. 1975 – 27 Aug. 1994[13]
Mahoney, Patrick	18 July 1983 – 31 Oct. 1994[14]
Marceau, Louis	18 July 1983 – present[15]
Hugessen, James	18 July 1983 – present
Stone, Arthur	18 July 1983 – present
MacGuigan, Mark	29 June 1984 – present
Lacombe, Bertrand	29 Oct. 1985 – 7 Dec. 1989
Desjardins, Alice	29 July 1987 – present
Décary, Robert	14 Mar. 1990 – present
Linden, Allen	5 July 1990 – present
Létourneau, Gilles	13 May 1992 – present
Robertson, Joseph	13 May 1992 – present
McDonald, Francis	1 Apr. 1993 – present
Strayer, Barry	30 Aug. 1994 – present

Judges of the Federal Court – Trial Division

Cattanach, Alexander	1 June 1971 – 26 July 1984
Gibson, Hugh	1 June 1971 – 14 Dec. 1981
Walsh, Allison	1 June 1971 – 30 June 1986[16]
Kerr, Roderick	1 June 1971 – 1 Sept. 1975
Pratte, Louis	10 June 1971 – 25 Jan. 1973
Heald, Darrel	30 June 1971 – 4 Dec. 1975
Collier, Frank	16 Sept. 1971 – 31 Dec. 1992[17]
Mahoney, Patrick	13 Sept. 1973 – 18 July 1983
Decary, Raymond	13 Sept. 1973 – 31 Jan. 1984
Addy, George	17 Sept. 1973 – 29 Sept. 1990[18]
Dubé, Jean-Eudes	9 Apr. 1975 – present[19]
Marceau, Louis	23 Dec. 1975 – 18 July 1983

12 Urie became a supernumerary judge on 31 December 1988.
13 Heald became a supernumerary judge on 2 January 1993.
14 Mahoney became a supernumerary judge on 1 August 1994.
15 Marceau became a supernumerary judge on 6 February 1992.
16 Walsh became a supernumerary judge on 1 June 1984.
17 Collier became a supernumerary judge on 1 November 1987.
18 Addy was the first Federal Court judge to become supernumerary, on 1 September 1983.
19 Dubé became a supernumerary judge on 6 November 1991.

Rouleau, Paul	9 Aug. 1982 – present
Muldoon, Francis	18 July 1983 – present
Strayer, Barry	18 July 1983 – 30 Aug. 1994
McNair, John	18 July 1983 – 31 Aug. 1990
Reed, Barbara	17 Nov. 1983 – present
Denault, Pierre	29 June 1984 – present
Pinard, Yvon	29 June 1984 – present
Joyal, Louis-Marcel	29 June 1984 – present[20]
Cullen, Bud	26 July 1984 – present
Martin, Leonard	29 Oct. 1985 – 24 Nov. 1991
Teitelbaum, Max	29 Oct. 1985 – present
MacKay, Andrew	2 Sept. 1988 – present
McGillis, Donna	13 May 1992 – present
Rothstein, Marshall	24 June 1992 – present
Noël, Marc	24 June 1992 – present
McKeown, William	1 Apr. 1993 – present
Gibson, Frederick	1 Apr. 1993 – present
Simpson, Sandra	10 June 1993 – present
Nadon, Marc	10 June 1993 – present
Wetston, Howard	16 June 1993 – present
Tremblay-Lamer, Danièle	16 June 1993 – present
Richard, John	30 Aug. 1994 – present
Campbell, Douglas	8 Dec. 1995 – present

20 Joyal became a supernumerary judge on 19 July 1994.

YEAR OF BIRTH, PROVINCE, LEGAL TRADITION, AND POSITION HELD AT THE TIME OF APPOINTMENT

Notes: The judges are listed in order of seniority of appointment to the bench of the Exchequer Court or the Federal Court.

'Province' refers to the province with which the judge had the greatest connection in his or her legal career. This may not necessarily be the province in which the judge was born and raised (see chapter 22).

'Legal tradition' refers to either the law of England ('common law') or the civil law of continental Europe. When Quebec is indicated, the judge's legal education and experience have been in the civil law of Quebec; for judges with a connection to other provinces, the education and experience have been in the law of England. Only two judges have had formal exposure to both traditions, Gerald Le Dain and Louis-Marcel Joyal, as noted in the table.

Judges of the Supreme Court of Canada
(Exchequer Court Judges, 1875–1887)

	Year of birth	Province (legal tradition)	Position at appointment
Richards, William	1815	Ont.	Judge
Ritchie, William	1813	N.B.	Judge
Strong, Henry	1825	Ont.	Judge
Taschereau, Jean-Thomas	1814	Que.	Judge
Fournier, Télesphore	1823	Que.	Minister (Can.)
Henry, William	1816	N.S.	Lawyer
Taschereau, Henri-Elzéar	1836	Que.	Judge
Gwynne, John	1814	Ont.	Judge

Judges of the Exchequer Court

	Year of birth	Province (legal tradition)	Position at appointment
Burbidge, George	1847	N.B.	Public servant (Can.)
Cassels, Walter	1845	Ont.	Lawyer
Audette, Louis-Arthur	1856	Que.	Registrar, Exchequer Court
Maclean, A.K.	1869	N.S.	MP (Can.)
Angers, Eugene-Réal	1883	Que.	Lawyer

Thorson, Joseph	1889	Man.	Minister (Can.)
O'Connor, Charles	1890	Alta.	Lawyer
Cameron, Charles	1891	Ont.	Judge
Archibald, Maynard	1891	N.S.	Judge
Kearney, John	1893	Que.	Ambassador
Fournier, Alphonse	1893	Que.	Minister (Can.)
Potter, William	1890	N.S.	Lawyer
Ritchie, Louis	1894	N.B.	Lawyer
Dumoulin, Jacques	1898	Que.	Lawyer
Thurlow, Arthur	1913	N.S.	Lawyer
Noël, Camilien	1912	Que.	Lawyer
Cattanach, Alexander	1909	Sask.	Public servant (Can.)
Jackett, Wilbur	1912	Sask.	Lawyer
Gibson, Hugh	1916	Ont.	Lawyer
Walsh, Allison	1911	Que.	Lawyer
Kerr, Roderick	1902	N.S.	Public servant (Can.)

Judges of the Federal Court of Canada

Pratte, Louis	1926	Que.	Professor of Law
Heald, Darrel	1919	Sask.	Minister (Sask.)
Collier, Frank	1922	B.C.	Lawyer
Urie, John	1920	Ont.	Lawyer
Mahoney, Patrick	1929	Alta.	Minister (Can.)
Decary, Raymond	1921	Que.	Lawyer
Addy, George	1915	Ont.	Judge
Ryan, William	1920	N.B.	Public servant (Can.)
Dubé, Jean-Eudes	1926	N.B.	Minister (Can.)
Le Dain, Gerald	1924	Que.[1]	Professor of Law
Marceau, Louis	1927	Que.	Ombudsman (Que.)
Jerome, James	1933	Ont.	Speaker, House of Commons
Rouleau, Paul	1930	Ont.	Judge
Hugessen, James	1933	Que.	Judge
Stone, Arthur	1929	Ont.	Lawyer
Muldoon, Francis	1930	Man.	Public servant (Can.)
Strayer, Barry	1932	Sask.	Public servant (Can.)

1 Le Dain was a Professor of Law at Osgoode Hall Law School of York University, Toronto, a common law institution. He had been selected as dean of the faculty in 1967, although he had a civil law background. He served as dean until 1972.

McNair, John	1923	N.B.	Lawyer
Reed, Barbara	1937	Ont.	Public servant (Can.)
Denault, Pierre	1938	Que.	Lawyer
MacGuigan, Mark	1931	Ont.	Minister (Can.)
Pinard, Yvon	1940	Que.	MP (Can.)
Joyal, Louis-Marcel	1924	Ont.[2]	Lawyer
Cullen, Bud	1927	Ont.	Minister (Can.)
Lacombe, Bertrand	1932	Que.	Lawyer
Martin, Leonard	1931	Nfld.	Lawyer
Teitelbaum, Max	1932	Que.	Lawyer
Desjardins, Alice	1934	Que.	Judge
Iacobucci, Frank	1937	Ont.	Public servant (Can.)
MacKay, Andrew	1929	N.S.	Ombudsman (N.S.)
Décary, Robert	1944	Que.	Lawyer
Linden, Allen	1934	Ont.	Public servant (Can.)
Isaac, Julius	1928	Ont.	Judge
Létourneau, Gilles	1945	Que.	Public servant (Can.)
Robertson, Joseph	1949	N.B.	Professor of Law
McGillis, Donna	1951	Ont.	Public servant (Can.)
Rothstein, Marshall	1940	Man.	Lawyer
Noël, Marc	1948	Que.	Lawyer
McDonald, Francis	1933	Ont.	Judge
McKeown, William	1936	Ont.	Judge
Gibson, Frederick	1935	Ont.	Public servant (Can.)
Simpson, Sandra	1949	Ont.	Lawyer
Nadon, Marc	1949	Que.	Lawyer
Wetston, Howard	1947	N.S.	Public servant (Can.)
Tremblay-Lamer, Danièle	1946	Que.	Public servant (Can.)
Richard, John	1934	Ont.	Lawyer
Campbell, Douglas	1945	B.C.	Judge

2 Joyal was educated at McGill University and was admitted to the Quebec bar following graduation, just before to joining the Ontario bar.

Appendix B

Interviews

George Addy
Alexander Cattanach
Jean-Eudes Dubé
Darrel Heald
Frank Iacobucci
James Jerome
Mark MacGuigan
Patrick Mahoney
Louis Marceau
Louis Pratte
William Ryan
Arthur Thurlow
John Urie
Allison Walsh

(Interviewer: Christine Kates)

Frank Collier
Bud Cullen
Robert Décary
Alice Desjardins

James Hugessen
Louis Joyal
Gilles Létourneau
Allen Linden
Andrew MacKay
Frank Muldoon
Marc Nadon
Barbara Reed
Paul Rouleau
Arthur Stone
Barry Strayer

(Interviewer: Lynne Watt)

Francis McDonald
Donna McGillis
Marc Noël
Joseph Robertson
Howard Wetston

(Interviewer: Marnie McCall)

Julius Isaac
Wilbur Jackett

(Interviewer: Ian Bushnell)

OTHERS

Robert Biljan, Administrator of the Court
Pauline Bratt, Judicial Administrator, Trial Division
Donald Christie, Associate Chief Judge, Tax Court of Canada; Assistant
  Deputy Minister of Justice during the creation of the Federal Court,
  1970–71
Monique Giroux, Regional Director, Federal Court, Montreal, Quebec
Hugette Narum, Judicial Administrator, Appeal Division
Pierre Trudeau, Prime Minister of Canada during the creation of the Fed-
  eral Court, 1970–71

(Interviewer: Christine Kates)

John Turner, Minister of Justice during the creation of the Federal Court
  of Canada, 1970–71; Prime Minister of Canada, 1984

(Interviewer: Ian Bushnell)

Mrs Gordon Maclaren (Margaret Maclean), daughter of A.K. Maclean,
  President of the Exchequer Court, 1923–1942
Jean Maclean, daughter of A.K. Maclean, President of the Exchequer
  Court, 1923–1942
Kenneth Maclaren, grandson of A.K. Maclean, President of the Exchequer
  Court, 1923–1942

(Interviewer: Lynne Watt)

Margot (Ritchie) Russell, daughter of Louis Ritchie, judge of the
  Exchequer Court, 1955–56 (in writing)

(Interviewer: Ian Bushnell)

Notes

CHAPTER ONE

1 The title of a recent study for the Canadian Judicial Council makes this clear: 'A Place Apart' (Martin L. Friedland, *A Place Apart: Judicial Independence and Accountability in Canada*, A Report Prepared for the Canadian Judicial Council, May 1995). The title was based on a statement by Senator Arthur Meighen in 1932: 'a judge is in no sense under the direction of the Government ... The judge is in a place apart' (Senate, *Debates*, 1932, 457).

2 House of Commons, *Debates*, 1880, 80.

3 Bora Laskin, 'Certiorari to Labour Boards: The Apparent Futility of Privative Clauses' (1952), 30 *Canadian Bar Review* 986–1003 at 1001.

4 'A Gift of Freedom,' a special edition of W5, CTV network, Sunday, June 8, 1986. The primary reason for the program was a discussion of the Canadian Charter of Rights and Freedoms.

5 S.R. Peck, 'The Supreme Court of Canada, 1958–1966: A Search for Policy through Scalogram Analysis' (1967), 45 *Canadian Bar Review* 666–725, and 'A Behavioural Approach to the Judicial Process: Scalogram Analysis,' (1967), 5 *Osgoode Hall Law Journal* 1–28.

6 R.M. Willes Chitty, 'Sniping at the Judiciary' (1968), 16 Chitty's Law Journal 74–6.

7 Peter Russell, 'An Evaluation by a Political Scientist' (paper presented at the 20th Anniversary Symposium, June 26, 1991) and published in *The Federal Court of Canada – An Evaluation* (Ottawa: Federal Court of Canada 1991), 19–26 at 25.

8 Section 3: 'Every citizen of Canada has the right to vote in an election of members of the House of Commons or of a legislative assembly and to be qualified for membership therein.'

9 *Muldoon and Teitlebaum v. The Queen* (November 3, 1988), T-2048–88 (Fed. T.D.).

10 W.R. Lederman, 'The Independence of the Judiciary,' in *The Canadian Judiciary*, ed. A.M. Linden (Toronto: Osgoode Hall Law School 1976), 8, quoting R.M. Dawson, *The Government of Canada*, 2d ed. (Toronto: University of Toronto Press 1954), 486.

11 J.K. Hugessen, 'Comment: The Judge and the Public: The Law of Contempt,' in *The Canadian Judiciary*, supra note 10 at 224–31. Such views have been around for some time: see Ian Bushnell, *The Captive Court: A Study of the Supreme Court of Canada* (Montreal & Kingston: McGill-Queen's University Press 1992), 479–81.

12 See, for example, House of Commons, *Debates*, 1891, 1418, 1423; Senate, *Debates*, 1951, 518.

13 Senate, *Debates*, 1955, 734–5.

14 'Code of Professional Conduct' (Canadian Bar Association), c. 13, 'The lawyer should encourage public respect for and try to improve the administration of justice.' See letter to the editor by Thomas G. Heintzman, President, Canadian Bar Association, *Law Times*, August 27, 1995, p. 7. Provincial law societies have similar requirements, for example, in the 'Rules of Professional Conduct' (Law Society of Upper Canada), maintaining public confidence in the administration of justice is a dominant concern, appearing in the Foreword and in Rules 11 and 21.

15 '[*Stare decisis* in the House of Lords] rests chiefly on the repeated assertions of one judge, Lord Campbell.' Pollock, *First Book of Jurisprudence*, 2d ed. (London: Macmillan 1904), 325. Campbell's assertions can be seen in *Bright v. Hutton* (1852), 3 HLC. 341, 10 ER 133 at 153, *Attorney General v. Dean and Canons of Windsor* (1860), 8 HLC 369, 11 ER 472 at 481, and *Beamish v. Beamish* (1861), 9 HLC 274, 11 ER 735.

16 *London Tramways Co. v. London County Council*, [1898] AC 375 (HL).

17 Blackstone, *Commentaries*, 1795 (London: Dawson of Pall Mall 1966), 70. It is important to note, however, that Blackstone accepted that a previous decision might be overruled if it was seen as evidently contrary to reason, or manifestly absurd or unjust.

18 See J.W. Gough, *Fundamental Law in English Constitutional History* (Oxford: Clarendon Press 1961), 6–7.

19 John Austin, *The Province of Jurisprudence Determined*, 2d ed. vol. 2 (London: J. Murray 1861–63), 102, s. 919.

20 There was an acceptance in the nineteenth century of absolutism in social values. This can be seen in the classic work of John Stuart Mill, *On Liberty*, written in 1859. Mills criticizes the amount of social values being taken for granted, for which there was a demand for conformity of behaviour.

21 See, for example, Senate, *Debates*, 1887, 443.

22 In the nineteenth century scientific principles were considered fixed and unchangeable, and it was common to see a reference to someone being a 'scientific' lawyer.

23 *Sussex Peerage case* (1844), 11 Cl. & Fin. 85, 8 ER 1034; *Abley v. Dale* (1851), 11 CB 391, 138 ER 519; *Grey v. Pearson* (1857), 6 HLC. 61, 10 ER 1216.

24 The most famous was *Heydon's Case* (1584), 3 Co. Rep. 7a, 76 ER 637. This decision was based on *Stradling v. Morgan* (1560), 1 Plowd. 199, 75 ER 305.

25 *Law of the Constitution*, 10th ed. (London: Macmillan & Co. 1964).

26 See Canadian Charter of Rights and Freedoms, preamble: 'Whereas Canada is founded upon principles that recognize the supremacy of God and the rule of law[.]'

27 *Reference re Language Rights under Section 23 of the Manitoba Act, 1870, and Section 133 of the Constitution Act, 1867* (*Re Manitoba Language Rights*), [1985] 1 SCR 721.

28 Charles Van Doren, *A History of Knowledge* (New York: Ballantine Books 1992), 300.

29 Dicey's connection to the principle has been so close that some have credited him with creating it, while others are prepared to give him credit for coining the phrase 'rule of law': Morton J. Horwitz, *The Transformation of American Law, 1870–1960* (New York: Oxford University Press 1992), 225. Originally published by Harvard University Press in 1977.

30 Dicey, supra note 25 at 188.

31 Horwitz, supra note 29 at 225–7.

32 Ibid., 226.

33 J.A. Corry, 'The Prospects for the Rule of Law' (1955), 21 *Canadian Journal of Economics and Political Science* 405–15; reprinted in *Canadian Public Administration*, ed. J.E. Hodgetts and D.C. Corbett) (Toronto: Macmillan Co. of Canada 1960), 544–55. See H.W. Arthurs, 'Rethinking Administrative Law: A Slightly Dicey Business' (1979), 17 *Osgoode Hall Law Journal* 1–45.

34 Dicey, supra note 25 at 188.

35 For an analysis of the judicial process in greater detail see chapters 5 and 6 of Bushnell, *Captive Court*, supra note 11 (47–72), and in particular 60–61 for a discussion of the contexts of decision making.

36 Roscoe Pound, 'Mechanical Jurisprudence' (1908), 8 *Columbia Law Review* 605–23; Roscoe Pound, 'The Scope and Purpose of Sociological Jurisprudence'

(1910–11), 24 *Harvard Law Review* 591–619 and (1911–12), 25 *Harvard Law Review* 140–68, 489–516; E. Russell Hopkins, 'The Literal Canon and the Golden Rule' (1937), 25 *Canadian Bar Review* 689–96; Roscoe Pound, 'Sociology of Law and Sociological Jurisprudence' (1943–44), 5 *University of Toronto Law Journal* 1–20. See also Roscoe Pound, 'The Theory of Judicial Decision' (1924), 2 *Canadian Bar Review* 263–80, 335–55, 443–60. In particular see Benjamin N. Cardozo, *The Nature of the Judicial Process* (New Haven, Connecticut: Yale University Press 1921). This classic publication of a series of lectures has been reprinted repeatedly over the years.

37 Steven M. Quevedo, 'Formalist and Instrumentalist Legal Reasoning and Legal Theory' (1985), 73 *California Law Review* 119–57.

38 H.W. Arthurs, *'Without the Law': Administrative Justice and Legal Pluralism in Nineteenth-Century England* (Toronto: University of Toronto Press 1985).

39 H. Wade MacLauchlan, 'Approaches to Interpretation in Administrative Law' (1988), 1 *Canadian Journal of Administrative Law & Practice* 293–317.

40 *The Queen v. Big M Drug Mart Ltd.*, [1985] 1 SCR 295 at 344.

41 Bushnell, *Captive Court*, supra note 11, chapters 5 and 6, 47–72.

42 *Watkins v. Olafson*, [1989] 2 SCR 750 at 760.

43 'The Limits of Judicial Creativity' (1977–78), 63 *Iowa Law Review* 1–13 at 2, 5.

44 Arthurs, supra note 38 at 5.

CHAPTER TWO

1 For a detailed discussion of the creation of the Supreme Court of Canada, from which this account is drawn, see Ian Bushnell, *The Captive Court: A Study of the Supreme Court of Canada* (Montreal and Kingston: McGill-Queen's University Press 1992), 3–37.

2 A.I. Silver, *The French-Canadian Idea of Confederation 1864–1900* (Toronto: University of Toronto Press 1982), 112.

3 At the Quebec Conference of 1864, Resolution 31 was adopted, which stated: 'The General Parliament may also, from time to time, establish additional Courts, and the General Government may appoint Judges and officers thereof, when the same shall appear necessary or for the public advantage, in order to the due execution of the laws of Parliament.'

4 British North America Act, 1867 (UK), 30 & 31 Vict., c. 3, known since 1982 as the Constitution Act, 1867.

5 While the existence of the proposed appellate court and the federal courts had been kept distinct in the Resolutions that came out of the Quebec Conference of 1864 and the London Conference of 1866, they became linked in the drafting of the provision that was ultimately enacted by Westminster as section 101 of the British North America Act, 1867.

6   See W.L. Morton, 'Confederation, 1870–1896: The End of the Macdonaldian Constitution and the Return to Duality' (1966), 1 *Journal of Canadian Studies*, No. 1, 11–24.

7   Section 17.

8   Sections 69, 71, 88.

9   Section 58.

10   Section 90.

11   Section 96.

12   Section 101.

13   Section 94.

14   Section 92, and in particular head number 16.

15   Section 91. There were other notable centralizing provisions. There was subsection 93(3), which allowed an appeal to the federal executive with respect to denominational education, and subsection 93(4), which allowed for remedial legislation by Ottawa even though education was otherwise securely within provincial authority. The Dominion was given concurrent powers with the provinces over agriculture and immigration, but the Dominion law was given paramountcy over any conflicting provincial law (section 95). Section 92(10)(2) gave Ottawa the power to declare local works to be for the general advantage of Canada or for two or more provinces and thereby assume control. While Ottawa was given the power to raise money by any means under section 91(3), the provinces were restricted to the (at the time) relatively insignificant means of direct taxation within the province by section 92(2), meaning that virtually all the revenue would go to Ottawa and that, through the power of the purse, the central authority might assume control. Under section 132, the Parliament of Canada was given the authority to deal with provincial matters if they were the subject of a treaty. Ottawa also, under section 146, had the power to create new provinces. Last, under section 91, Ottawa had the power to enact 'laws for the peace, order and good government of Canada,' which was at the time a verbal formula indicating the power to enact laws of any kind; the provincial authority to enact laws under section 92 had to be perceived as merely an exception to the authority under section 91.

16   Copies of the 1869 bill were sent to judges throughout Canada for their opinions. See Bushnell, *Captive Court*, supra note 1 at 9.

17   Strong's strong pro-province attitude was demonstrated in the very first constitutional case to reach the Supreme Court of Canada, *Severn v. The Queen* (1878), 2 SCR 70.

18   Bushnell, *Captive Court*, supra note 1 at 9–10.

19   House of Commons, *Debates*, 1870, 525

20   House of Commons, *Debates*, 1870, 524.

21 House of Commons, *Debates*, 1875, 285. The statute was titled The Supreme and Exchequer Court Act, SC 1875, c. 11, s. 81, but the pages of the statute were headed using the word 'Courts.' In the Revised Statutes of 1886 the Act appeared as The Supreme and Exchequer Courts Act, RSC 1886, c. 135, s. 1.
22 House of Commons, *Debates*, 1875, 288.
23 House of Commons, *Debates*, 738 (Palmer, Conservative, New Brunswick), 745 (Aemilius Irving, Liberal, Ontario).
24 House of Commons, *Debates*, 738 (Palmer, Conservative, New Brunswick).
25 SC 1875, c. 11. The Exchequer Court was dealt with in sections 58–67.
26 Ibid., s. 80.

CHAPTER THREE

1 The provisions of The Supreme and Exchequer Court Act, SC. 1875, c. 11, dealing with the jurisdiction of the Exchequer Court were sections 58 and 59:

58. The Exchequer Court shall have and possess concurrent original jurisdiction in the Dominion of Canada, in all cases in which it shall be sought to enforce any law of the Dominion of Canada relating to the revenue, including actions, suits, and proceedings, by way of information, to enforce penalties and proceedings by way of information *in rem*, and as well in *qui tam* suits for penalties or forfeitures [see below] as where the suit is on behalf of the Crown alone; and the said Court shall have exclusive original jurisdiction in all cases in which demand shall be made or relief sought in respect of any matter which might in England be the subject of a suit or action in the Court of Exchequer on its revenue side against the Crown, or any officer of the Crown.

59. The Exchequer Court shall also have concurrent original jurisdiction with the Courts of the several Provinces in all other suits of a civil nature at common law or equity in which the Crown in the interest of the Dominion of Canada is plaintiff or petitioner.

The *qui tam* suit referred to in section 58 consisted of an action brought by an informer. Such an action would come under a statute which established a penalty for the commission or omission of a certain act and provided that that penalty would be recoverable in a civil action, with part of it going to the person who brought the action and the remainder going to the state or some other institution. *Qui tam* is Latin for 'who as well ....': the plaintiff stated that the suit was brought for the state *as well* as for himself (*Black's Law Dictionary*, 6th ed., St Paul, Minnesota: West Publishing Co. 1991).

2 Sir Geoffrey Gilbert, *A Treatise on The Court of Exchequer* (London: Henry
Lintot 1758), 1. Gilbert (1674–1726) had been Lord Chief Baron of the Court
of Exchequer. Of the other sources that I examined regarding the history of
England's Court of Exchequer, the following were the most useful: Sir
William Holdsworth, *A History of English Law*, 3d ed. (London: Methuen &
Co. / Sweet and Maxwell, 1944; reprinted 1966), 1:42–4, 231–42; Thomas
Madox, *The History and Antiquities of the Exchequer of the Kings of England*, 2d
ed., 2 vs. (1769; reprinted, New York: A.M. Kelley 1969); Theodore F.T.
Plucknett, *A Concise History of the Common Law*, 5th ed. (London: Butterworth & Co. 1956), 146–7, 159–62, 170–1, 175, 185–6. See also Louis Arthur
Audette, *The Practice of the Exchequer Court of Canada* (Ottawa: Thorburn &
Co. 1895), 23–31; reprinted in 2d ed. (Ottawa: Copeland-Chatterson-Crain
1909), 40–50.
3 Gilbert, supra note 2 at 2.
4 Holdsworth, supra note 2 at 1:239.
5 The equity jurisdiction refers to the jurisdiction of the Court of Chancery,
which developed beginning in the fourteenth century to alleviate defects
within the common law system. There thus came into being essentially two
legal systems, that is, two judicial systems which applied their own principles
in the settlement of disputes. The rules of equity, however, supplemented
those of the common law by providing remedies in the name of justice, meaning substnative justice and not the notion of justice as simply following a set of
predetermined rules; equity was said to follow the law. The rules of the common law and the rules of equity were fused in England by the Judicature Act,
1873 (36 and 37 Vict., c. 66). In the case of a matter not provided for, or a conflict, the rules of equity were to prevail. See David M. Walker, *The Oxford
Companion to Law* (Oxford: Clarendon Press 1980), 424–7. In England the
equity jurisdiction was removed from the Exchequer Court and transferred
to the Court of Chancery in 1842 (5 Vict., c. 5), except for revenue cases:
J. Paterson, H. MacNamara, and W. Marshall, *The New Practice of the Common
Law* (London: New Times Office 1858), 1:12, note 10. See also Audette, *The
Practice of the Exchequer Court of Canada*, supra note 2, 1st ed., 28 (note), 2d ed.,
46 (note).
6 Paterson, MacNamara, and Marshall, supra note 5 at 1:11–12.
7 Supreme Court of Judicature Act, 1873 (UK), 36 & 37 Vict., c. 66. The operation
of the 1873 statute had been postponed until November 1875: Supreme Court
of Judicature (Commencement) Act, 1874 (UK), 37 & 38 Vict., c. 83.
8 Plucknett, supra note 2 at 185. See W.H. Bryson, *The Equity Side of the Exchequer*
(London: Cambridge University Press 1975).
9 The Supreme and Exchequer Court Act, SC 1875, c. 11, s. 58.

10 House of Commons, *Debates*, 1876, 291 (Edward Blake).

11 An Act to make further provision in regard to the Supreme Court and the Exchequer Court of Canada, SC 1876, c. 26, s. 18. In addition, by section 19, a reference to 'revenue side' that had appeared in section 61 of the original statute was removed and replaced by the words 'similar suits.' The legislation received royal assent on April 12, 1876.

12 The device used to acquire a jurisdiction over disputes between private individuals was the writ *quo minus*. The plaintiff would assert that he was a debtor to the sovereign and because of the injury or damage caused to him by the defendant he could not pay his debt to the Crown. In this way the revenue was engaged, and the court acquired jurisdiction: Holdsworth, *A History of English Law*, 1:240. *Attorney-General v. Halling* (1846), 15 M. & W. 687, 153 E.R. 1027

13 SC 1875, c. 11, s. 58.

14 Legislative Assembly of United Canada, *Debates*, 1846, 5:1591, 1631.

15 Ibid., 1630.

16 An Act to amend the Law constituting the Board of Works, SC 1846, c. 37. Three arbitrators were to be appointed for each of Upper and Lower Canada. Later, provision was made for private arbitrators to be selected by the parties rather than using the provincial arbitrators: An Act to amend the Laws relating to Public Works, SC 1853, c. 160. In 1859, three arbitrators were appointed for all of Canada: An Act to amend and consolidate the several Acts respecting the Public Works, SC 1859, c. 3.

17 An Act respecting the Public Works of Canada, SC 1867, c. 12.

18 Ibid. s. 44.

19 An Act to extend the powers of the Official Arbitrators, SC 1870, c. 23.

20 An Act to authorize the construction of railways in this Province, SNB 1856, c. 15; An Act relating to the recovery of Damages against the Commissioners of the European and North American Railway, in certain cases, SNB 1859, c. 24.

21 House of Commons, *Debates*, 1867, 305.

22 The following information is drawn from Sir William Holdsworth, *A History of English Law*, 3d ed. (London: Methuen & Co. / Sweet and Maxwell 1944; reprinted 1966), 9:30–45; W.S. Holdsworth, 'The History of Remedies Against the Crown' (1922), 38 *Law Quarterly Review* 141–64, 280–96.

23 *Pawlett v. The Attorney-General* (1667), Hardres 465, 145 ER 550.

24 See supra, note 2, for the sources of the information about the early years of the Exchequer Court.

25 Supra note 23.

26 Following a reference to the court to hear and determine a claim for payment of a debt due from the Crown, the Court of Exchequer would issue a writ of

liberate authorizing payment if that was determined to be appropriate. The last payment by writ of *liberate* in England occurred in 1844.

27 (1843), 1 Phillips 306, 41 ER 648. This case is of added interest because of a coincidence. The petitioner, Viscount Canterbury, had been Speaker of the House of Commons and had occupied a residence on the premises of the Houses of Parliament. On October 16, 1834, the Houses of Parliament were destroyed by fire and with them items of furniture, books, prints, and other belongings of his. The fire had started from overheated stoves after employees of the Commissioners of Woods and Forests had been directed to remove some old sticks from a room on the premises and burn them. The sticks were 'tallies,' shaped pieces of wood representing sums of money; they had been used by the Exchequer for accounting purposes to prevent fraud. Each was cut into two and when the parts were fitted together exactly a claim was substantiated: Madox, *Antiquities*, supra note 2 at 285. They had been used until 1785.

28 23 & 24 Vict. (UK), c. 34.

29 *Thomas v. The Queen*, LR 10 QB 31.

30 House of Commons, *Debates*, 1875, 803.

31 SC 1875, c. 12.

32 In section 2 the court with jurisdiction is defined: 'the court, (being such as would have cognizance of the subject matter of such petition or any material part thereof, if the same had been a matter of dispute between subject and subject).' The provincial courts would have had jurisdiction if the matter of dispute had been between subject and subject.

33 See House of Commons, *Debates*, 1876, 85 (Edward Blake, Minister of Justice).

34 SC 1876, c. 27.

35 House of Commons, *Debates*, 466: The Minister of Justice, Edward Blake, stated that the 1875 statute had excluded nine out of every ten cases of contracts entered into with the Department of Public Works.

36 House of Commons, *Debates*, 463 (Edward Blake).

37 The Petition of Right Act, 1876, SC 1876, c. 27, s. 19(3)(b).

38 House of Commons, *Debates*, 671.

39 Ibid.

40 An Act respecting the Official Arbitrators, SC 1879, c. 8.

41 SC 1881, c. 25, s. 40.

CHAPTER FOUR

1 Joseph Schull, *Edward Blake* (Toronto: Macmillan 1976), 150.

2 Dale C. Thomson, *Alexander Mackenzie: Clear Grit* (Toronto: Macmillan 1960), 235.

3 'Judicial Appointments to the Supreme Court' (1875), 11 *Canada Law Journal* 265–6 at 266.

4 Ibid.

5 Gordon Bale and E. Bruce Mellett, 'Sir William Johnstone Ritchie,' *Dictionary of Canadian Biography* (Toronto: University of Toronto Press 1966), 12:895–900 at 899. See Gordon Bale, *Chief Justice William Johnstone Ritchie* (Ottawa: Carleton University Press 1991).

6 See Bale, supra note 5 at 45–61.

7 'The Late Sir Henry Strong' (1909), 29 *Canadian Law Times* 1044–5 at 1045. See also Ian Bushnell, *The Captive Court: A History of the Supreme Court of Canada* (Montreal & Kingston: McGill–Queen's University Press 1992), 41.

8 The Supreme and Exchequer Court Act, SC 1875, c. 11, s. 4.

9 House of Commons, *Debates*, 1879, 506 (Alexander Mackenzie, Prime Minister).

10 See Bushnell, *Captive Court*, supra note 7 at 15–18.

11 Henry had been at the Charlottetown, Quebec, and London conferences. He is credited with preparing the draft of the constitution, the British North America Act. See George Patterson, 'Hon. William A. Henry' (1940), 18 *Canadian Bar Review* 762–75. Cf. Phyllis R. Blakeley, 'William Alexander Henry,' *Dictionary of Canadian Biography* (Toronto: University of Toronto Press 1982), 11:398–400.

12 Bushnell, *Captive Court*, supra note 7 at 42.

13 'Judicial Appointments to the Supreme Court' (1875), 11 *Canada Law Journal* 265–66. The writer in the Ontario journal thought that there should be three judges from that province, not merely two. In essence, Henry was occupying the position that should have gone to an Ontario judge, since the choice of Ritchie was unassailable.

14 See J.G. Snell, 'Relations between the Maritimes and the Supreme Court of Canada: The Pattern of the Early Years,' in 'Law in a Colonial Society; the Nova Scotia Experience, Dalhousie/Berkeley Lectures on Legal History' (1984), 8 *Dalhousie Law Journal* 143–63. See also James G. Snell and Frederick Vaughan, *The Supreme Court of Canada: History of the Institution* (Toronto: The Osgoode Society 1985), 14 and 43–4, in which the negative assumption regarding Henry's ability must have coloured the analysis of the case being discussed. In Phyllis R. Blakeley, 'William Alexander Henry,' *Dictionary of Canadian Biography* (Toronto: University of Toronto Press 1982), 11:398–400, the author, an archivist in the provincial archives, quotes two of Henry's colleagues who made disparaging remarks about him, without any apparent reflection on their credibility.

15 See Bushnell, *Captive Court*, supra note 7 at 87–8.

16 See ibid., 88–9.

17 (1878), 2 SCR 70 at 95. For a detailed discussion of the case see Bushnell, *Captive Court*, supra note 7 at 80–6.

18 (1878), 2 SCR 70 at 140.

19 Ibid., 142.

20 Ibid., 99.

21 Ibid., 103.

22 Ibid., 119.

23 *Observations of the Chief Justice of New Brunswick* (Fredericton 1870). See Bushnell, *Captive Court*, supra note 7 at 9.

24 An Act to make further provision in regard to the Supreme Court and the Exchequer Court of Canada, SC 1876, c. 26, s. 20.

25 House of Commons, *Debates*, 1876, 291.

26 Of the cases heard in this period, 31 per cent were appeals from the Official Arbitrators.

27 For example, *Boyd v. The Queen* (1887), 1 Ex. CR 186. There were two referees, one of whom was the registrar. In *Robertson v. The Queen* (4 April 1887), file no. 40, the registrar was directed to ascertain the amount of damages in a contract action. Referees were used in only one other case, *McLean and Roger v. The Queen* (3 Oct. 1883), file no. 45, but this aspect of the case was not reported. A judgment dismissing a demurrer, however, was reported and appealed to the Supreme Court: *The Queen v. McLean and Roger* (1881), 8 SCR 210.

CHAPTER FIVE

1 'The Supreme Court' (1878), 14 *Canada Law Journal* 3–5.

2 *Robertson v. The Queen* (1880), 6 SCR 52 at 61, aff'd (1882), 6 SCR 52. It was held that the federal authorities could not issue a licence to fish.

3 *Attorney General of British Columbia v. Attorney General of Canada* (1887), 14 SCR 345. The decision of the Supreme Court in favour of Ottawa was reversed by the Privy Council: (1889), 14 App. Cas. 295.

4 See Gordon Bale, *Chief Justice William Johnstone Ritchie* (Ottawa: Carleton University Press 1991), 206–8; James G. Snell and Frederick Vaughan, *The Supreme Court of Canada: History of the Institution* (Toronto: Osgoode Society 1985), 40; Ian Bushnell, *The Captive Court: A Study of the Supreme Court of Canada* (Montreal & Kingston: McGill–Queen's University Press 1992), 90, 114.

5 NA, Sir John A. Macdonald Papers, MG 26A, vol. 329, No. 148624–640, Strong to Macdonald, February 9, 1880.

6 See Bushnell, *Captive Court*, supra note 4 at 163–5.

7 Strong accused Ritchie of not paying enough attention to his judicial work and

being tardy in rendering his judgments. Strong's solution was to propose a rule that all cases for which judgments were delayed for more than one month should be laid before Parliament with the reasons for the delays.

8 *Thomas v. The Queen*, LR 10 QB 31.

9 *Wood v. The Queen* (1877), 7 SCR 634.

10 *Hall v. The Queen* (1893), 3 Ex. CR 373, at 376.

11 *The Queen v. Henderson* (1898), 28 SCR 425.

12 *Chevrier v. The Queen* (1880), 4 SCR 1 at 127.

13 The trial judge had been Jean-Thomas Taschereau, who had found in favour of the Crown: *Chevrier v. The Queen* (1878), 4 SCR 1 at 7.

14 The judgments in the two cases are discussed in more detail in Bushnell, *Captive Court*, supra note 4 at 121–7.

15 (1881), 7 SCR 216 at 221.

16 *The Queen v. McFarlane* (1882), 7 SCR 216 at 234.

17 Ibid. 239.

18 Ibid. 246.

19 (1883), 8 SCR 1.

20 *McLeod* v. *The Queen* (1882), 8 SCR 1 at 2, 6.

21 Ibid., 27.

22 Ritchie had also concluded that there was no contract.

23 The Government Railways Act, 1881, SC 1881, c. 25, ss. 27(3), 40.

24 10 SCR 1 at 3.

25 Ibid., 6.

26 Ibid., 11.

27 *The Queen v. Smith* (1883), 10 SCR 1.

28 Ibid., 78.

CHAPTER SIX

1 See Gordon Bale, *Chief Justice William Johnstone Ritchie* (Ottawa: Carleton University Press 1991), 218–30.

2 *Glassman v. Council of the College of Physicians and Surgeons*, [1966] 2 OR 81 at 97.

3 See *Mayor, etc. of Montreal v. Brown* (1876), 2 App. Cas. 168 at 184 (PC).

4 It should be noted that, in an *en banc* system, all the judges of the court would sit, but when so sitting the court was not a court of appeal. The full court when constituted *en banc* would consider questions of law arising on a demurrer, and points of procedure, and at best could grant a motion for a new trial.

5 An Act to make further provision for the due Administration of Justice, SO 1874, c. 7, s. 9.

6 The Judicial Committee Act, 1871 (UK), 34 & 35 Vict., c. 91, s. 1.

7 Senate, *Debates*, 1889, 403. The legislation was enacted as An Act further to Amend the Supreme Court and Exchequer Courts Act, SC 1889, c. 37, s. 1.

8 House of Commons, *Debates*, 1876: 86, 467 (John A. Macdonald); 466 (Edward Blake).

9 Henry Borden, ed., *Robert Laird Borden: His Memoirs* (Toronto: Macmillan 1938), 27.

10 *Robertson v. The Queen* (1880), 6 SCR 52 at 61. See 101–2.

11 *The Queen v. Robertson* (1882), 6 SCR 52.

12 See Ian Bushnell, *The Captive Court: A Study of the Supreme Court of Canada* (Montreal & Kingston: McGill–Queen's University Press 1992), 92–6. The bill was introduced on April 21, 1879; the first hearing had been conducted on June 5, 1876: See *Captive Court*, chapter 7, 75–7. For the Exchequer Court it appears from the docket book that the first hearing was conducted by Mr Justice J.-T. Taschereau at Quebec City in *Berlinguet v. The Queen* (1877), 13 SCR 26 at 29 in early July 1876.

13 House of Commons, *Debates*, 1879, 1376 (Luther Holten, Liberal, Quebec).

14 House of Commons, *Debates*, 1880–1, 1302.

15 *Berlinguet v. The Queen*, supra note 12.

16 The suppliants had spent $35,000, the government $16,000: House of Commons, *Debates*, 1880, 236.

17 House of Commons, *Debates*, 1880, 236.

18 House of Commons, *Debates*, 1880, 255–6.

19 House of Commons, *Debates*, 1880, 242 (Cameron, Conservative, Ontario), 256 (Edward Blake, Liberal, Ontario).

20 Ibid., 258 (Girouard, Conservative, Quebec).

21 Ibid., 1880, 261 (D'Alton McCarthy, Conservative, Ontario).

22 Ibid., 263 (David Mills, Liberal, Ontario)

23 Ibid., 262.

CHAPTER SEVEN

1 *Farnell v. Bowman* (1887), 12 App. Cas. 643 at 649. See Ian Bushnell, *The Captive Court: A Study of the Supreme Court of Canada* (Montreal & Kingston: McGill–Queen's University Press), 127.

2 An Act to amend the Law constituting the Board of Works SC 1846, c. 37, s. 24.

3 See Morton Horwitz, *The Transformation of American Law, 1780–1860* (New York: Oxford University Press 1992), originally published by Harvard University Press in 1977.

4 House of Commons, *Debates*, 1887, 812 (John Thompson, Minister of Justice).

5 House of Commons, *Debates*, 1887, 810 (John Thompson, Minister of Justice).

6 See House of Commons, *Debates*, 1887, 810–811; Senate, *Debates*, 442, 444. By the end of the nineteenth century there were three exclusionary rules. The first two excluded evidence of character and evidence in the form of an opinion. The third, the most characteristic and best-known rule of the common law legal system, the hearsay rule, excluded evidence of what someone had said or written at another time out of court that was being offered as proof of what had been asserted. These rules, it should be noted, were rules of the law of England, not civil law.

7 Senate, *Debates*, 1887, 425 (John Abbott, Conservative, Quebec).

8 See Louis Arthur Audette, *The Practice of the Exchequer Court of Canada*, 1st ed. (Ottawa: Thorburn & Co. 1895), 46, reprinted in the 2d ed. (Ottawa: Copeland-Chatterson-Crain Ltd. 1909) 67.

9 Bill 93, 1885. See House of Commons, *Debates*, 1885, 449, 777, 2439.

10 P.B. Waite, *The Man from Halifax: Sir John Thompson, Prime Minister* (Toronto: University of Toronto Press 1985), 186.

11 Ibid.

12 An Act to amend "The Supreme and Exchequer Courts Act," and to make better provision for the Trial of Claims against the Crown, SC 1887, c. 16.

13 Ibid., ss. 11 (Official Referees), 58, 59. Section 59 provided that all matters pending before the Official Arbitrators would be transferred to the Exchequer Court when the Act came into force. By General Order dated March 7, 1888, unless otherwise specified any matter that had been heard or partly heard by the Arbitrators would be continued before them as Official Referees, and they would report to the court as if there had been a reference under section 26 of the 1887 Act: *Rioux v. The Queen* (1889), 2 Ex. CR 91, 92.

14 The provision establishing the position of Official Referee was repealed in 1928: An Act to amend the Exchequer Court Act, SC 1928, c. 23. In the debate, it was said, 'It is queer that this particular section should have been retained in the statute when the men to whom it applies were dead long ago' (House of Commons, *Debates*, 1928, 2265).

15 House of Commons, *Debates*, 1887, 813.

16 (1878), 2 SCR 70.

17 *Bank of Toronto v. Lambe* (1887), 12 App. Cas. 575.

18 *Valin v. Langlois* (1879), 3 SCR 1.

19 *Citizen's Insurance Co. of Canada v. Parsons* (1881), 7 App. Cas. 96.

20 See The Quebec Act 1774 (UK), 1774, 14 Geo. 3, c. 83, s. VIII.

21 *Liquidators of the Maritime Bank of Canada v. Receiver-General of New Brunswick*, [1892] AC 437 (PC); *Attorney-General for Ontario v. Attorney-General for Canada (Local Prohibition)*, [1896] AC 348 (PC).

CHAPTER EIGHT

1 The Exchequer Court Act was proclaimed in force on October 1, 1887: Louis Arthur Audette, *The Practice of the Exchequer Court of Canada*, 1st ed. (Ottawa: Thorburn & Co. 1895), 67.

2 Desmond H. Brown, *The Genesis of the Canadian Criminal Code of 1892* (Toronto: Osgoode Society 1989), 121, 123.

3 P.B. Waite, *The Man from Halifax: Sir John Thompson, Prime Minister* (Toronto: University of Toronto Press 1985), 187.

4 Senate, *Debates*, 1887, 442, 444.

5 House of Commons, *Debates*, 1887, 812.

6 An Act to amend 'The Supreme and Exchequer Courts Act,' and to make better provision for the Trial of Claims against the Crown, SC 1887, c. 16, s. 26.

7 Audette's appointment as registrar was as of November 8, 1887.

8 An Act to amend the law respecting the Exchequer Court of Canada, SC 1889, c. 38, s. 1.

9 See Louis Arthur Audette, supra note 1, 92; 'Case Comment' (1894), 30 *Canada Law Journal* 562.

10 See *Price v. The King* (1906), 10 Ex. CR 105.

11 House of Commons, *Debates*, 1904, 1790.

12 The account that follows is based on surveying the first three Docket Books of the court for information about the use of referees.

13 In addition Audette acted as interpreter: House of Commons, *Debates*, 1907, 7256.

14 SC 1887, c. 16, s. 3(5).

15 Ibid., s. 3(6).

16 A.V. Dicey, *Introduction to the Study of the Law of the Constitution*, 10th ed. (London: Macmillan & Co. 1964), 329. The first edition was published in 1885, the second in 1886, and a third in 1889.

17 See H.W. Arthurs, 'Rethinking Administrative Law: A Slightly Dicey Business' (1979), 17 *Osgoode Hall Law Journal* 1–45.

18 The specific wording of the provisions dealing with jurisdiction was as follows:

> **15.** The Exchequer Court shall have exclusive original jurisdiction in all cases in which demand is made or relief sought in respect of any matter which might in England, be the subject of a suit or action against the Crown, and for greater certainty, but not so as to restrict the generality of the foregoing terms, it shall have exclusive original jurisdiction in all cases in which the land, goods or money of the subject are in the possession of the Crown, or in which the claim arises out of a contract entered into by or on behalf of the Crown.

16. The Exchequer Court shall also have exclusive original. jurisdiction to hear and determine the following matters: –

(a) Every claim against the Crown for property taken for any public purpose;

(b) Every claim against the Crown for damage to property, injuriously affected by the construction of any public work;

(c) Every claim against the Crown arising out of any death or injury to the person or to property on any public work, resulting from the negligence of any officer or servant of the Crown, while acting within the scope of his duties or employment;

(d) Every claim against the Crown arising under any law of Canada or any regulation made by the Governor in Council;

(e) Every set off, counter claim, claim for damages, whether liquidated or unliquidated, or other demand whatsoever, on the part of the Crown, against any person making claim against the Crown.

17. The Exchequer Court shall have and possess concurrent original jurisdiction in Canada, –

(a) in all cases relating to the revenue, in which it is sought to enforce any law of Canada, including actions, suits, and proceedings, by way of information, to enforce penalties and proceedings by way of information *in rem*, and as well in *qui tam* suits for penalties or forfeitures as where the suit is on behalf of the Crown alone;

(b) In all cases in which it is sought at the instance of the Attorney General of Canada, to impeach or annul any patent of invention, or any patent, lease, or other instrument respecting lands;

(c) In all cases in which demand is made or relief sought against any officer of the Crown for anything done or omitted to be done in the performance of his duty as such officer;

(d) In all other actions and suits of a civil nature at common law or equity in which the Crown is plaintiff or petitioner.

19 See Audette, supra note 1, 74.
20 *The Queen v. McLeod* (1883), 8 SCR 1. See supra, chapter 5. The reference to an action in the Court of Exchequer in England in the original statute was replaced by a reference simply to an action in England, thereby eliminating the words which had the potential (albeit extremely remote) of bringing the tort

liability jurisdiction into existence. See *Pawlett v. Attorney General* (1667), Hardres 465, 145 ER 550; W.S. Holdsworth, 'The History of Remedies against the Crown' (1922), *Law Quarterly Review* 141–64, 280–96.

21 SC 1887, c. 16, s. 16(c).

22 Ibid., s. 23.

23 Section 23. By Order in Council of October 15, 1887, all references by the head of a department were to be made through the minister of justice: Audette, supra note 1, 91.

24 *Carter, Macy & Co. v. The Queen* (1890), 2 Ex. CR 126, aff'd (1890) 18 SCR 706n. See Audette, supra note 1, 115.

25 Section 51.

26 An Act to amend 'The Exchequer Court Act,' SC 1890, c. 35. The case was heard in the Supreme Court on March 21, 1890, and the legislation was introduced on March 28; assent was given on May 16, 1890.

27 The Supreme and Exchequer Court Act, SC 1875, c. 11, s. 52.

28 House of Commons, *Debates*, 1875, 286.

29 See J.F. Davison, 'The Constitutionality and Utility of Advisory Opinions' (1937–38), 2 *University of Toronto Law Journal* 254–79 at 258–60.

30 An Act to amend Chapter 135 of the revised Statutes intituled 'An Act respecting the Supreme and Exchequer Courts,' SC 1891, c. 25, s. 4. The amendment also provided for taking evidence in the reference cases, if needed.

31 House of Commons, *Debates*, 1908, 4837, 4842 (Sir A.B. Aylesworth).

32 Moffatt Hancock, 'Book Review: *Handbook of Admiralty Law in the United States*' (1941–42), 4 *University of Toronto Law Journal* 204–6 at 204. Hancock referred to Admiralty Law as an 'obscure and difficult topic.' P.D. Lowry, 'Book Review: *Federal Court Practice – 1988*' (1989), 47 *The Advocate* 128.

33 There are numerous accounts of the jurisdiction of the Court of Admiralty. The information that follows is drawn from Alfred A. Stockton, *Reports of the Cases Decided in the Vice-Admiralty Court of New Brunswick from 1879 to 1891* (St John, N.B.: J. & A. McMillan 1894), Introduction, xxxv–lxxv; Sir William Holdsworth, *A History of English Law*, 3d ed. (London: Methuen & Co./Sweet and Maxwell 1944: reprinted 1966), 1:548–68; *Benedict on Admiralty*, 7th ed. rev., (New York: Matthew Bender, 1974), vol. 1, chapters 1–5; F.L. Wiswall Jr, *The Development of Admiralty Jurisdiction and Practice Since 1800* (Cambridge: Cambridge University Press 1970).

34 1389 (Eng.), 13 Rich. II, c. 5: only something done upon the sea; 1391 (Eng.), 15 Rich. II, c. 3: not matters of contract or wreck.

35 Thomas Madox, *The History and Antiquities of the Exchequer of the Kings of England* (1769; reprinted New York, A.M. Kelley 1969), 82.

36 Added to the notion of universality was the idea of timelessness, which

increased the mystique surrounding admiralty law. The laws of the sea were traced back to the ancient laws of the Island of Rhodes at the eastern end of the Aegean Sea, centuries before the rise of Rome, which had found their way into the laws of the Roman Empire and later appeared in various medieval codes of law. The laws of the Island of Oleron, off the Atlantic coast of France, were of particular interest because they had been adopted by Richard I in the twelfth century for use in England. See Stockton, note 33.

37 Holdsworth, supra, note 33 at 553.

38 *Bottomry* is the name of a contract in the form of a bond by which money is borrowed using the ship or cargo as a pledge in order to allow a voyage to be completed, for example, when money for repair is needed. *Respondentia* is the term applied when the cargo alone is pledged. There is no change of possession and hence such a pledge is not known in the common law; these contracts originated in the civil law. If the ship is lost on the voyage the lender loses the money, while, if the voyage is completed, the lender recovers the loan with interest: Edward C. Mayers, *Admiralty Law and Practice in Canada* (Toronto: Carswell Co. 1916), 72.

39 While exercising jurisdiction over matters of prize, the Admiralty Court was called the Prize Court; when exercising its jurisdiction over other matters, it was called the Instance Court.

40 The Admiralty Court Act (UK), 3 & 4 Vict., c. 65; The Admiralty Court Act, 1861 (UK), 24 & 25 Vict., c. 10.

41 The Admiralty Court Act (UK), 3 & 4 Vict. c. 65, s. 23.

42 The Admiralty Court Act, 1861 (UK), 24 & 25 Vict., c. 10, s. 14.

43 The Supreme Court of Judicature Act, 1873 (UK), 36 & 37 Vict., c. 66

44 Joseph Henry Smith, *Appeals to the Privy Council from the American Plantations* (New York: Octagon Books 1965), 88–93. See Arthur J. Stone, 'The Admiralty Court in Colonial Nova Scotia' (1994), 17 *Dalhousie Law Journal* 363–429, for a highly informative article about the institutional aspects of the Vice-Admiralty Court in Nova Scotia and its judges. The article also contains useful information about the developments between Confederation and the enactment of the Canadian legislation of 1891. Arthur Stone is a judge of the Federal Court of Appeal.

45 Alfred Howell, *Admiralty Law, Canada* (Toronto: Carswell 1893), xv.

46 Vice-Admiralty Courts Act, 1863 (UK), 26 Vict., c. 24, and an amendment act passed in 1867, 30 & 31 Vict., c. 45.

47 Stockton, supra note 33, lxvi.

48 Canada did undertake to pay the salaries of the Vice-Admiral judges: The British North America Act, 1867 (UK), 30 & 31 Vict., c. 3, s. 100.

49 Sir Joseph Pope, *Correspondence of Sir John Macdonald* (Toronto: Oxford University Press 1921), 81–2, letter from S.H. Strong to John A. Macdonald, December 30, 1868.

50 This was defined as 'all oceans, seas, bays, channels, rivers, creeks and waters below low-water mark where great ships do generally go': E.C. Mayers, *Admiralty Law and Practice* (Toronto: Carswell 1916), 38.

51 The maritime lien was a claim on maritime property for service done to it or injury caused by it (Mayers, supra note 50, p. 55). It arose by operation of law and became a charge upon the property, taking priority over other claims. The property could be the ship and its contents, the cargo, or the proceeds of their sale. Maritime liens arose for bottomry and *respondentia* bonds, seaman's wages, wages, disbursements, and liabilities of the master, damage, salvage, life salvage, fees and expenses of a receiver or wreck, and damage sustained by the owner or occupier of lands used to facilitate the rendering of assistance to a wreck (Mayers, supra note 50, p. 25). The lien attached to the property and stayed with it even though the ownership might change. Such a lien was unique to admiralty law. The benefit of the lien would be realized in a proceeding *in rem*, which was also unique to admiralty law. In instances when a maritime lien would not be created, such as for the supply of necessaries, the party seeking compensation could still bring an action *in rem* in its own right. The ship itself (the *res*) could be arrested for any claim and dealt with accordingly.

52 See (1869), 5 *Canada Law Journal* 143 at 148 (section 58).

53 Stone, supra note 44, 418 note 225.

54 SC 1877, c. 21. The title was changed to The Maritime Court Act in the revised statutes of 1886: RSC 1886, c. 137, s. 1.

55 Ibid., ss. 1, 2.

56 Stone, supra note 44 at 419.

57 House of Commons, *Debates*, 1882, 1541.

58 Mills suggested the military and naval defence power as the constitutional basis for the legislation.

59 The only reference to the matter that I found in subsequent years was a statement in 1884 in the House of Commons that no answer had been received: House of Commons, *Debates*, 1884, 965 (Sir John A. Macdonald).

60 See Stone, supra note 44 at 420–5.

61 Ibid., 422.

62 See supra, chapter 5.

63 1890 (UK), 53 & 54 Vict., c. 27, assented to on July 25, 1890.

64 Stone, supra note 44 at 422.

65 Section 16(1).

66 House of Commons, *Debates*, 1891, 142 (John Thompson).

67 The British North America Act, 1867 (UK), 30 & 31 Vict., c. 3.

68 House of Commons, *Debates*, 1891, 1416 (Louis Davies, P.E.I.), 1419 (David Mills, Ontario); Senate, *Debates*, 1891, 229 (Power).

69 House of Commons, *Debates*, 1891, 1416 (Louis Davies, P.E.I.).

70 Ibid., 1419, 1424 (David Mills, Ontario).

71 Ibid., 1418 (John Thompson).

72 Ibid., 1419.

73 Ibid., 1732.

74 Senate, *Debates*, 1891, 231 (Lawrence Power, Liberal).

75 House of Commons, *Debates*, 1891, 1432 (Louis Davies, P.E.I.).

76 Under section 6 of the Colonial Court of Admiralty Act, 1890 (UK), 53–54 Vict., c. 27, an appeal as of right existed from a judgment of the Supreme Court on an appeal on an admiralty matter to the Judicial Committee of the Privy Council. Other appeals required the granting of leave to appeal. As the Court of Admiralty for Canada the Exchequer Court would also be designated in times of war as the Prize Court. See 6 *Exchequer Court Reports* 469–73, for the Imperial despatch and warrant to the Judge of the Exchequer Court of 1899.

77 The Exchequer Court Amendment Act, 1891, SC 1891, c. 26, s. 4:

The Exchequer Court shall have jurisdiction, as well between subject and subject as otherwise, –

(a) In all cases of conflicting applications for any patent or invention, or for the registration of any copyright, trade mark or industrial design;

(b) In all cases in which it is sought to impeach or annul any patent of invention, or to have any entry in any register of copyrights, trade marks or industrial designs made, expunged, varied or rectified;

(c) In all other cases in which a remedy is sought respecting the infringement of any patent of invention, copyright, trade mark or industrial design.

78 British North America Act, 1867 (UK), 30 & 31 Vict., c. 3, s. 91(22).

79 The Patent Act of 1869, SC 1869, c. 11; The Patent Act of 1872, SC 1872, c. 26.

80 See Harold G. Fox, *The Canadian Law and Practice relating to Letters Patent for Inventions*, 4th ed. (Toronto: Carswell 1969), 5–7, for a very brief historical discussion.

81 An Act to amend 'The Supreme and Exchequer Courts Act,' SC 1887, c. 16, s. 17(b).

82 An Act to amend 'The Patent Act,' SC 1890, c. 13, s. 1. The question of giving the court jurisdiction over patents had been raised in the House of Commons

debate in 1887 when the new Exchequer Court was being created. The government stated that the matter had been considered, but it wanted first to let the new court get on its feet: House of Commons, *Debates*, 1887, 880 (John Thompson).

83 The conditions were that the patented invention had to be constructed or manufactured within two years of the date of issue of the patent, and that the invention had not, after a year had passed following the issue of the patent, been imported into Canada: SC 1890, c.13, s. 2 (s. 37 repealed and substituted).

84 See Harold G. Fox, *The Canadian Law of Trade Marks and Unfair Competition*, 2nd ed. (Toronto: Carswell 1956), Chapter 1, 'Historical Introduction,' 1–29.

85 The Trade Mark and Design Act of 1868, SC 1868, c. 55.

86 The Trade Mark and Design Act of 1879, SC 1879, c. 22, s. 15.

87 An Act to amend the Act respecting Trade Marks and Industrial Designs, SC 1890, c. 14.

88 An Act further to amend the Act respecting Trade Marks and Industrial Designs, SC 1891, c. 35. The jurisdiction conferred by this statute was confirmed by the amendment to the Exchequer Court Act: The Exchequer Court Amendment Act, *1891*, SC 1891, c. 26, s. 4.

89 An Act to amend the law of copyright, 1842 (UK), 5–6 Vict., c. 45.

90 The Canada Copyright Act, 1875 (UK), 38–39 Vict., c. 53. The Canadian statute, The Copyright Act, SC 1875, c. 88, appeared in SC 1876, at page xvii.

91 An Act to amend 'The Copyright Act,' SC 1890, c. 12; An Act to amend the Copyright Act, SC 1891, c. 34.

CHAPTER NINE

1 *Toronto Railway Co. v. The Queen* (1894), 4 Ex. CR 262 at 270. The conclusion reached by Burbidge in the case was affirmed by a 3-2 majority in the Supreme Court, (1895), 25 SCR 24, but that decision was ultimately reversed by the Privy Council, [1896] AC 551. Formalists called this approach to the interpretation of statutes the rule in *Heydon's case* (from an early description of the approach in this sixteenth-century case (1584), 3 Coke 7a, 76 ER 637). However, although given a name by formalists, it is rarely even mentioned by them, since it runs counter to the requirements of the model. Contextualists feel no need to identify the approach as a rule; rather, as with Burbidge, they see it as simply the proper form of analysis.

2 *Hall v. The Queen* (1893), 3 Ex. CR 373. Richards' decision was *Wood v. The Queen* (1877), 7 SCR 634, which is discussed supra, chapter 5.

3 *Hall v. The Queen* (1893), 3 Ex. CR 373 at 376.

4 *The Queen v. Henderson* (1898), 28 SCR 425. Burbidge at the trial had naturally

continued to follow his own previous decision, which had been based on Richards' work: *Henderson v. The Queen* (1897), 6 Ex. CR 39.

5 *The Queen v. McLeod* (1883), 8 SCR 1. See supra, chapter 5.

6 See *Larose v. The Queen* (1900), 6 Ex. CR 425; *Paul v. The King* (1904), 9 Ex. CR 245.

7 An Act to amend 'The Supreme and Exchequer Courts Act,' and to make better provision for the Trial of Claims against the Crown, SC 1887, c. 16, s. 16(c), later, Exchequer Court Act, RSC 1906, c. 140, s. 20(c).

8 *Larose v. The Queen* (1900), 6 Ex. CR 425; aff'd (1901), 31 SCR 206. While the Supreme Court was happy with the decision reached by Burbidge, the government did recognize changing values; under legislation enacted in 1904 the government would 'be liable to make compensation for the death of any person, or for any injury to the person ... arising from the use of any ... rifle range under the control of the Department of Militia': The Militia Act, SC 1904, c. 23, s. 59.

9 *Chamberlin v. The King* (1909), 42 SCR 350.

10 *Letourneux v. The Queen* (1900), 7 Ex. CR 1; rev'd, *Letourneux v. The King* (1903), 33 SCR 335 on the issue of jurisdiction, without comment on the issue of the meaning of the words 'on a public work.'

11 *Paul v. The King* (1904), 9 Ex. CR 245; *Price v. The King* (1906), 10 Ex. CR 105.

12 *Chamberlin v. The King* (1909), 42 SCR 350. The trial in the Exchequer Court had been conducted by Judge Burbidge, but he had died before hearing argument. The case was argued before Judge Cassels, who succeeded Burbidge as the judge of the Exchequer Court.

13 Ibid., 354.

14 Supra, chapter 7.

15 (1887), 12 App. Cas. 643. The judgment of the Privy Council was rendered on July 23, 1887, a month after the new Exchequer Court of Canada came into being as a court of claims against the government. By coincidence the hearing in the *Farnell* case was conducted on June 23, 1887, the day the Exchequer Court Act received Royal Assent.

16 Ibid., 649.

17 Ibid., 648.

18 *Leprohon v. The Queen* (1894), 4 Ex. CR 100 at 111.

19 It appeared briefly in a 1934 decision by the then judge of the Court, A.K Maclean: *Dubois v. The King*, [1934] Ex. CR 195 at 211. Much more will be said about this case in chapter 11, infra.

20 *McArthur v. The King*, [1943] Ex. CR 77 at 102.

21 *The Queen v. Martin* (1892), 20 SCR 240, rev'g *Martin v. The Queen* (1891), 1 Ex. CR 328.

22 SC 1881, c. 25.

23 Ibid., s. 27(3).

24 Patterson, *The Queen v. Martin* (1892), 20 SCR 240 at 257; Louis Arthur Audette, *The Practice of the Exchequer Court of Canada* (Ottawa: Thorburn & Co. 1895), 78.
25 See *The Queen v. Filion* (1895), 24 SCR 482 at 483 (per Henri-Elzéar Taschereau).
26 *Lavoie v. The Queen* (1892), 3 Ex. CR 96 at 100, 101.
27 *The Hamburg American Packet Co. v. The King* (1901), 7 Ex. CR 119 at 155.
28 *City of Quebec v. The Queen* (1894), 24 SCR 420.
29 *Paul v. The King* (1906), 38 SCR 126 at 135.
30 *Chamberlin v. The King* (1909), 42 SCR 350.
31 *Armstrong v. The King* (1907), 11 Ex. CR 119 at 122. On appeal to the Supreme Court of Canada, Burbidge's opinion of the law was adopted: *The King v. Armstrong* (1908), 40 SCR 229.
32 (1894), 24 SCR 420 at 429, quoted in *Armstrong v. The King* (1907), 11 Ex. CR 119 at 124.
33 House of Commons, *Debates*, 1904, 4000.
34 See supra, chapter 6.
35 *In re Representation in the House of Commons* (1903), 33 SCR 475 at 592–3.
36 (1902), 38 *Canada Law Journal* 697.
37 See Ian Bushnell, *The Captive Court: A Study of the Supreme Court of Canada* (Montreal & Kingston: McGill–Queen's University Press 1992), 169ff.
38 See Bushnell, *Captive Court*, supra note 37 at 165–6; House of Commons, *Debates*, 1903, 2351–73.
39 House of Commons, *Debates*, 1907–8, 4839; Constitution Act, 1867, s. 92 (14).
40 The docket book is unfortunately incomplete for the period before 1887, but, although a firm conclusion is not possible, it seems fairly clear that the Quebec judges, J.-T. Taschereau, Fournier, and Henri-Elzéar Taschereau, heard the cases from Quebec.
41 C.M., 'The Late Mr. Justice Burbidge' (1908), 28 *Canadian Law Times* 222–3.
42 *Attorney General of British Columbia v. Attorney General of Canada* (1886), 14 SCR 345 at 346–7. This case involved the constitutional issue of the ownership of the precious metals in the railway belt in British Columbia. The province had conveyed to the Dominion government public land along the railway in order to facilitate the construction of the railway. The case made its way to the Privy Council, which held in favour of the province: *Attorney-General of British Columbia v. Attorney-General of Canada* (1889), 14 App. Cas. 295.
43 See (1908), 11 Ex. CR at 252, 254, 256, 258, 261, 263, 267, 269, 271.
44 (1908), 44 *Canada Law Journal* 141.
45 C.M., supra note 41 at 222–3.

CHAPTER TEN

1 House of Commons, *Debates*, 1901, 3178.

2 Senate, *Debates*, 1908, 845.

3 An Act to amend the Exchequer Court Act, SC 1908, c. 27. There was also a provision to deal with the problem that had arisen when Sir Thomas Taylor was appointed as a substitute for Burbidge; Taylor's authority to act lapsed on Burbidge's death. There were cases for which judgment had not been rendered, and this legislation gave validity to these judgments and allowed him to complete his outstanding work: section 1, adding section 8(4).

4 An Act to amend the Supreme and Exchequer Courts Act, SC 1905, c. 47. The 1905 provision subsequently appeared in the *Judges Act*, RSC 1906, c. 138, s. 33, where it was made applicable to all federally appointed judges.

5 'The Independence of the Bench and Extra Judicial Duties' (1910), 46 *Canada Law Journal* 473–6; 'Judges Engaged in Other than Judicial Duties' (1910), 46 *Canada Law Journal* 523–4; 'Judges and Royal Commissions' (1911), 47 *Canada Law Journal* 92–3.

6 House of Commons, *Debates*, 1908, 8506, 8508.

7 'The Exchequer Court and Royal Commissions' (1908), 44 *Canada Law Journal* 289–92.

8 An Act to amend the Exchequer Court Act, SC 1912, c. 21.

9 Charles Morse, who had been appointed law reporter in 1891, was made the new registrar.

10 House of Commons, *Debates*, 1876, 794. A quorum of the Supreme Court is five judges, with the possiblility of four in certain situations.

11 (1882), 5 *Legal News* 105; (1896), 16 *Canadian Law Times* 246.

12 See David Ricardo Williams, *Duff: A Life in the Law* (Vancouver: University of British Columbia Press 1984), 90–4.

13 House of Commons, *Debates*, 1918, 240. From its inception in 1876, the Supreme Court had sat with a full bench of six judges and 3–3 splits had been accepted, so it seems probable that the concern in 1918 was more the size of the bench than the possibility of an even split.

14 An Act to amend the Supreme Court Act, SC 1918, c. 7, s. 1, adding section 31A.

15 See House of Commons, *Debates*, 1918, 241.

16 House of Commons, *Debates*, 1918, 531, 533.

17 See House of Commons, *Debates*, 1918, 523, 531.

18 The Supreme Court Act, RSC 1927, c. 35, s. 30.

19 See House of Commons, *Debates*, 1918, 241 (Rodolphe Lemieux, Liberal, Quebec), and 1919, 4437 (Andrew McMaster, Liberal, Quebec), 1920, 2201 (Hyacinthe-Adelard Fortier, Liberal, Quebec).

20 House of Commons, *Debates*, 1919, 4437.

21 An Act to amend the Exchequer Court Act, SC 1920, c. 26, s. 2.

22 An Act to amend the Judges Act, SC 1919, c. 59.

23 An Act to amend the Judges Act, SC 1920, c. 56.

24 House of Commons, *Debates*, 1919, 4217.

25 *Chamberlin v. The King* (1909), 42 SCR 350.

26 An Act to amend the Government Railways Act, SC 1908, c. 31.

27 An Act to amend the Exchequer Court Act, SC 1910, c. 19.

28 Senate, *Debates*, 1909–10, 157.

29 House of Commons, *Debates*, 1909, 6751–2.

30 House of Commons, *Debates*, 1917, 1422.

31 (1916), 53 SCR 626, affirming a decision by Cassels in the Exchequer Court that was unreported.

32 Ibid., 630.

33 Ibid., 631.

34 Ibid., 632.

35 SC 1917, c. 23, s. 2. While the wording differed from that proposed by Lapointe, the new law was identical in substance.

36 House of Commons, *Debates*, 1917, 2568, 3631.

37 *Wolfe Co. v. The King* (1921), 20 Ex. CR 306. The decision was affirmed by the Supreme Court: (1921), 63 SCR 141.

38 *Conrod v. The King* (1913), 14 Ex. CR 472.

39 *Coleman v. The King*, (1918), 18 Ex. CR 263.

40 *Thompson v. The King* (1921), 20 Ex. CR 467; *Alderson v. The King* (1922), 21 Ex. CR 359.

41 The first ad hoc judge to sit was Joseph Lavergne of the Quebec Court of King's Bench, in *Power v. The King* (1918), 56 SCR 499. The only article ever written on the topic was by Reynald Boult, Librarian of the Supreme Court of Canada: 'Ad Hoc Judges of The Supreme Court of Canada' (1978), 26 *Chitty's Law Journal* 289–95.

42 Bill 151, 1909. See House of Commons, *Debates*, 1909, 4695–6, 6744–56; Senate, *Debates*, 1909, 626, 639–50, 653–4, 671–2.

43 Senate, *Debates*, 1909, 639 (Power), 642 (Ross), 647 (Dandurand).

44 Mr Justice Mignault, 'Sir Walter Cassels' (1923), 1 *Canadian Bar Review* 210–13; Sir William Ralph Meredith, 'An Appreciation: Sir Walter Gibson Pringle Cassels' (1923), 1 *Canadian Bar Review* 297–8.

CHAPTER ELEVEN

1 See House of Commons, *Debates*, 1919, 3783, in which the speaker assumes that the judge's replacement will also be a Protestant. Maclean was a Presbyterian, and Burbidge and Cassels had both been Anglicans.

2 An Act to amend the Exchequer Court Act, SC 1927, c. 30.

3 An Act to amend the Exchequer Court Act, SC 1908, c. 27, s. 2.

4 Mr Justice Thibaudeau Rinfret in *The King v. Krakowec*, infra, note 15 and accompanying text.

5 [1924] Ex. CR 167, aff'd [1925] SCR 434.

6 SC 1912, c. 27.

7 Section 95(7), added by SC 1919, c. 40.

8 [1925] SCR 434 at 456.

9 Mr Justice Idington in the Supreme Court agreed with Maclean's analysis, while Mr Justice Rinfret concurred with Mr Justice Duff. Chief Justice Anglin rendered a dissenting judgment.

10 Alexander Smith, *The Commerce Power in Canada and the United States* (Toronto: Butterworths & Co. 1963), 127.

11 David Ricardo Williams, *Duff: A Life in the Law* (Vancouver: University of British Columbia Press 1984), 274, 275.

12 [1931] Ex. CR 137.

13 *Excise Act*, RSC 1927, c. 60, s. 181.

14 Supra, note 12, at 142.

15 *The King v. Krakowec* (1931), [1932] SCR 134 at 142.

16 Ibid., 143.

17 *The King v. National Fish Co. Ltd.*, [1931] Ex. CR 75.

18 *Smith v. Attorney General of Canada*, [1924] Ex. CR 193; rev'd, *Smith v. Minister of Finance*, [1925] SCR 405; rev'd, *Minister of Finance v. Smith* (1926), [1927] AC 193.

19 *Minister of Finance v. Smith*, [1927] AC 193 at 198.

20 *Re Indian Reserve, Sydney, Cape Breton* (1916), 17 Ex. CR 517 at 521.

21 Together they sat for 100 of the 207 sittings.

22 *Bayer Co. Ltd. v. American Druggists Syndicate Ltd.*, [1924] SCR 558, rev'g *American Druggists Syndicate Ltd. v. Bayer Co. Ltd.*, [1923] Ex. CR 65.

23 See Ian Bushnell, *The Captive Court: A Study of the Supreme Court of Canada* (Montreal & Kingston: McGill-Queen's University Press 1992), 211–14.

24 *In re Board of Commerce Act and Combines and Fair Prices Act, 1919* (1920), 60 SCR 456.

25 Ibid., 487, 489.

26 Ibid., 512–13.

27 [1922] 1 AC 191.

28 Senate, *Debates*, 1920, 848.

29 Gordon Hewart (Baron), *The New Despotism* (London: E. Benn 1929).

30 'The Crown as Litigant: Report of the Committee on Comparative Provincial Legislation and Law Reform' (1936), 14 *Canadian Bar Review* 606–14.

31 Ibid., 613. Section 6 of the draft bill provided that 'This Act shall not be deemed to authorize or sanction the bringing or institution of any proceedings or actions against the Crown except in the courts of the Province.'

32 E.M. Hall, 'Extension of Civil Remedies against the Crown' (1938), 5 *Saskatchewan Bar Review* 51–6 at 53.

33 Ibid.

34 Sir Carleton Kemp Allen, *Law in the Making*, 1st ed. (Oxford: The Clarendon Press 1927), 331.

35 House of Commons, *Debates*, 1937, 2114.

36 [1925] Ex. CR 167.

37 *The King v. Schrobounst*, [1925] SCR 458.

38 C.M., 'Crown's Liability for Negligence of Its Servants: Case Comment' (1925), 3 *Canadian Bar Review* 333–4.

39 *Joubert v. The King*, [1931] Ex. CR 113 at 116, 117.

40 Supra, note 37 at 459.

41 [1934] Ex. CR 195.

42 *The King v. Mason*, [1933] SCR 332 at 334–5.

43 *Wolfe Co. v. The King*(1921), 63 SCR 141.

44 Supra note 41 at 200.

45 Ibid., 201.

46 Rinfret agreed that the appeal should be allowed, but did not render any reasons.

47 *The King v. Dubois*, [1935] SCR 378.

48 Ibid., 381.

49 Ibid.

50 Ibid., 394.

51 *Jokela v. The King*, [1937] Ex. CR 132 at 133.

52 *Salmo Investments Ltd. v. The King*, [1939] Ex. CR 228.

53 Ibid., 232.

54 Ibid., 234.

55 See *Hochelaga Shipping and Towing Co. Ltd. v. The King*, [1940] Ex. CR 199, and *Yukon Southern Air Transport Ltd. and Phoenix Assurance Co. Ltd. v. The King* (1941), [1942] Ex. CR 181.

56 *Toman v. The King*, [1934] Ex. CR 161 (French), trans. [1935] 2 DLR 289.

57 Ibid., [1934] Ex. CR 161 at 181, [1935] 2 DLR 289 at 307.

58 *The King v. Dubois*, [1935] SCR 378 at 381.

59 It is obvious that there was support for their position within the profession. See H.W. Riley, 'Case Comment' (1934–35), 1 *Alberta Law Quarterly* 210–18.

60 Moffatt Hancock, 'Case Comment' (1935), 13 *Canadian Bar Review* 602–4 at 602.

61 *The King v. Cliche*, [1935] SCR 561. See F.R. Scott, 'Case Comment' (1936), 14 *Canadian Bar Review* 252–7.

62 House of Commons, *Debates*, 1936, 3000–5, 3105–16 (Charles Cahan, Conservative, Quebec).

63 An Act to amend the Exchequer Court Act, SC 1938, c. 28.
64 House of Commons, *Debates*, 1938, 3359 (Ernest Lapointe, Minister of Justice).
65 SC 1934, c. 31.
66 (UK), 22–23 Geo. V, c. 4.
67 Colonial Courts of Admiralty Act, 1890 (Imp.), 53–54 Vict., c. 27, s. 2(2).
68 *SS Woron v. Canadian American Shipping Co. Ltd.* (1926), [1927] Ex. CR 1 at 12 (Ex. Ct., British Columbia Admiralty District).
69 Edward C. Mayers, *Admiralty Law and Practice in Canada* (Toronto: Carswell Co. 1916), 4–5. This book had been dedicated to Martin himself.
70 *SS Woron v. Canadian American Shipping Co. Ltd.* (1926), [1927] Ex. CR 1.
71 Colonial Laws Validity Act (Imp.), 28–29 Vict. (1865), c. 63, s. 1.
72 *The Woron*, [1927] AC 906.
73 The Admiralty Act, 1934, SC 1934, c. 31.
74 House of Commons, *Debates*, 1934, 3625–7.
75 An Act to amend the Admiralty Act, 1934, SC 1935, c. 35.
76 House of Commons, *Debates*, 1935, 3447, 3694. There is one reported decision of an appeal heard by both Maclean and Angers, *Robin Hood Mills Ltd. v. Paterson Steamships Ltd.*, [1935] Ex. CR 207. The appeal was from a decision rendered by Demers L.J.A. of the Quebec District and was heard on May 1, 1935. The judgment of the court, dismissing the appeal, was rendered by Maclean on July 17, 1935.
77 *Canadian National Railway Co. v. Lewis*, [1930] Ex. CR 145 at 150. The italics are in the original.
78 *Canadian National Railway Co. v. Boland*, [1925] Ex. CR 173.
79 *Reference re Railway Act and Expropriation Act; Canadian National Railway Co. v. Boland* (1925), [1926] SCR 239.
80 A. Brady, 'The State and Economic Life in Canada' (1933), 3 *University of Toronto Quarterly* 422–41.
81 Bill No. 26, 1933. See House of Commons, *Debates*, 1933, 2121, 2202ff.
82 House of Commons, *Debates*, 1924, 3337.

CHAPTER TWELVE

1 An Act to amend the Exchequer Court Act, SC 1944–45, c. 3.
2 An Act to amend the Exchequer Court Act, SC 1946, c. 22.
3 House of Commons, *Debates*, 1946, 3178 (L.S. St Laurent).
4 (1946–47), 16 *Fortnightly Law Journal* 75.
5 Cameron sat on several cases as a deputy judge in 1945, the year before his appointment to the court.
6 An Act to amend the Railway Act, the Exchequer Court Act and The Judges Act, 1946, SC 1947–48, c. 66.

7 House of Commons, *Debates, 1947–48,* 4888–9, 5151, 5222–36, 5294–301; Senate, *Debates, 1947–48,* 601–3.

8 See Carl Vincent, *No Reason Why: The Canadian Hong Kong Tragedy – An Examination* (Stittsville, Ont.: Canada's Wings 1981).

9 House of Commons, *Debates,* 1947–48, 5297.

10 House of Commons, *Debates,* 1880, 262. For the 1880 debate, see the end of chapter 6.

11 An Act to amend the Railway Act, SC 1951 (2nd Sess.), c. 22.

12 An Act to amend the Judges Act and the Exchequer Court Act, SC 1960, c. 38.

13 An Act to amend the National Defence Act, SC 1959, c. 5.

14 The National Defence Act, SC 1950, c. 43, s. 190.

15 Only one of the other members of the Court Martial Appeal Board was a judge, A.G. McDougall, County Court judge for the County of Carleton. The others were lawyers. Two were of special interest: L.C. Audette, son of Louis Arthur Audette, and George Addy, an Ottawa lawyer with considerable military experience, who would join the Federal Court of Canada in 1973. There were ten members in all.

16 The bill introduced in the legislature had included a provision allowing for the appointment of military advisers, who were to act in the same manner as assessors in admiralty cases. The Senate removed the provision, since it felt that the judges would be able to appreciate the evidence without help and, if help were actually needed, it could be supplied by the use of expert witnesses.

17 An Act to amend the Exchequer Court Act, SC 1920, c. 26, s. 2.

18 There were six sittings in Quebec, and two at Ottawa.

19 *In re Storgoff,* [1945] SCR 526.

20 *City of Saskatoon v. Shaw* (1944), [1945] SCR 42.

21 House of Commons, *Debates,* 1944, 1845.

22 *McArthur v. The King,* [1943] Ex. CR 77.

23 House of Commons, *Debates,* 1943, 3367.

24 An Act to amend the Exchequer Court Act, SC 1943–44, c. 25.

25 See House of Commons, *Debates,* 1943, 4912*ff.*

26 *Beauchemin v. The King* (1946), [1947] Ex. CR 102.

27 *Burton v. The Queen,* [1954] Ex. CR 715.

28 *Darowany v. The Queen,* [1956] Ex. CR 340.

29 *Harris v. The Queen,* [1955] Ex. CR 75; *Meredith v. The Queen,* [1955] Ex. CR 156.

30 An Act to amend the Statute Law, SC 1950, c. 51.

31 An Act to amend the Petition of Right Act, SC 1951, c. 33.

32 Crown Proceedings Act, 1947 (UK), 10 & 11 Geo. VI, c. 44 (in force January 1, 1948), and the American Federal Tort Claims Act, ch. 753, Title IV, 60 Stat. 842

(1946). These changes received prominent coverage in the twenty-fifth anniversary issue of the *Canadian Bar Review* in 1948 (vol. 26).

33 SC 1952–53, c. 30.

34 O. Hood Phillips, *Constitutional and Administrative Law*, 4th ed. (London: Sweet & Maxwell 1967), 678. The first edition was published in 1952.

35 See Senate, *Debates*, 1951, 507–9, 512–21.

36 House of Commons, *Debates*, 1952–53, 3268.

37 See Senate, *Debates*, 1951, 516.

38 See chapter 7.

39 See Senate, *Debates*, 1951, 515, 517, 519; House of Commons, *Debates*, 1952–53, 3276.

40 See House of Commons, *Debates*, 1947–48, 5296–7.

41 S.I. Bushnell, 'Crown Privilege' (1973), 51 *Canadian Bar Review* 551–82.

42 House of Commons, *Debates*, 1951, 3484; Senate, *Debates*, 1951, 517, 521.

43 J.M. Evans, 'Developments in Administrative Law: The 1986–87 Term' (1988), 10 *Supreme Court Law Review* 1–59 at 56.

44 W.H. Kerr, 'Letter to the Editor' (1878), 1 *Legal News* 140; Sir William Mulock, 'Address of the Chief Justice of Ontario' (1934), 12 *Canadian Bar Review* 35–41 at 37.

45 *Rahey v. The Queen*, [1987] 1 SCR 588 at 645, per La Forest J.

46 [1947] Ex. CR 486.

47 See Ken Adachi, *The Enemy That Never Was* (Toronto: McClelland & Stewart 1991), 319–34.

48 [1964] Ex. CR 649.

49 SC 1968–69, c. 54.

50 (1974), [1975] 1 SCR 138.

51 For a detailed discussion of the *Thorson* case see Ian Bushnell, *The Captive Court: A Study of the Supreme Court of Canada* (Montreal & Kingston: McGill-Queen's University Press 1992), 395–9.

52 *Jones v. Attorney General of New Brunswick* (1974), [1975] 2 SCR 182.

53 *The King v. British Columbia Electric Railway Co.*, [1945] Ex. CR 82. This was a taxation case. Thorson's decision was reversed by the Supreme Court on its merits, [1946] SCR 235, and that decision was affirmed by the Privy Council, [1946] AC 527.

CHAPTER THIRTEEN

1 In 1958 the Progressive Conservatives won 208 of 265 seats, 78.5 per cent. The same party under Brian Mulroney won more seats in 1984, 211, but of the 282 seats available, this was only 74.8 per cent.

2 John G. Diefenbaker, *One Canada: Memoirs of the Right Honourable John G. Diefenbaker, vol. 2, The Years of Achievement, 1957–1962* (Toronto: Macmillan of Canada 1976), 52–5.
3 An Act to amend the Judges Act and the Exchequer Court Act, SC 1964–65, c. 14.
4 Senate, *Debates*, 1964, 527.
5 National Transportation Act, SC 1966–67, c. 69, s. 7.
6 *City of Fredericton v. The Queen* (1880), 3 SCR 505 at 561.
7 Constitution Act, 1867, s.92(12).
8 Ibid., s. 91(26).
9 See S. Ian Bushnell, 'Family Law and the Constitution' (1978), 1 *Canadian Journal of Family Law* 202–31 at 204–5.
10 Ibid., 212–13.
11 See House of Commons, *Debates*, 1919, 3783; 1942, 380–2; 1943, 110–13, 138.
12 House of Commons, *Debates*, 1919, 3784 (Jacques Bureau, Liberal, Quebec; William Nickle, Conservative, Ontario).
13 See Senate, *Debates*, 1942, 380 (Louis Athanase, Liberal, Quebec); 1943, 111 (Charles-Philippe Beaubien, Conservative, Quebec).
14 The grounds for divorce were those recognized in England as of July 15, 1870, and as subsequently amended by Canadian legislation such as The Divorce Act, SC 1925, c. 41, which gave a wife the right to divorce her husband for his adultery.
15 See Senate, *Debates*, 1956, 294–5; House of Commons, *Debates*, 1960, 6128.
16 House of Commons, *Debates*, 1960, 6126.
17 Dissolution and Annulment of Marriages Act, SC 1963, c. 10.
18 See Allison A.M. Walsh, 'Divorce by Resolution of the Senate' (1967), 13 *McGill Law Journal* 1–22, for a detailed discussion of the topic.
19 Senate, *Debates*, 1964, 562, 566.
20 House of Commons, *Debates*, 1967, 5014 (Pierre Trudeau, Minister of Justice).
21 Divorce Act, SC 1967–68, c. 24.
22 Ibid., s. 23. See also sections 2(e) and (f).
23 Ibid., s. 22. The Governor in Council could issue proclamations declaring the Superior Court of Quebec and the Supreme Court of Newfoundland to have jurisdiction, on the recommendations of their respective provincial governments.
24 House of Commons, *Debates*, 1967, 5015.
25 Supra note 21, s. 2(f), 17.
26 Supra note 21, s. 5(2)(b).
27 *Randolph v. The Queen* (1965), [1966] Ex. CR 157; rev'd, *The Queen v. Randolph*, [1966] SCR 260.

28 *Hopson v. The Queen* (1965), [1966] Ex. CR 608.

29 *Gamache v. Jones* (1967), [1968] 1 Ex. CR 345.

30 At the time, the relevant legislation was The Customs Act, RSC 1952, c. 58, s. 143; The Excise Act, RSC 1952, c. 99, s. 78; The Narcotic Control Act, SC 1960–61, c. 35, s. 10; The Food and Drugs Act, SC 1952–53, c. 38, s. 36, am. SC 1960–61, c. 37.

31 *In re Writs of Assistance*, [1965] 2 Ex. CR 646.

32 Ibid., 647.

33 Criminal Law Amendment Act, 1985, SC 1985, c. 19, s. 200.

34 *The Queen v. Sieben*, [1987] 1 SCR 295; *The Queen v. Hamill*, [1987] 1 SCR 301. The Charter prohibition is s. 8.

35 SC 1960, c. 44.

36 An Act to amend the Combines Investigation Act and the Criminal Code, SC 1960, c. 45.

37 See Ian Bushnell, *The Captive Court: A Study of the Supreme Court of Canada* (Montreal & Kingston: McGill-Queen's University Press 1992), chapter 23, 312–21, and 'Freedom of Expression – The First Step' (1977), 15 *Alberta Law Review* 93–121.

38 The result of the judges' interpretation was so pronounced that Mr Justice Brown of the British Columbia Supreme Court referred to 'the judicially emasculated *Canadian Bill of Rights*' in his judgment in *Re Regina v. Lapinsky* (1965), [1966] 3 CCC 97 at 100.

39 Elmer A. Driedger, 'The Enactment and Publication of Canadian Administrative Regulations' (1966), 19 *Administrative Law Review* 129–36 at 132. Driedger was deputy minister of justice from 1961 to 1965, succeeding Jackett in the position.

40 *The Queen v. Gonzales* (1962), 32 DLR (2d) 290 (BCCA) (per Davey J.A.); *Benning v. Attorney-General for Saskatchewan* (1963), 39 DLR (2d) 426 (Sask.). As a canon or rule of interpretation, the Bill of Rights would give way before the plain words of a statute. The Supreme Court of Canada rejected this approach in 1969 in *The Queen v. Drybones*, [1970] SCR 282, but the court then recoiled so strongly from the implications of what it had done in the *Drybones* case, when it had for the first time rendered a law inoperative, that the Bill was subsequently stripped of all significance legally.

41 *R. v. Goldstein* (1961), 34 WWR 236 (BC Mag. Ct.); *The Queen v. Jensen* (1962), 39 WWR 321 (BC Mag. Ct.). Some cases simply took the position that the Bill would be used for subsequent legislation only: *Bergeron v. La Société de Publication Merlin Ltée.* (1970), 14 CRNS 52 (Que.); *Magda v. The Queen* (1963), [1964] SCR 72; *The Queen v. Fulmer* (1960), 129 CCC 142 (Ont. Mag. Ct.). And when, in the first significant case to reach the Supreme Court, it was said that one

should look to the law prior to 1960 to give meaning to the language of the Bill, the same thing was accomplished: *Robertson and Rosetanni v. The Queen*, [1963] SCR 651; *The Queen v. Judges of the Provincial Court* (1970), 2 CCC (2d) 469 (Ont. CA).

42 *Attorney General of Canada v. Lavell; Isaac v. Bedard*, [1974] SCR 1349. The point was affirmed in *Miller and Cockriell v. The Queen* (1976), [1977] 2 SCR 680.

43 *Attorney-General of British Columbia v. McDonald* (1961), 131 CCC 126 (BC Co. Ct.); *Benning*, supra note 40; *The Queen v. Dick, Penner and Finnigan* (1964), [1965] 1 CCC 171 (Man. CA).

44 *R. v. Martin* (1961), 35 WWR 385 (Alta. SC, AD); *Attorney-General of British Columbia v. McDonald*, supra note 43; *Rebrin v. Bird*, [1961] SCR 376; *Louie Yuet Sun v. The Queen* (1960), [1961] SCR 70; *The Queen v. Jensen*, supra note 41; *The Queen v. Collins* (1962), 39 WWR 32 (Man. CA).

45 *Martin*, supra note 44.

46 *Gunn v. The Queen* (1965), [1966] Ex. CR 118 (Jackett).

47 (1965), [1966] Ex. CR 157.

48 Ibid., 162.

49 *Jones* v. *Gamache* (1968), [1969] SCR 119, Cartwright, Fauteux, Abbott, Martland, Judson, Ritchie, and Spence.

50 *The Queen v. Randolph*, [1966] SCR 260 at 265.

51 RSC 1952, c. 212, s. 40.

52 *Gamache v. Jones* (1967), [1968] 1 Ex. CR 345.

53 Canadian Bill of Rights, SC 1960, c. 44, s. 2(e).

54 Cartwright, Fauteux, Ritchie, Spence, and Pigeon.

55 *Bokor v. The Queen*, [1970] Ex. CR 842.

56 *In re Almaas*, [1968] 2 Ex. CR 391.

57 W.R. Jackett, 'Foundations of Canadian Law in History and Theory,' in Otto Lang, ed., *Contemporary Problems of Public Law in Canada* (Toronto: University of Toronto Press 1968), 3–30.

58 W.R. Jackett, 'Practice and Procedure in the Twentieth Century with Special Reference to the Exchequer Court,' Pitblado Lectures (Winnipeg: Law Society of Manitoba 1968), 67–82; and 'Practice and Procedure in the Exchequer Court' (1968), 11 *Canadian Bar Journal* 45–65.

59 See *The Queen v. Murray*, [1965] 2 Ex. CR 663; aff'd, [1967] SCR 262.

60 *Pouliot v. Minister of Transport* (1964), [1965] 1 Ex. CR 330.

61 In all there are seven judgments with appendices: (1) *The Queen v. Murray*, [1965] 2 Ex. CR 663, an action by the Crown for loss of services of a serviceman as a result of a motor vehicle accident. The issue was the applicability of provincial legislation in the case. There were two appendices: Appendix A contained a list of representative authorities concerning the prerogative and

statutory rules that the Crown was not bound by legislation unless the legislation was made applicable to it either expressly or by necessary implication, and that the Crown might, nevertheless, take advantage of such legislation. Appendix B began with the statement 'The principle that I have adopted for the decision of this case would achieve the result (although not by the same reasoning) by the Privy Council in the *Dominion Building Corporation* case.' The Privy Council case was discussed with respect to why it should not be considered a binding authority.

(2) *Union Carbide Canada Ltd. v. Trans-Canadian Feeds Ltd.* (1965), [1966] Ex. CR 884, a patent infringement case in which the specification in the patent is examined in an appendix.

(3) *Viking Food Products Ltd. v. MNR*, [1967] 2 Ex. CR 11, an income tax case. In an appendix, Jackett addressed an argument that counsel for the appellant had made in written submissions.

(4) *Koninklijke Nederlandsche Stoombootmaatschappil NV*, [1967] 2 Ex. CR 22, an application to strike out part of a petition of right arising as a result of a collision between two ships. In an appendix, Jackett dealt with the differences in terminology and practice between the courts of Quebec and the common law provinces. The discussion is about material facts and evidentiary facts and pleading.

(5) *Wilkinson Sword (Canada) Ltd. v. Juda* (1966), [1968] 2 Ex. CR 137, a trade mark infringement action. In an appendix, Jackett stated, 'I have, to the best of my ability, done justice to the arguments made to me in this case.' He went on to consider a provision in which 'distinctive' was defined.

(6) *Lagacé v. MNR*, [1968] 2 Ex. CR 98, an income tax case. In an appendix Jackett states, 'So that there may be no misunderstanding as to the view upon which I have acted in deciding this case, I should like to make it clear that, as I see it, there is a clear distinction in principle between ...,' and he went on to discuss the distinction.

(7) *National Capital Commission v. Marcus* (1968), [1969] 1 Ex. CR 327, an expropriation case. In the appendix Jackett set out the reasons of Roland Ritchie in a Supreme Court decision, saying 'I regard the reasoning in that case as being so analogous that I have set out the relevant portion of Mr. Justice Ritchie's reasons in an appendix to these reasons.'

62 Allison Walsh in *The Queen v. Scheer Ltd.* (1971), [1970] Ex. CR 956 at 972.
63 See House of Commons, *Debates*, 1969–70, 3371 (Gordon Blair, Liberal, Ontario).
64 House of Commons, *Debates*, 1967, 3796, 3798.

65 House of Commons, *Debates*, 1968–69, 835, 880.

66 Ibid., 1218, 1219.

67 Ibid., 1229.

68 Ibid., 1219.

69 Ibid., 1229.

70 Ibid., 2990.

71 House of Commons, *Debates*, 1969–70, 652–4, 3363–71; House of Commons, Standing Committee on Justice and Legal Affairs, 28th Parliament, 2nd Session (1969–70), *Minutes of Proceedings and Evidence*, nos. 2–5; House of Commons, *Debates*, 1970, 703.

72 House of Commons, Standing Committee on Justice and Legal Affairs, 28th Parliament, 2nd Session (1969–70), *Minutes of Proceedings and Evidence*, no. 2, 11 (Minister of Justice).

73 See House of Commons, *Debates*, 1969–70, 3370 (Minister of Justice).

74 House of Commons, Standing Committee on Justice and Legal Affairs, 28th Parliament, 2nd Session (1969–70), *Minutes of Proceedings and Evidence*, no. 2, 17, 19, 21.

75 *Attorney General of British Columbia v. Smith*, [1967] SCR 702.

76 House of Commons, *Debates*, 1969–70, 654.

77 André Fortin, a *Créditiste* member of Parliament, was in the habit of moving amendments to eliminate references to following the procedure of English courts: House of Commons, *Debates*, 1968–69, 6507; *Debates*, 1969–70, 537.

78 House of Commons, *Debates*, 1970, 668 (F.J. Bigg, Conservative, Alberta).

79 House of Commons, Standing Committee on Justice and Legal Affairs, 28th Parliament, 2nd Session (1969–70), *Minutes of Proceedings and Evidence* no. 5, 25 (Minister of Justice).

80 Report of the Quebec Royal Commission of Inquiry on Constitutional Problems (Quebec: Province of Quebec, 1956).

81 See Sheila McLeod Arnopoulos, *The English Fact in Quebec* (Montreal: McGill–Queen's University Press 1980).

82 SC 1969, c. 54.

83 [1970] *Exchequer Court Reports*.

CHAPTER FOURTEEN

1 SC 1970, c. 1, included as RSC 1970 (2nd Supp.), c. 10, in the Revised Statutes that were coming out at the time.

2 Section 3. The marginal note reads 'Original Court continued.'

3 House of Commons, *Debates*, 1969, 6015, 6017. See also 6018.

4 Untitled memorandum from D.S.M. to the minister of justice, dated July 2, 1968. I would like to thank Richard Pound, who is presently working on a

biography of Wilbur Jackett, for making this memorandum, and other material obtained from the Department of Justice, available to me.

5 House of Commons, Debates, 1968–69, 1219 (October 16, 1968).

6 House of Commons, Debates, 1968–69, 2981 (November 20, 1968).

7 Canada, *Report of the Royal Commission on Taxation* [Carter Commission] (Ottawa: Queen's Printer 1967).

8 It would also serve as an appeal court for practice rulings, which were not at the time being heard by the Supreme Court of Canada. The new appeal court was envisaged as having more time to hear appeals for which there was voluminous evidence, such as in patent, expropriation, and admiralty litigation.

9 There were also the District Judges in Admiralty, from whom an appeal lay to either the Exchequer Court or the Supreme Court.

10 *Canadian Fishing Co. Ltd. v. Smith*, [1962] SCR 294. For a discussion of the litigation see H.W. Arthurs, 'Comment' (1962), 40 *Canadian Bar Review* 505–11. In the memorandum of July 2, 1968, the deputy minister stated that Arthurs had proposed the solution of giving a federal court exclusive supervisory jurisdiction over federal administrative tribunals in this case comment.

11 *Re Vantel Broadcasting Co. Ltd. and Canada Labour Relations Board* (1962), 35 DLR (2d) 620.

12 *The Queen v. Canada Labour Relations Board, ex parte Martin* [1966] 2 OR 684.

13 *Le Conseil canadien des relations ouvrières v. Agence Maritime Inc.* (1967), [1968] BR 381.

14 Bill C-192; first reading took place on March 2, 1970.

15 House of Commons, *Debates*, 1970, 5470.

16 The government's concern with the workload of the Supreme Court also showed in the passage of legislation that eliminated appeals as of right in civil cases on questions of fact: An Act to amend the Supreme Court Act, RSC 1970, c. 44 (1st Supp.).

17 See House of Commons, *Debates*, 1944, 1845, and 1949, 2150.

18 House of Commons, *Debates*, 1970, 5474.

19 House of Commons, *Debates*, 1970–72, 2735. Other parts of the continuum of law reform concerned the expropriation law, Tax Review Board Act, and National Law Reform Commission, as well as the Statutory Instruments Act.

20 See Alan W. Mewett, 'The Ontario Police Act, 1964' (1965–66), 16 *University of Toronto Law Journal* 184–6.

21 Order in Council, dated May 21, 1964, reproduced in *Report of the Royal Commission of Inquiry into Civil Rights* [McRuer Commission](Toronto: Queen's Printer 1968), vol. 1, xi. For an account of the establishment of the McRuer Commission see Patrick Boyer, *A Passion for Justice: The Legacy of James Chalmers McRuer* (Toronto: Osgoode Society 1994), 298–301.

22 The Statutory Powers Procedure Act, 1971, SO 1971, c. 47; The Judicial Review Procedure Act, 1971, SO 1971, c. 48; The Public Inquiries Act, 1971, SO 1971, c. 49.

23 April 22, 1972, p. 6, and April 24, 1972, p. 6.

24 D.W. Mundell, *Manual of Practice on Administrative Law and Procedure in Ontario* (Department of Justice and Attorney General 1972), Foreword by the Minister of Justice and Attorney General Allan F. Lawrence.

25 *Three Rivers Boatman Ltd. v. Canada Labour Relations Board*, [1969] SCR 607 (in French), 12 DLR (3d) 710 (translation).

26 Constitution Act, 1867, s. 129.

27 In a Special Lecture of the Law Society of Upper Canada in 1992, Madame Justice Alice Desjardins of the Federal Court of Appeal placed the origin of the Federal Court squarely on the decision in *Three Rivers Boatman*. She had been a legal counsel in the Privy Council Office from 1969 to 1974. See Alice Desjardins (Honourable Madame Justice), 'Review of Administrative Action in the Federal Court of Canada: The New Style in a Pluralist Setting,' in *Administrative Law* Special Lectures of the Law Society of Upper Canada 1992 (Toronto: Carswell 1993), 405–437.

28 House of Commons, *Debates*, 1970, 5471.

29 Federal Court Act, RSC 1970 (2nd Supp.), c. 10, s. 23. Constitution Act, 1867, s. 91, head 18 ('Bills of Exchange and Promissory Notes'); head 29, with reference to section 92, head 10(a) ('Works and Undertakings connecting the Province with any other or others of the provinces, or extending beyond the Limits of the Province'). Aeronautics was effectively created as an additional head of power through the general power of 'Peace, Order, and good Government': *In re Regulation and Control of Aeronautics in Canada*, [1932] AC 54 (PC).

30 House of Commons, *Debates*, 1970, 5474.

31 Federal Court Act, RSC 1970 (2nd Supp.), c. 10, s. 22. See also s. 2(b).

32 John Mahoney was introduced by the Minister of Justice at the Committee hearings as 'a well reputed lawyer and advocate and a proctor in marine law, who has been retained by the Department of Justice and by the Department of Transport to work out a completely new marine maritime code over the next three or four years.' (House of Commons, Standing Committee on Justice and Legal Affairs, 28th Parliament, 2nd Session (1969–70), *Minutes of Proceedings and Evidence*, no. 26, 7).

33 J.J. Mahoney, Notes with Respect to Admiralty Provisions, dated June 12, 1969, 3. Provided by Richard Pound, supra, note 4.

34 Constitution Act, 1867, section 91, head 10.

35 House of Commons, *Debates*, 1970: see G.H. Aiken (Progressive Conservative, Ontario) at 5481, and Robert McCleave (Progressive Conservative, Nova Scotia) at 5477.

36 House of Commons, Standing Committee on Justice and Legal Affairs; 28th Parliament, 2nd Session (1969–70), *Minutes of Proceedings and Evidence*, nos. 26–28, 31, 33.

37 See G.V.V. Nicholls, 'Federal Proposals for Review of Tribunal Decisions' (1970), 18 *Chitty's Law Journal* 254–63.

38 The witnesses were Jean Beaudry, Executive Vice-President, and A. Andras, Director of Government Employees and Legislation. See supra note 36, no. 31.

39 During the clause-by-clause examination of the bill which followed, the committee also focused on a letter from Claude Thomson, chairman of a subcommittee of the Administrative Law section of the Ontario Branch of the Canadian Bar Association. The letter had been addressed to a Conservative member of the committee, Lincoln Alexander. It contained concerns about administrative law, which were addressed by the deputy minister of justice. The letter is reproduced at supra note 36, no. 33, 100–4, as Appendix D.

40 One of them, Stephen A. Scott, a professor of law, at McGill University, raised certain constitutional points with respect to the bill. The Canadian Bar Association informed Senator Connolly that a committee had been established to deal with the admiralty part of the bill. No member of the Bar Association's committee appeared before the Senate committee, but the Senate committee received a letter from one of the members, Francis Gerity. Apparently Gerity had written on his own behalf and not on behalf of the Bar Association. The discussion before the Senate committee was conducted by John Mahoney, the lawyer retained by the Department of Justice to develop the admiralty jurisdiction provisions in the bill.

41 'A Brief from the Bar of the Province of Quebec to the Government of Canada on Bill C-172,' Senate, Standing Committee on Legal and Constitutional Affairs, 28th Parliament, 3rd Session, *Minutes and Proceedings*, no. 3, 16–20, Appendix B.

42 Senate, Standing Committee on Legal and Constitutional Affairs, 28th Parliament, 3rd Session, *Minutes and Proceedings*, no. 3, 11.

43 House of Commons, Standing Committee on Justice and Legal Affairs, 28th Parliament, 2nd Session, *Minutes of Proceedings and Evidence*, no. 27, 10.

44 House of Commons, *Debates*, 1971, 6665 (Albert Béchard, Parliamentary Secretary to the Minister of Justice).

CHAPTER FIFTEEN

1 Theodore F.T. Plucknett, *A Concise History of the Common Law*, 5th ed. (London: Butterworth & Co. 1956), 197.

2 See supra, chapter 12.

3 F.W. Maitland, *The Constitutional History of England* (Cambridge, U.K.: Cambridge University Press 1911), 382–7.

4 John Willis, 'Three Approaches to Administrative Law: The Judicial, the Conceptual, and the Functional' (1935), 1 *University of Toronto Law Journal* 53–81 at 54. See also Theodore Plucknett, supra note 1 at 233, where he wrote of a national antipathy between the public and the functionary.

5 John Willis, 'Administrative Law in Canada' (1961), 39 *Canadian Bar Review* 251–65 at 253; R.C.B. Risk, 'Lawyers, Courts, and the Rise of the Regulatory State' (1984), 9 *Dalhousie Law Journal* 31–54 at 38.

6 'Aspects of Administrative Law in Canada' (1934), 46 *Juridical Review* 203–29.

7 See supra, chapter 11.

8 *Dyson v. Attorney General*, [1911] 1 KB 410 at 424.

9 See supra, chapter 7.

10 *Barter v. Smith*, 2 Ex. CR 455.

11 Ibid., 481.

12 John Willis, ed., *Canadian Boards at Work* (Toronto: Macmillan Co. of Canada 1941); John P. Humphrey, 'Judicial Control over Administrative Action with Special Reference to the Province of Quebec' (1939), 5 *Canadian Journal of Economics and Political Science* 417–31 at 430. See also Morton J. Horwitz, *The Transformation of American Law 1870–1960: The Crisis of Legal Orthodoxy* (New York: Oxford University Press 1991), chapter 8, 213–46, particularly 216.

13 'Note' (1905), 41 *Canada Law Journal* 205–6.

14 W.P.M. Kennedy, supra note 6; John Willis, supra note 4; John P. Humphrey, 'Judicial Control over Administrative Action with Special Reference to the Province of Quebec' (1939), 5 *Canadian Journal of Economics and Political Science* 417–31; John Willis ed., *Canadian Boards at Work* (Toronto: Macmillan Co. of Canada Ltd., 1941); R.C.B. Risk, 'Lawyers, Courts, and the Rise of the Regulatory State' (1984), 9 *Dalhousie Law Journal* 31–54. Risk wrote, at 42: 'One cause may have been the threat that regulation would limit the power of the lawyers and their clients, but another was the threat that these changes made to the foundation of ideals that had shaped their understanding of law and their constitutional beliefs, as well as their perceptions of reality and the justifications of their role.'

15 J.A. Corry, 'Introduction – The Genesis and Nature of Boards,' in John Willis, ed., *Canadian Boards at Work* (Toronto: Macmillan Co. of Canada 1941), xxxi–xxxii.

16 John P. Humphrey, supra note 14 at 430.

17 Morton J. Horwitz, *Transformation of American Law 1870–1960*, supra, note 12 at 215.

18 David J. Mullan, 'Administrative Tribunals: Their Evolution in Canada from

1945 to 1984', *Regulations, Crown Corporations and Administrative Tribunals*, ed.
Ivan Bernier and Andrée Lajoie (Toronto: University of Toronto Press 1985),
155–202 at 187.

19 Hampden was the first cousin of Oliver Cromwell and a leader of the opposition to King Charles I. An attempt to arrest him for treason failed. In the ensuing civil war Hampden was killed, but Cromwell and the opposition to the
King won; the King was executed, and the Commonwealth established with
Cromwell as Protector.

20 Saturday, January 20, 1934, 1, 2. The speech also received front-page coverage
in the *Toronto Daily Star* that day, and was mentioned by the *London Free Press*
on page 9. The *Ottawa Journal* covered the speech the following week on January 27, 6.

21 'Address of the Chief Justice of Ontario' (1934), 12 *Canadian Bar Review*
35–41.

22 Roscoe Pound, 'Mechanical Jurisprudence' (1908), 8 *Columbia Law Review*
605–23.

23 See Jerome Hall, 'Nulla Poena Sine Lege' (1937), 47 *Yale Law Journal* 165–93 at
190–1.

24 Benjamin N. Cardozo, *The Nature of the Judicial Process* (New Haven, Conn.:
Yale University Press 1921). This work has gone through numerous reprint-
ings up to the present day. See Morton J. Horwitz, *Transformation of American
Law 1870–1960*, supra note 12, for a discussion of the conflict between formalism and contextualism in the United States.

25 In Robert F. Reid, *Administrative Law and Practice* (Toronto: Butterworth & Co.
1971), the following examples are given (180): (1) no action may be brought to
disturb a decision or action of a tribunal, e.g., 'No decision, order, direction,
declaration or ruling of the Board shall be questioned or reviewed in any court
and no order shall be made or process entered, or proceedings taken in any
court, whether by way of injunction, declaratory judgment, *certiorari, mandamus*, prohibition, *quo warranto*, or otherwise to question, review, prohibit or
restrain the Board or any of its proceedings.' (2) the decisions of a tribunal
shall be 'final,' or 'final and conclusive,' or 'final and binding,' or the like.
(3) 'exclusive jurisdiction' clauses provide that a tribunal shall have exclusive
jurisdiction to decide certain matters, or even all matters arising before it.

26 Ibid., 179.

27 'Certiorari to Labour Boards: The Apparent Futility of Privative Clauses'
(1952), 30 *Canadian Bar Review* 986–1003 at 990. The struggle over privative
clauses was fiercest in the area of labour law. Judicial antipathy to labour legislation is well known. See Bora Laskin, ibid., 993; Mullan, supra, note 18, 155–
202 at 187; and Roger Carter, 'The Privative Clause in Canadian Administra-

tive Law, 1944–1985: A Doctrinal Examination' (1986), 64 *Canadian Bar Review* 241–82 at 242.

28 A.V. Dicey, *Introduction to the Study of the Law of the Constitution*, 10th ed. (London: Macmillan & Co. 1964).

29 Morton J. Horwitz,*Transformation of American Law 1870–1960*, supra note 12 at 221, 226.

30 See Kennedy, supra note 6.

31 Supra note 6 at 205.

32 Supra note 4 at 54.

33 'Administrative Law: 1923–1947' (1948), 26 *Canadian Bar Review* 268–85 at 268–9.

34 D.M. Gordon, 'Administrative Tribunals and the Courts' (1933), 49 *Law Quarterly Review* 94–120 at 110, 120.

35 Humphrey, supra note 12 at 420. One writer notes politely that identifying the judicial function as involving no discretion, which must mean choice, is 'rather artificial': René Dussault, Relationship between the Nature and the Acts of the Administration and Judicial Review: Quebec and Canada' (1967), 10 *Canadian Public Administration* 298–318. Clearly the legal profession has not universally accepted the distinction between administrative decision making and judicial decision making. See P.J. Millward, 'Judicial Review of Administrative Authorities in Canada' (1961), 39 *Canadian Bar Review* 351–95.

36 C. Lloyd Brown-John, *Canadian Regulatory Agencies* (Toronto: Butterworths 1981).

37 There is also the writ of *mandamus* by which someone is commanded to do a certain act, but which is not of particular interest in this context.

38 The word 'writ' simply means the directive of a superior court.

39 Robert Reid has said that 'tribunal' is 'a basket word embracing many kinds and sorts' of decision maker: supra, note 25 at 220.

40 John Willis, 'Administrative Law and the British North America Act' (1939), 53 *Harvard Law Review* 251–81 at 280.

41 Dussault, supra note 35.

42 Supra, note 25 at 461.

43 See David Mullan, 'Reform of Administrative Law Remedies – Method or Madness' (1975), 6 *Federal Law Review* 340–66.

44 Mullan, supra note 18 at 188.

45 John Willis, 'The McRuer Report: Lawyers' Values and Civil Servants' Values' (1968), 18 *University of Toronto Law Journal* 351–60 at 351.

46 *Report of the Committee on Ministers' Powers, 1932*, Cmd. 4060, noted by John Willis, 'Three Approaches to Administrative Law,' supra note 4 at 67–8, 73, 74.

47 Supra note 6 at 228.

48 *Federal Court Act*, RSC 1970 (2nd Supp.), c. 10.

49 House of Commons, *Debates*, 1970, 5471 (John Turner, Minister of Justice).

50 See Reid, supra, note 25, chapter 14, 367–77.

51 The original version (as it appeared in the bill) of section 28(1)(c) provided for judicial review if the decision of the administrative agency had been made 'without due regard for the material before it.' Jean Beaudry, Executive Vice-President of the Canadian Labour Congress, expressed concern in his presentation to the House of Commons committee that the bill created the possibility of an appeal on questions of fact. Claude Thomson, chairman of a subcommittee of the Administrative Law section of the Ontario Branch of the Canadian Bar Association, wrote a letter also objecting to the possibility of such a wide review power, and Andrew Brewin of the New Democratic Party added his voice in opposition to it. As a result the word 'due' was removed. The effect had been seen as restricting judicial review to the question of whether the decision of the agency was made without any evidentiary base, as opposed to an assessment of the weight given to the evidence. In the end section 28(1)(c) would turn out to be essentially a dormant provision; any potential it had to create an appeal on a question of fact was never fully tested. See House of Commons, Standing Committee on Justice and Legal Affairs, 28th Parliament, 2nd Session (1970), *Minutes of Proceedings and Evidence*, nos. 31, 33.

52 See the statement of the minister of justice, John Turner, in House of Commons, *Debates*, 1968–69, 1219.

53 House of Commons, *Debates*, 1969–70, 5475 (Robert McCleave, Conservative, Nova Scotia), 5477 (Andrew Brewin, New Democrat, Ontario).

54 Willis, supra note 5 at 262.

55 House of Commons, Standing Committee on Justice and Legal Affairs; 28th Parliament, 2nd Session, *Minutes of Proceedings and Evidence*, no. 31, 21 (Douglas Hogarth, Liberal, British Columbia).

56 Ibid., 30 (Terrence Murphy, Liberal, Ontario).

57 Senate, Standing Committee on Legal and Constitutional Affairs, 28th Parliament, 3rd Session, *Minutes and Proceedings* no. 1, 10 (Donald Maxwell, Deputy Minister of Justice).

58 Laskin, supra note 27 at 1001.

59 Scott, supra note 33 at 276.

60 House of Commons, *Debates*, 1970–72, 2735.

61 House of Commons, *Debates*, 1969–70, 5478.

62 House of Commons, Standing Committee on Justice and Legal Affairs, 28th Parliament, 2nd Session, *Minutes of Proceedings and Evidence*, no. 26, May 7, 1970, 25.

63 An example offered was a refusal to act when there was a purely adminis-

trative jurisdictional decision. In that event an order, known as a writ of
mandamus, could be sought, and the administrative body ordered to
proceed.

64 House of Commons, Standing Committee on Justice and Legal Affairs, 28th
Parliament, 2nd Session, *Minutes of Proceedings and Evidence,* no. 26, May 7,
1970, 28.

65 Ibid., 29.

66 G.V.V. Nicholls, 'Federal Proposals for Review of Tribunal Decisions' (1970),
18 *Chitty's Law Journal* 254–63.

67 Supra note 64, no. 27, 27.

68 Ibid., 46.

69 Ibid., 39.

70 *Proposals to Amend the Federal Court Act* (Ottawa: Department of Justice 1983),
para. 19(iii).

71 Supra note 25 at 449–53.

72 Peter Russell, *The Judiciary in Canada: The Third Branch of Government* (Toronto:
McGraw-Hill Ryerson 1987), 311.

CHAPTER SIXTEEN

1 The admiralty districts and the 'District Judges in Admiralty' had been abolished, which made the judges of the Trial Division admiralty trial judges, a
function the judges of the Exchequer Court had started to carry out under
President Jackett.

2 *Federal Court Act,* RSC 1970 (2nd Supp.), c. 10, s. 16(3).

3 Long gone was the thinking that allowed the judges of the Supreme Court
who sat on the Exchequer Court to participate in the hearing of an appeal from
their own decision.

4 *Manual for Federal Court Judges,* Appendix J.

5 This restriction on a trial judge and an appellate judge discussing a decision
existed until 1992. On October 22, 1992, it was decided at a meeting of all
judges that discussion be allowed once the appeal was decided. However, the
Manual for Federal Court Judges, Appendix J, cautions that any such discussion
could be extremely awkward and that some appeal court judges may resent a
trial judge raising any such matter.

6 *Federal Court Act,* RSC 1970 (2nd supp.), c.10, s. 5(1).

7 Ibid, s. 5.

8 'Memorandum to the Cabinet from Minister of Justice, Re: Revision of the
Exchequer Court Act and the Admiralty Act,' Cabinet Document No. 1269/69,
December 23, 1969, 5.

9 The establishment of a rota of judges was authorized by the *Federal Court Act*, RSC 1970, (2nd Supp.), c.10, s. 7(2).

10 Untitled memorandum from D.S.M. to the Interim Minister of Justice, dated July 2, 1968, 17. Provided by Richard Pound, supra chapter 14, note 4.

11 See Ian Bushnell, *The Captive Court: A Study of the Supreme Court of Canada* (Montreal & Kingston: McGill-Queen's University Press 1992), 40, 91, 103; see also S.J.R. Noel, *Patrons, Clients, Brokers* (Toronto: University of Toronto Press 1990), 281, 298.

12 Walter Cassels had been a judge from 1908 to 1923; from 1946 to the end, when there were more than two judges, there had been only a single Ontario judge.

13 *An Act to amend the Judges Act*, SC 1973–74, c. 17.

14 The number of judges from Quebec was left unchanged at a required minimum of four.

15 Mr Justice Dubé has written his autobiography: *Du Banc d'école au banc fédéral* (Montreal: Guerin 1993).

16 House of Commons, *Debates*, 1975, 4759.

17 *Federal Court Act*, SC 1970, c. 1, 16(1); later RSC 1970 (2nd Supp.), c. 10.

18 *An Act to amend the Judges Act and the Finance Administration Act*, SC 1970–71, c. 55.

19 PC 1971–1422, dated July 13, 1971.

20 PC 1973–6/1953, dated July 10, 1973.

21 *American Cyanamid Co. v. Novopharm Ltd.*, [1972] FC 739 (Jackett, Bastin D.J., Sweet D.J.); *Hawrish v. MNR* (1976), 14 NR 381 (Jackett, Greschuk D.J., Maguire D.J.).

CHAPTER SEVENTEEN

1 David Mullan, 'The Federal Court – Comment,' in *Proceedings* of the Administrative Law Conference, University of British Columbia, October 18–19, 1979 (Vancouver: UBC Law Review 1981), 38–42 at 38, 42.

2 See Pierre Lamontagne, 'Notes on the Federal Court' (1977), 35 *The Advocate* 139–42 at 140–1.

3 D.M.M. Goldie, 'Notes on the Federal Court' (1977), 35 *The Advocate* 17–24 at 17.

4 A. Lorne Campbell, D.M.M. Goldie, and B.A. Crane, *Report of the Canadian Bar Association on the Federal Court* (Ottawa: Canadian Bar Association 1977).

5 *The National*, August 1978, 15–21 at 15. In some respects this excellent summary of the report adds to the original.

6 Supra note 4 at 63.

7 House of Commons, *Debates*, 1977, 6153.

8 Supra note 4 at 65.

9 House of Commons, *Debates*, 1970–72, 2735 (John Turner).

10 Law Reform Commission of Canada, *Administrative Law: Federal Court, Judicial Review*, Working Paper 18 (Ottawa: Law Reform Commission of Canada 1977); David J. Mullan, *The Federal Court Act: Administrative Law Jurisdiction* (Ottawa: Law Reform Commission of Canada 1977). The latter was essentially a mini-textbook.

11 Robert F. Reid, *Administrative Law and Practice* (Toronto: Butterworth & Co. (Canada) 1971), 2.

12 (1973), 23 *University of Toronto Law Journal* 14–53.

13 H. Wade MacLauchlan, 'Developments in Administrative Law: The 1989–90 Term' (1991), 2 *Supreme Court Law Review* (2d) 1–82 at 69.

14 Supra note 12 at 29; see also p. 32.

15 Mullan, supra note 10 at 76.

16 Ibid., 66, 76.

17 Ibid., 53.

18 The commission was chaired at the time by Antonio Lamer, currently the Chief Justice of Canada.

19 Working Paper 18, supra, note 10 at 4, 5.

20 Ibid., 17, 18.

21 D. Carrier et P. Verge, 'Chronique de législation: Loi concernant la Cour fédérale du Canada' (1971), 12 *Cahiers de Droit* (Université Laval) 207–11.

22 Supra note 10 at 36.

23 Ibid., 42.

24 Law Reform Commission of Canada, *Judicial Review and the Federal Court*, Report 14 (Ottawa: Law Reform Commission of Canada 1980), 2.

25 Ibid., 9.

26 P.S.A. Lamek, 'Jurisdiction of the Federal Courts and the Superior Courts' in *The Constitution and the Future of Canada*, Special Lectures Law Society of Upper Canada 1978, Toronto: Richard de Boo 1978), 87–108.

27 Ibid., 88.

28 Ibid., 91.

29 Ibid., 92.

30 Ibid., 108.

CHAPTER EIGHTEEN

1 In the language of the prerogative writs named in section 18, what was sought was first an order of *mandamus*; the alternative application was by way of the

writ of *certiorari*, with the final order sought being once again by way of *mandamus*.

2 *The Unjust Society: The Tragedy of Canada's Indians* (Edmonton: M.G. Hurtig 1969).

3 *National Indian Brotherhood v. Juneau (No. 1)*, [1971] FC 66 at 68–9.

4 *National Indian Brotherhood v. Juneau (No. 1)*, [1971] FC 66.

5 SC 1967–68, c. 25, s. 19(2)(c).

6 Federal Court Act, RSC 1970 (2nd Supp.), c. 10, s. 28(3).

7 *National Indian Brotherhood v. Juneau (No. 2)*, [1971] FC 72.

8 Federal Court Act, RSC 1970 (2nd Supp.), c.10, s. 61(1).

9 Supra note 7 at 79.

10 Ibid.

11 David J. Mullan, 'The Federal Court Act: Administrative Law Jurisdiction' (Ottawa: Law Reform Commission of Canada 1977), 65.

12 In law it would be termed *obiter dicta*.

13 *National Indian Brotherhood v. CTV Television Network Ltd.*, [1971] FC 127.

14 *National Indian Brotherhood v. Juneau (No. 3)*, [1971] FC 498. No further action had been taken before the Court of Appeal with respect to a motion to quash: Jackett had apparently proved too convincing that the matter would be quashed.

15 Ibid., 516.

16 *Toronto Star*, July 17, 1971, 76.

17 [1971] FC 347.

18 *The Queen v. Drybones* (1969), [1970] SCR 282.

19 *Bray v. Bray* (1970), [1971] 1 OR 232 (Wright J.).

20 The following argued in favour of the challenged law: The Indian Association of Alberta, the Union of British Columbia Indian Chiefs, the Manitoba Indian Brotherhood Inc., the Union of New Brunswick Indians, the Indian Brotherhood of the Northwest Territories, the Union of Nova Scotia Indians, the Union of Ontario Indians, the Federation of Saskatchewan Indians, the Indian Association of Quebec, the Yukon Native Brotherhood, the National Indian Brotherhood, and the Treaty Voice of Alberta Association. The following opposed the law: Rose Wilhelm (an Indian woman from Ontario who had married a non-Indian), the Alberta Committee on Indian Rights for Indian Women Inc. (a group of 250 Indian women), Viola Shannacaffo (a Manitoba Indian who disagreed with the stance of the Manitoba Indian Brotherhood), the University Women's Club of Toronto and the University Women Graduates Limited (equal rights for women), the North Toronto Business and Professional Women's Club Inc. (status of women), and Monica Agnes Turner (an Indian woman from Ontario who had married a non–Band member).

21 *The Attorney General of Canada v. Lavell; Isaac v. Bedard* (1973), [1974] SCR 1349.

See Ian Bushnell, *The Captive Court: A Study of the Supreme Court of Canada* (Montreal & Kingston: McGill–Queen's University Press 1992), 360–4, for a full discussion of the Supreme Court's decision.

22 The other judges who made up the majority of five were: Gérald Fauteux, Ronald Martland, Wilfred Judson, and Louis-Philippe Pigeon.

23 The other judges who agreed with Laskin were: Emmett Hall, Wishart Spence, and Douglas Abbott. Abbott expressed regret at what he was doing, but saw no way to distinguish the *Drybones* case, which he considered binding on him.

24 *An Act to amend the Indian Act*, SC 1985, c. 27.

25 In *Sawridge Band v. Canada* (1995), [1996] 1 FC 3 (T.D., Muldoon). The validity of the amendment was upheld, but the Federal Court of Appeal overturned the decision and ordered a new trial on the ground that the trial judge had displayed a 'reasonable apprehension of bias': [1997] FCJ No. 794 (Isaac CJ, Strayer, Linden).

26 *Federal Court Act*, RSC 1970 (2nd Supp.), c. 10, s. 2(g).

27 J.E. Côté, 'Comment: Jurisdiction of Federal Court – What Is 'Federal Board Commission or other tribunal' – When Judge of Provincial Court Included' (1972), 50 *Canadian Bar Review* 519–22.

28 [1972] FC 1976.

29 *U.S.A. v. Link*, [1955] SCR 183.

30 The concurring judges were Fauteux, Martland, Ritchie, and Dickson.

31 (1973), [1975] 1 SCR 228 at 232.

32 The Federal Court was also said to have jurisdiction over criminal matters when the decision was made by a 'federal board, commission or other tribunal.'

33 The unanimous bench was made up of Laskin (by this time chief justice of Canada), Martland, Ritchie, Pigeon, Dickson, Beetz, and Yves Pratte (brother of Louis Pratte).

34 *The Deputy Attorney General of Canada v. Brown*, [1965] SCR 84.

35 (1977), 20 NR 70 at 74 (Fed. CA).

36 (1978), [1979] 1 SCR 729.

37 [1982] 2 SCR 518.

38 (1980), 44 NR 626 (Fed. CA).

39 Pollock, *First Book of Jurisprudence*, 2nd ed. (London: Macmillan & Co. 1904), 325. The cases referred to were *Bright v. Hutton* (1852), 10 ER 133, *Attorney General v. Dean and Canons of Windsor* (1860), 11 ER 472, and *Beamish v. Beamish* (1861), 11 ER 735.

40 *London Tramways Co. v. London County Council*, [1898] AC 375.

41 W.R. Jackett, Foreword to Harold G. Fox, *The Canadian Law of Trade Marks and Unfair Competition*, 3rd ed. (Toronto: Carswell 1972).

42 See [1966] 3 All E.R. 77.

43 *Conway v. Rimmer*, [1968] AC 910, [1968] 1 All ER 874.

44 *McNamara Construction (Western) Ltd. v. The Queen,* [1977] 2 SCR 654.

45 *Murray v. Minister of Employment and Immigration* (1978), [1979] 1 FC 518 (Jackett, Heald, MacKay D.J.).

46 *The Queen v. Zelensky,* [1978] 2 SCR 940.

47 *Federal Court Act,* RSC 1970 (2nd Supp.), c. 10, s. 2(g).

48 *Re Paulette's Application to file a Caveat,* [1973] 6 WWR 97 at 98.

49 Ibid., 99.

50 Ibid., 100.

51 Page 3.

52 'Government vs. the Law: An Historic Power Confrontation,' *London Free Press,* August 13, 1973.

53 *Attorney General of Canada v. Morrow J.,* [1973] FC 889.

54 Collier added that he would not have issued the writ of prohibition even if he had the jurisdiction to do so since it was a matter of discretion, there was no error on the face of the record, and also the points could be dealt with by the appeal process.

55 For an account by Morrow of the episode see *Northern Justice: The Memoirs of Mr Justice William G. Morrow,* ed. W.H. Morrow (Toronto: Osgoode Society 1995), 156–79.

56 *Paulette v. The Queen* (1976), [1977] 2 SCR 628; aff'g *Re Paulette and Registrar of Land Titles* (1975), 63 DLR (3d) 1 (NWT CA), rev'g (1973), 39 DLR (3d) 45 (NWT).

57 [1973] FC 1018, aff'd (1974), [1976] 1 SCR 453.

58 The Supreme Court granted leave to appeal.

59 See, for example, David Phillip Jones, 'Case Comment – Howarth v. National Parole Board (1975), 21 *McGill Law Journal* 434–41; S. Silverstone, Comment: Administrative Law – Judicial Review – Parole Revocation – Section 28 Federal Court Act – Rules of Natural Justice – Duty to Act Fairly' (1975), 53 *Canadian Bar Review* 92–102.

CHAPTER NINETEEN

1 The Anti-dumping Tribunal had been established in 1969 to deal with questions about the dumping of goods into Canada and the impact on Canadian production of such goods: *Anti-dumping Act,* SC 1968–69, c. 10.

2 *In re Anti-Dumping Tribunal and re transparent sheet glass,* [1972] FC 1078 (TD).

3 *In re Anti-Dumping Tribunal and re transparent sheet glass,* [1973] FC 745 (CA).

4 David J. Mullan, *The Federal Court Act: Administrative Law Jurisdiction* (Ottawa: Law Reform Commission of Canada 1977), 56.

5 (1975), [1976] 2 SCR 739 at 749. Laskin went on to say that in any case, since

certiorari is a discretionary remedy, not only when a private person moves to quash but also when the Crown does so, the case was 'an eminently proper one for the exercise of discretion to refuse the relief sought.' The reasons were that there had been a two-year delay, that none of the parties affected had taken exception, and that there had been an insufficient taint of the decision by the signature.

6 Ibid, 741.

7 Mullan, supra note 4 at 56.

8 (1976), [1978] 1 SCR 369.

9 (1975), [1976] 1 FC 20 (CA).

10 Five-judge panels were used only three times in the 1970s, all in 1975. The first case was *Canadian Pacific Ltd. v. Governments of Alberta, Saskatchewan, Manitoba and Ontario; Canadian National Railway Co. Ltd. v. Governments of Alberta, Saskatchewan, Manitoba and Ontario*, [1975] FC 171 (Thurlow, Pratte, Heald, Urie, Ryan). At stake was an increase in freight rates by the railways, to which the western provinces objected. The second was *Re Shell Canada Ltd.*, [1975] FC 184 (Jackett, Thurlow, Pratte, Urie, Ryan). The Director of Investigation and Research under the Combines Investigation Act sought an order directing the police to obtain from Shell Canada Ltd. all documents of the company. A judge of the Ontario High Court refused to issue the order and the government applied for judicial review. The issue was whether solicitor–client privilege could be claimed for the documents. What was involved was an obvious conflict in values – the power of the state to investigate corporations versus the value inherent in solicitor-client privilege. A unanimous court came down on the side of the privilege, in a precedent-setting case. Note also that the case involved a review of a decision of a provincial court judge. The third case was *In re Canadian Arctic Gas Pipeline Ltd.*, the one being discussed in the text.

11 The Court of Appeal raised the issue of whether it had jurisdiction to deal with the particular question. Section 28(4) of the Federal Court Act was said not to create a purely advisory function for the court; there had to be a dispute involved. In the end the court determined that the perceived problem was a matter of the way the particular question was worded. None of the parties had argued that the court lacked jurisdiction. The court held that it had jurisdiction. This was an example of the preoccupation that the members of the court had with its jurisdiction.

12 Supra note 9 at 29.

13 The three were the Committee for Justice and Liberty Foundation, the Consumers' Association of Canada, and the Canadian Arctic Resources Committee.

14 The other judges were Ritchie, Spence, Pigeon, and Dickson.

15 The dissenting judges, de Grandpré, Martland, and Judson, did not identify the board as having to decide in accordance with rules that would operate with a judicial process; rather, they considered it an administrative body which relied on the experience and expertise of its members. De Grandpré stated, 'Members of administrative boards acquire their expertise by virtue of previous exposure to the industry which they are appointed to regulate. The system would not work if it were not premised on an assertion of faith in those appointed to adjudicate' ([1978] 1 SCR 369 at 398).

16 (1976), [1977] 2 SCR 422.

17 *Federal Court Rules*, r. 307.

18 Supra note 16 at 453.

19 Ibid., 444.

20 Ibid., 428.

21 Ibid., 432.

22 Ibid., 433.

23 *MacDonald v. Vapor Canada Limited* (1976), [1977] 2 SCR 134 at 175.

24 *Manitoba Fisheries Ltd. v. The Queen* (1976), [1977] 2 FC 457 at 471, 472 (TD).

25 See, for example, *The Queen v. Smith* (1883), 10 SCR 1, discussed in chapter 5.

26 Canadian Bill of Rights, SC 1960, c. 44, s. 1(a).

27 *Manitoba Fisheries v. The Queen* (1977), [1978] 1 FC 485 at 497 (CA).

28 The other judges were Spence, Pigeon, Dickson, Beetz, Estey, and Pratte.

29 *Manitoba Fisheries Ltd. v. Canada* (1978), [1979] 1 SCR 101. Given Ritchie's attitude towards the Bill of Rights (mentioned in chapter 13), it is not surprising that the Bill was completely ignored in the Supreme Court's decision.

30 *Martineau v. Matsqui Institution Inmate Disciplinary Board*, [1976] 2 FC 198.

31 *Martineau and Butters v. Matsqui Institution Inmate Disciplinary Board* (1977), [1978] 1 SCR 118. The split among the judges is even worse when the reasons for judgment are examined – there was a 4–1–4 result.

32 *In re the Penitentiary Act and in re Thomas Martineau* (1977), [1978] 1 FC 312 at 318 (TD).

33 *Matsqui Institution Disciplinary Board v. Martineau*, [1978] 2 FC 637 (CA).

34 Ibid., 640.

35 (1978), [1979] 1 SCR 311.

36 *Martineau v. Matsqui Institution Disciplinary Board* (1979), [1980] 1 SCR 602.

37 Ibid., 637.

38 Ibid., 608.

39 *Blais v. Basford*, [1972] FC 151. Thurlow articulated the same idea in *Armstrong v. State of Wisconsin and U.S.A.*, [1972] FC 1228.

40 David Mullan, 'The Federal Court – Comment,' *Proceedings* of the Administra-

tive Law Conference, University of British Columbia, October 18–19, 1979 (Vancouver: UBC Law Review 1981), 38–42 at 42.

41 D.M.M. Goldie, 'The Federal Court,' Proceedings of the Administrative Law Conference, University of British Columbia, October 18–19, 1979, 10–18 at 18.

42 D.J. Mullan, 'Fairness: The New Natural Justice?' (1975), 25 *University of Toronto Law Journal* 281–316 at 300.

CHAPTER TWENTY

1 J.M. Evans, 'Comment: Federal Jurisdiction – A Lamentable Situation' (1981), 59 *Canadian Bar Review* 124–53 at 124.

2 *Quebec North Shore Paper Co. v. Canadian Pacific Ltd.* (1976), [1977] 2 SCR 1054.

3 The jurisdiction of the Federal Court was made concurrent with that of the provincial courts.

4 *Canadian Pacific Ltd. v. Quebec North Shore Paper Co.* (1975), [1976] 1 FC 405.

5 *Quebec North Shore Paper Co. v. Canadian Pacific Ltd.* (1975), [1976] 1 FC 646.

6 Since there was no legislation of the Parliament of Canada involved, in the end the resolution of the problem depended on the meaning of the words 'or otherwise' in section 23.

7 [1930] SCR 531.

8 [1932] SCR 419. For the Privy Council decision, see infra, note 23.

9 Supra note 7 at 534.

10 Supra note 2 at 1063.

11 Ibid. See also the mention of this same idea at 1066.

12 Ibid., 1065–6.

13 Laskin noted that Addy in the Trial Division had not dealt with s. 101 and had appeared to assume jurisdiction if there was an interprovincial enterprise involved. Laskin also pointed out that Thurlow in the Court of Appeal had overlooked the words in section 23.

14 The contract between Quebec North Shore Paper and Canadian Pacific specified that Quebec law was to be used in any dispute.

15 The legislative authority of the Parliament of Canada over 'trade and commerce' given by the constitution, had been expressed in the widest of terms, and was recognized initially by the Supreme Court of Canada to be the power to regulate business: *Severn v. The Queen* (1878), 2 SCR 70. However, even at the moment when this federal power was at its greatest extent (before it was restricted in the name of provincial autonomy), contracts were accepted as coming within provincial control, as an ingredient of provincial authority over 'civil rights': *Citizens' Insurance Co. v. Parsons* (1880), 4 SCR 215. 'Property and civil rights' (Constitution Act, 1867, section 92, head 13) was the primary

source of provincial legislative power and it was not surprising that there was no 'applicable and existing federal law' dealing with contractual matters, since it would have faced a formidable challenge from the provinces, particularly Quebec.

16 The words used by Chief Justice Anglin in *The King v. Consolidated Distilleries Ltd.*, [1930] SCR 531, when he stated categorically that there was no power under section 101 'to set up a court competent to deal with matters purely of civil right as between subject and subject,' were not referred to.

17 *McNamara Construction (Western) Ltd. v. The Queen*, [1977] 2 SCR 654.

18 Federal Court Act, s. 17(4)(a).

19 Constitution Act, 1867, section 91, head 28: (1975), [1976] 2 FC 29 2(CA).

20 *Farwell v. The Queen* (1894), 22 SCR 553 at 562; *The King v. Petite*, [1933] Ex. CR 186 (Angers).

21 22 SCR 553.

22 Bora Laskin, 'Note on Federal Jurisdiction and Federal Common or Decisional Law,' in *Canadian Constitutional Law*, 3rd ed. (Toronto: Carswell 1966), 817–23 at 823.

23 *Consolidated Distilleries Ltd. v. The King*, [1933] AC 508 at 522.

24 *McGregor v. The Queen*, [1977] 2 FC 520 at 527.

25 See *Johannesson v. Rural Municipality of West St. Paul* (1951), [1952] 1 SCR 292; *The Queen v. Pearsall* (1977), 80 DLR (3d) 285 (Sask. CA); *Schwella v. The Queen*, [1957] Ex. CR 226 (Thurlow).

26 *Canadian Pacific Ltd. v. United Transportation Union*, [1977] 2 FC 712 (TD).

27 *Dome Petroleum Ltd. v. Hunt International Petroleum* (1977), [1978] 1 FC 11 (TD).

28 *Blanchette v. Canadian Pacific Ltd.* (1977), [1978] 2 FC 299 (CA, Urie, MacKay D.J., Kerr D.J.). The judgment of the court was rendered by Urie.

29 *Blanchette v. Canadian National Railway Co.* (1976), [1977] 2 FC 431 at 435.

30 *Alda Enterprises Ltd. v. The Queen* (1977), [1978] 2 FC 106 (TD, Collier). Regarding the previous Supreme Court decision of *Ship 'Sparrows Point' v. Greater Vancouver Water District*, [1951] SCR 396, Collier stated at 113, 'The 'Sparrows Point' is distinguishable on its particular facts, and must now be read in the light of the *Quebec North Shore* and *McNamara* decisions.' The main impact that the *'Sparrows Point'* case would have had was to require that a grant of jurisdiction be interpreted in a way that favoured convenience and justice.

31 [1978] 2 FC 710 at 712–14.

32 This opinion was also accepted within the academic community: see Robert W. Kerr, 'Constitutional Limitations on the Admiralty Jurisdiction of the Federal Court' (1979), 5 *Dalhousie Law Journal* 568–83 at 572; John B. Laskin and Robert J. Sharpe, 'Constricting Federal Court Jurisdiction: A Comment on Fuller Construction' (1980), 30 *University of Toronto Law Journal* 283–306 at 284;

and Peter W. Hogg, 'Federalism and the Jurisdiction of Canadian Courts' (1981), 30 *University of New Brunswick Law Journal* 9–25 at 18. The Special Committee of the Canadian Bar Association treated it as a common assumption: A. Lorne Campbell, D.M.M. Goldie, and B.A. Crane, *Report of the Canadian Bar Association on the Federal Court* (Ottawa: Canadian Bar Association 1977), 9.

33 See supra note 23.

34 Supra note 2 at 1063.

35 This seems to be an expression of the idea associated with the well-known exclusiveness doctine in constitutional adjudication: Neil Finkelstein, ed., *Laskin's Canadian Constitutional Law*, 5th ed. (Toronto: Carswell, 1986), 250.

36 Supra, chapter 2.

37 E. Douglas Armour, 'Provincial Jurisdiction over Civil Procedure' (1882), 2 *Canadian Law Times* 513–26.

38 E. Douglas Armour, 'The Laws of Canada' (1883), 3 *Canadian Law Times* 334–5. The occasion appears to have been the issue of the extent of British Columbia's legislative authority over its Supreme Court regarding procedure and the residence of judges. A reference to the Supreme Court of Canada was required to resolve the issue: *Sewell v. British Columbia Towing Co. (The Thrasher Case)* (1883), *Cass. Dig.* 480.

39 Armour, 'Laws of Canada,' supra note 38 at 334.

40 *Valin v. Langlois* (1879), 3 SCR 1.

41 Ibid., 62, 63. The Judicial Committee of the Privy Council refused special leave to appeal. In the judgment refusing leave to appeal the Judicial Committee entertained no doubt that the courts in Canada had correctly decided the question: *Valin v. Langlois* (1879), 5 App. Cas. 115. A five-member panel sat, made up of Lord Selborne, Sir James W. Colville, Sir Barnes Peacock, Sir Montague E. Smith, and Sir Robert P. Collier.

42 Supra, chapter 2.

43 (1891), 11 *Canadian Law Times* 113–26, 137–52, 233–48, at 147 (emphasis added).

44 See supra, note 20 and accompanying text.

45 Constitution Act, 1867, s. 92, head 13.

46 Ibid., s. 91, head 27.

47 *City of Quebec v. The Queen* (1894), 24 SCR 420 at 428–9.

48 *The British Tradition in Canadian Law* (London: Stevens 1969), 112–13.

49 *The King v. Armstrong* (1908), 40 SCR 229 at 248 (per Davies J.).

50 Laskin, *The British Tradition in Canadian Law*, supra note 48 at 129.

51 *Federal Court Act*, RSC 1970 (2nd Supp.), c. 10, s. 2(b)

52 *The Robert Simpson Montreal Ltd. v. Hamburg-Amerika Linie Norddeutecher*, [1973] FC 1356 (CA).

53 Laskin, *The British Tradition in Canadian Law*, supra note 48 at 131.

54 *Hawker Industries Ltd. v. Santa Maria Shipowning and Trading Co. SA* (1978), [1979] 1 FC 183 (CA). Justices Pratte and Urie concurred in Jackett's judgment.

55 In an earlier case Jackett had offered an explanation of the two Supreme Court of Canada cases which would have minimized their impact. He stated that they would come into play only when constitutionally Ottawa could have made a special law, such as in relation to banking or the Crown, but had not done so, and thus provincial law in relation to civil rights would continue to govern: *Associated Metals & Minerals Corp. v. Ship 'Evie W'* (1977), [1978] 2 FC 710 (CA, Jackett, Pratte, Le Dain). This explanation was swept away in the ensuing confusion.

56 *The Queen v. Canadian Vickers Ltd.* (1977), [1978] 2 FC 675 (TD).

57 *Federal Court Act*, RSC 1970 (2nd Supp.), c.10, s. 2(2)(n).

58 [1979] 2 SCR 157.

59 SC 1891, c. 20, s. 4.

60 (UK), 24 Vict., c. 10, s. 6.

61 *The Queen v. Canadian Vickers Ltd.* (1979), [1980] 1 FC 366 (CA).

62 *Intermunicipal Realty & Development Corp. v. Gore Mutual Insurance Co.* (1977), [1978] 2 FC 691 (T.D.).

63 RSC 1970 (2nd Supp.), c. 10, s. 2, 'Canadian maritime law.'

CHAPTER TWENTY-ONE

1 (1979), [1980] 1 SCR 695.

2 *Foundation Co. of Canada Ltd. v. The Queen* (1978), [1979] 1 FC 877 (CA). The other judges were Heald and Ryan.

3 *Thomas Fuller*, supra note 1 at 706.

4 Ibid., 707.

5 Ibid.

6 Ibid., 713.

7 (1977), [1978] 1 FC 198 (TD).

8 (1977), [1978] 1 FC 356 (TD).

9 Smith D.J. in *The Queen v. Saskatchewan Wheat Pool* (1977), [1978] 2 FC 470 at 479 (TD).

10 *The Queen v. Prytula*, [1979] 2 FC 516 (CA); *The Queen v. Rhine*, [1979] 2 FC 651 (CA).

11 Constitution Act, 1867, s. 91, head 15.

12 The federal head of legislative power, banking, included the common law of contracts.

13 *Attorney-General for Canada v. Attorney-General for Ontario*, [1898] AC 700.

14 *Rhine v. The Queen; Prytula v. The Queen*, [1980] 2 SCR 442.

15 Ibid., 447.
16 House of Commons, Standing Committee on Justice and Legal Affairs, 28th Parliament, 2nd Session, *Minutes of Proceedings and Evidence*, no. 26, 34.
17 *Pacific Western Airlines Ltd. v. The Queen*, [1979] 2 FC 476 at 483 (TD).
18 Peter W. Hogg, *Constitutional Law of Canada*, 3rd ed. (Toronto: Carswell 1992), 178.
19 (1978), [1979] 2 FC 235 (TD).
20 Hogg, supra, note 18 at 180.
21 Laskin had said, 'I would, however, observe that if there had been jurisdiction in the Federal Court there could be some likelihood of proceedings for contribution or indemnity being similarly competent, at least between the parties, in so far as the supporting federal law embraced the issues arising therein': [1977] 2 SCR 654 at 664.
22 [1951] SCR 396.
23 *Alda Enterprises Limited v. The Queen*, [1978] 2 FC 106 (TD).
24 *Pacific Western*, supra note 17 at 490.
25 *Pacific Western Airlines Ltd. v. The Queen* (1979), [1980] 1 FC 86 (CA).
26 Ibid., 89.
27 [1979] 2 FC 575 (CA).
28 John N. Turner, 'The Origin and Mission of the Federal Court of Canada,' paper presented at the 20th Anniversary Symposium, June 26, 1991, and published in *The Federal Court of Canada – An Evaluation* (Ottawa: Federal Court of Canada 1991), 1–17 at 11–12.
29 In 1924 Frank Anglin was promoted over John Idington and Lyman Duff.
30 *Harrison v. Carswell* (1975), [1976] 2 SCR 200 at 205, 209.
31 Bora Laskin, 'The Role and Functions of Final Appellate Courts: The Supreme Court of Canada' (1975), 53 *Canadian Bar Review* 469–81 at 472. He did, however, acknowledge that the power to create a dual system existed within section 101.
32 [1979] 2 SCR 227. For *Nicholson*, see chapter 19.
33 David J. Mullan, 'Developments in Administrative Law: The 1978–79 Term' (1980), 1 *Supreme Court Law Review* 1–76; Brian Etherington, 'Arbitration, Labour Boards and the Courts in the 1980s: Romance Meets Realism' (1989), 68 *Canadian Bar Review* 405–47.
34 Mullan, supra note 33 at 75.
35 J.M. Evans, 'Comment: Federal Jurisdiction – A Lamentable Situation' (1981), 59 *Canadian Bar Review* 124–53. See especially 151.
36 John B. Laskin and Robert J. Sharpe, 'Constricting Federal Court Jurisdiction: A Comment on Fuller Construction' (1980), 30 *University of Toronto Law Journal* 283–306; Denis Lemieux, 'Supervisory Judicial Control of Federal and Provin-

cial Public Authorities in Quebec' (1979), 17 *Osgoode Hall Law Journal* 133–59 at 156.

37 James C. MacPherson, 'Developments in Constitutional Law: The 1979–80 Term' (1981), 2 *Supreme Court Law Review* 49–123 at 101, 106.

CHAPTER TWENTY-TWO

1 See House of Commons, *Debates*, 1971, 6664.

2 See ibid., 6665.

3 See supra, chapter 16.

4 *An Act respecting the Tax Court of Canada and to amend the Federal Court Act, the Judges Act and the Unemployment Insurance Act, 1971*, SC 1980–81–82–83, c. 158.

5 House of Commons, *Debates*, 1983, 26884 (Mark MacGuigan, Minister of Justice).

6 House of Commons, *Debates*, 1971, 6666.

7 RSC 1985, c. 41 (1st Supp.).

8 The two judges were Frank Collier, who was sworn in at Vancouver, and who was known as the British Columbia judge because of the rota (the system whereby a judge would be assigned to Vancouver on a continuing basis), and Raymond Decary, who was sworn in at Montreal.

9 See House of Commons, Legislative Committee on Bill C-38, An Act to amend the Federal Court Act, the Crown Liability Act, the Supreme Court Act and other Acts in consequence thereof, 34th Parliament, 2nd Session, *Minutes of Proceedings and Evidence*, no. 1, 20.

10 Ibid.

11 Ibid.

12 Ibid.

13 *Report of the Canadian Bar Association Committee on the Appointment of Judges in Canada* (Ottawa: The Canadian Bar Foundation 1985), 65.

14 *Ottawa Citizen*, Saturday, July 21, 1984, 17.

CHAPTER TWENTY-THREE

1 R.A. Macdonald, 'Federal Judicial Review Jurisdiction under the Federal Court Act: When is a 'federal board, or commission or other tribunal' not a 'federal board, commission or tribunal?' (1981), 6 *Dalhousie Law Journal* 449–70 at 469.

2 D. Michael M. Goldie, 'Judicial Review under Common Law Remedies and the Statutory Code of Section 28 of the "Federal Court Act,"' The Cambridge Lectures, 1980 (Toronto: Butterworths 1981), 247–55.

3 *Proposals to Amend the Federal Court Act* (Ottawa: Department of Justice Canada 1983).
4 Ibid., 2, 18.
5 'Tribunals Would Ease Court Work: MacGuigan,' *The National*, September 1983, p. 2.
6 See Goldie, supra note 2.
7 *Saskatchewan Wheat Pool v. The Queen* (1980), [1981] 2 FC 212 at 217 (CA). Urie and Kelly D.J. concurred.
8 *Canadian National Railway Co. v. Canadian Human Rights Commission*, [1985] 1 FC 96 (CA), rev'd *Action Travail des Femmes v. Canadian National Railway Co.*, [1987] 1 SCR 1114.
9 *Egmont Towing & Sorting Ltd. v. Ship 'Telendos'* (1982), 43 NR 147. Mr Justice Pratte and Mr Justice Verchere sitting as a deputy judge concurred.
10 *Guy v. Public Service Commission Appeal Board* (1984), 55 NR 105 (Fed. CA).
11 H. Wade MacLauchlan, 'Approaches to Interpretation in Administrative Law' (1988), 1 *Canadian Journal of Administrative Law and Practice* 293–317.
12 [1986] 1 FC 437 (TD).
13 Ibid., 441 n. 1.
14 [1979] 2 FC 575 (CA).
15 [1980] 2 SCR 442 at 447.
16 Supra note 12 at 445.
17 [1951] SCR 396.
18 Quoted in supra note 12 at 450.
19 Keith Farquhar, 'A New Development in the Jurisdiction of the Federal Court' (1988), 33 *McGill Law Journal* 387–99.
20 [1987] 1 FC 155 (TD).
21 [1987] 2 FC 535 (CA).
22 Ibid., 541.
23 [1989] 1 SCR 322.
24 Ibid., 333.
25 *Bensol*, supra note 14.
26 [1988] 2 FC 454 at 461. This was an appeal from a decision of Madame Justice Reed, who had naturally maintained the opinion that she had stated in the *Marshall* case: *Varnam v. Minister of National Health and Welfare*, [1987] 3 FC 185.
27 Rand J. in *Ship 'Sparrows Point' v. Greater Vancouver Water District*, [1951] SCR 396.
28 The Court of Appeal had unanimously asserted earlier that convenience or advantage was not a reason for extending jurisdiction beyond statutory limits: *Canadian Saltfish Corp. v. Rasmussen* (1986), 68 NR 379 (Thurlow, Heald, MacGuigan). That still left the question of what the statutory limits were.

29 J.M. Evans and Brian Slattery, 'Case Note: Federal Jurisdiction – Pendent Parties – Aboriginal Title and Federal Common Law – Charter Challenges – Reform Proposals: *Roberts v. Canada'* (1989), 68 Canadian Bar Review 817–42.

30 *Oag v. Canada*, [1987] 2 FC 511 (CA).

31 [1986] 1 FC 472 (TD).

32 [1987] 3 FC 45 (TD).

33 Ibid., 54.

34 Ibid., 57.

35 *Stephens' Estate v. MNR* (1982), 40 NR 620 (Fed. CA).

36 *Wilder*, supra note 32 at 57.

37 *Wilder v. Canada*, [1988] 2 FC 465 (CA) (Pratte, Urie, MacGuigan).

38 [1990] 3 F.C. 32 (CA).

39 *Heafey v. Canada* (1991), 46 FTR 123.

40 See Joyal in *Heafey v. Canada*, ibid.

41 [1986] 1 SCR 752.

42 *Marubeni America Corp. v. Mitsui OSK Lines Ltd.*, [1979] 2 FC 283 (TD; Marceau).

43 *Miida Electronics Inc. v. Mitsui OSK Lines Ltd.* (1981), [1982] 1 FC 406 (CA).

44 The Supreme Court did acknowledge that a limitation existed, in that matters of provincial concern involving property and civil rights would be excluded. It would be difficult to know when such a limitation would reduce the maritime jurisdiction.

45 [1964] SCR 144.

46 *ITO*, supra note 41 at 801.

47 *Domestic Converters Corporation v. Arctic Steamship Line* (1980), [1984] 1 FC 211 (CA).

48 (1980), 46 NR 195 (Fed. CA). It was four years before the case was reported in the Federal Court Reports: [1984] 1 FC 211.

49 *ITO*, supra note 41 at 766.

50 *Wilder v. Canada*, [1987] 3 F.C. 45 (TD, Muldoon).

CHAPTER TWENTY-FOUR

1 Pierre Elliott Trudeau, Minister of Justice, *A Canadian Charter of Human Rights* (Ottawa: Queen's Printer 1968).

2 Canadian Charter of Rights and Freedoms, [Part I of the Constitution Act, 1982, being Schedule B of the Canada Act 1982 (UK) 1982, c. 11], s. 33.

3 Constitution Act, 1982, being Schedule B to the Canada Act 1982 (UK) 1982, c. 11.

4 House of Commons, *Debates*, 1980–83, 26886.

5 Madame Justice B.M. McLachlin, 'The Charter: A New Role for the Judiciary (1991), 29 *Alberta Law Review* 540–59, at 540–48.

6 October 7, 1983, 1, 9. The article was written by Marina Strauss.

7 *Operation Dismantle Inc. v. The Queen*, [1983] 1 FC 429 (TD), at 432, 436.

8 In addition to Thurlow, the other judges who did not sit were Urie, Heald, Stone, and Mahoney. The unusual five-judge panel suggests that there may have been a careful selection of the judges who would constitute it; however, no obvious selection criteria present themselves. Four of the judges on the panel were Quebec lawyers and four had academic backgrounds, while none of the five judges omitted had either background.

9 *The Queen v. Operation Dismantle Inc.*, [1983] 1 FC 745 (CA).

10 Ibid., 784.

11 Ibid., 751.

12 Ibid., 765.

13 *R. v. Chandler and Others* (1962), [1964] AC 763 at 771 (CCA), aff'd, *Chandler v. Director of Public Prosecutions* (1962), [1964] AC 763 (HL). The classic legal writing consisted of Chitty on *Prerogatives of the Crown* (1820), Blackstone and his eighteenth-century *Commentaries* on the laws of England, and Halsbury's *Laws of England*, an encyclopedic digest of English law.

14 Andrew J. Roman, 'Operation Dismantle: An Acute Case of *Obiter Dicta*,' *Ontario Lawyers Weekly*, March 2, 1984, 8–9, 15.

15 *Operation Dismantle Inc. v. The Queen*, [1985] 1 SCR 441. See Ian Bushnell, *The Captive Court: A Study of the Supreme Court of Canada* (Montreal & Kingston: McGill-Queen's University Press 1992), 449–54.

16 A seventh judge, Roland Ritchie, resigned for reasons of health after the hearing.

17 Estey, McIntyre, Chouinard, and Lamer concurred.

18 In her extensive treatment of the issue Bertha Wilson did discuss when review would be appropriate, but left it very vague.

19 [1985] 1 FC 85 (CA).

20 RSC 1970, c. C-41, tariff item 99201–1 of Schedule C.

21 Section 2(b).

22 The following summary is taken from S.I. Bushnell, 'Historical Dimensions of Obscenity Laws and Morality: The Censored Society,' paper delivered June 10 at the Law in History Conference, Carleton University, Ottawa, Ontario, June 8–10, 1987.

23 *An Act to amend the Customs Act*, SC 1947–48, c. 41, s. 49.

24 Ibid., s. 49(3).

25 *Dell Publishing Co. v. Deputy Minister of National Revenue for Customs and Excise* (1958), 2 TBR 154.

26 *An Act to amend the Customs Act*, SC 1958, c. 26, s. 3.
27 *Minister of National Revenue for Customs and Excise v. Tache* (1982), 40 NR 559, 65 CCC (2d) 250 (Fed. CA).
28 Toronto *Globe and Mail*, March 18, 1985, 1, 2.
29 *Windsor Star*, March 19, 1985, D8.
30 House of Commons, *Debates*, 1985, 3603.
31 *An Act to amend the Customs Tariff*, SC 1985, c. 12.

CHAPTER TWENTY-FIVE

1 *Denison Mines Ltd. v. Attorney-General of Canada*, [1973] 1 OR 797.
2 See *Cuddy Chicks Ltd. v. Ontario Labour Relations Board*, [1991] 2 SCR 3 at 14, where Mr Justice La Forest, for a majority of the Supreme Court, pointed this out, regarding a Charter issue, as a fundamental principle of constitutional law.
3 John N. Turner, 'The Origin and Mission of the Federal Court of Canada,' paper presented at the 20th Anniversary Symposium, June 26, 1991, and published in *The Federal Court of Canada – An Evaluation* (Ottawa: Federal Court of Canada 1991), 1–17 at 10.
4 *Denison*, supra note 1.
5 *Hamilton v. Hamilton Harbour Commissioners*, [1972] 3 OR 61.
6 Dale Gibson, 'Comment: Constitutional Law – Power of Provincial Courts to Determine Constitutionality of Federal Legislation' (1976), 54 *Canadian Bar Review* 372–80.
7 *Thorson v. Attorney General of Canada* (1974), [1975] 1 SCR 138, rev'g [1972] 2 OR 340 (CA). This case is also discussed in chapter 12.
8 *Borowski v. Minister of Justice of Canada* (1980), [1981] 1 WWR 1 (Sask. CA), aff'g [1980] 5 WWR 283 (Sask. QB).
9 *Minister of Justice of Canada v. Borowski*, [1981] 2 SCR 575.
10 *Attorney General of Canada v. Law Society of British Columbia; Jabour v. Law Society of British Columbia*, [1982] 2 SCR 307.
11 *Law Society of British Columbia v. Attorney-General of Canada* (1980), 108 DLR (3d) 753 (BCCA), affirming (1978), 92 DLR (3d) 53 (BCSC, in chambers).
12 *Jabour*, supra, note 10 at 326.
13 Ibid., 327.
14 Supra, chapter 21.
15 *Jabour*, supra, note 10 at 328.
16 [1983] 1 SCR 147.
17 Mr Justice Estey participated in the *Paul L'Anglais* case, but concurred with Chouinard.

18 See S.I. Bushnell, 'Leave to Appeal Applications to the Supreme Court of Canada: A Matter of Public Importance' (1982), 3 *Supreme Court Law Review* 479–558 at 547–9. This article identified the 1979–80 term as the beginning of the trend of a high percentage of unanimous decisions (89 per cent), compared with the previous decade when the average had been in the mid–70 per cent range. The trend continued, with the percentage over 80, until the 1987–88 term. The highest percentage of unanimous decisions occurred in the 1981–82 term, with 90 per cent.

19 *Northern Telecom Canada Ltd. v. Communications Workers of Canada*, [1983] 1 SCR 733.

20 *Paul L'Anglais Inc. v. Canada Labour Relations Board*, [1979] 2 FC 444 (CA; Jackett, Pratte, Le Dain).

21 *Attorney General of Canada v. Cylien*, [1973] FC 1166 (CA; Jackett, Thurlow, Pratte); *British Columbia Packers Ltd. v. Canada Labour Relations Board*, [1973] FC 1194 (CA; Jackett, Thurlow, Sheppard D.J.).

22 *Re Lavers and Minister of Finance* (1985), 18 DLR (4th) 477 at 480 (BCSC, in chambers). Only Mr Justice Barry Strayer of the Federal Court appeared conscious of a difference between a case in which a constitutional issue was raised in a proceeding otherwise within the jurisdiction of a provincial court, and a request for a declaration in a proceeding brought solely for that purpose: *Re Groupe des Éleveurs and Canadian Chicken Marleting Agency* (1984), [1985] 1 FC 280 at 304 (TD).

23 (1992), 11 OR (3d) 65 (CA).

24 *The Queen v. Reza*, [1994] 2 SCR 394. The judges were La Forest, L'Heureux-Dubé, Sopinka, Gonthier, Cory, McLachlin, and Major.

25 *Beauregard v. The Queen*, [1981] 2 FC 543 at 551–2 (TD, Addy). See also Alice Desjardins (Honourable Madame Justice), 'Review of Administrative Action in the Federal Court of Canada: The New Style in a Pluralist Setting,' in *Administrative Law*, Special Lectures of the Law Society of Upper Canada 1992, Administrative Law (Toronto: Carswell 1993), 405–37 at 408.

26 See, for instance, *Three Rivers Boatman Ltd. v. Canada Labour Relations Board*, [1969] SCR 607.

27 See J.W. Gough, *Fundamental Law in English Constitutional History* (Oxford: Clarendon Press 1961), 5.

28 *Northern Pipeline Agency v. Perehinec*, [1985] 2 SCR 513 at 521 (per Estey J.). David Mullan commented that this view was set up as an operating presumption against giving section 17 of the Federal Court Act a broad interpretation: 'Developments in Administrative Law: The 1983–84 Term' (1985), 7 *Supreme Court Law Review* 1–61 at 35.

29 *Attorney General of Canada v. Canard* (1975), [1976] 1 SCR 170 at 203.

30 (UK), 30 & 31 Vict., c. 3.

31 (UK), 28 & 29 Vict., c. 63, s. 2.

32 P.W. Hogg, 'Is Judicial Review of Administrative Action Guaranteed by the British North America Act?' (1976), 54 *Canadian Bar Review* 716–30.

33 Bora Laskin, 'Certiorari to Labour Boards: The Apparent Futility of Privative Clauses' (1952), 30 *Canadian Bar Review* 986–1003 at 989.

34 *Crevier v. Attorney-General for Quebec*, [1981] 2 SCR 220.

35 David J. Mullan, 'Developments in Administrative Law: The 1983–84 Term' (1985), 7 *Supreme Court Law Review* 1–61. Mullan noted that there had been a common assumption in 1979–80 that judicial review of administrative action did not have a protected, constitutional position and could be excluded by an appropriately worded provision.

36 David J. Mullan, 'The Uncertain Constitutional Position of Canada's Administrative Appeal Tribunals' (1982), 14 *Ottawa Law Review* 239–69.

37 [1979] 2 SCR 227.

38 Brian Etherington, 'Arbitration, Labour Boards and the Courts in the 1980s: Romance Meets Realism' (1989), 68 *Canadian Bar Review* 405–47.

39 *Canada Labour Relations Board v. Syndicat des employés de production du Québec et de L'Acadie*, [1984] 2 SCR 412.

40 Ibid., 444.

41 Roderick A. Macdonald, 'Big Government and Its Control: Legislative Initiatives of the Past Decade,' in *Decade of Adjustment*, ed. Julio Menezes (Toronto: Butterworths 1980), 57–77.

42 J.M. Evans, 'Developments in Administrative Law: The 1984–85 Term' (1986), 8 *Supreme Court Law Review* 1–52: 'an unpleasant surprise' (26), 'threatens much of the progress made over the past six years' (30), 'meagre and conclusionary reasoning' (36). Brian A. Langille, 'Judicial Review, Judicial Revisionism and Judicial Responsibility' (1986), 17 Revue générale de droit 169–216: 'has redrawn the map of judicial review abruptly, illogically, and against all rational grounds of persuasion' (171), 'a radical rewriting' (214), 'aberrational decision' (215). Dianne Pothier, 'Institutional Relationships between Tribunals and Courts: Review of Neil R. Finkelstein and Brian MacLeod Rogers, eds., *Recent Developments in Administrative Law*' (1988), 8 *Windsor Yearbook of Access to Justice* 381–411: 'unequivocally retreated from *New Brunswick Liquor*' (393), 'Beetz's distinction is both confusing and lacking in justification' (396).

43 The bench consisted of Justices Dickson, Beetz, Estey, McIntyre, Chouinard, and Wilson. Chief Justice Laskin was at the hearing, but died before judgment was rendered.

44 Supra note 18.

45 *Syndicat des employés de production du Québec et de l'Acadie v. Canada Labour Relations Board* (1981), [1982] 1 FC 471 (CA).

46 One commentator blamed the Court of Appeal for re-inventing a distinction between provisions that do and do not confer jurisdiction, which was used by Beetz: Dianne Pothier, supra note 42.

47 D. Carrier and P. Verge, 'Chronique de législation: Loi concernant la Cour fédérale du Canada (1971), 12 *Cahiers de Droit* (Université Laval) 207–11; J.M. Evans, 'The Trial Division of the Federal Court: An Addendum' (1977), 23 *McGill Law Journal* 132–43; P.S.A. Lamek, 'Jurisdiction of the Federal Courts and the Superior Courts' in *The Constitution and the Future of Canada*, Special Lectures of the Law Society of Upper Canada 1978 (Toronto: Richard de Boo 1978), 87–108; R.A. Macdonald, 'Federal Judicial Review Jurisdiction under Section 2(g) of the Federal Court Act: The Position of Section 96 Judges' (1979), 11 *Ottawa Law Review* 689–711.

48 A.M. Linden, ed., *The Canadian Judiciary* (Toronto: Osgoode Hall Law School 1976).

49 The fact that the Exchequer Court and the Supreme Court had constituted a federal court system, albeit on a relatively small scale, was not mentioned; the conference also ignored the existence of the Admiralty Districts, which did resemble a 'system,' and which had been created with a federal system in mind (see chapter 8).

50 Supra, chapter 17.

51 *Attorney General of Ontario v. Pembina Exploration Canada Ltd.*, [1989] 1 SCR 206; *Monk Corporation v. Island Fertilizers Ltd.*, [1991] 1 SCR 779; *Hunt v. Lac d'Amiante du Québec Ltée.*, [1993] 4 SCR 289; *Tolofson v. Jensen*, [1994] 3 SCR 1022. James C. MacPherson, 'Developments in Constitutional Law: The 1979–80 Term' (1981), 2 *Supreme Court Law Review* 49–123 at 100–2. Martin L. Friedland, in his recent report for the Canadian Judicial Council, took it for granted that 'we have one integrated legal system': *A Place Apart: Judicial Independence and Accountability in Canada*, May 1995, p. 264.

52 J.M. Evans, 'Developments in Administrative Law: The 1988–89 Term' (1990), 1 *Supreme Court Law Review* (2d) 1–79.

53 See *Martineau v. The Matsqui Institution Inmate Disciplinary Board*, [1976] 2 FC 198 (CA).

54 P.W. Hogg, 'The Supreme Court of Canada and Administrative Law, 1949–1971' (1973), 11 *Osgoode Hall Law Journal* 187–223 at 189.

55 H. Wade MacLauchlan, 'Developments in Administrative Law: The 1989–90 Term' (1991), 2 *Supreme Court Law Review* (2d) 1–82 at 7.

56 Julius A. Isaac, 'Recent Developments in the Federal Court of Canada' (1995), 11 *Canadian Intellectual Property Review* 251–5.

57 *Re Lavers and Minister of Finance* (1985), 18 DLR (4th) 477 at 479 (BC SC, in chambers).
58 RSC 1970 (2nd Supp.), c. 10, s. 3 (now RSC 1985, c. F-7, s. 3).
59 RSC 1970, c. E-11, s. 3.
60 *Valin v. Langlois* (1879), 3 SCR 1. Section 129 reads, 'Except as otherwise provided by this Act, all Laws in force in Canada, Nova Scotia, or New Brunswick at the Union, and all Courts of Civil and Criminal Jurisdiction, and all legal Commissions, Powers, and Authorities, and all Officers, Judicial, Administrative, and Ministerial, existing therein at the Union, shall continue in Ontario, Quebec, Nova Scotia, and New Brunswick respectively, as if the Union had not been made; subject nevertheless (except with respect to such as are enacted by or exist under Acts of the Parliament of Great Britain or of the Parliament of the United Kingdom of Great Britain and Ireland), to be repealed, abolished, or altered by the Parliament of Canada, or by the Legislature of the respective Province, according to the Authority of the Parliament or of that Legislature under this Act.'
61 *Valin v. Langlois*, ibid.; *Re Bell Telephone Co. v. Minister of Agriculture* (1884), 7 Ont. 605 (CP).

CHAPTER TWENTY-SIX

1 Duff was a member of the Supreme Court of Canada for thirty-seven years and three months, from September 27, 1906, to January 7, 1944.
2 The first two were George Burbidge (1887–1908) and Wilbur Jackett (1964–79).
3 Arthur Thurlow's promotion from associate chief justice to chief justice has been the only departure from the practice to date.
4 Gerald Le Dain, the first, moved to the Supreme Court of Canada on May 29, 1984.
5 Marina Strauss, 'Courts Impede Change: Linden,' May 29, 1984, 1, 2.
6 J.M. Evans and Brian Slattery, 'Case Note: Federal Jurisdiction – Pendent Parties – Aboriginal Title and Federal Common Law – Charter Challenges – Reform Proposals: *Roberts v. Canada*' (1989), 68 *Canadian Bar Review* 817–42.
7 Ibid., 817.
8 Ibid., 818.
9 Ibid., 842.
10 See David Mullan, 'Judicial Review,' paper presented at the 20th Anniversary Symposium, June 26, 1991, and published in *The Federal Court of Canada – An Evaluation* (Ottawa: Federal Court of Canada 1991), 27–41 at 30.
11 Quicklaw, Margot Sinclair, Canadian Press, June 6, 1989.
12 *Rudolph Wolff & Co. Ltd. v. The Queen*, [1990] 1 SCR 695; *Dywidag Systems*

International, Canada Ltd. v. Zutphen Brothers Construction Ltd., [1990] 1 SCR 705.

13 *Rudolph Wolff & Co.*, supra note 12 at 703.
14 House of Commons, *Debates*, 1989–90, 5413–15.
15 House of Commons, *debates*, 1989–90, 5414.
16 House of Commons, Legislative Committee on Bill C-38, An Act to amend the Federal Court Act, the Crown Liability Act, the Supreme Court Act and other Acts in consequence thereof, 34th Parliament, 2nd Session, *Minutes of Proceedings and Evidence*, no. 1, 16.
17 Ibid., no. 6, 6.
18 Vol. 2, No. 2.
19 Canadian Bar Association, Resolution M-01-91.

CHAPTER TWENTY-SEVEN

1 *Weatherall v. Attorney General of Canada; Conway v. The Queen; Spearman v. Disciplinary Tribunal of Collins Bay Penitentiary* (1987), [1988] 1 FC 369 (TD, Strayer).
2 *The Queen v. Conway* (1990), [1991] 1 FC 85 at 107 (CA).
3 Ibid., 108, quoting Lamer in *The Queen v. Collins*, [1987] 1 SCR 165 at 282–3.
4 *The Queen v. Conway*, supra note 2 at 91.
5 Ibid., 94.
6 L'Heureux-Dubé, Sopinka, Gonthier, McLachlin, Iacobucci, and Major concurred.
7 *Conway v. The Queen*, [1993] 2 SCR 872 at 877.
8 *Thomson v. Canada*, [1988] 3 FC 108 (CA).
9 *Thomson v. The Queen*, (1988), [1989] 1 FC 86, (TD).
10 *Thomson v. The Queen*, [1990] 2 FC 820 (CA).
11 *The Queen v. Thomson*, [1992] 1 SCR 385. L'Heureux-Dubé dissented and agreed with Stone's judgment in the Court of Appeal.
12 *Federal Court Act*, RSC 1970 (2nd Supp.), c. 10, s. 2, 'federal board, commission or other tribunal.'
13 *An Act to amend the Federal Court Act, the Crown Liability Act, the Supreme Court Act and other Acts in consequence thereof*, SC 1990, c. 8, s. 1(3), amending the definition of 'federal board, commission or other tribunal.'
14 *Schachter v. The Queen*, [1988] 3 FC 515 at 536 (TD).
15 *The Queen v. Schachter*, [1990] 2 FC 129 (CA).
16 Ibid., 150. He quoted Estey J. in *Law Society of Upper Canada v. Skapinker*, [1984] 1 SCR 357.
17 *The Queen v. Schachter*, [1990] 2 FC 129 at 140 (CA).
18 *The Queen v. Schachter*, [1992] 2 SCR 679.

19 Sopinka, Gonthier, Cory, and McLachlin concurred. La Forest rendered a concurring judgment with which L'Heureux-Dubé concurred.
20 Supra note 18 at 705.
21 Ibid., 723. There were difficulties with the case that tended to be overlooked in
   the publicity involved. Lamer registered the court's dissatisfaction with the
   state in which the case had come before it, and La Forest also commented on
   the unsatisfactory manner in which the case had been presented. The problem
   was that the government had chosen to concede that there had been a viola-
   tion of equality rights, and appealed only on the issue of a remedy. This,
   Lamer said, created 'a factual vacuum,' which affected the question of an
   appropriate remedy. It was questionable that the highest court would have
   found discrimination, and La Forest, with L'Heureux-Dubé concurring, said
   as much. Possibly, in light of the considerable public awareness that the case
   had generated, it would not have been in the court's best interest to reject the
   remedial weapon fashioned in the Federal Court. Instead the court blunted its
   use, but that action was overwhelmed by the acceptance of the power, albeit
   limited. Within a month the *Schachter* case was forever locked into history, as
   imperfect as it may have been, by the much more politically sensitive decision
   of the Ontario Court of Appeal in *Haig and Birch v. The Queen* (1992), 9 OR (3d)
   495 (CA, Lacourcière, Krever, McKinlay). The Ontario court had held its decision back waiting for the Supreme Court decision in *Schachter*. Sexual orientation was said to be an analogous ground of discrimination under section 15 of
   the Charter. Following *Schachter*, the appeal court took the language of section
   3(1) of the Canadian Human Rights Act: 'For all purposes of this Act, race,
   national or ethnic origin, colour, religion, age, sex, marital status, family status, disability and conviction for which a pardon has been granted are prohibited grounds of discrimination,' and added to the list the words 'sexual
   orientation.' The appeal was from a decision rendered on September 23, 1991,
   by Mr Justice F.J. McDonald of the General Division (who was appointed to
   the Federal Court of Appeal on April 1, 1993). He had declared the provision
   to be discriminatory but ordered his decision to be stayed for six months.
   Rather than appeal the *Haig* decision, the federal government announced that
   they were accepting it on October 30, 1992.
22 *Symes v. The Queen*, [1989] 3 FC 59 at 71 (TD).
23 Ibid., 72.
24 Ibid., 87.
25 *The Queen v. Symes*, [1991] 3 FC 507 at 523, 525 (CA).
26 Ibid., 529.
27 Ibid., 532.
28 *Symes v. The Queen*, [1993] 4 SCR 695.

29 Chief Justice Lamer and Justices La Forest, Sopinka, Gonthier, Cory, and Major concurred.

30 *Symes v. The Queen*, supra, note 28 at 766.

31 Ibid., 776.

32 Ibid., 786.

33 *Veysey v. Correctional Service of Canada* (1990), 109 NR 300 (FCA, Iacobucci, Urie, Décary), aff'g [1990] 1 FC 321 (TD, Dubé).

34 The intervenors were (1) in support of the government, the Salvation Army, Focus on the Family Association Canada, REAL Women, the Pentecostal Assemblies of Canada, and the Evangelical Fellowship of Canada; (2) in support of the tribunal's decision, the Canadian Rights and Liberties Federation, Equality for Gays and Lesbians Everywhere, the National Association of Women and the Law, the Canadian Disability Rights Council, and the National Action Committee on the Status of Women.

35 This was the Ontario Court of Appeal decision in *Haig and Birch v. The Queen* (1992), 9 OR (3d) 495, discussed supra, note 21.

36 *Attorney General of Canada v. Mossop* (1990), [1991] 1 FC 18 at 33 (CA).

37 *Canadian Human Rights Commission v. Attorney General of Canada*, [1993] 1 SCR 554.

38 Chief Justice Lamer rendered a judgment, with which Sopinka and Iacobucci concurred, and La Forest rendered a short concurring judgment in which he added some comments. Iacobucci also concurred with La Forest.

39 The issue in *Mossop* returned to the Federal Court in 1991 when James Egan and Jack Nesbit claimed that they had been discriminated against when they applied for spousal benefits under the Old Age Security Act. They were turned down since as a gay couple they were not spouses. Mr Justice Leonard Martin decided against them: *Egan v. The Queen* (1991), [1992] 1 FC 687 (TD). For him the unit of husband and wife was the basic unit of society, on which it depended for its continuing existence, and by definition a gay relationship could not be a 'spousal' relationship. An appeal to the Federal Court of Appeal created a 2–1 split. Mahoney and Robertson agreed with Martin for the same definitional reason, but Linden dissented and considered that the purpose of the pension legislation, not a pre-ordained meaning of words, should determine eligibility: *Egan v. The Queen*, [1993] 3 FC 401 (CA). The appeal to the Supreme Court was dismissed by a 5–4 split: *Egan and Nesbit v. The Queen*, [1995] 2 SCR 513. The division among the judges showed that a division existed within society, but not necessarily to the same degree. Mossop had failed to have a gay relationship recognized by the judiciary as a 'family,' with the judges divided 7–3; Egan and Nesbit failed to have their union recognized as 'spousal' with a division of 8–5.

40 Demurrage is remuneration to the owner of a ship for detaining the ship beyond the agreed-on time for loading and unloading.

41 *Monk Corporation v. Island Fertilizers Ltd.* (1988), 19 FTR 220 (TD).

42 *Island Fertilizers Ltd. v. Monk Corporation,* (1989), 97 NR 384 (Fed. CA).

43 Chief Justice Lamer, Justices La Forest, Sopinka, Gonthier, Cory, McLachlin, and Stevenson concurred.

44 *Monk Corporation v. Island Fertilizers Ltd.,* [1991] 1 SCR 779.

45 See supra, chapter 21.

46 See J.M. Evans, 'Developments in Administrative Law: The 1988–89 Term' (1990), 1 *Supreme Court Law Review* (2d) 1–79 at 78.

47 See H. Wade MacLauchlan, 'Developments in Administrative Law: The 1989–90 Term' (1991), 2 *Supreme Court Law Review* (2d) 1–82 at 7; and 'Developments in Administrative Law: The 1990–91 Term' (1992), 3 *Supreme Court Law Review* (2d) 29–71 at 31, 71.

48 *Harris Steel Group Inc. v. Minister of National Revenue* [1985] FCJ No. 124 (A-893-84)(QL)(CA, Heald, Ryan, MacGuigan).

49 *Lor-Wes Contracting Ltd. v. The Queen* (1985), [1986] 1 FC 346 (CA, Pratte, Marceau, MacGuigan). The Supreme Court decisions were *Morguard Properties Ltd. v. City of Winnipeg,* [1983] 2 SCR 493, and *Stubart Investments Ltd. v. The Queen,* [1984] 1 SCR 536.

50 The initial decision in which the 'words-in-total-context' approach was enunciated was not reported, supra note 48, and subsequent references to it are to *Lor-Wes Contracting Ltd. v. The Queen,* (1985), [1986] 1 FC 346 (CA).

51 *Cashin v. Canadian Broadcasting Corp.,* [1988] 3 FC 494 (CA, Heald, Mahoney, MacGuigan).

CHAPTER TWENTY-EIGHT

1 Federal Court Act, RSC 1985, c. F-7, ss. 45.1, 46, as amended by SC 1990, c. 8, ss. 13, 14.

2 Federal Court Act, RSC 1985, c. F-7, s. 28, as amended by SC 1990, c. 8, s. 8.

3 An Act to amend the Immigration Act and other Acts in consequence thereof, SC 1992, c. 49.

4 See Brian A. Crane, 'Constitutional Restraints on the Federal Court in Relation to Crown Litigation' (Canada) (1992), 2 *National Journal of Constitutional Law* 1–26.

5 The speech was published in (1990), 11 *Advocates' Quarterly* 319–26.

6 The present chief justice, Julius Isaac, presented a historical paper in 1993 as part of the Continuing Legal Education Program of the Canadian Bar Association, at its annual meeting. It was entitled 'The Federal Court of Canada: Its

Past, Its Present, and Some Thoughts on Its Future,' and was part of a block entitled 'Specialized Litigation in the Federal Court.'

7 Included in the published work were two papers that were considered to be of interest, but had been delivered on other occasions, one by former Chief Justice Iacobucci and the other by Mr Justice Heald.

8 See Ian Bushnell, *The Captive Court: A Study of the Supreme Court of Canada* (Montreal & Kingston: McGill Queen's University Press 1992) 39–43, passim.

9 See supra, chapter 16.

10 Strayer was appointed to the Court on the same day as Hugessen and Stone, but his Order in Council was signed later than theirs.

11 In the report of the Canadian Judicial Council, *'Delays Project,'* it was pointed out that the writing of judgments assumed greater significance in an appeal court since the court had a role not only in correcting errors in trial judgments, but also in clarifying and developing the law. The report also said, 'it is fundamental that any proposal for expediting an appeal court's processes must take into account the potential impact it will have on the quality of the court's judgments' (Ottawa: Canadian Judicial Council 1992), 5.

12 W.R. Jackett, 'Foundations of Canadian Law in History and Theory,' in Otto Lang, ed., *Contemporary Problems of Public Law in Canada* (Toronto: University of Toronto Press 1968), 3–30.

13 Supra, chapter 4.

14 See Rosalie Silberman Abella, 'The Civil Litigation Process under Siege: Roscoe Pound Redux' (1994), 28 *Gazette* [Law Society of Upper Canada] 213–22, for an articulate and vigorous attack on the formalism of the legal profession by a justice of the Ontario Court of Appeal. It is interesting that the attack was made in an address in 1991, but not published until 1994.

15 See House of Commons, Legislative Committee on Bill C-38, An Act to amend the Federal Court Act, the Crown Liability Act, the Supreme Court Act and other Acts in consequence thereof, 34th Parliament, 2nd Session, *Minutes of Proceedings and Evidence*, no. 4, 12 (A.M. Linden, chair of the Canada Law Reform Commission, and now a justice of the Federal Court of Appeal); David Mullan, 'Judicial Review,' paper presented at the 20th Anniversary Symposium, June 26, 1991, and published in *The Federal Court of Canada – An Evaluation* (Ottawa: Federal Court of Canada 1991), 27–41; Gordon F. Henderson, 'Comments on Review of Administrative Action by Federal and Ontario Courts,' in *Administrative Law*, Special Lectures of the Law Society of Upper Canada, 1992 (Toronto: Carswell 1993), 445–53. Robert F. Reid has made a call for the creation of specialized administrative appeal courts: 'Judicial Review: A Poor Way to Run a Railroad,' in *Administrative Law*, Special Lectures of the Law Society of Upper Canada, 1992 (Toronto: Carswell 1993), 455–60.

16 Alice Desjardins (Honourable Madame Justice), 'Review of Administrative Action in the Federal Court of Canada: The New Style in a Pluralist Setting,' in *Administrative Law*, Special Lectures of the Law Society of Upper Canada, 1992, (Toronto: Carswell 1993), 405–37; Beverley McLachlin, 'Rules and Discretion in the Governance of Canada' (1992), 56 *Saskatchewan Law Review* 167–79.
17 Supra note 14 at 219.

Index of Cases

The name of a case discussed in the book may appear in the text or in a note. To facilitate going from this index to the appropriate pages in the text, page numbers are indicated for all cases discussed at any length. If the name of a case discussed in the text appears only in a note, the note is identified in parentheses: For example, *McNamara Construction (Western) Ltd. v. The Queen* (1977) SCC, 237–9 (408 n17) indicates that the case is discussed on pages 237 to 239 of the text and is identified by name in note 17, which appears on page 408.

ABBREVIATIONS

AD	Appellate Division
BCCA	British Columbia Court of Appeal
CA	Court of Appeal
CCA	Court of Criminal Appeal
Ch.	Court of Chancery
Co. Ct.	County Court
CP	Court of Common Pleas
Eng.	England
Ex.	Exchequer Court
Ex. Adm.	Admiralty District Court, Exchequer Court of Canada
FCA	Federal Court of Appeal
FCTD	Federal Court Trial Division

Index of Names and Terms

1981 David F. Flaherty, ed., *Essays in the History of Canadian Law: Volume I*

1982 Marion MacRae and Anthony Adamson, *Cornerstones of Order: Courthouses and Town Halls of Ontario, 1784–1914*

1983 David H. Flaherty, ed., *Essays in the History of Canadian Law: Volume II*

1984 Patrick Brode, *Sir John Beverley Robinson: Bone and Sinew of the Compact*
      David Williams, *Duff, A Life in the Law*

1985 James Snell and Frederick Vaughan, *The Supreme Court of Canada: History of the Institution*

1986 Paul Romney, *Mr Attorney: The Attorney General for Ontario in Court, Cabinet and Legislature, 1791–1899*
      Martin Friedland, *The Case of Valentine Shortis: A True Story of Crime and Politics in Canada*

1987 C. Ian Kyer and Jerome Bickenbach, *The Fiercest Debate: Cecil A. Wright, the Benchers, and Legal Education in Ontario, 1923–1957*

1988 Robert Sharpe, *The Last Day, the Last Hour: The Currie Libel Trial*
      John D. Arnup, *Middleton: The Beloved Judge*

1989 Desmond Brown, *The Genesis of the Canadian Criminal Code of 1892*
      Patrick Brode, *The Odyssey of John Anderson*

1990 Philip Girard and Jim Phillips, eds., *Essays in the History of Canadian Law: Volume III – Nova Scotia*
      Carol Wilton, ed., *Essays in the History of Canadian Law: Volume IV – Beyond the Law: Lawyers and Business in Canada, 1830–1930*

1991 Constance Backhouse, *Petticoats and Prejudice: Women and Law in Nineteenth-Century Canada*

1992 Brendan O'Brien, *Speedy Justice: The Tragic Last Voyage of His Majesty's Vessel* Speedy
      Robert Fraser, ed., *Provincial Justice: Upper Canadian Legal Portraits from the Dictionary of Canadian Biography*

1993 Greg Marquis, *Policing Canada's Century: A History of the Canadian Association of Chiefs of Police*
      F. Murray Greenwood, *Legacies of Fear: Law and Politics in Quebec in the Era of the French Revolution*

1994 Patrick Boyer, *A Passion for Justice: The Legacy of James Chalmers McRuer*
      Charles Pullen, *The Life and Times of Arthur Maloney: The Last of the Tribunes*
      Jim Phillips, Tina Loo, and Susan Lewthwaite, eds., *Essays in the History of Canadian Law: Volume V – Crime and Criminal Justice*

Brian Young, *The Politics of Codification: The Lower Canadian Civil Code of 1866*

1995 David Williams, *Just Lawyers: Seven Portraits*

Hamar Foster and John McLaren, eds., *Essays in the History of Canadian Law: Volume VI – British Columbia and the Yukon*

W.H. Morrow, ed., *Northern Justice: The Memoirs of Mr Justice William G. Morrow*

Beverley Boissery, *A Deep Sense of Wrong: The Treason, Trials and Transportation to New South Wales of Lower Canadian Rebels after the 1838 Rebellion*

1996 Carol Wilton, ed., *Essays in the History of Canadian Law: Volume VII – Inside the Law: Canadian Law Firms in Historical Perspective*

William Kaplan, *Bad Judgment: The Case of Mr Justice Leo A. Landreville*

F. Murray Greenwood and Barry Wright, eds., *Canadian State Trials Series: Volume I – Law, Politics, and Security Measures, 1608–1837*

1997 James W. St.G. Walker, *'Race,' Rights, and the Law in the Supreme Court of Canada: Historical Case Studies*

Lori Chambers, *Married Women and Property Law in Victorian Ontario*

Patrick Brode, *Casual Slaughters and Accidental Judgments: Canadian War Crimes Prosecutions, 1944–1948*

Ian Bushnell, *The Federal Court of Canada: A History, 1875–1992*